International Law and Diplomacy

Ambassador Andrew Jacovides addressing the United Nations General Assembly

International Law and Diplomacy

Selected Writings by
Ambassador Andrew Jacovides

with the Assistance of Nani Jansen

Foreword by Dame Rosalyn Higgins

MARTINUS
NIJHOFF
PUBLISHERS

LEIDEN • BOSTON
2011

This book is printed on acid-free paper.

Library of Congress Cataloging-in-Publication Data

Jacovides, Andrew.
International law and diplomacy : selected writings / by Andrew Jacovides.
p. cm.
Includes index.
ISBN 978-90-04-20167-5 (hardback : alk. paper) 1. International law. 2. Diplomacy.
3. Foreign relations administration. I. Title.

K3240.J338 2011
341—dc22

2011018277

ISBN 978 90 04 20167 5

FSC
www.fsc.org
MIX
Paper from responsible sources
FSC® C008919

PRINTED BY AD DRUK BV - ZEIST, THE NETHERLANDS

Contents

Foreword ix
Acknowledgement xiii

Introduction: Careers in Diplomacy and International Law 1

PART A
INTERNATIONAL LAW

State Responsibility
State Responsibility: Reflections on the ILC's Draft Articles 11

Law of Treaties
Treaties Conflicting with Peremptory Norms of International Law and the Zurich-London 'Agreements' 17
The Role of International Law in the World Today and Tomorrow ... 57

Law of the Sea
Peaceful Settlement of Disputes in Ocean Conflicts: Does UNCLOS III Point the Way? 69
A Review of the 2004 General Assembly Discussions on the Law of the Sea 75
Statement at the Inaugural Meeting of the General Assembly of the International Seabed Authority 87
Some Aspects of the Law of the Sea: Islands, Delimitation, and Dispute Settlement Revisited 91
The Contribution of the International Tribunal for the Law of the Sea to International Law 113
Current Issues of the Law of the Sea and Their Relevance to Cyprus 115

International Dispute Resolution
International Tribunals: Do They Really Work for Small States? 125
Great Expectations: Where Does the Proliferation of International Dispute Resolution Tribunals Leave International Law? 133
U.N. Reform and the International Court of Justice: Introductory Statement 141

UN Peacekeeping
A View from Within: The Role of Small States and the Cyprus Experience 149
The Cyprus Problem and United Nations Peace-Keeping 179
The United Nations Peacekeeping: A View of the First 50 Years at the Brink of a New Century 195
Remarks at the Ceremony to Honour the Canadian Armed Forces for Their Contribution to UNFICYP 205

Terrorism
International Law Aspects of Combating Terrorism 211

International Law and Diplomacy
The Role and Work of the Diplomatic Corps in Washington 217
Recent Trends towards International Legal Order 225
The Role of International Law in Diplomacy 231
The UN Decade on International Law: Progress and Promises 243
UN Reform Forum, America's Interests in the United Nations 251
International Law and Diplomacy, Some Reflections 255

PART B
CYPRUS

The Cyprus Problem and the United Nations 273
The Cyprus Question: Its Dimensions, Implications, and Prospects for a Solution 289
Cyprus: The International Law Dimension 305
The Cyprus Problem: The International Dimension 315
The Cyprus Problem 319
Cyprus: Prospects for a Solution 327
European Union Expansion: The Old and the New 335

Book Review (Excerpt) of *An International Relations Debacle: The UN Secretary-General's Mission of Good Offices in Cyprus 1999–2004* by Claire Palley, Hart Publishing, 2005 341
Letter to the Editor of the New York Times 347
Turkish Flexibility Would Solve Cyprus 351
Fifty Year Anniversary of the Republic of Cyprus (1960–2010) 353
Turkey Needs to Be Sincere on Cyprus 363
Letter to the Editor of Foreign Affairs 365

PART C
RELATED TOPICS

Remarks at the 75th Anniversary Commonwealth Day Celebration of the British Officers' Club of Haverford 369
Remarks at the Kennedy Center on the Occasion of the Presentation of an Ancient Amphora by the Cyprus Government 375
The United Nations Programme of Assistance in the Training, Study, Dissemination, and Wider Appreciation of International Law 379

Index 381

Foreword

Andreas Jacovides and I have been friends – good friends – for what feels like a lifetime. We met while studying for a Master's Degree in international law at the University of Cambridge. It was not simply that we attended classes together. A group of us from that year's intake formed a particular bond and spent time together socializing and also discussing legal issues beyond the confines of the upcoming examination.

It was a rather strong year: among others, there was John McMahon, who died in tragic circumstances in 1969. Already he had shown his exceptional promise, with a publication in the British Yearbook of International Law and a junior posting at the United Nations. Philip Allott was also in our group. He was to become a legal adviser at the Foreign Office, and then a don at Trinity College, Cambridge, producing highly original books on legal theory. And Andreas Jacovides – "Andrew" as he was content to be known to his Cambridge friends – was widely regarded by his peers as extraordinarily clever, and was duly awarded a First in his examination papers. (He had already achieved a double first class in the Law Tripos and had in 1958 graduated top of his year with a starred First.) In achieving these examination results, he never gave the appearance of being overwhelmed with the volume of work required of him. I now realise that he was already evidencing a trait that has remained with him all his life – namely a voracious appetite for his chosen subject, the study of which would be for him a constant joy and not a burden.

He was at Harvard Law School as a Henry Fellow while I was at Yale as a Commonwealth Fund Fellow. We stayed in touch, both benefiting immeasurably from this transatlantic exposure. How could it not be formative to be the research assistant to Louis Sohn and Richard Baxter?

Andreas Jacovides' career has in every way fulfilled this brilliant start in the law as a student. His classmates from Cambridge were still pursuing further studies or seeking first employment when the news came through that our friend was already a member of Cyprus' Permanent Mission to the United Nations, going there upon Cyprus' independence in 1960. He rapidly rose in the ranks of the Mission and was over the years to become one of the most highly regarded and long-serving diplomats at the United Nations. From 1971 right through 1996, matters relating to the law of the sea took up more and more of Jacovides' time, and required him to travel to many countries.

It is fair to say that he has known all there is to know about the workings of the United Nations, serving in the Cyprus delegation in every regular session of the General Assembly since Cyprus was admitted to the United Nations.

He was Cyprus' Permanent Representative to the United Nations in 1992–1993. He also gave long service to Cyprus at the Sixth Committee of the Assembly, and was a familiar figure on a multitude of UN Committees, notable among them the Special Committee on the Definition of Aggression, the Special Committee on the Review of the Charter, the Committee on Host Country Relations (Chairman of the Committee 1992–1993), and the Committee on the Peaceful Uses of the Seabed and the Ocean Floor Beyond the Limits of National Jurisdiction. In all of these Jacovides could bring to bear his legal skills and deep knowledge of the personalities and politics of the United Nations.

It is easy to think of him as having a rich life in the world of international organizations – not only at UN Headquarters, but also at the World Bank, the International Monetary Fund, and the Organization of American States.

But it should also be recalled that he twice served as Ambassador of Cyprus to the United States – 1979–89 and again 1993–1996. He was as well known in diplomatic circles in Washington as in New York. And from 1990 to 1992, he combined bilateral with multilateral diplomacy, serving as Cyprus' Ambassador to the Federal Republic of Germany and Permanent Representative to the IAEA, and to the UN agencies in Vienna.

To be elected as a Member of the International Law Commission is a notable achievement for any international lawyer. Andreas Jacovides was three times elected to that prestigious body; in 1991, he was Vice-Chairman. This is one of many ways in which he avoided over-narrow specialization (though he had a considerable expertise in the law of the sea). He interested himself in the broad range of international law issues there under consideration.

There are a handful of international civil servants who have managed to combine careers with important academic writings. There are perhaps even fewer members of the diplomatic corps who have also earned respect for their academic works. Jacovides has over the years actively participated in academic ventures and written trenchant observations throughout his time as a diplomat. It is in every way appropriate that these writings are now brought together in one volume.

The breadth of the topics covered reflect the wide range of intellectual and professional interests of Andreas Jacovides. In festschriften for two great figures – Louis Sohn and Carl-August Fleischer – he has written on Peaceful Settlement in Ocean Conflicts and on Islands, Delimitation and Dispute Settlement. There are a cluster of pieces on law of the sea. His interest in dispute settlement has gone beyond maritime matters. The reader will find thoughtful pieces on small states and international tribunals and on the potential problems associated with the proliferation of dispute resolution tribunals. There are also some pithy thoughts on UN reform and the International Court of Justice. The reader will also find some well-articulated reflections on UN Peacekeeping, on international law, on terrorism, and on the law of treaties.

Of particular interest is the section given over to international law and diplomacy – matters not readily to be found elsewhere. A wide variety of institutions have been the beneficiary of this expertise.

Of course, what he has to say in the major section entitled "Cyprus" will attract special attention. Here a cluster of speeches, letters, and book reviews are gathered together.

Jacovides' contributions over the years have generally been thoughtful and low-key rather than didactic. But from the very outset of Cyprus' independence, he has challenged the compatibility of certain provisions in the independence treaties with peremptory norms of international law. A 1966 28-page paper, along with other later pieces in 1976, 1977, 1995 and elsewhere reflect a continuing preoccupation with this matter – and with the foreign policy problems that Cyprus faces. There seems little evidence of serious engagement by others on these legal issues in Jacovides' contentions; they would seem to merit a response that has not been forthcoming.

These short remarks on the career of Andreas Jacovides, and what may be found in this useful volume, must be supplemented with a further comment.

Behind the glittering diplomatic career and the expertise gathered in a variety of areas, lies a fine human being. Andreas Jacovides is a man of warmth, who takes the trouble to nurture his friends. He wants to know about their work, their health, their families – and when they might all get together. Nurturing one's friends is high on my list of admirable human qualities. He is ready to appreciate the work of others and all colleagues are treated with respect.

Equally impressive is the high degree of interest and enthusiasm in the United Nations, and in international law generally, that Jacovides continues to display in his retirement. He has, of course, his own interesting life to lead, both as regards work and with his wife, Pamela. But his days are also filled in listening to the lectures of others, attending debates, following in great depth all the major controversies of the day. He will be willing to talk, if asked – but it is not mostly his own voice that he wishes to hear. The freshness of his interest in all these matters reveal a man who has loved his chosen path in life.

Dame Rosalyn Higgins
DBE QC, former President of the International Court of Justice

Acknowledgement

This book would not have been produced if it were not for Pieter Bekker, the brilliant and accomplished Dutch international lawyer, who suggested the idea and introduced me to his countrywoman, young lawyer Nani Jansen, whose diligence and conscientious assistance has made it possible to put it together. In addition to helping collect and organize the papers included in this volume, Nani's pleasant but firm personality helped persuade me that more is not necessarily better and thus kept the 'Selected Writings' in manageable proportions.

It would not be possible to expressly mention all those who, over the years, helped me at different stages over half a century to develop the themes dealt with in this book. They include, in addition to my teachers at Cambridge and at Harvard, present and past Cyprus Ambassadors like the late Elias Ipsarides, Costas Malliotis, Andreas Pirishis, Loria Markides, Kornelios Korneliou, Leonidas Markides, Euripides Evriviades, James Droushiotis, Pavlos Anastasiades, Andreas Kakouris, Joseph Stephanides, Michael Stavrinos; Press Officers like Marios Evriviades, Miltos Miltiadou, Maria Zoupanioti; and such towering Cypriot figures as Presidents Makarios, Spyros Kyprianou, George Vassiliou, Glafkos Clerides; Foreign Ministers John Christophides, Nicos Rolandis, George Iacovou; and, of course, Ambassador Zenon Rossides to mention only a few of those I served under and with.

But my greatest tribute is due to Pamela, my dear wife of some decades, who, besides being a constant inspiration and the sunshine of my life, has been a source of unceasing support and encouragement over the years and, more recently, also supplemented my minimal typing and computer skills!

To all of them, I am sincerely grateful.

Andrew Jacovides
New York, April 2011

Introduction: Careers in Diplomacy and International Law*

On the basis of experience I can say with conviction that, given the appropriate circumstances, international law and diplomacy interact and expertise in one can be of great relevance and usefulness in the conduct of the other.[1]

When I was asked to contribute a piece to the series "Careers in International Law," I was somewhat hesitant to do so. From the time of joining my country's first delegation to the United Nations in 1960, soon after the independence of Cyprus, until nearly thirty-seven years later when I retired from the Foreign Service, I held key diplomatic positions, including two postings as Ambassador to the United States (fourteen years) and Dean of the Diplomatic Corps in Washington, three postings to the United Nations, including as Permanent Representative (sixteen years), Chairman of the Host Country Relations Committee, Ambassador to Germany, and Permanent Secretary of the Ministry of Foreign Affairs. In addition, I had multiple non-resident accreditations as Ambassador to such diverse countries as Brazil, Ecuador, Austria, Denmark, Canada and the Caribbean Commonwealth, and international organizations such as the International Atomic Energy Agency, UNIDO, ICAO, International Monetary Fund, International Bank for Reconstruction and Development, Organization of American States and the United Nations in Vienna. I also represented Cyprus at numerous conferences of the Non-Aligned Movement and the Commonwealth, and carried out several bilateral diplomatic missions to world capitals (London, Beijing, New Delhi, Moscow, and others).

Even though my diplomatic duties included such activities as signing the Multilateral Investments Guarantee Agreement (MIGA) Convention at the World Bank, the Customs Cooperation and the Avoidance of Double Taxation Agreements with the United States, and the Double Taxation Agreement

---

* Previously published in *Careers in International Law, 2003–2004 Edition*, American Society of International Law, 2003.

[1] See *International Law in International Diplomacy*, 77 ASIL Proc. 99–105 (1983); International Law Commission, International Law on the Eve of the 20th Century – Views from the International Law Commission 69–78 (1997).

with Canada, on behalf of Cyprus, these actions were in the course of political representation rather than as an international lawyer. Helping to set the course of Cyprus' application to join the European Union in 1990 as Permanent Secretary of the Ministry of Foreign Affairs and systematically cultivating its advance as Ambassador in the just re-united Germany with its pivotal role in Maastricht and later in the United States, was also more diplomatic than legal activity. Signing the 1969 Vienna Convention of the Law of Treaties and the 1982 Law of the Sea Convention, on the other hand, could be considered a more legal function since both of these were major law-making treaties, following protracted negotiations in which I participated.

By training, choice and inclination, I also had a parallel career in international law, having studied the subject at Cambridge University, the Inns of Court and Harvard Law School; as a representative of Cyprus to the Sixth (Legal) Committee of the United Nations General Assembly from 1960 to the present; as a College Supervisor in international law at St. Johns College, Cambridge (1958–1959); and as a Professor of UN Law at the New School for Social Research (NY 1963–1965). I was also a three-term member of the UN International Law Commission (1982–1996) and a panelist for ASIL on such topics as UN Peacekeeping (1969), the Law of the Sea (1977), UN Decade of International Law (1995), State Responsibility (2001), and Proliferation of International Tribunals (2002), and I served as a judge at the Philip C. Jessup International Moot Court Competition. With my retirement from the Foreign Service at the mandatory age of sixty, I have a greater opportunity and more time to further pursue this interest. The evolving law of the sea, the new institutions of criminal justice and, more particularly, the nascent Permanent International Criminal Court – which I had advocated in various forums decades earlier – and the items currently on the agenda of the Sixth Committee including international terrorism, human cloning and international criminal jurisdiction, provide ample opportunity for meaningful, continued and intensified engagement. When this is combined with arbitration and other legal work, as well as consulting in the field, it can be not only interesting but also financially rewarding.

Looking back over more than four decades of involvement in the international legal field, a number of thoughts emerge. Some have to do with promoting one's own country's concerns and some are of broader interest and matters of personal conviction. As far as the former are concerned, I have always considered that it is in the national interest of Cyprus to be, and to be perceived as being, an "international law-minded" state. Constructive participation in conferences leading to major law-making treaties such as the Vienna Convention on the Law of Treaties (1968–1969) and the Convention on the Law of the Sea (1973–1982), and promoting concepts such as peremptory norms of international law in the former and the position of islands, the median line for delimitation and compulsory dispute settlement in the latter, has been one way of furthering this perception. Another way is through acting for the acceptance of the optional clause of the Statute of the International Court of Justice (ICJ) and the declared willingness to have the legal aspects of the Cyprus problem clarified by reference to the ICJ, whether in contentious or advisory proceedings; the adoption of universal and regional conventions for the protection of human rights; and voluntary contributions, even in token amounts, to funds dedicated to the promotion of teaching international law and to judicial settlement. Cyprus has indeed pursued the rights of its citizens in many international, regional and national courts – including those of the United States, as in the Kanakaria Mosaics case[2] – with positive results.

In the broader sense, perhaps I might indicatively touch on three areas where, in the course of my involvement with international law, I endeavored to make a modest contribution based on my conviction of what is right. First, in the early 1960s, with the great expansion of membership of the international community through decolonization, the question was hotly debated whether newly independent states, which had not participated in creating the rules of international law, should be bound by such rules if the states considered the rules to run counter to their interest. In my first statement in the Sixth Committee[3] as a brand new 23-year-old delegate, I stated that I "viewed with some apprehension the suggestion that new States need not be bound by rules of international law which they had not helped to create and which ran counter to their interests". "National interests," I stressed, "could not be allowed more weight than the concept of international legal obligations." Twenty-two years later, speaking at the final session of the Conference of the Law of the Sea in Montego Bay, on December 8, 1982, addressing the same issue in the context of the Law of the Sea, I stated that "the newly independent states and the developing countries are fully capable of contributing constructively in exhibiting the proper sense of responsibility for the common good… It has been demonstrated that, through a process of compromise and consensus, in most instances, the conference did strike a judicious balance between, on the one hand, the new and even revolutionary approach required by the technological, political and economic changes and trends of our time and, on the other hand, the retention of those positive rules of traditional international law which have stood the test of time and have served well the interest of the international community. The concept that the

[2] Autocephalous Greek-Orthodox Church of Cyprus v. Goldberg & Feldman Fine Arts, Inc., 917 F.2d 278 (7th Cir. 1990); *see* M.-Christine Bourloyannis & Virginia Morris, International Decision, 86 AJIL 128 (1992).

[3] UN GAOR 6th Comm., 15th Sess., 668th mtg., A/C.6/SR668 (1960) at 93.

resources of the seabed beyond national jurisdiction are the national heritage of mankind and the creation of an appropriate machinery for administering them for the benefit of mankind as a whole is an example of the former. The principle that islands are entitled to the same rights as continental territories in terms of their entitlement to the zones of maritime jurisdiction is an example of the latter. The elements of progressive developments and codification of the international law of the sea are evident throughout the Convention."

Second, in terms of the peaceful settlement of disputes, the third party dispute settlement has been a firm position that I put forward in the context of all law-making treaties, including most recently, before the International Law Commission (ILC) and in the Sixth Committee on the draft Convention on State Responsibility. To quote from my statement (in the plenary of the Law of the Sea Conference on April 6, 1976): "We are for an effective, comprehensive, expeditious and viable dispute settlement system entailing a binding decision regarding all disputes arising out of the substantive provisions of the Convention. We are convinced that such a system is a necessary corollary to the substantive rules in the Convention and should form an integral part of it. This position is dictated both by reason of our attachment to the general principle of equal justice under the law and by reason of our national self-interest as a small and militarily weak state which needs the protection of the law, impartially and effectively administered, in order to safeguard its legitimate rights under the Law of the Sea Convention."[4] Whether the state of development of international law allows for the adoption of such a system in all cases is, of course, debatable. But then one could try and keep trying if one is convinced this is the right approach, even if others consider it too doctrinaire or impractical.

Third, it has long been my conviction that international law, as it has evolved in this era of the United Nations, has come to include several progressive notions, especially under the topics of the law of treaties, state responsibility and international criminal jurisdiction, such as peremptory norms of international law from which no state may derogate by agreement (*jus cogens*), of obligations erga omnes and the notion of international crime or a variant thereto. These notions, though not free from controversy as to their exact legal content, and subject to further elaboration and refining as legal rules, deserve their place in the present-day corpus of public international law. It is frequently said, and in my view correctly, that the principle of the prohibition of the use of force in international relations contained in

[4] Third United Nations Conference on the Law of the Sea at 25, U.N. Doc. *A/CONF.62/WP.9* and Add.l.

Article 2 para. 4 of the UN Charter is *jus cogens*. Having strongly supported the adoption of *jus cogens* in the Law of Treaties Conference (1968–1969), as a member of the ILC and as a delegate to the Sixth Committee, I persistently put forward papers and proposals urging the process to go forward in providing the exact legal meaning to *jus cogens* and of filling the legal vacuum that surrounds this concept.[5]

Some of the readers may be familiar with the United Nations Programme of Assistance in the Training, Study, Dissemination and Wider Appreciation of International Law. I had the privilege of being an early supporter of this Programme in the Sixth Committee. I helped establish it in 1965 through General Assembly Resolution 2099 (XX) and have served for the bulk of the intervening period on its Advisory Committee as representative of Cyprus. It is a very sound Programme which, modestly and quietly, performs valuable and constructive work in its various manifestations in New York, The Hague and in Geneva. I was fortunate, as a member of the UN International Law Commission, to give two lectures to the Geneva International Law Seminar ("Three Aspects of the Law of the Sea: Islands, Delimitation and Dispute Settlement" and the "Role of International Law in Diplomacy") and to conduct a seminar at the Hague International Law Fellowship Programme on "Alternative Means of Dispute Settlement: The United Nations Compensation Commission and the Claims Resolution Tribunal for Dormant Swiss Accounts" (August 2000), which are self-explanatory as to the range and importance of the topics dealt with under this Programme, which deserves much more financial and other support than it has been receiving.

So how is all this of relevance or usefulness to young men and women seeking careers in international law? At first glance, it would appear that my case is *sui generis* and therefore not particularly relevant. Nonetheless, with the recent increase in members of the international community and the United Nations through the break up of the former Yugoslavia and the Soviet Union and the recent admission of several small states from Europe and elsewhere to the United Nations, there might be parallels for young ASIL members in pursuing careers in diplomacy combined with careers in international law.

Let me conclude by leaving young men and women embarking on a career in international law with two notions to remember: one, it can indeed be rewarding and satisfying to contemplate combining a career in international law with a career in diplomacy; and, two, it is important that the international

[5] *See, e.g.* UN Doc. *A/CN.4/454*, at 16–26, 105–1199 Nov. 1993, UN Doc. *A/C6/46 SR23A/C6/47/SR21*. Treaties conflicting with Peremptory Norms of International Law and the Zurich/London Agreements (Nicosia 1966).

lawyer of today should be knowledgeable in both public and private international law.

It has been a pleasure for me over the years, as a diplomat, a UN delegate and a member of the ILC, to be as helpful as I could to aspiring young international lawyers, an attitude that was reciprocated and mutually rewarding. I would be very glad to continue to do so in my present capacity.

Part A

International Law

State Responsibility

State Responsibility: Reflections on the ILC's Draft Articles*◊

My exposure to state responsibility goes back to the academic year 1959–1960, when Harvard law school was engaged in the Project of State Responsibility for Injury to Aliens under Professors Richard Baxter (later a judge of the International Court of Justice) and Louis B. Sohn. I was one of a small team of research assistants (another was Keith Highet, later a president of the American Society of International Law) assigned to produce a "statement of existing law" to be attached to the draft articles on state responsibility.

The preponderance of doctrine and state practice at that time was that an espoused claim was indeed that of the state concerned, which, in turn, was entitled to waive, compromise or settle it in its dealings with other states. In doing so, a state needed to pay little or no attention to the individual claimant – a view that underwent considerable evolution in the intervening four decades.

As a three-term member of the International Law Commission (through 1996) and as a representative of my country, Cyprus, to the Sixth (Legal) Committee of the UN General Assembly, I repeatedly had occasion to comment on the topic of state responsibility, expressing regret at the slow progress on this topic in the ILC, urging that its consideration be given top priority, and even expressing the hope that the state responsibility project would be completed during the UN Decade of International Law, thus marking a major contribution by the ILC toward the objectives of the Decade.

I observed that, with the completion of the state responsibility project, several of the problems, primarily of scope, encountered in the context of the topic of the draft Code of Crimes against the Peace and Security of Mankind and the topic of Injurious Consequences Arising Out of Acts Not Prohibited by International Law would be obviated – for instance, the aspect of the

* Previously published in *American Society of International Law Proceedings of the 94th Annual Meeting 2000*, pp. 14–17.

◊ Other selected writings by Andrew Jacovides on State Responsibility: Article 25 Statement of Existing Law, Research Paper as part of the State Responsibility Project of Harvard Law School 1960, 201 pages (not published, on file with the author).

criminal responsibility of a state, as distinct from the criminal responsibility of the individual.

Turning to the current text of draft articles on state responsibility, I am glad to note that the current Special Rapporteur, James Crawford, has done an outstanding job, in his customary energetic style, in grappling with the many remaining problems while modernizing and streamlining the text of the draft articles. Indeed, the prospect of completing the second reading of the draft articles during the term of office of the ILC's present members, that is, by 2001, is in sight.

On the whole, I find myself in agreement with the Special Rapporteur's approach both in substance and in drafting. I can see the practical reason for a distinction between states specifically injured by an international wrongful act and other states that have a legal interest in the performance of the relevant obligation but that do not suffer economically quantifiable injury. While the legal interest exists for both categories of states, in the practice of states it is the specifically injured state that has the right to such reparations. I also agree that a wrongdoing state must provide compensation to the specifically injured state, to include, in addition to the principal amount of pecuniary damage, interest and loss of profit.

On the issue of countermeasures, my view has been that, if they are to be retained at all, their scope should be narrowly defined since they lend themselves to abuse at the expense of weaker states; that they should be aimed at restitution and reparation or compensation rather than punishment; that there should be an extensive third-party dispute settlement system; and that if they be applied at all, it be done objectively and not abusively. I would also stress that armed countermeasures are prohibited under Article 2(4) of the UN Charter, which has become a customary rule of international law.

On the question of dispute settlement in the context of state responsibility, but also generally in multilateral law-making treaties concluded under UN auspices, the position I have persistently and consistently advocated as a delegate of Cyprus is: "We are for an effective, comprehensive, expeditious and viable dispute settlement system entailing a binding decision regarding all disputes arising out of the substantive provisions of the Convention. We are convinced that such a system is a necessary corollary of the substantive rules of the Convention and should form an integral part of it. This position is dictated both by reason of our attachment to the general principle of equal justice under the law and by reason of our national self-interest as a small and relatively weak state which needs the protection of the law, impartially and objectively administered, in order to safeguard its legitimate rights."[1]

[1] From author's statement at the Plenary of the Law of the Sea Conference, April 6, 1976.

Whether the state of development of international law allows for the adoption of so broad a system is, of course, debatable. But I believe one should keep trying if one is convinced that this is the right approach, even if others consider it, for the present at least, too doctrinaire or impractical. This applies also to the state responsibility convention, should there be one.

Let me observe also that in the context of State Responsibility, the concept of *jus cogens*, or peremptory norms of international law, needs to be clarified as to its scope and applications. The issue of consent, which must in any case be freely given, should be approached with great caution. The essence of peremptory norms is that they cannot be derogated by agreement between the parties *inter se* because this would be contrary to international public policy. If Article 2(4) of the UN Charter incorporates a peremptory norm prohibiting the use of force, any purported derogation from it by agreement is invalid and inoperative under the Vienna Convention on the Law of the Treaties and customary international law, even if the agreement obtained is not through an imposed or unequal treaty.

It could be argued that there may be other ways, such as through a chapter VII binding Security Council resolution, to cover the requirements of particular situations in a pragmatic fashion with the consent of the state concerned, but in my view the principle that peremptory norms may not be modified by agreements of the patties *inter se* must remain intact.

On the question of crimes, as distinct from delicts, I would be interested to hear the views of others as to the latest developments of this issue in the present draft. The controversy on the issue may be diffused through a change in terminology, but the substance ought to be retained. Similarly, I would reserve my position on the basic question of whether the situation calls for a convention or for a model law. My own preference would be that, as practicable, the subject is too important and too much time and effort have gone into it to let it be treated by way of a model law.

Allow me a brief diversion from the theory of the draft articles of the ILC to the presently existing practical aspect of state responsibility at work. I am referring to the UN Compensation Commission (UNCC), which was established as a subsidiary organ of the UN Security Council in order to process claims and pay compensation for losses resulting from Iraq's 1990 invasion and occupation of Kuwait.

Iraq's legal responsibility and liability was established in Security Council Resolution 687 (1991), adopted under chapter VII of the UN Charter, which confirmed that "Iraq... is liable under international law for any direct loss, damage, including environmental damage, and the depletion of natural resources, or injury to foreign Governments, nationals and corporations, as a result of Iraq's unlawful invasion and occupation of Kuwait." Iraq accepted the terms of Resolution 687 (1991), and, by its Resolution 692 (1991), the

Security Council created on May 20, 1999, the UN Compensation Fund (which receives a percentage of the proceeds from the sales of Iraqi oil) and the UN Compensation Commission. The UNCC operates through several panels of commissioners, examining claims, verifying their validity, evaluating losses, assessing payments and resolving disputed claims, all within parameters set by the Security Council, which has the final say, as governing council, in approving the reports and recommendations of the Panels of Commissioners.

It is not for the present to go into the constantly evolving jurisprudence of the UNCC, which presents many interesting international-law features. But it is relevant to note that, as far as I know, the formation of the UNCC marked the first time the United Nations established a major claims resolution facility to deal effectively and on a large scale with the financial consequences of a state's responsibility for the violation of its international law obligations.

Two brief observations will help bring the matter into perspective. One is that the declaration in Security Council Resolution 687 (1991) regarding Iraq's liability is consistent with established customary international law holding states responsible for damages caused by their unlawful actions.[2] The governing principle is that damages should be awarded that are sufficient to wipe out the consequences of the illegal act and reestablish the situation that would, in all probability, have existed if that act had not been committed.

The second observation is that one can envisage several other situations in which unlawful acts generally, and unlawful invasion and occupation in particular, have occurred without the victim states receiving any remedy. Indeed, it was a rare convergence when unanimous support in the Security Council for the adoption of a chapter VII binding resolution occurred simultaneous with the availability of resources, in this case Iraqi oil, to satisfy the resultant claims. In a world where the rule of law applies, this exceptional situation ought to be the rule rather than the exception.

---

2 *Factory at Chorzow* (Ger. v. Pol), 1928 PCIJ (ser. A) No. 17.

Law of Treaties

Treaties Conflicting with Peremptory Norms of International Law and the Zurich-London 'Agreements'*◊

The purpose of the present paper is to consider the question whether international law recognises the existence within its legal order of rules having the character of *jus cogens* i.e. rules from which the law does not permit any derogation by agreement between the parties *inter se* as distinct from *jus dispositivum* i.e. rules which the parties may freely regulate by such agreement.[1] This inquiry will touch upon such material as is available in the writings of scholars, the pronouncements of international tribunals and international practice, with particular emphasis on the work of the International Law Commission on the subject and the views expressed thereon by the representatives of States, both in the Sixth (Legal) Committee of the United Nations General Assembly and through written comments of Governments.

Certain considerations and reflections will be put forward regarding the theoretical justification for the existence of the *jus cogens* doctrine, its effect

---

* Privately published, 1966. Paper prepared at the Dag Hammarskjöld Foundation Seminar on the Law of Treaties, Uppsala, Sweden 1966.

◊ For other selected writings by Andrew Jacovides on the Law of Treaties see: Official Records of the General Assembly, Twenty-second Session, Sixth Committee, Summary Records of Meetings 19 September–14 December 1967, New York, pp. 126–128; Use of Force, May 2, 1968, United Nations Conference on the Law of Treaties, First Session, Vienna, 26 March–24 May 1968, Official Records, Summary Records of the plenary meetings and of the meetings of the Committee of the Whole, A/CONF.39/11, pp. 279–280; Jus Cogens, May 3, 1968, United Nations Conference on the Law of Treaties, First Session, Vienna, 26 March–24 May 1968, Official Records, Summary Records of the plenary meetings and of the meetings of the Committee of the Whole, A/CONF.39/11, pp. 305–306; and Jus Cogens, Outlines Prepared by Members of the Commission on Selected Topics of International Law, General Assembly A/CN.4/454, 9 November 1993, pp. 16–26 and Annex pp. 105–119.

1 For bibliography see generally Wright, Conflicts between international law and treaties, AJIL, Vol. 2 (1917), pp. 566–579; Lauterpacht, H., The Covenant as the "Higher Law", BYIL, 1936, pp. 54–65; Jenks, C.W., The Conflict of Law-making treaties, BYIL, 1953, pp. 401–453; Verdross, A. Von, Forbidden Treaties in international law, AJIL, Vol. 31 (1937), pp. 571–577; Verdross, A. Von, Jus dispositivum and Jus cogens in international law, AJIL, Vol. 60 (1966), pp. 55–63; Schwarzenberger, G., "International jus cogens" Texas Law Review, March, 1965, pp. 455–478; Suy, E., Le jus cogens en droit international public, Conference de droit international, Lagonissi, (Grece 3–8 avril 1966); Murty, B. S., *Jus cogens* in international law, International Law Conference, Lagonissi (Greece 3–8 April, 1966).

upon the law of treaties generally and the means for determining whether a given rule does or does not merit the description of *jus cogens* at a given time. Certain principles will then be cited and broadly examined which, in the view of the writer, fall within this category.

The attempt will then be made to illustrate the problem by applying the findings of such inquiry in order to test the validity of the Zurich-London 'Agreements' of February 1959, and of the resultant "Treaties" signed at Nicosia on 16th August, 1960.[2] While the emphasis will be placed upon the consideration of the validity of these 'Agreements' in the light of the present rules of general international law regarding *jus cogens*, it will also be necessary, in order to present a complete picture of the legal situation regarding these instruments, to sketch the factual background of these 'Agreements' and to touch very briefly upon certain other aspects of the law of treaties, as well as of United Nations law, which are of direct relevance to the issue.

Historical Background and Recent Developments

It may be readily accepted that the general rule of the law of treaties is that States are competent, by agreement between themselves, to conclude treaties on any subject whatsoever and thus regulate their relations with each other at discretion.

From a very early stage of the development of international law, however, this sweeping character of this rule did not remain unchallenged. As early as the middle of the eighteenth century eminent writers such as Christian Wolff[3] and Emeric Vattel[4] were distinguishing between the necessary law, which nations cannot alter by agreement, and the voluntary law created by the will of the parties. Likewise, A.W. Heffter[5] declared, a century later, that treaties were void if their object was physically or morally impossible and by moral impossibility he understood that the object of the treaty was contrary to the ethics of the World.

In more recent times opinion among writers was more divided. Nineteenth century positivism had a significant effect and it was widely accepted that international law did not impose any restrictions upon the freedom of States to conclude any treaty irrespective of its object. Modern writers who,

[2] Conference on Cyprus; H.M.'s Stationery Office, 1959, Cmnd 679; and Cyprus, H.M.'s Stationery Office, 1960, Cmnd 1093. U.N.T.S., Vol. 382 (1960), Nos. 5475, 5476; U.N.T.S. Vol. 397 (1961), No. 5712.

[3] Wolff, Jus Gentium, paras. 5 and 25 (1764).

[4] Vattel, Le droit des Gens, Introduction paras. 9 and 27 (1758).

[5] A.W. Heffter, Das Europaische Volkerrecht der Gegenwatt 156 (4th ed. 1861).

with various degrees of emphasis, have shared this view include such prominent scholars as Charles Rousseau,[6] Gaetano Morelli,[7] Paul Guggenheim[8] and G. Schwarzenberger.[9]

On the other hand, certain recent developments in international law, such as the conclusion of the Kellogg-Briand Pact of 1928 and the decisions of the Nuremberg and Tokyo tribunals and even more important, such fundamental landmarks in the direction of organised international society as the Covenant of the League of Nations and the Charter of the United Nations, have served to reverse this trend. Another such factor is the recent transformation in the composition of the society of nations through the emergence of a considerable number of new States which put their own imprint on the process of developing international law. All these factors have had a decisive effect in reviving and reinforcing the notion that, besides jus dispositivum rules which can be departed from by agreement, there exist certain rules and principles of general international law having the character of jus cogens from which the parties cannot derogate by agreement between themselves.

It has been persuasively argued[10] that the very fact of the existence of norms determining which persons are endowed with the capacity to act in international law, what intrinsic and extrinsic conditions must be fulfilled so that an international treaty may come into existence, what juridical consequences are attached to the conclusion of an international treaty, militates against accepting the view that the whole international law system is dependent on the agreement of the wills of States.

These rules of *jus cogens* do not exist in order to satisfy the needs of individual States but in order to serve the higher interests of the international community as a whole, and the ultimate justification for their existence is that they rest upon the common expression of the conscience of the international community.

Various terms have been used to describe this notion and to explain the basis upon which it rests. Lauterpacht, referring to the Covenant of the League of Nations, wrote in 1936 that "...the substance of its law differs so radically from other international conventions in its scope and significance as a purposeful instrument in the process of political integration of mankind as to deserve the designation of a 'higher law'...".[11] McNair writing in 1930

[6] Rousseau, Principes du Droit International Public 340–341 (1944).
[7] Morelli, Nozioni di Diritto Internazionale 37 (3rd ed. 1951).
[8] Guggennheim, Traité de Droit International Public 57 (1953) – but see footnote (19).
[9] Schwarzenberger, International Law 352–3, 425–7 (1957) and op. cit. footnote (1).
[10] Verdross, Forbidden Treaties in International Law, op. cit. footnote (1).
[11] Lauterpacht op. cit. footnote (1).

and referring both to the Covenant and to the Kellogg-Briand Pact, says[12] that these instruments created "a kind of public law transcending in kind and not merely in degree the ordinary agreements between States". These views, expressed in the inter-war years, would have equal, if not greater, validity in relation to the United Nations Charter. The terms "international public policy" and "international public order" (*ordre public*) have also been used to underscore the notion that these rules of *jus cogens* or peremptory norms are firmly based upon the conscience of mankind, that they represent some higher social needs and that they are the minimum of rules of conduct necessary to make orderly international relations possible.

Writers who have shared and promoted a position in favour of the existence of *jus cogens* include, in addition to Lauterpacht[13] and McNair,[14] such eminent jurists as Balladore Pallieri,[15] Kelsen,[16] and Tunkin.[17] The eminent Austrian international jurist Verdross[18] deserves a particular place among these writers. It now appears to be the general trend, even among those who previously held different views, with the notable exception of Schwarzenberger, to accept the notion of *jus cogens.*[19]

The issue of *jus cogens* received scant attention before international tribunals. The instances quoted where the matter was touched upon are not directly on point. These are the celebrated individual opinion of Judge Anzilotti in *the Austro-German Customs Union* case[20] (where he questioned whether there is not a contradiction in the fact of obliging a State to live and of putting it at the same time into a situation which renders its life extremely difficult-and see post, on the principle of sovereign equality) and of the dissenting opinion of Judge Schucking in the *Oscar Chinn* case,[21] where he stressed that the Court would never apply a convention the contents of which were contrary to *bonos mores.* In its Advisory Opinion concerning *Reservations to the Genocide Convention*[22] the Court, referring to the Genocide Convention, "adopted for a purely humanitarian and civilising purpose", commented that "the contracting States do not have any interest of their own: they merely

[12] McNair, The functions and differing legal character of treaties, BYIL 11 (1930), 112.
[13] See also Oppenheim-Lauterpacht, 8th Edition (1955) p. 896 to the effect that "immoral obligations cannot be the object of an international treaty".
[14] See also McNair, Law of Treaties 213–4 (1961).
[15] Balladore Pallieri, Diritto Internazionale Publico 282 (8th ed. 1962).
[16] Kelsen, Principles of International Law, 89, 323, 344 (1952).
[17] Tunkin, Das Volkerrecht der Gegenwart, 95–96 (1963).
[18] Verdross, Von, op. cit. footnote (1).
[19] Suy op. cit. footnote (1) at p. 55.
[20] P.C.I.J., Series A/B No. 41.
[21] P.C.I.J., Series A/B, No. 63 p. 149.
[22] I.C.J. Reports, 1951, 23.

have, one and all, a common interest, namely, the accomplishment of those high purposes which are the raison d'être of the Convention".[23]

The Work of the International Law Commission and Issues Arising Therefrom

The process of the acceptance of the *jus cogens* doctrine as part of contemporary international law was further promoted through the work of successive Special Rapporteurs of the International Law Commission on the law of treaties and culminated during the fifteenth session of the Commission in 1963. It will be recalled that the Commission, after extensive discussion of the subject[24] and after fully considering the various aspects of the text submitted by its latest Special Rapporteur, Sir Humphrey Waldock,[25] reached the unanimous conclusion that:

> A treaty is void if it conflicts with a peremptory norm of general international law from which no derogation is permitted and which can be modified only by a subsequent norm of general international law having the same character. (Draft Article 37).[26]

The Commission also took the further step, which was only the logical corollary of its adoption of the draft Article cited above, of adopting a further draft Article 45,[27] covering the case of the emergence of a new peremptory norm of general international law, through either custom or a general multilateral treaty, and its effect upon treaties:

> 1. A treaty becomes void and terminates when a new peremptory norm of general international law of the kind referred to in Article 37 is established and the treaty conflicts with that norm.
> 2. Under the conditions specified in Article 46,[28] if only certain clauses of the treaty are in conflict with the new norm those clauses alone shall become void.[29]

---

23 For an extensive collection of material from the international jurisprudence, including references to individual and dissenting opinion, on the subject see Suy, op. cit. footnote No. (1), pp. 76–84.

24 Yearbook of the International Law Commission, 1963, Vol. I, pp. 62–78.

25 A/CN.4/156.

26 Official Records of the General Assembly, Eighteenth Session, Supplement No. 9 (A/5509), p. 11.

27 Op. cit. footnote (26) at p. 23.

28 Op. cit. footnote (23) at p. 26.

29 As is pointed out by the Special Rapporteur in the course of the debate in the ILC, the nineteenth century conventions for regulating the slave-trade were valid when drawn up but subsequently became void by the development of a new rule of international law prohibiting the slave-trade altogether.

The close study of the records of the Commission's debate of this matter,[30] the commentary accompanying the text,[31] the records of the debate in the Sixth (Legal) Committee of the General Assembly on the Commission's Report,[32] the comments of Governments[33] regarding draft Article 37, as well as the Special Rapporteur's comments as set out in his Fifth Report,[34] furnishes a wealth of evidence to demonstrate that the principle as stated in the draft Article meets with general approval, if not with complete unanimity.[35]

The examination of these records also reveals the significant role which the new States which came into existence subsequently to the Second World War, as well as the East European States,[36] played in helping establish the existence of this rule, although the contribution of the Latin American as well as of several Western European States is in no way underestimated. On the whole, it may be said that it is particularly the smaller and weaker States which have a greater interest in the recognition of the existence and the strengthening of a public order placing checks upon an unlimited freedom of contract, as opposed to a situation which, under the respectable guise of the unlimited freedom of contract, exposes them to the real danger of unequal and inequitable treaties under which the stronger State would, in the nature of things, take the lion's share.[37]

The rule which finds expression in draft Article 37 corresponds to the rule in municipal systems of law[38] to the effect that an agreement to commit a crime or one which is otherwise contrary to public policy is null and void and cannot be construed as conferring any rights upon the parties to it (*ex injuria non oritur jus*). The recognition on the part of the Commission of the existence of the equivalent rule in public international law constitutes a most

30 Op. cit. footnote (24).

31 Op. cit. footnote (26).

32 Official Records of the General Assembly, Eighteenth Session, Report of the ILC (item 69).

33 A.CN.4/175 et Addenda.

34 A/CN.4/183 Add 1.

35 While comments on the part of Governments were favourable, with several shades of enthusiasm, only the Government of Luxembourg was openly negative to the notion, while the Government of Turkey took also a negative but more guarded approach.

36 Both of these categories of States are characterised by their own approach to international law. For a Western view of these approaches see e.g. Higgins, Conflicts of Interest-London, 1965, and Lissytzin, International Law Today and Tomorrow, New York, 1965.

37 In the course of the discussion in the ILC on draft Article 37 the distinguished Spanish jurist Dr. de Luna observed: "The contractual conception of international law, which did not recognise *jus cogens*, belonged to the time when international law had been only a law for the Great Powers. But modern international law has become universalised and socialised".

38 A rule which may undeniably be described as a general principle of law recognised by civilised nations within the meaning of Article 38 of the Statute of the International Court of Justice.

constructive contribution by the Commission in pursuance of its mandate not only to codify but also to further the progressive development of international law. As was epigrammatically put by Dr. El Erian, in the course of the subsequent debate in the 6th Committee of the General Assembly, "the recognition of the notion... marked a transition from classical international law to the modern law of the United Nations".

The Commission has been criticised for its formulation of draft Articles 37 and 45 on two grounds. Firstly, that they involve the creation of a new ground on which treaty obligations can be denied; and secondly, that they would furnish to third States the right to discuss the legal validity of agreements to which they are not parties and which normally would not be their concern. It is argued that particularly the former ground creates the great danger that, since the rules of *jus cogens* cannot be precisely identified and stated, the recognition of their existence enables every State wishing to denounce a treaty, to put forward a plea of nullity alleging the repugnance of such a treaty with *jus cogens.*

While this danger cannot be denied and the principle of *jus cogens* can indeed be abused, it is believed by the present writer that it can, and should, be minimised if not completely eliminated through as exact a delimitation of the rules of international law falling within the category of *jus cogens* as possible (see post) rather than by ignoring the existence of such rules altogether. In this respect the analogy with the equivalent municipal law rule is instructive: No one denies the existence in municipal law of rules of public policy even though these, too, are not always clearly and exactly defined or definable. It may of course be retorted that in the case of municipal law systems, whenever there arises a doubt as to whether in a given case such a rule does or does not apply, the matter can always be referred to and be settled by a competent tribunal.

There may indeed be a lot to be said in favour of making the determination as to whether a given situation is or is not covered by a rule of *jus cogens*, especially when the plea of nullity is contested by one of the parties, subject to the decision of an impartial tribunal. In his Report to the International Law Commission, Lauterpacht phrased the relevant Article as follows:

> A treaty, or any of its provisions, is void if its performance involves an act which is illegal under international law and if it is declared so to be by the International Court of Justice.[39]

[39] Yearbook of the International Law Commission, 1953, Vol. II, p. 154.

Likewise, Verdross[40] had suggested that all disputes concerning the interpretation and application of a norm having the character of *jus cogens* must be submitted to arbitration.

It is axiomatic that if the rule of law among nations is to acquire its full meaning, the jurisdiction of an International Court (whether in its present or other form) ought to be universal and the means should be provided whereby its decisions would be enforced. International institutions, however, cannot be raised from the co-operative to the organic level until we have a society of States which is far more closely bound together than are the States of today. In the present imperfect stage of development of the international society, with the Court's jurisdiction dependent on the consent of the individual States and suffering from a variety of other inhibiting factors, it would, it is believed, be plainly unrealistic to tie the principle of *jus cogens* to adjudication by the International Court and the International Law Commission acted in accordance with the hard facts of the international life of today.

The absence of compulsory adjudication, however, does not mean that international law in general, or its *jus cogens* in particular, lacks binding legal force. Moreover, there exist a number of other means for the peaceful settlement of disputes between States including, in addition to negotiation, conciliation, mediation and arbitration, recourse to the Security Council and the General Assembly of the United Nations.

In particular, Article 14 of the Charter, which empowers the General Assembly to make recommendations for the peaceful adjustment of any situation regardless of origin, is certainly sufficiently broad to enable the General Assembly to pronounce itself upon disputes between Member States involving the inconsistency of treaty provisions with rules of *jus cogens*,[41] especially if such disputes are basically political in nature.

As for the second ground of criticism, viz. the possibility for third states to concern themselves with situations to which they were not parties, it may be said that this may have been well-founded in the past. However, it must be accepted that in an interdependent world intended to be regulated in a number of respects by such a fundamental instrument as the Charter of the

[40] Op. cit. footnote (1).

[41] Indeed General Assembly resolution 2077 XX, on the Question of Cyprus, furnishes a good illustration of the point. And see the statement of Mr. Paredes who, in the course of the debate in the International Law Commission on the more specific rule of a treaty imposed upon a State by the threat or use of force in violation of the principles of the Charter and consequently in violation of the relevant *jus cogens* rule, stated that, in the absence of compulsory international adjudication, "the only remedy would be… that the victim of aggression should be able to appear before the United Nations Security Council and declare the treaty void because of vitiation" – Yearbook of the International Law Commission, 1963, Vol. I, p. 61.

United Nations, it would be anachronistic to claim that third States should have no voice when patent illegalities are perpetrated against one or more of the members of the society of nations.

Turning now to the question of what effect the conflict of a *jus cogens* rule has upon a treaty, the members of the Commission were unanimous in their view that the treaty becomes null and void *ab initio*, rather than simply voidable at the instance of one or more of the parties. The legal consequences of this view are far-reaching for "the consequence of voidance *ab initio* was simply that there was no treaty".[42] Likewise, Verdross[43] takes the view that the formal voidance of immoral contracts is unnecessary and that the burdened State has the right simply to refuse the fulfillment of such an obligation. It would therefore, appear that, at least according to these views, and in the absence of any provision in the Article for third party determination, such treaties as conflict with *jus cogens* can simply be taken as non-existent i.e. as not requiring any further act declaring such treaty to be not binding.[44]

The Commission, after considering the possibility of severance of the offending provisions from the rest of the treaty, under the conditions laid down in Article 46 of the Draft, took the view of the majority of its members who considered that rules of *jus cogens* are of so fundamental a character that, when parties conclude a treaty which conflicts in any of its clauses with an already existing rule of *jus cogens*, the treaty must be considered totally invalid and the sanction of nullity should extend to the whole transaction.

By contrast, in the case of a new peremptory norm emerging (Article 45, supra) the effect of the rule is not to render the treaty provision in question void *ab initio* but to invalidate it only from the date when the new rule of *jus cogens* was established i.e. to forbid further performance. Likewise, the Commission took the view that, under the conditions provided in Draft Article 46, severance is permitted in the case of Draft Article 45, with the result that provisions not affected by the emergence of the *jus cogens* rule in question would be regarded as still valid.

---

[42] Rosenne op. cit. footnote (41) at p. 55.

[43] Op. cit. footnote (1).

[44] This might indeed in some cases be too drastic a remedy and it might, when the illegality is disputed, strengthen the argument that the doctrine is subject to abuse. One might wonder whether, on the analogy of null marriages, it would not be appropriate for a formal act to take place in order to "take it off the book". In that case, however, it would seem that it would be for the party contesting the plea of nullity and relying on the treaty in question to prove its legality.

The Relationship between Article 103 of the Charter and Article 37 of the International Law Commission's Draft

The interesting question which arises in this connection is the relationship between the effect of Article 103[45] of the Charter of the United Nations and Article 37 (and 45) of the International Law Commission's draft. Reference to the preparatory work regarding Article 103 shows that that Article does not provide for the automatic abrogation of treaties conflicting with the Charter, but rather requires that obligations under the Charter shall prevail.[46]

In the course of the discussion of the International Law Commission's draft by the Sixth Committee of the General Assembly many representatives pointed out that Article 103, by proclaiming that obligations under the Charter prevailed over obligations under any other international agreement, had aided greatly in creating the *jus cogens rule*. Yet, as various representatives stated, its logical consequences had not been recognised, and it was that gap which the International Law Commission had filled by stating that an international treaty was void if it conflicted with a peremptory norm of international law.[47] The matter occupied again the attention of the Commission when, in its commentary on draft Article 63, it recognised the primacy of the rule in Article 103, in the context of the relative priority of incompatible treaty obligations. As the Special Rapporteur pointed out, however, while the Commission appreciated that there may be certain areas of overlap in the application of the *jus cogens* provisions of Articles 37 and 45 and of Article 103 of the Charter because certain provisions of the Charter, notably those of Article 2(4), are of a *jus cogens* character, it nevertheless considered the invalidity of a treaty under Articles 37 and 45 of the draft Articles, by reason of a conflict with a rule of the *jus cogens*, to be a distinct and independent question.[48] In other words, while Article 103 refers to *priority* or conflicting obligations, draft Articles 37 and 45 refer to *invalidity* of obligations – yet they may, and do, overlap in certain areas. While the writer shares the view

[45] Which provides that "in the event of a conflict between the obligations of the Members of the United Nations under the present Charter and their obligations under any other international agreement, their obligations under the present Charter shall prevail".

[46] The Committee on Legal Problems, Committee 2, decided that "it would be inadvisable to provide for the automatic abrogation by the Charter of obligations inconsistent with the terms thereof. It has been deemed preferable to have the rule depend upon and be linked with the case of a conflict between the two categories of obligations. In such a case the obligations of the Charter would be pre-eminent and would exclude any other" – Report of the Rapporteur of Committee IV/2, U.N. Doc. 933, IV/2/42, U.N. Conf. Int.'l Org. docs. 707 (1945).

[47] Official Records of the General Assembly, Eighteenth Session-Agenda item 69, document A/5601, para. 18.

[48] A/CNA/183/Add. 1 pp. 23–24.

of Sir Humphrey Waldock that not all rules contained in the Charter are necessarily peremptory norms and, conversely, there are peremptory norms that are not contained in the Charter, it is believed that the area of overlap is considerably greater than merely the principle contained in Article 2 (4) of the Charter (see post).

The Question of What Rules of International Law Fall within the Category of Peremptory Norms

While it appears that the principle of the existence of peremptory norms from which no derogation by treaty is permitted, has won overwhelming approval both within and outside the International Law Commission, the question of what specific rules of international law fit under this description, in other words, what is the exact juridical content of this principle, is considerably less clear.

The International Law Commission was unable to arrive at any generally recognised criterion by which to identify a general rule of international law as having the character of *jus cogens*. Certain examples were suggested by some of the members of the Commission "of the most obvious and best settled rules of *jus cogens*" in order to indicate the general nature and scope of the rule, and indeed some of these had originally appeared in the body of the draft Article as presented by the Special Rapporteur. These included, in addition to the case of the threat or use of force contrary to the principles of the Charter (a subject to which we shall return, see post), a treaty contemplating the performance of any act criminal under international law; a treaty contemplating or conniving at the commission of acts, such as trade in slaves, piracy or genocide, in the suppression of which every State is called upon to cooperate; treaties violating human rights; treaties violating the right to self-determinations.[49] Some members of the Commissions[50] stressed that the examples given should include unequal treaties.

In the end, however, the Commission, bearing in mind the comparatively recent emergence of these rules and the rapid development of international law, decided against including any specific examples and of leaving "the full content of the rule to be worked out in State practice and in the jurisprudence of international tribunals". The Commission reached this conclusion (a) because it thought that to include certain examples and not others might lead to a misunderstanding regarding the position of other cases not expressly

[49] Op. cit. footnote (26) at pp. 11–12.
[50] Mr. Lachs and Mr. Tunkin, op. cit. footnote (24).

mentioned; and (b) because it feared that, if it were to draw up, even on a selective basis, a list of the rules meriting the description of *jus cogens*, it might find itself engaged in a prolonged study of matters which did not fall within the ambit of the law of treaties. It may well be that the Commission, in the particular circumstances of its work, acted wisely in adopting this cautious approach. While the first reason given is not a very convincing one (it would always be possible to furnish an illustrative list of examples, thereby giving concrete expression to the principle generally stated in the draft Article, and to stress that this is not an exhaustive list) the second reason, which in any case is connected with the first, presents a much more real problem. As was pointed out in the course of the Commission's debate,[51] the problem, reduced to its simplest terms, was how to define illegality in international law and this, in view of the widely-divergent political theories and conflicting interests involved, is indeed a formidable task[52] if the unanimity which prevailed in the adoption of the principle was to be preserved. The danger of opening a Pandora's Box of disagreements and the consequent weakening of the very principle which was so painstakingly reached by unanimity is only too clearly visible to be ignored.

At the same time the impression should not be permitted to be created that the notion of *jus cogens* is merely a philosophical or theoretical idea devoid of any real meaning. Nor can the suggestion be entertained that the principle so clearly formulated by the Commission means all things to all people but has no practical significance in present day international law. The almost unanimous reception of the principle by the representatives of Governments[53] militates against any such cynical evaluation of the Commission's work on this subject – an evaluation which offends the legitimate expectations of the vast majority of the members of the international community and outrages the social conscience of mankind upon which, in the last analysis, the notion of *jus cogens* ultimately rests.

It is therefore to be regretted that the difficulties which confronted the Commission prevented it from going the full way and from spelling out the content of the principle it enunciated, thereby completing the process which it had so admirably initiated and advanced. The door is left open to the danger on the one hand of too broad a definition of what constitutes *jus cogens* with the consequent risk of abuse and stretching the principle to the point

---

[51] By Mr. Amado, op. cit. footnote (24).

[52] As the efforts to define aggression and, more recently, the current efforts in the Sixth Committee and its Special Committee to arrive at an agreed formulation of the principles of international law governing friendly relations and co-operation in accordance with the Charter of the United Nations, illustrate.

[53] Op. cit. footnotes (32) and (33).

of breaking and, on the other hand, to too narrow or restrictive a definition thereby robbing the principle of any real meaning and negativing its effect.

The question arises whether there exists no other body within the machinery of the organised international society of today, which might usefully undertake the task at the point where the International Law Commission left it. One such possible forum which comes readily to mind is the Sixth (Legal) Committee of the General Assembly. If one bears in mind that *jus cogens* is formed through the expression of the collective conscience of the community of nations there might be a lot to recommend the Sixth Committee – where, unlike the International Law Commission, all Member States are represented – acting possibly through a special committee, whereon States would be represented by jurists, to undertake the task of defining what rules of general international law constitute peremptory norms for the purpose of the *jus cogens* doctrine. Undoubtedly the Committee would be faced by the same real difficulties as the Commission was. Likewise any resolution, or declaration, that it might be able to arrive at by the requisite majority might be open to the objection that it did not itself constitute a source of law and was not binding. Nonetheless any such resolution, especially a unanimous or near-unanimous one though not in itself a source of law, might be taken as confirming the existing law on the subject and would in any case carry considerable weight as the expression of the general opinion of States.[54]

Another possibility might be offered by the proposed. Conference of Plenipotentiaries to be convened in 1968 in order to adopt a multilateral convention on the law of Treaties.

Quite independently, however, of these possibilities there is no doubt that in the light of the principle unanimously adopted by the Commission and overwhelmingly approved by States and by international jurists, there exists considerable material upon which to base the conclusion that there exist today a considerable number of rules of general international law which have a legitimate claim to be regarded as peremptory norms (*jus cogens*). Indeed several were mentioned in the Commission's discussion and are referred to above.[55] The present writer shares the view of Mr. Rosenne who stated in the course or the International Law Commission's discussion[56] that 'there existed

---

[54] E.g. see the statements of Mr. Yasseen and Mr. Bartos, also shared by Mr. Waldock, on the effect of General Assembly resolution as expressing rules of *jus cogens* op. cit. footnote (24).

[55] It is sometimes stated e.g. Verdross op. cit. footnote (1), that treaties encroaching upon the rights of third states are contrary to *jus cogens*. If appears the better view, now recognised also by Verdross, that this falls properly under the *pacta tertiis nec nocent nec prosunt* rule. While these treaties are illegal if the third State does not give its consent, in the ordinary case it would not be contrary to *jus cogens*.

[56] Op. cit. footnote (24).

elements which made it possible to determine with a reasonable degree of accuracy whether a given rule constituted *jus cogens*'. What is intended here, however, is not to attempt any full enumeration of such rules but, instead, to concentrate on four principles, which, it is believed, particularly in view of recent trends and developments in international law and organisation, do fall within the principle covered by draft Article 37 and merit the description of *jus cogens*.

These are:

(A). The principle that States should refrain from the threat or use of force their international relations.
(B). The principle of the peaceful settlement of international disputes.
(C). The principle of non-intervention in the internal affairs of any State.
(D). The principle of the sovereign equality of all States.[57]

(A) *The Principle that States Should Refrain from the Threat or Use of Force in Their International Relations*

It may be safely asserted that, unlike the accepted doctrine of earlier times, the combined effect of the Covenant of the League of Nations and the Kellogg-Briand Pact and especially the clear-cut prohibition of the threat or use of force in Article 2 (4) of the United Nations Charter,[58] together with the practice of the Organisation itself, establish quite conclusively that the prohibition of the threat or use of force in international relations constitutes *lex lata* in the international law of today.

This prohibition is absolute, the only possible exceptions being provided in the Charter itself viz. under Article 42 i.e. action decided upon by the Security Council, and under Article 51 i.e. in self-defence if an armed attack occurs and until the Security Council has taken appropriate measures. It appears to be the prevalent view that both of these exceptions should be interpreted

---

[57] It would be beyond the scope of the present paper to deal fully with the contents of these principles. The matter has received a great deal of attention during successive sessions of the Sixth Committee of the General Assembly under the heading "Consideration of Principles of International Law Concerning Friendly Relations and Cooperation in accordance with the Charter of the United Nations" – see Official Records of the General Assembly regarding this item during the 17th, 18th and 20th Sessions. Likewise see the Report of the Special Committee at its meetings in Mexico City UN doc. A/5764 and New York, A/AC.125/L.38 et addenda. Statements by the delegation of Cyprus contained in A/C.61 SR.768; 822; 824; The written views of the Government of Cyprus are contained in UN Document A/5725 of 22 July 1964. This material is drawn upon freely in discussing the scope of these principles.

[58] Article 2 (4) reads: "All members shall refrain in their international relations from the threat or use of force against the territorial integrity or political independence of any state, or in any other manner inconsistent with the Purposes of the United Nations".

stricto sensu. This is particularly true in the case of the use of force in reliance upon Article 51. Since the establishment of the United Nations a State which found itself threatened by war preparations from another State can have immediate recourse to the Security Council rather than resort to any measures of anticipatory self-defence as it might have done under previously existing rules of traditional international law. "The final result is that Article 2 (4) prohibits entirely any threat or use of armed force between independent States except in individual or collective self-defence under Article 51 or in execution of collective measures under the Charter for maintaining or restoring peace. Armed reprisals to obtain satisfaction for an injury or armed intervention as an instrument of national policy otherwise than for self-defence is illegal under the Charter."[59]

Regarding the meaning of the term "force" as employed in Article 2 (4), some doubt may exist as to whether economic, psychological or other coercion comes within its purview even though this is supported by a strong body of opinion. But there is no room for doubt that the use of threat of armed force falls definitely within this paragraph. Likewise "threat" may take the form not only of action but also of words. Moreover the practice of the United Nations indicates that the fomenting of civil strife in a State in the interest of a foreign Power constitutes use of force under this paragraph.

Concerning the term "international relations" as used in Article 2 (4), it is evident that the prohibition of the threat or use of force applies only to disputes between States and has no application in the field of civil war or other disturbances *within* a State. Consequently a State is not precluded from using force in the event of civil war, or similar occurrence, in order to put down a rebellion within its own territory.

The employment of the words "against the territorial integrity or political independence of any state" in Article 2 (4) was clearly not intended to imply any limitation to the prohibition of the threat or use of force. In fact they were inserted into the text in San Francisco in order to give to smaller and weaker States an *express* guarantee of their territorial integrity and political independence. The wording used clearly does not imply that a State may use force against another State on the ground that this force is not directed against the territorial integrity or political independence of the latter State, but is done on the allegation that it is simply designed to support constitutional order or to protect a minority or other pretext, such as a treaty right, and is not intended permanently to interfere with the territorial integrity or political independence of the latter State. To accept such a contention would

[59] Waldock, "The regulation of the use of force by individual States in international law," Academie de droit international, Recueil des cours, 1952–11 at p. 493.

be to nullify the very purpose of Article 2 (4) and it appears to be the better view that such interpretation has no foundation.

It is likewise clear that the term "any State" as used in the paragraph under consideration means that the prohibition extends to the use of force against any member of the society of nations, including non-members of the United Nations.[60] Obviously, however, it applies *a fortiori* in relation between Member States.

In addition to the obvious cases of the use of force, such as the invasion of a State's territory by the armed forces of another State or the aerial bombing or naval bombardment of such territory, there exist several other situations which may be cited as constituting violations of the principle embodied in Article 2 (4). Thus if armed forces of one State found themselves present in the territory of another State under an arrangement which could be taken to imply the latter's consent to such presence and this consent was subsequently withdrawn, the refusal of the authorities of the former State to withdraw its forces would amount to a violation of the principle in Article 2 (4). This would be so *a fortiori* if the reason for the withdrawal of such consent was the flagrant and persistent violation of the said arrangement by the troops in question which deployed themselves as an army of occupation and did not recognise the authority of the host State.

The prohibition to the threat or use of force being absolute, it logically follows that any alleged right to use or to threaten to use force by one State against another under a treaty is non-existent in modern international law. Any provision in any treaty purporting to give such a right would be invalid in international law as being contrary to a fundamental rule of *jus cogens* as well as under Article 103 of the Charter,[61] in the same way as an agreement to commit a crime would be invalid in municipal law as being contrary to public policy.

(B) *The Principle of the Peaceful Settlement of International Disputes*

A second principle of *jus cogens* and one which finds expression in Article 2 (3) of the Charter, is that States are under an obligation to settle disputes arising in their international relations by peaceful means on the basis of international law and of justice and within the framework of the principles of the Charter. It follows logically that since disputes do, in the nature of things, arise between States, and since these can no longer be solved through the threat or use of force, they must be settled by peaceful means. Under

---

[60] This interpretation is indeed clearly supported by the wording of Article 2 (6).

[61] See footnote (45), supra.

Article 33 of the Charter,[62] States are free to choose from among a variety of means for settlement. Of these negotiation is the most frequent, and, in relations among sovereign States, the most appropriate method provided that it is conducted on the basis of equality. It is of course to be recognised that in instances where the parties hold widely divergent and hardened positions this method has obvious limitations. Inquiry, mediation, conciliation and arbitration may also prove useful methods for arriving at a peaceful settlement.

With regard to judicial settlement through the International Court of Justice there is no doubt that the ideal position should be that the Court's jurisdiction should be broader and its decisions always enforced. At the same time it must be recognised that this is a position which does not correspond to the realities of the present-day development of the international community which is far from perfect. Particularly as regards the International Court its jurisdiction may be said to suffer from certain inhibiting factors due to its composition, the notion of representation upon it (as exemplified by the need for a provision for *ad hoc* judges), the inability of the parties to predict the Court's decision with any degree of reasonable certainty and the absence of specific means for enforcing the Court's decision otherwise than by recourse to the Security Council – a recourse which is subject to the veto. Moreover it should be borne in mind that there exist situations where a strict application of the letter of the law may well produce a result inconsistent with universally accepted notions of justice.

In such situations the courts are unable properly to serve the cause of peace by pronouncing upon conflicts basically political in nature for which the proper, remedy is new legislation and not judicial decision. Such situation could be best settled out of court or, if brought before a tribunal, such tribunal should be empowered to decide *ex aequo et bono*.

Apart from the judicial organ of the United Nations, however, the Security Council, the General Assembly and the Secretary-General can each play, and do play, a vital part in the peaceful settlement of disputes. The functions of the Security Council in this field are well established but are not always satisfactorily discharged owing to the coming into play of power politics and of the occasionally indiscriminate use of the veto power. The experience of the General Assembly, on which all Member States are represented, acting on the basis of the dynamic interpretation of Articles 10, 11 and 14 of the Charter, has been more rewarding and can indeed he further utilised. Again, the

[62] It reads: "All Members shall settle their international disputes by peaceful means in such a manner that international peace and security, and justice are not endangered".

Secretary-General, acting either in person or through special representatives or fact-finding missions, has been of incalculable assistance in ascertaining facts, clarifying positions and exerting a moderating influence through the prestige of his office on the parties to disputes of an explosive nature. His functions in this respect, even apart from specific powers granted to him under resolutions of the political organs of the Organisation, may be said to go further than the mere exercise of good offices or mediation for it is generally recognised that, by virtue of the nature of his office, the Secretary-General is presumed to possess the moral authority and impartiality which place him in a unique position in the peaceful settlement of disputes.

Whatever may be the specific method selected by the parties for the settlement of their dispute, the cardinal factor remains that it must be peaceful, and this is a peremptory norm of international law. The parties may not agree, as they might have done in the past, "to fight it out between them". If they do, such agreement falls within the scope of the principle draft 37 of the International Law Commission's draft and is null and void.[63]

(C) *The Principle of Non-Intervention in the Internal Affairs of Any State*

Particularly since the adoption of the Charter, the system of which is squarely based on the principles of sovereign equality[64] and political independence,[65] it has come to be established that intervention in the sense of dictatorial interference by one State in the internal affairs of another State, on whatever ground, is inadmissible as part of modern international law.

Even before the adoption of the Charter there existed a body of opinion for the view that intervention was illegitimate.[66] More recently, however, it

---

63 In relation to principles A and B the following excerpt from Verdross, op. cit. footnote (1), is particularly instructive: "Another group of rules having the character of *jus cogens* was introduced by the Charter. It deals with the use of force, and is composed of three interconnected rules. The first obliges the Member States to refrain in their international relations from the threat or use of force other than in individual or collective self-defence (Article 2 (4) and Article 51). The second rule obliges the Member States to settle their international disputes by peaceful means (Article 2 (3))... It is clear that these rules exist in the common interest of all humanity. Therefore bilateral or multilateral treaties concluded in violation of these norms are void. The contracting parties are not bound inter se by such treaties. Never could the International Court or an arbitral tribunal consider them as valid".

64 See D, post.

65 See A, supra.

66 E.g. Hall, A Treatise on International Law, 4th edition, 1895, p. 305 wrote: "It may perhaps at one time have been an open question whether a right or a duty of intervention could be set up by a Treaty of Guarantee binding a State to maintain a particular form of government in the state to which the guarantee applied. But the doctrine that intervention on this ground is either due or permissible involves the assumption that independent States have not the right to change their government at will and is in reality a relic of... exploded notion(s)".

has come to be reaffirmed and elaborated upon through such instruments as the charters of the Organisation of American States, the League of Arab States and the Organisation of African Unity, the decisions of the Asian-African Conferences in Bandung, of the Belgrade and Cairo Conference of the Heads of State or Government of Non-Aligned countries, the declaration of subversion adopted at Accra by the Heads of State and Government of the African States and the conferences held at Montevideo, Buenos Aires, Chapultepec and Bogota. The process culminated in the adoption by the 20th General Assembly, without any dissenting vote, of resolution 2131 (XX) entitled 'Declaration on the Inadmissibility of Intervention in the Domestic Affairs of States and the Protection of Their Independence and Sovereignty'. This resolution solemnly declared that "No State has the right to intervene, directly or indirectly, for any reason whatever, in the internal or external affairs of any other State". This trend is also aptly expressed in the judgment of the International Court of Justice in the *Corfu Channel* case where the alleged right of intervention was described by the Court as "the manifestation of a policy of force such as has in the past given rise to most serious abuses and such as cannot, whatever be the present defects in international organisation, find a place in international law".[67]

This pronouncement on the part of the highest international judicial tribunal, combined with the overwhelming weight of the other authorities, leaves little scope for doubt that the rule against intervention by one State in the internal affairs of another State,[68] such intervention being inconsistent with the basic principles of the political independence and the sovereign equality of States, falls within the description of *jus cogens* and constitutes a peremptory norm of international law. Consequently, States are not competent to derogate from it by treaty arrangement.[69]

---

67 I.C.J. reports 1949 at p. 35.

68 It would be going beyond the scope of the present paper to attempt to cover in detail the aspects of this rule the precise definition of which is admittedly difficult to arrive at. E.g. a considerable weight of authority, as expressed e.g. in General Assembly resolution 2131 (XX) as quoted above would extend the rule to cover external as well as internal affairs. Likewise intervention by invitation of the Government of the state in question poses various questions. See e.g. E. Lauterpacht – Intervention by invitation, The Times, London, 24 August, 1960, p. 9. On principle such invitation should be restrictively interpreted because it is apt to lend itself to abuse.

69 E.g. Stowell, writing as early as 1921, stated "Treaties which record an agreement to interfere in the internal affairs of the signatory or of other sovereign states are Without any standing in international law and cannot be made to justify the interference which they contemplate." Ellery Stowell, Intervention in International Law, 1921, at p. 439.

(D) *The Principle of the Sovereign Equality of all States*

The principle of the sovereign equality of States, which is clearly stated in Article 2 (1) of the Charter[70] as the foundation of the United Nations, carries within it two notions viz. that States are sovereign and that States are juridically equal. It means that a State is sovereign and its authority over its territory is supreme and that, in relation to all other States it is independent and equal. Indeed, in this sense, "sovereignty is independence"[71] and to that extent, the analysis which follows applies to the notion of "political independence" as used in Article 2 (4) and principle A, supra. It likewise carries with it the notion that every State, in the exercise of its sovereignty has the right to determine freely its own destiny and its political, constitutional and social system – in other words, the right of self-determination as a State.

In stressing the above the fact is not overlooked that States do not exist in a vacuum but are in continuous economic, political, social and other relations with each other. Undoubtedly a State can, through agreements freely negotiated and validly arrived at, enter into international obligations which hamper it, more or less, in the management of its external or even internal affairs and *protanto* limit its sovereignty. This is a principle which lies at the root of the law of treaties and was fully recognised in the decision of the Permanent Court of International Justice in the S. S. *Wimbledon* case[72] where it was stressed that every sovereign State has the power to limit the exercise of its sovereignty. No doubt Schwarzenberger is right in stating that "every state is free to alienate a part or the whole of its territory, transform itself into a dependent state, retain or give up its international personality, constitute itself into a new international entity",[73] provided, it should be stressed, that this is done in the free exercise of the will of the people and without dictation from outside. Indeed, there have been several instances in recent years when one State, in the exercise of its sovereignty, freely decided to divest itself of its sovereignty and to merge with another State (e.g. Syria merged with Egypt in 1958 in order to form the United Arab Republic; Zanzibar merged with Tanganyika in 1964 in order to form the United Republic or Tanzania).

However, it should be equally clear that, in the case where a sovereign State continues to exist and is universally recognised as such and, more particularly, it is a Member State of the United Nations, such a State cannot, it is submitted, at the same time by treaty divest itself of the essential manifestations

---

[70] It reads: "The Organisation is based on the principle of the sovereign equality of all its Members".
[71] E.g. Oppenheim-Lauterpacht, International Law; Vol. I, eighth edition at p. 286.
[72] P.C.I.J. Sec. A, No. 1, 1923.
[73] Op. cit. footnote (1) at p. 458.

of its sovereignty for, in that case, it would be unable to carry out its basic duties and responsibilities as a sovereign State and a United Nations member.[74] To quote Oppenheim-Lauterpacht[75] "independence is a question of degree and it is therefore also a question of degree whether the independence of a State is destroyed or not by certain restrictions". The question whether, in any given case, the derogation from the State's sovereignty and independence is of such a nature as to go to the root or substance of such State's sovereignty and independence depends on the particular circumstances of the case.

It would be instructive to quote Oppenheim again as to what rights and responsibilities constitute the substance of such sovereignty and independence: "In consequence of its internal independence and territorial supremacy, a State can adopt any constitution it likes, arrange its administration in any way it thinks fit, enact any laws it pleases, organise its forces on land and sea, adopt any commercial policy and so on".[76] It is submitted that a State cannot, by treaty or otherwise, validly contract out of the substance of its sovereignty and independence and still purport to be considered a sovereign and independent State[77] and that this constitutes a basic rule and a peremptory norm of present day international law. A State's membership in the United Nations furnishes conclusive evidence of the fact that such a State is entitled to be considered as an independent and sovereign State. Its international rights and obligations are governed primarily by the principles of the Charter. In the event of a conflict between these principles, including the principle of sovereign equality, and any undue and excessive limitations imposed under any other treaty, the Charter prevails under its Article 103. Moreover, any such undue limitations would be null and void under the *jus cogens* rule of international law regarding state sovereignty.[78]

---

[74] Verdross supra footnote (1) where he cites as treaties contra bonos mores those "which restrict the liberty of one contracting party in an excessive or unworthy manner or which endanger its most important rights". See also Anzilotti supra footnote (20).

[75] Op. cit. footnote (1) p. 289

[76] Ibid. p. 287. See also Fenwick, International Law, 3rd Edition, 1952, p. 249.

[77] See the minority opinion of the seven judges of the Permanent Court of International Justice in the Austro-German Customs Union case, op. cit. supra, footnote (20), in which it is stressed that a State would not be independent in a legal sense if it ceased exercising within its territory the *summa potestas* or sovereignty, or if it lost the right to exercise its discretion in the taking of the decisions necessary for the governing of its territory.

[78] As early as the Lausanne Conference the Government of Turkey, in attempting to justify its unilateral denunciation of the Capitulations in 1914 stated "...according to modern legal conception each State, in order to be considered as an independent State, must enjoy within the limits of its frontiers, a complete and full independence". AJIL, vol. 29 (1935) Suppl. Part III, p. 1114. Murty, supra footnote (1), writing as late as 1966, in reference to both principle C and principle D says "There have been two basic objectives sought in the past two or three centuries in developing prescriptions, and they are, first the maintenance

Another area in which the doctrine of equality of States is of practical significance today is that of unequal, imposed, unjust or inequitable treaties. While the exact legal content of this doctrine has still to be worked out it appears clear that the trend[79] today is that private law analogies of the invalidation of contracts arrived at in circumstances of duress or undue influence should be borne in mind in determining the validity of international agreements arrived at when the two (or more) parties to such agreements were in an unequal bargaining position with the result that the treaty was unjust, inequitable or Imposed. If a treaty was imposed upon a State without its free consent in violation of the Charter and its fundamental principles, it would be for the State concerned to take its free decision with regard to the maintenance or not of such a treaty after it found itself in a position of legal equality with the at her State or States.[80] This observation would be even more pertinent if such a treaty was imposed upon a people prior to, and as a condition for, such a people being permitted to accede to independence.

Consequences of the Conflict of a Treaty Provision with Any of These Principles

In the light of the above, it follows that a treaty which, directly or by necessary implication, purports to permit to the parties to It to resort to the threat or use of force otherwise than under Article 2 (4) of the Charter; or to settle their disputes not by peaceful means, as provided in Article 2 (3) and Article 33 of the Charter; or would purport to license intervention in matters which are manifestly of domestic jurisdictions; or would purport to deprive a State on the essential attributes of its sovereignty, such a State continuing to exist us a sovereign and independent State, are null and void and the sanction of nullity extends to the whole transaction. This would *a fortiori* be so if a treaty

of a minimum order of peace and security, and second, of certain standards of civilisation and humanity. The first objective was sought in a system based upon the *principles of sovereignty, equality, non-intervention; in internal affairs, territorial and personal supremacy, etc*... What the U.N. Charter has done in relation to the maintenance of minimum order is to provide prescriptions furnishing less escape doors, and an organised machinery of decision regarding, and response to, unauthorised acts of coercion... In a general way it may be stated that *treaties the objective and/or outcome of performance of which conflict with these goals are liable to be regarded as invalid*".

79 See e.g. footnote (50) for a suggestion that these treaties are specifically mentioned as examples of violation of *jus cogens*. Likewise, during the debate in the 6th Committee on the ILC's report in 1963 several representatives, notably the East Europeans but also several others notably of Algeria, Cyprus and Panama stressed that such treaties should be regarded as invalid.

80 See generally debate in 6th Committee on draft Article 36 of the I.L.C.'s Report in 1963.

containing such vitiated provisions was imposed upon a State in circumstances of duress or undue influence and, even more so, if it was imposed upon a people prior to and as a condition for such people for permitting such people to accede to independence.

Peremptory Norms of International Law and the Zurich-London 'Agreements'

We may now turn to the second part of the present paper viz. the consideration of whether and, if so to what extent, the Zurich-London 'Agreements',[81] conflict with any of the rules of *jus cogens* and more particularly those indicated above.

Background

Before, however, embarking upon this task it will be necessary to give a brief description of the background and the circumstances in which these 'Agreements' were entered into and to touch upon certain of their provisions.

It will be recalled that the island of Cyprus (which, under the Treaty of Defensive Alliance between Great Britain and Turkey of 1878, had been assigned by the latter to the former Power for the purpose of occupation and administration) was annexed by Great Britain on 5 November 1914. This annexation was expressly recognised by Turkey in Article 20 of the Treaty of Lausanne of 1923. Moreover Turkey, under Articles 16 and 27, respectively, of the same Treaty, renounced any right or title over Cyprus and divested itself of the exercise of any power or jurisdiction in political, legislative or administrative matters over the nationals of Cyprus. By Letters Patent of 1925, Cyprus was declared to be a British Crown Colony.

It was administered as such when on 1 April, 1955, an armed struggle was initiated on the part of the Greek Cypriot population of the island, among

[81] For bibliography on the Zurich-London 'Agreements' see generally Emilianides, The Zurich and London Agreements and the Cyprus Republic, Mélanges Seferiades, Athens, 1961; Tornaritis, The Legal Aspects of the Question of Cyprus, Nicosia, 1965; Zoupanos, The Invalidity and the Inapplicability of the Treaty of guarantee of Cyprus, Corfu, 1964 (in Greek); Zotiades, The Treaty of Guarantee and the Principle of Non-intervention, 1965; Tsatsos in 'Kathimerini' newspaper 9 and 10 December, 1964 (In Greek); Tenekides, Chypre, Editions Nagel, 1964; Tornaritis, Talarides and Ipsarides in Cyprus To-day, Vol. II, Nos. 3–4, 1964. See also statements by the Minister of Foreign Affairs of Cyprus Mr. S. Kyprianou before the Security Council and the General Assembly and notably his statement in the Official Records of the Security Council 10 the 1098th meeting.

whom the objective of uniting the island with Greece had always been a cherished ideal, in order to force the Colonial Power to recognise the applicability to the case of the people of Cyprus of the right of self-determination.

After four years of armed struggle and repeated recourses to the United Nations General Assembly (which, however, being still dominated by the Colonial Powers, failed to give, by the requisite majority, any clear-cut directive notwithstanding the express provisions of the Charter) and after considerable secret diplomatic activity in certain Western capitals, an agreement was reached on 11 February, 1959, in Zurich, Switzerland, between the then Prime Ministers of Greece and Turkey, Mr. Karamanlis and Mr. Menderes, respectively, laying down the structure of a new State, the Republic of Cyprus. It should be noted that this agreement was worked out by Turkey and Greece without the participation of the people directly concerned viz. the people of Cyprus, and in a manner which would reconcile their mutual interests.[82]

The two Prime Ministers initialed three documents viz. (*a*) a draft Basic Structure of the Republic of Cyprus; (*b*) a draft Treaty of Guarantee between the Republic of Cyprus on the one part and Greece, Turkey and the United Kingdom on the other part; and (*c*) a draft Treaty of Alliance between Cyprus, Greece and Turkey. These became known as the Zurich Agreement.

On the same day, the Ministers for Foreign Affairs of Greece and of Turkey flew to London to consult the Secretary of State for Foreign Affairs of the United Kingdom. It was agreed between them, as a result of these consultations, that certain areas of Cyprus should be retained under the sovereignty of the United Kingdom and that an additional article should be inserted in the draft Treaty of Guarantee, providing for the respect of the integrity of these areas as well as the use and enjoyment of various rights in connection thereto to be secured to the United Kingdom. In addition, the British Government asked, and this was also agreed upon, that certain other matters be provided for in the settlement.[83]

It was only at this stage that the documents initialed at Zurich, together with the British declaration and its acceptance by the Ministers for Foreign Affairs of Greece and Turkey, were put before Archbishop Makarios, the acknowledged leader of the Greek Cypriots, and to Dr. F. Kutchuk, as the leader of the Turkish Cypriots who were invited to London for that purpose.[84] They were asked to accept or to reject these documents as they stood-no margin was permitted for any alterations or amendments. Dr. Kutchuk,

[82] As subsequently stated by the Government of Turkey, U.N. document A/C 1/914 at p. 16.
[83] See Cmnd 679, op. cit. footnote (2), pp. 11–13.
[84] This procedure was employed in view of the absence of any form of national representative government in Cyprus and differs from the usual case of granting of independence to non-self-governing territories.

for self-evident reasons, was quite willing to accept these documents. This was not the case with Archbishop Makarios. It was clear however, and was made explicitly so from many quarters during the tense days which ensued, that "rejection of the Agreements would have meant denial of independence and increased bloodshed".[85] The circumstances which compelled Archbishop Makarios to accept the documents placed before him are best expressed by himself as follows: "At the Conference at Lancaster House on 15 February, 1959, which I was invited to attend as leader of the Greek Cypriots, I raised a number of objections and expressed strong misgivings regarding certain provisions of the agreement arrived at in Zurich between the Greek and the Turkish Governments and adopted by the British Government. I tried very hard to bring about the change of at least some of those provisions. I failed, however, in that effort and I was faced with the dilemma either of signing the agreement as it stood or of rejecting it with all the grave consequences that would have ensued. In the circumstances I had no alternative but to sign the agreement. This was the course dictated to me by necessity".[86]

It was under these circumstances, which precluded free choice and with the parties being in grossly unequal positions to negotiate, that on 19 February, 1959, in a ceremony at Lancaster House, Archbishop Makarios initialed the relevant documents as the representative of the Greek Cypriot population. Dr. Kutchuk also affixed his initials for the Turkish Cypriots.

On the same day provision was made, and was initialed by the three Foreign Ministers, for the setting up of three committees in order to give final form to what had been 'agreed upon': (*a*) a Joint Commission for drafting the constitution (with representatives from Greece and Turkey as well as from the Greek and Turkish Cypriots); (*b*) a Transitional Committee for the transfer of authority to the Republic of Cyprus; and (*c*) a Joint Committee for the purpose of preparing the final treaties giving effect to the conclusions of the London Conference.[87]

At this stage the Prime Ministers of the United Kingdom, Greece and Turkey signed a memorandum by which they adopted, on behalf of their respective Governments, the documents as "the agreed foundation for the final settlement of the problem of Cyprus".[88]

85 As Archbishop Makarios put it in addressing the Non-Aligned Conference as President of Cyprus in Cairo on 9 October, 1964.

86 From the document dated 30 November 1963 entitled "Suggested measures to facilitate the smooth functioning of the State and to remove certain causes of intercommunal friction". Cyprus Today, Vol. I, No. 6, 1963.

87 Cmnd 679, supra footnote (2) pp. 14–15.

88 Ibid., p. 4.

Conflict with the Rule against Imposed and Unequal Treaties

These were the circumstances in which what began in Zurich was concluded and the London 'Agreement' came into existence. Having regard to these circumstances one would indeed find it difficult to disagree with the Foreign Minister of Cyprus who declared, before the Security Council, that "the parties were in an unequal bargaining position and the Greek Cypriot side did not give its consent freely." These treaties which contained onerous provisions were thus imposed on the majority of the people of Cyprus making the doctrine of unequal, inequitable and unjust treaties relevant.[89] Such treaties offend the rule of the *jus cogens* regarding sovereign equality and more specifically the rule of the *jus cogens* regarding unequal treaties (above). This inequality is further aggravated if it is borne in mind that these 'agreements' were imposed, not by independent States upon another independent State but by two independent States and by a Colonial Power upon a people prior to, and as a condition for, such people acceding to independence. Indeed it could also be argued that, having regard to the circumstances of the conclusion of the Zurich-London 'Agreements', not only is the rule of unequal treaties applicable but also the principle expressed in draft Article 36 of the Law of Treaties[90] is also relevant and applicable.

For the sake of completing the picture, the following facts regarding the transitional period between the conclusion of the London Conference and the proclamation of the independence of Cyprus are also relevant:

The Joint Commission completed its work[91] on the draft Constitution on 6 April 1960 and the document was signed on that date.[92] It came into force on 16 August[93] upon its signature by the then Governor of Cyprus on behalf of the British Government, by the representatives of the Governments of Greece and Turkey and by Archbishop Makarios and by Dr. Kutchuk, who had been returned as President-elect and Vice-President-elect, respectively, as a result of elections held in December 1959.

[89] Official Records of the Security Council, 1098th meeting, p. 20.

[90] To the effect that "any treaty the conclusion of which was procured by the threat or use of force in violation of the principles of the charter of the United Nations shall be void".

[91] It is pertinent to stress, in reply to the unfounded argument occasionally put forward that there could have been an improvement to the Zurich framework as a result of the work in this Commission, that this body was strictly enjoined under the Agreed Measures, Cmnd 679, p. 15, to "have regard to and... scrupulously to observe the points contained in the documents of the Zurich Conference and to fulfill its task in accordance with the principles there laid down".

[92] Cmnd 1093, supra footnote (2), p. 3.

[93] By Order-in-Council S.l. 1368/1960 made under the Cyprus Act, 1960.

The London Joint Committee, after protracted talks in London and Nicosia, completed its work on 1 July, 1960.[94]

The Constitution having been signed, as indicated above, and the Treaties of Establishment, of Guarantee and of Alliance having also been signed by their respective parties,[95] Cyprus was declared to be an independent sovereign Republic on 16 August, 1960.[96]

The Republic of Cyprus was admitted to membership in the United Nations on 20 September, 1960, through the unanimous vote of the General Assembly acting upon the recommendation of the Security Council. Turkey, Greece and the United Kingdom were among those Member States which, without any reservation, voted for admission.[97–98]

Conflict with the Principle of Sovereignty and Non-Intervention

We should now turn to consider certain aspects of the Constitution which was foisted upon the people of Cyprus in the circumstances described above, in so far as this is relevant to our present inquiry. It would be going beyond the scope of the present paper to examine in any detail the provisions of the thus imposed Constitution. It will suffice to say that it was intended to place on an equal footing and keep separate and divided two ethnic groups of grossly unequal size (the Greek Cypriots being over 80% and the Turkish Cypriots being less than 18% of the population of Cyprus) and, as a result, under the

94 Cmnd 1093, supra footnote (2), p. 4.

95 See generally ibid., Cmnd 1093, in which a variety of other arrangements of a legal nature are also set out.

96 In so far as United Kingdom constitutional law was concerned, Cyprus became independent as a result of Order-in-Council S.l. 1368/1960 made under the authority of the Cyprus Act, 1960.

97 The argument has been put forward in a letter to the New York Times dated 26 June, 1964, by the Permanent Representative of Cyprus to the United Nations, that by voting for admission and by not raising any objection or making any reservation at the time as to the qualified or restricted nature of the sovereignty of the Republic, the three 'Guarantor' Powers forfeited any right they may have had under the Treaty of Guarantee and are estopped from alleging that Cyprus is not a sovereign and independent State within the meaning of the Charter.

98 The Treaty of Establishment and the Treaty of Guarantee were registered with the United Nations Secretariat under Article 102 of the Charter by the United Kingdom on 12 December, 1960 – op. cit. footnote (2) – while the Treaty of Alliance was registered through the unusual procedure of joint registration by Turkey and Greece, though not by Cyprus on 12 June, 1961 – op. cit. footnote (2). It is the accepted United Nations practice that the registration of treaties under Article 102 is performed by the Secretariat as an administrative or mechanical act and in no way denotes any acceptance of the validity of the instrument in question.

guise of protecting the minority, contains many *sui generis* features[99] which conflict with the internationally recognised principles of democratic government, such as the principle of universal suffrage on the basis of 'one man one vote' and the trends of our times against discrimination and division on the basis of race, creed or ethnic origin.[100]

On a more practical level, these *sui generis* provisions soon proved, despite the goodwill shown on the part of the Greek Cypriot side, to be constant sources of friction between the Greek majority and the Turkish minority and to result in serious instances of abnormality and even breakdown of the governmental machinery.[101] As time was going by it was becoming increasingly clear that, owing to the inherent peculiarities of the provisions of the Constitution on the one hand and to the intransigence of the minority – inspired and encouraged from the outside – the Constitution was proving increasingly unworkable.

But the most striking feature of the Constitution, and the one which is most relevant to our present task, is the fact that it not only embodies fully the provisions agreed upon in Zurich between the Prime Ministers of Greece and of Turkey, but also provides[102] that "the articles or parts of articles of this Constitution set out in Annex III hereto which have been incorporated from the Zurich Agreement dated 11 February, 1959, are the basic articles of this Constitution and cannot, in any way, be amended, whether by way of variation, addition or repeal". The Constitution thus purported to declare the constitutional structure it embodied as immutable for ever in so far as the people of Cyprus were concerned thus precluding them from exercising within their own territory the most basic right of sovereignty. It cannot be denied that, in modern times, this is an unprecedented example of denial of democratic principles and, incidentally, irreconcilable with the letter of the

---

[99] Including, separate municipalities; separate administration of justice; separate simple majority of the Turkish Cypriot members of the House of Representatives in certain matters; absolute veto on the part of the Turkish Vice-President – who is elected by the members of his community above – against laws or decisions of the House of Representatives, or decisions of the Council of Ministers, relating to foreign affairs, security or defence; privileged position on the part of the Turkish Cypriots who even though less than 18% of the population as stated above, were said to be entitled to 30% of the posts in the public service, and security forces and 40% in the army – the strength of which was arbitrarily fixed in Zurich at 2,000 men – 3 out of the 10 posts on the Council of Ministers and 15 out of the 50 posts in the House of Representatives.

[100] Such as those embodied in the United Nations Declaration on the Elimination of All Forms of Racial Discrimination, adopted without a dissenting vote by the 18th General Assembly, Resolution 1904 XVIII.

[101] Such as the situation when the Turkish members of the House of Representatives, by misusing their right of separate voting, refused to support the Income Tax Bill, with the result that the Republic remained without a unitary income tax legislation since 1 January, 1962 and subsidiary devices had to be employed.

[102] In Article 182 (1).

Constitution itself which, in its Article I, declares Cyprus to be "an independent and sovereign Republic".

But that was not considered to be sufficient and, under Article 181 of the Constitution, both the Treaty of Guarantee and the Treaty of Alliance were declared "to have constitutional force". Moreover, under Annex III of the Constitution, both Article 181 and Article 182 were included in the list of the 'basic articles of the Constitution' i.e. they could not "in any way, be amended, whether by way of variation, addition or repeal".

We shall have occasion subsequently to deal more fully with these Treaties. But at this juncture it would be relevant to note that, while under the Treaty of Alliance provision was made for the presence in the Republic of Cyprus of military contingents from Turkey and from Greece (Article IV thereof), under the Treaty of Guarantee these two Powers as well as the United Kingdom guaranteed "the state of affairs established by the Basic Articles of the Constitution" (Article II thereof) and "in the event of a breach of the provisions of the present Treaty, Greece, Turkey and the United Kingdom undertook to consult together with respect to the representations or measures necessary to ensure observance of those provisions. In so far as common or concerted action may not prove possible, each of the three guaranteeing Powers reserved the right to take action with the sole aim of re-establishing the state of affairs created by the present Treaty" (Article IV thereof).

It is submitted that these interlocking provisions, the combined effect of which was to arrest the constitutional and political development of the Republic by putting it into a straight jacket at its infancy as a sovereign entity,[103] and to subject it to the will of three outside Powers, created a state of affairs inconsistent with the basic elements of the principles of sovereign equality and non-intervention, as developed supra.

Indeed, independence is a question of degree but it is plain and self-evident that if a State cannot at will alter its constitution, pass the necessary laws regarding the operation of its internal services, arrange for its local government, its administration of justice, its police force, etc., but all these – and many others – matters are dependent upon the will of three outside Powers or anyone of them, then such a State cannot be considered to be a sovereign and independent State. Conversely, if it is a sovereign and independent State, and the Republic of Cyprus is stated so to be in Article I of its Constitution and its membership of the United Nations and of many other international organisations furnishes conclusive evidence of the fact that it is and is so recognised by the members of the family of nations, then

[103] As aptly remarked by the Foreign Minister of Cyprus before the Security Council, Official Records 1098th meeting, p. 20.

such undue and excessive restrictions, being inconsistent with the rules of *jus cogens* regarding sovereign equality and non-intervention, are null and void. This is so independently from and in addition to the operation of the contractual remedy available under Article 103 of the Charter (supra).

Conflict with the Principle of the Prohibition of the Use of Force

Let us now turn to consider the more specific question of whether Article IV of the Treaty of Guarantee (cited in full *supra* in connection with the principles of sovereign equality and non-intervention) can be taken to permit to the 'Guarantor Powers', and each one of them, the right to intervene by force in the affairs of the Republic and, if so, whether this is consistent with the principle regarding the prohibition of the threat or use of force in international relations.

Indeed, on the basis of the text as it stands, it might be argued that the term 'representations or measures' in the first paragraph, and the term 'action' in the second paragraph, of the said Article contain an element of ambiguity. Consequently, in accordance with the principle of interpretation of reasonableness and consistency with generally recognised principles of international law,[104] as well the rule of construction contained in the maxim *ut res magis valeat quam pereat* (principle of effectiveness), these terms should be interpreted as referring only to such 'measures' or 'action' as would not conflict with the principle of the Charter – and part of the *jus cogens* – regarding the prohibition of the threat or use of force. In other words (and quite independently of the validity of this Article under other principles, as set out above) it could be argued that Article IV should not be interpreted as permitting an unqualified licence to intervene in Cyprus by the use of armed force.[105–106]

---

104 E.g. Oppenheim-Lauterpacht, supra p. 952. Jenks, op. cit. supra footnote (1).

105 Indeed this was the interpretation given by the representative of Greece, Official Records of the Security Council 1097th meeting, while the representative of the United Kingdom was more equivocal, Official Records of the Security Council 1098th meeting.

106 As early as March, 1959, i.e. a few weeks after the signature of the 'Agreements' and more than a year before they were formally put into effect, the present writer, in a paper introduced to the Cambridge University International Law seminar dealing with several aspects of those documents, pointed out the danger inherent in the wording used which could easily lend itself to an interpretation purporting to permit unilateral use of force. He had stressed that such an interpretation would be illegal under the post-Charter notions of international law regarding the use of force in international relations and suggested the possibility of employing a form of words that would remove this danger. More specifically he had suggested that the word "such" be used before and the words "as is permitted under international law" after the word "action" in the draft text, with the result that the relevant part of the Article would read: "…such action as is permitted under international law…" if the draft Treaty were not to be struck with nullity *ab initio*. These observations

It is, however, clear that at least one party to the Treaty of Guarantee, viz. Turkey, has not only claimed[107] that Article IV of the said Treaty gives to it the right to intervene by force in Cyprus but also, in pursuance of this interpretation, it has, deliberately and repeatedly, so intervened as early as 25 December, 1963, and most flagrantly on 8 and 9 August, 1964. It is submitted therefore that, in accordance with the principle considered under A, above, and more specifically, through the interplay of Articles 2 (4) and 103 of the Charter on the one hand and the rule of *jus cogens* regarding the prohibition of the use of force and draft Article 37 of the International Law Commission's conclusions (which in this respect overlap) on the other hand, it can be validly contended that Article IV of the Treaty of Guarantee, as interpreted by at least one of the 'Guarantors', and by extension the whole Treaty, is inconsistent with the Charter and is null and void as being in conflict with a peremptory norm of general international law. To accept the opposite would have the effect of taking a giant step backwards because it would imply the endorsement of the untenable proposition that States may, by agreement *inter se*, legalise what is manifestly illegal in general international law.

Other Grounds on which the Zurich-London 'Agreements' Are Not in Force – Termination, Fundamental Change of Circumstances

What has been said so far covers, in broad terms, the position of the Zurich-London 'Agreements' in the light of the relevant rules of *jus cogens* viz. the violation of the principles of equality and sovereignty, the violation of the principle of non-intervention, the violation of the principle of the prohibition of the threat or use of force. It by no means exhausts the legal grounds that could be invoked in support of the case that these 'Agreements', if they ever did, no longer have any validity or effect.

---

were also submitted to the Greek Cypriot representative to the London Joint Committee which was about to start its work on the draft instruments. It is understood that the effort was made in the Committee on the part of this representative to improve the text in such or a similar way. However, the final text is identical to that agreed upon in Zurich and this would support the view that the ambiguity may well have been intended from the beginning.

[107] See e.g. statement by the Turkish Foreign Minister before the London Conference in January, 1964, cited in the 1098th meeting of the Security Council Official Records pp. 15–16; note by the Turkish Government to the Cyprus Government dated 12 March, 1964; statement by the Turkish representative before the Security Council on 8 August 1964; S/PV 1142 p. 38; and numerous statements by political personalities in Turkey reported in the press.

Thus, it may be argued in the alternative that both the Treaty of Guarantee and the Treaty of Alliance can be, and have been validly, terminated by virtue of the repeated and material violation of their essential provisions on the part of Turkey.

In so far as the Treaty of Guarantee is concerned, Turkey has repeatedly and flagrantly violated its undertaking (in Article II thereof) to respect "the political independence, territorial integrity and security" of the Republic and has systematically pursued, through its agents in Cyprus, a policy of subversion (in violation of its obligation under the said Article) with the aim of bringing about the partition of the island and the annexation of part, if not the whole of it, to Turkey, contrary to the wishes of the vast majority of the people of Cyprus.

As regards the Treaty of Alliance,[108] the professed purpose of which was "to resist any attack or aggression, direct or indirect, directed against the independence or the territorial integrity of the Republic" (Article II thereof), the breach occurred as early as 25 December, 1963, when the Turkish military contingent stationed in Cyprus under the terms of the said Treaty, moved out of its barracks and took battle positions in hostile occupation of part of the territory of the Republic, in flagrant violation both of the basic purpose of the said Treaty as cited above and of Article V, paragraph 2, of the Application Agreement thereof. Two days after the establishment of the United Nations Force in Cyprus viz. on 29 March 1964, the President of the Republic Archbishop Makarios in a letter of that date addressed to the then Prime Minister of Turkey, formally demanded that the illegally deployed Turkish contingent return to its barracks by 1 April, 1964. After the negative reply of the Turkish Prime Minister was received, the President of Cyprus informed him by letter, dated 4 April, 1964, that the Republic of Cyprus considered the Treaty of Alliance as terminated in consequence of its material breach on the part of Turkey.[109]

Likewise, it may be argued with good reason that Turkey's belligerent gestures and actions towards the Republic of Cyprus (beginning with the threatening over-flights of Turkish jets over Nicosia and the move of the Turkish contingent in order to occupy the Kyrenia road on 25 December, 1963, referred to above, and culminating in the brutal bombings by waves of jet bombers, using rockets and napalm incendiary bombs, against the civilian population centres of the Tylliria area in Cyprus on 8 and 9 August, 1964),

---

108 It will be recalled that treaties of alliance because of their very nature are especially susceptible of denunciation when the underlying basis for the alliance no longer exists e.g, Hall, International Law, 8th Edition p. 405; Oppenheim, supra p. 938; McNair op. cit. supra pp. 501–505; Fizmanrice, Second Report of the Law of Treaties, Yearbook of the ILC, 1952, Vol. II, p, 22.

109 And see Tornaritis, the Treaty of Alliance, Cyprus To-day, Suppl. No. 4, 1964.

being inconsistent with the very notion and purpose of alliance or of guarantee, have made nonsense of any claim of the continuing validity of any Treaty of Alliance or of any Treaty of Guarantee between Turkey and Cyprus.[110]

Similarly, the contention can be put forward that, in particular with regard to the Treaty of Guarantee, it should be considered to be at an end since it has become apparent that the Constitution, which is the principal subject-matter guaranteed thereunder, has proved to be a completely unworkable instrument (partly as a result of its inherent unworkability and partly as a result of the recalcitrant and intransigerit attitude of the Turkish Cypriot minority which resulted in thwarting the normal functioning of the State). It may also be argued, in the alternative, that this unworkability of the Constitution represents a fundamental change of circumstances from those envisaged as being the foundation of the Treaty of Guarantee and that consequently the *rebus sic stantibus* doctrine has become relevant.

While none of these arguments is developed here for the reason that they do not fall under the scope of the present paper, they all serve to demonstrate that because of a variety of reasons, the Zurich-London 'Agreements' cannot properly be described as treaties *in force* for the purposes of the *pacta sunt servanda rule.*

The Principle of the Peaceful Settlement of Disputes and the Zurich-London 'Agreements'

What now remains for us is to consider the effect and relevance of the remaining of the four principles stated above as constituting peremptory norms of international law, namely that international disputes should be solved by peaceful means, in the context of the Zurich-London 'Agreements'.

Once it became manifest that the Constitution, with its cumbersome, undemocratic and inherently unworkable provisions, as we have seen above, was becoming increasingly difficult to operate, the President of Cyprus, Archbishop Makarios, after carefully considering the issues involved, on 30 November, 1963, presented to the then Vice-President Dr. Kutchuk a document entitled 'Suggested Measures to Facilitate the Smooth Functioning of the State and to Remove Certain Causes of Intercommunal Friction',[111] setting out thirteen points on the basis of which the Constitution might appropriately be amended. The intention was that these points should be

[110] Cf. R. Layton, The Effect of Measures Short of War on Treaties, University of Chicago Law Review Vol. 30 1962; a good illustration is also furnished by the Egyptian decree of January, 1957, denouncing the Anglo-Egyptian Suez Canal Base Agreement of 1954, following the hostilities against Egypt by the United Kingdom over Suez in 1956.

[111] Op. cit. footnote (86).

discussed with Dr. Kutchuk, as the leader of the Turkish Cypriot minority, with a view to arriving at an amicable and peaceful settlement of the difficulties that had arisen as an internal matter in Cyprus. Copies of this document were simultaneously forwarded to the Governments of Greece, Turkey and the United Kingdom for their information.

Nonetheless, the Turkish Government took it upon itself to 'reject' outright the contents of this document, even though it had not been submitted to it except for information, and it did so before Dr. Kutchuk had even had a chance to reply for the Turkish Cypriots. There followed increased tension in the Island and a series of incidents of violence originated with Turkish Cypriot extremists, culminating in the withdrawal of the Turkish Cypriot Ministers from the Government, the declaration by Dr. Kutchuk that the Republic was dead and the active involvement of Turkey in the affairs of the Republic (some of which have been referred to above).

It was the Government of Cyprus which hastened to place the problem posed by Turkey's aggression and intervention before the Security Council[112] and the Council, in the proper discharge of its responsibilities for the maintenance of international peace and security, discussed the situation in an emergency meeting[113] called by the Representative of Cyprus during the night of 27 December, 1963. The Council remained seized of this question ever since that time.

The Government of Cyprus spared no effort to arrive at a peaceful settlement of the crisis on the spot. But when interference on the part of Turkey took unacceptable proportions, the President of Cyprus, in a Message dated 1 January 1964 addressed to all Heads of State, described the Treaty of Guarantee and the Treaty of Alliance as "the source of our present anomalous situation" and announced His decision to bring them to an end – as clarified subsequently – "by appropriate means".

Moreover, the Government of Cyprus in addition to negotiating on the spot, agreed, despite certain reservations of principle, to refrain, for the time being, from pressing its case before the Security Council and to try to exhaust the other means for peaceful settlement provided for in Article 33 of the Charter. Thus it participated with the utmost goodwill in the abortive London Conference of January 1964 even though it was apparent that Turkey's attitude of instransigence did not permit many hopes for an agreement. Prior to the date when the Conference was due, however, the Cyprus Government requested and the Secretary-General of the United Nations agreed to appoint

---

[112] By letter dated 26 December, 1963, U.N. document S/5488.
[113] The 1085th meeting, see Official of the Security Council.

a Personal Representative to be available on the spot in Cyprus, as a form of United Nations presence.[114]

It was only after the failure of the London Conference and after rejecting two sets of unacceptable proposals which, if accepted, would have the effect of placing the Republic under virtual protectorate, that the Government of Cyprus insisted and succeeded in placing[115] the matter effectively within the jurisdiction of the Security Council by reactivating its complaint on 15 February, 1964. After a protracted and complicated debate, the Security Council on 4 March, 1964[116] passed a resolution on this question which, though a compromise, had far-reaching implications. In so far as 'the treaties signed at Nicosia on 16 August, 1960' were concerned, the Council did not endorse Turkey's claim to 'affirm' them but simply 'noted' in the preamble of the Resolution 'the positions taken by the parties' in relation thereto, at the same time explicitly recalling Article 2 (4) of the Charter, which would seem to have the effect of negating the validity at least of Turkey's claims of a right to unilateral military intervention. The Council, likewise, referred to the 'sovereign' Republic of Cyprus, the Government of which had 'the responsibility for maintenance of law and order', and, in addition to providing for the setting up of a United Nations Force in Cyprus, authorised the appointment of a mediator charged with 'promoting an agreed solution and a peaceful settlement in accordance with the Charter of the United Nations'.

It is only reasonable to take the view that, while the Security Council did not pass directly upon the legality or illegality of the 'Nicosia Treaties' (indeed it was not within its province to do so nor did the Cyprus Government so request or expect), by reminding Turkey that the use of force in international relations is forbidden and by appointing a mediator to seek a new solution, the Security Council did accept that the Zurich-London framework was far from satisfactory.

After the Cyprus Government once again demonstrated its good will by promptly consenting to the stationing of the United Nations Force[117] in Cyprus, the Security Council and the Secretary-General continued to be closely associated with the subsequent developments of the situation in Cyprus.

---

[114] See U.N. documents S/5514 and S/5516 and correspondence referred to therein. The other three Governments eventually joined in making the request.

[115] The British delegation attempted to 'steal a march' by submitting its own request for convening the Security Council some 30 minutes prior to the submission of the Cyprus request, after it had been announced in Nicosia that a special delegation, consisting of the Minister of Foreign Affairs and the President of the House of Representatives, would be leaving for New York to present the case for Cyprus.

[116] Resolution S/5575 during its 1102th meeting, see Official Records of the Security Council.

[117] See UN document S/5578.

When it became clear that the mediation effort, though the Mediator appointed under the Security Council's Resolution of 4 March, 1964, did not offer any practical prospects for a peaceful settlement owing to the arbitrary rejection of the Report[118] of the United Nations Mediator, Dr. Galo Plaza, by the Turkish Government, the Cyprus Government placed its case before the General Assembly and sought a recommendation upon which the solution of the problem could be peacefully resolved.[119]

The Cyprus Government did not ask the General Assembly to pronounce itself upon the validity or invalidity of 'the Nicosia Treaties'. What it did ask was that the Assembly, being the most representative body in the Organisation and, in a sense, the keeper of the conscience of mankind, to pronounce itself upon whether the principles of the Charter – the most notably the principle of the prohibition of the use of force, the principle of the prohibition of intervention, the principle of sovereignty – were merely abstract principles or whether they were more than that and were applicable to concrete cases, in this instance to the Republic of Cyprus, a Member of the United Nations. The Assembly, after a long debate in which all the aspects of the problem were considered, answered this call in a most positive manner and, after noting in the preamble the Security Council's previous resolutions and a number of consideranda favourable to the Cyprus Government's case, declared, quite categorically, that "the Republic of Cyprus, as an equal Member of the United Nations, is, in accordance with the Charter, entitled to, and should enjoy, full sovereignty and complete independence without any foreign intervention or interference".[120]

Turkey voted against this Resolution and subsequently indicated that it did not consider it as binding upon it, thereby demonstrating once again, the negative and sterile attitude it has shown towards the United Nations Mediator's Report, as we have already seen. The matter remains within the jurisdiction of the Security Council, primarily in so far as it concerns the question of the maintenance of international peace, even though the mediation effort is at present at a standstill owing to Dr. Plaza's forced resignation. The Council periodically meets to renew the United Nations Force's mandate, while the Special Representative of the Secretary-General in Cyprus has been authorised by all concerned to carry out certain quasi-mediational functions.

The brief account given above demonstrates, it is believed, that the Cyprus Government has done its utmost in order to seek a solution of the political

[118] UN document S/6253.

[119] Originally by letter dated 24 September, 1964, followed by the submission of the explanatory memorandum, see U.N. doc. A/5752, supplemented on 22 September 1965, see U.N. doc. A/5934/ add. 1.

[120] Resolution 2077 (XX).

problem through peaceful means: It has attempted to foreclose the crisis by inviting the Turkish Cypriot leadership to talks on the basis of the thirteen points. After the crisis erupted it referred the matter to the Security Council and continued negotiating both on the spot and, on a regional level, at the London Conference. It has made use of the office of the Secretary-General (through the early appointment of a Personal Representative and subsequently a Special Representative of the Secretary-General), of the Security Council, in so far as the maintenance of peace and security were concerned, as well as of the peace-keeping force and of the mediation effort under the Council's resolutions. Moreover it has resorted to the General Assembly in order to seek its assistance for the solution of the long-term political problem. Since the problem is basically political in nature it has not resorted to the International Court of Justice (and in this connection the considerations set out with regard to the Court, supra, would seem to be relevant) but, if it did, it is believed that it would have a good case on a number of grounds.

Indeed, the question arises what was the effect of the General Assembly's resolution upon the Zurich-London 'Agreements'. (We have already touched upon the question of the effect of the Security Council's resolution of 4 March 1964). That the Assembly, under Articles 10, 11 and 14 of the Charter, has competence to consider all the matters which come before the Organisation is not open to dispute. It is less clear whether the General Assembly may, under Article 14, recommend any measures regarding the peaceful adjustment of any situation, regardless of origin, and this would also include the setting aside of a treaty. But this was really not the point in the present context. What the General Assembly was requested to do, and what it did do, was to declare that certain principles of the Charter – viz. sovereignty, independence, non-use of force, non-intervention – applied to the case at issue, viz. the question of Cyprus. If any or all of these principles were inconsistent with any or all of the provisions of any treaties allegedly applicable to this case, such provisions were subordinated to the principles – not necessarily because the Resolution said so but because the Charter, which is binding upon all the parties, so provides in its Article 103. In other words, the argument is not that it was the Assembly's resolution which set aside the controversial treaty provisions (even though this might be argued also) but that the Charter provisions, as reaffirmed and declared applicable to the problem of Cyprus in the General Assembly's resolution, had this effect. Moreover, what is involved is more than a question of compatibility of these treaty provisions with the relevant Charter principles since these Charter principles happen also to be peremptory norms of international law – as it has been submitted and elaborated upon in the present paper. In other words the issue is not merely one of incompatibility under Article 103 of the Charter but, more importantly and broadly, one of nullity because of conflict with *jus cogens* rules under the principle in Article 37 of the International Law Commission's draft.[121]

Apart, however, from the specific problem of Cyprus, there is a lot to be said for the suggestion that the General Assembly of the United Nations is a particularly qualified body for pronouncing itself upon primarily political disputes, involving as a side issue, the applicability or not of peremptory norms of international law. In representing the vast majority of the members of the family of nations the General Assembly is a proper forum where to ascertain how the conscience of the international community asserts itself at any given time regarding whether a given rule of the *jus cogens* does or does not apply. At the same time it has to be admitted that there does exist a danger inherent in the political nature of this body, which in turn might result in an arbitrary or non-legal approach to the applicable rule.

Concluding Remarks

Having reached the end of our inquiry it would now seem appropriate to set out certain general comments by way of conclusion:

The consensus of opinion among legal authorities clearly favours the acceptance of the view that peremptory norms of international law do exist. While there has been some difference of opinion as to what rules merit this description, there appears to be sufficient evidence that the principles of non-use of force in international relations, the principle of peaceful settlement of disputes, the principle of non-intervention and the principle of sovereign equality fall within this category. The question of Cyprus, with which the present writer has had some acquaintance, offers a first rate illustration of the invoking of such peremptory norms in the context of a burning political issue – indeed the only issue, as far as it could be ascertained, where considerable reliance was placed upon the *jus cogens* doctrine in presenting it before the United Nations. While complete objectivity on the part of the present writer might be too much to expect in the circumstances, it is

[121] It is interesting to cite the views expressed by the Foreign Minister of Turkey on the effect of resolution 2077 (XX) on the Nicosia Treaties: "…in the present text the paragraphs have been drafted in such a way that they… have the effect of setting aside treaties whose very purpose was to safeguard the territorial integrity of Cyprus. These treaties are permanent and cannot be repudiated or modified by the General Assembly…" A/PV 1402, p. 48. The Foreign Minister of Cyprus put it as follows: "The Zurich and London Agreements, following the UN General Assembly's resolution, which fully confirms our views on them, have no value at all, theoretical or practical. Cyprus is a fully independent and sovereign State entitled to decide its future, entitled to exercise its sovereign rights, and no one may interfere or intervene in its affairs" – Statement before the House of Representatives, 7 January, 1966.

nonetheless believed that the conclusions found in the text, to the effect that the Zurich-London 'Agreements' do conflict in a number of respects with peremptory norms, are valid and can be supported before any international tribunal. Finally the sketchy account of the processes applied in the effort to find a peaceful settlement of the problem of Cyprus might present some interest both in its variety and in the effect (or rather lack of it) that each of these processes has had so far in solving this problem.

The Role of International Law in the World Today and Tomorrow*

The title of this essay – "The Role of International Law in the World Today and Tomorrow" – is perhaps a little too ambitious. More accurately put, it would be some reflections on the role of international law in the world by someone who, for more than three decades, practised both bilateral and multilateral diplomacy in the service of his country (Cyprus) and who, because of training, experience and inclination, is strongly convinced that international law has a very important role to play in diplomacy and international affairs.

This is the half-way point of the United Nations Decade of International Law, proclaimed by the General Assembly in 1989,[1] the purpose of which is to enhance and solidify respect for international law, as well as to popularize it. It also happens that the year of writing of this essay coincides with the fiftieth anniversary of the founding of the United Nations when much thinking and soul-searching is going on in various forums, national and international, as to where the United Nations stands and where it is going after 50 years of its existence. This is particularly relevant since the United Nations and its Charter have, respectively, provided the forum and the basis of much of the activity in codifying and progressively developing international law during the past half century.

There have been times, particularly in the aftermath of the Second World War and, more recently, in the wake of crises such as that of the Falklands/Malvinas and the Gulf War, when high-sounding declarations have been made by world leaders proclaiming the value and relevance of international law in world affairs. It was hoped at the time, and it still should be hoped, that these declarations would be of lasting value, intended to govern relations among States in a "new world order" and to be applied universally and objectively. Yet, time and again, these hopes were dashed and these declarations

---

* Previously published in International Law on the Eve of the Twenty-First Century (views of the International Law Commission), United Nations (1997).

[1] Resolution 44/23 of 17 November 1989.

in many instances proved to be no more than convenient slogans applied selectively and according to temporary expediencies in a "new world disorder". In too many cases, double standards have been applied and aggressors have been able to defy with impunity the application of the relevant rules of international law and the collective will of the international community, as expressed in unanimous resolutions of the General Assembly and the Security Council of the United Nations. Bad precedents, when tolerated and condoned, tend to be repeated.

There are several themes upon which this essay is premised. These are that international law does indeed play an important role in diplomacy and international affairs; that the rules of international law must keep pace with the evolving conditions of international life; that these rules must be based on international morality and must be applied universally, not selectively; that the present world situation is conducive to enhancing the role of international law and its effectiveness; that attention should focus on the areas of law affecting present needs and that these should be defined and progressively developed; that the role of newly independent States is instrumental and has been constructive in developing such rules; that the role of the Legal Advisers to Foreign Ministries is essential and their opinion in any given situation should be sought and be given decisive weight by policy-makers before taking any policy decision on matters involving international law; and that the role of the International Law Commission and that of other expert bodies, on the universal and regional level, as well as that of major law-making conferences, are also very important.

Increased activity in the international legal field certainly provides a focal point for the Non-Aligned Movement in the changed circumstances of the world situation within the broad framework of the principles which dictated its creation. Likewise, the Commonwealth, which constitutes a principal legal system based on the common law, can play more of a role than heretofore in the international legal field.

It can be fairly stated that, by and large, States abide by their treaty obligations, despite the lack of an international legislature with binding powers or a standing international peace force or even a compulsory third-party adjudication system. Ultimately, the viability of any system of law depends upon the will of the community it seeks to regulate. The vast majority of States ordinarily observe their obligations under international law, even if motivated only by enlightened self-interest. Even when they do not observe such obligations, they tend to attempt to justify their actions or omissions by invoking legal arguments, however contrived, rather than admit that such actions or omissions violate the relevant rules of international law.

In any given situation, there may indeed be room for bona fide argument, different interpretations and lack of clarity, and certainly so – perhaps even more so – in international law as indeed in the other fields of law. But, if the rule of law is to have real meaning in international relations, as indeed in domestic situations, such rules as are clearly discernible and objectively valid need to be observed in practice in all situations. Before a decision is taken on policy regarding any given situation which is covered by rules of international law, the considered view of the legal aspect needs to be sought, formulated, communicated and be given due – indeed determining – weight by the policy-makers before deciding on the policy in that situation. This is true everywhere and particularly true in countries which proudly proclaim that they are nations of laws and not of people. The rule of law in international affairs means that narrow national interests are subordinated to international law, particularly where the relevant rules of international law are clear and unambiguous. National interests should be pursued in a way consistent with international law.

Looking back to my own experience of three and a half decades of diplomatic life, the principles and rules, of international law – whether in major issues of national survival or in mundane topics of everyday diplomatic life such as consular and diplomatic law, e.g., immunities and tax exemptions[2] – were frequently relied on and provided the framework in which diplomatic negotiations, arguments and positions were formulated and used.

While the role of international law in international diplomacy is often limited, it is not insignificant. In certain cases where law coincides with power, law is determining – as we have witnessed in the recent case of the Gulf War. In other cases, where law does not coincide with power, international law at least serves as a restraint on power by placing some constraints on its abuse by the strong and mighty and by providing the weak with arguments to buttress their position as well as international standards for third parties, not directly involved, to support these positions. Contemporary international law, as developed in the era of the United Nations with the participation of all members of the international community, and particularly of the newly independent States which brought some new perspectives to bear on the law-making process, has increasingly tended to sustain those who have justice on their side, particularly in such areas as decolonization, the protection of human rights, the law, of treaties and the law of the sea.

The role of international law in practice varies, of course, according to the field which it is supposed to regulate. While limited in the field of international peace and security, it is considerable in regulating international

[2] As acting Dean in Washington or as Chairman of the Committee on Relations with the Host Country in New York or as Permanent Secretary at the Ministry of Foreign Affairs in Nicosia.

relations, exchanges and behaviour in fields such as commerce, trade, finance, science, energy, art, etc.

How much a role international law is allowed to play varies from State to State and often depends on the attitudes of the individuals making the decisions. No general rule necessarily applies but, on the whole, it is small and weaker States which have more reason to rely on the law rather than on power in defending their sovereignty, independence, territorial integrity and other fundamental interests, and, more generally, in projecting their policies. Even though all States are supposed to be equal, some States are more "international law-minded" than others.[3]

Within the United Nations system, much work is being carried out in codifying and progressively developing international law. The highest judicial organ of the United Nations, the International Court of Justice, has of course made a great contribution to this end, both through its contentious and its advisory jurisdiction, in all areas of the law it has had the occasion to address. Its recently increased jurisdiction is undoubtedly a reflection of the confidence that the Court has been enjoying in recent years and is certainly to be encouraged to continue along the same lines. The Sixth (Legal) Committee of the General Assembly, a universal body of Government representatives from all Member States of the United Nations, also plays a major role through its three-month annual session, in itself and through several Committees and Working Groups, whether of the whole or with restricted membership, which examine and develop individual topics and report to the Sixth Committee, which in its turn considers these reports and recommends relevant resolutions for adoption by the General Assembly. Besides these bodies, much work in international law is carried out daily through the Security Council and other United Nations bodies and through the Office of Legal Affairs of the Secretariat – whether at Headquarters or in the specialized agencies. Major topics, such as the law of treaties or the law of the sea, to mention two of many examples, after appropriate preparatory work by expert or other preparatory bodies and relevant comments by Governments, are referred to major law-making conferences under United Nations auspices and result in landmark treaties which enter into force after the requisite number of ratifications by States are obtained.

Evidently, in an essay such as the present one, there is no possibility to examine even cursorily the substance of this enormous amount of

[3] It is my conviction that if the rules of international law had been applied, the Cyprus problem would not have arisen. And, if these rules were to be applied today, I believe the problem can be solved in conformity with the relevant United Nations resolutions, and in a manner that is fair for all parties concerned and in the interest of international peace in the volatile Eastern Mediterranean region.

international law-making within the United Nations system, let alone that carried out bilaterally and through other bodies or groupings of States-other essays in this volume deal with several of these issues. What I intend to do is to illustrate my thinking on the topic of this essay by touching on some of the aspects of the work of the International Law Commission in the light of the main themes I indicated earlier.

Since its creation by the General Assembly in 1947, the International Law Commission has made an enormous contribution to the codification and progressive development of international law.[4] On the basis of the Commission's present agenda, one can point to solid work having been accomplished on such subjects of "lawyers' law" as "jurisdictional immunities of States and their property" and "international watercourses", which have reached fruition, and, hopefully soon, the relevant respective conventions will be adopted. Much progress has been made 'on the challenging item on "international liability for injurious consequences arising from acts not prohibited by international law". To my mind, particularly relevant and significant for the role of international law in the world today are the topics of "State responsibility" and of the "Draft Code of Crimes against the Peace and Security of Mankind", which includes the establishment of an international criminal court.

"State responsibility" is a very broad subject which has been on the agenda of the International Law Commission for too long (and this because of reasons largely beyond the Commission's control) and should be finalized at the earliest possible time. It is important to observe that it has gone through considerable progressive development. Gone are the days when "State responsibility" primarily meant remedying injury to aliens and, in effect, catered to the needs and requirements of a small number of powerful developed States, often at the expense of weaker and less developed States.

With the coming into effect of the Charter of the United Nations, encompassing rules prevailing over the provisions of other treaties conflicting with such rules and with the acceptance in the 1969 Vienna Convention on the Law of Treaties of the principle of peremptory norms of international law which cannot be departed from by States by agreement between themselves (*jus cogens*), the topic of "State responsibility" has been placed on a much broader foundation. It is now recognized, also by the International Court of Justice, that there exist obligations *erga omnes* and that the interest of the international community as a whole needs to be duly taken into account.

[4] This is reflected in many books, including the handy United Nations publication The Work of the International Law Commission in its successive editions, the latest being the fifth, published in 1996 (Sales No. E.95.V.6).

"State responsibility" has thus been transformed as a proper expression of the application of progressive development.

On this topic, and in general, the Commission must ensure that the expectations of the international community and in particular of the newly independent States, which came into existence after the classical rules of international law were formulated, are not ignored. The Commission must keep pace with contemporary notions of international law such as international crimes. It must keep pace with the current developments in the international scene and not be slow in recognizing and capitalizing on the opportunities provided in recent shifts of attitude by major powers, particularly as these might facilitate acceptance of the principle of third-party settlement of disputes. The effective and expeditious third-party dispute settlement procedure, which unavoidably eluded the international community in past major projects such as the Convention on the Law of Treaties and less so in the United Nations Convention on the Law of the Sea, should be included as a matter of principle in all future multilateral law-making treaties. Every effort should be made to include such a system in the future convention on State responsibility, especially considering the need for authoritative judicial adjudication on the new notions on which it is based (*jus cogens*, international crimes, obligations *erga omnes*, among others).

The "Draft Code of Crimes Against the Peace and Security of Mankind", a topic which acquired additional importance and topicality in the light of recent and current developments on the world scene, deserves its rightful place in the corpus of present-day international law and can serve the important purpose of deterrence and punishment against present and future violators of its provisions. The International Law Commission's adoption of the Draft Code on first reading in 1991 was an important step forward and its adoption on second reading in 1996, appropriately slimmed down and concentrated on legally definable grave crimes, thus conforming to political realities, will hopefully lead to the final fruition of this major topic.

Closely connected with the Code, though not necessarily dependent on it, are recent developments regarding an international criminal judiciary. The creation of a permanent international criminal court is an institution long overdue. While a case could be made for a less minimalist approach and for broader jurisdiction of such a court, it is indisputable that the International Law Commission did an outstanding job in producing, in record time in response to the General Assembly's request, a draft statute for such a court. It now remains for the international community to exhibit the necessary political will – the momentum already exists – in order to overcome the remaining obstacles and to adopt at the earliest possible time the draft statute and establish such a permanent international court which would, in several respects, be preferable to ad hoc tribunals tailored for particular situations.

Such an institution would be a major contribution by the international community to the United Nations Decade of International Law.

Once the topics on the present agenda of the International Law Commission are brought to a satisfactory conclusion, it is important for the Commission and the Sixth Committee of the General Assembly to choose wisely which topics should be dealt with by the former in the years ahead. No doubt many factors apply in making such choice. To my mind the primary criterion is what is in the mainstream of the concerns of the international community and my preferred – albeit subjective – choice would include topics such as the implementation of United Nations resolutions, the binding nature of Security Council resolutions, the legal aspects of United Nations peacekeeping, a more comprehensive and binding system of peaceful settlement of disputes,[5] issues of environment and economic relations and defining the legal content of *jus cogens*.

With regard to the latter topic, I would like to note briefly a few basic points. Since the notion of *jus cogens* (peremptory norms of international law from which no State may derogate by agreement or otherwise) was incorporated into international law in the 1969 Vienna Convention on the Law of Treaties, it has been referred to in debates at the United Nations, including the Security Council, has been the subject of in-depth studies by scholars, has been raised in the proceedings of learned societies, has been alluded to by the International Court of Justice and is often referred to in debates and documents of the International Law Commission (particularly regarding the Draft Code of Crimes and State responsibility items). Yet, there exists no authoritative statement on what the peremptory norms are or where they may be found. It is frequently said – in my view correctly – that the principle of the prohibition of the use of force in international relations, contained in Article 2, paragraph 4, of the Charter of the United Nations, is *jus cogens*. Undoubtedly other principles and rules of international law exist for which the same status may be claimed. Evidently there is need to define the exact parameters of what comes under the rubric of *jus cogens* since the situation as it now stands is not conducive to the objectivity, transparency and predictability which should characterize a legal principle, especially one which has been solemnly incorporated in such a landmark treaty as the 1969 Vienna

[5] Perhaps on the lines proposed by Professor L. Sohn on the adaptation of the relevant Hague Conventions to the needs of the twenty-first century. See L. B. Sohn, "Preparation of a New Treaty for the Settlement of International Disputes", in M. Brus, S. Muller and S. Wiemers, eds., The United Nations Decade of International Law: Reflections on International Dispute Settlement (Dordrecht, Martinus Nijhoff, 1991), pp. 51–57. See also "Draft General Treaty on the Peaceful Settlement of International Disputes: A Proposal and Report", The International Lawyer, vol. 20 (1986), pp. 261–291 (prepared by Professor Sohn for the American Bar Association Standing Committee on World Order Under Law).

Convention on the Law of Treaties and also in the 1986 Vienna Convention on the Law of Treaties between States and International Organizations. At it stands, *jus cogens* can mean a great deal to some and very little to others. Without going into greater depth now, in my opinion it is important that this concept be considered by the International Law Commission, as a highly qualified authoritative body of experts which codified it in the first place in the 1960s, with a view to establishing which rules of international law are indeed peremptory.[6] I hope that a way will be found to do this during the United Nations Decade of International Law as an important contribution to the Decade, whether by the International Law Commission or otherwise.

We are living in interesting and challenging times, times full of opportunities but also of pitfalls in terms of politics, economics, and the development and the role of international law. We are witnessing developments of historic importance all over the world, with the end of the Cold War and the newly found unanimity among the permanent members of the Security Council. Several regional problems have been solved, especially those which had their origin in the competition between the two super-powers, but others have been created in the wake of the disappearance of communism as a world ideology and the unleashing of ethnic and religious tensions and conflicts, notably in parts of the former Soviet Union and the former Yugoslavia. Germany has been peacefully reunified, apartheid has been peacefully dismantled in South Africa, the Middle East is hopefully on the way to a more peaceful and prosperous future and so is Northern Ireland, to cite some of the most obvious cases, but other international and regional problems continue to fester.[7] Global interdependence and the need to protect the environment, promote sustainable development, provide equality for women are some of the themes of the day. In the wake of the disappearance of the nuclear confrontation, economic groupings have gained prominence in various parts of the world; since Maastricht the European Union has embarked on a different, more advanced, form of integration and the Organization for Security and Cooperation in Europe has taken on additional functions. The United Nations, despite its financial and administrative problems, has been revitalized and has taken on additional responsibilities under its Charter, which has stood well the test of time. Hopefully, the Organization can look to the future with confidence.

The clear objective is international legal order based on the supremacy of international law. If this objective is to be achieved, to my mind, the best formula is idealism tempered with realism. Politics, it has been said, is the

---

6 See United Nations document A/CN.4/454, pp. 16–26 and annex containing a further elaboration.

7 Cyprus being one such tragic anachronism.

art of the possible and the same is nearly as true of international law. We should strive to achieve what is ideal but we must also be prepared to compromise on the basis of what is achievable at any given time since the penalty for insisting on what is ideal may be to achieve no result at all. The prayer of the medieval theologian has relevance to many situations, including the development and application of international law: "Good Lord, give me the courage to change the things that can be changed, the serenity to accept the things that cannot be changed and the wisdom to know the difference between the two".

Law of the Sea

Peaceful Settlement of Disputes in Ocean Conflicts: Does UNCLOS III Point the Way?*◊

I would readily agree with Professor Sohn's basic thesis that the system for the peaceful settlement of disputes which may arise regarding the interpretation and application of the Law of the Sea Convention is one of the important accomplishments of the Third United Nations Law of the Sea Conference.

Seen in the context of past experience, as for instance in the 1958 Law of the Sea Conference which, despite a majority decision in the Committee for the compulsory reference of disputes to the ICJ, was in the end able to agree only to an optional protocol which very few states ratified, we now have a significant achievement. In the large majority of cases (and here I might be a little more skeptical than Professor Sohn who speaks optimistically that the "system… can lead in 90 percent of cases to a binding decision, which is likely to be accepted and complied with by the parties to the dispute") the possibility exists, as between the parties to the Convention, for an effective dispute settlement system.

Therefore, if the question is whether the international community and the rule of law are better served by this system than by no system at all or by an optional protocol as in 1958, the answer is a resounding yes.

If on the other hand, the question is whether the international community and the rule of law could have been better served by a more streamlined system, subject to fewer and less complicated exceptions, the answer in my view is also yes.

As Professor Sohn rightly points out, it was recognized early in the negotiations that the complex text drafted by the Conference would lack stability, certainty and predictability if the parties to the Convention retained the right of unilateral interpretation.

---

* Previously published in CONTEMPORARY ISSUES IN INTERNATIONAL LAW, ESSAYS IN HONOUR OF LOUIS B. SOHN, ed. T. Buergenthal, N.P. Engel (1984).

◊ For other selected writings by Andrew Jacovides on the Law of The Sea *see*: THIRD UNITED NATIONS CONFERENCE ON THE LAW OF THE SEA, OFFICIAL RECORDS, VOLUME V, Summary Records of Meetings, New York 1976 (UN New York 1977), pp. 25–26, 73 and 105; Three Aspects of the Law of the Sea; Islands, Delimitation, and Dispute Settlement, *Marine Policy*, Volume 3, number 4, October 1979, pp. 278–288.

I can say without fear of contradiction that no other person has done so much to bring about the present monumental "veritable code for the settlement of disputes" than Professor Sohn himself. Throughout the long drawn out period of negotiations, no one has demonstrated so much expert knowledge, ingenuity, sheer hard work and dogged determination in bringing about the – best possible result under the circumstances. Because no one doubted his good faith and because he deservedly enjoyed universal respect (not least from his many former students who belonged to diverse delegations), he was looked upon not so much as a leading member of the United States delegation which he also was, *but* as a benevolent and wise independent expert whose constructive ingenuity carried much weight and commanded general attention. In a way, it was like the E. F. Hutton television commercial: when Louis Sohn spoke, people listened! Therefore, in paying the warmest tribute to him, I want to make clear that any criticism that may emerge from my remarks is directed at the compromises made necessary because of political realities in the course of protracted negotiations and certainly not at Professor Sohn, whose heart I am convinced has always been in the right place and who – I have every reason to believe – would have been happier with a more all embracing system subject to fewer of the exceptions, qualifications and uncertainties required by the vagaries of political realities.

If I may turn to the formative stage of the Conference on this subject, the basic position of many delegations on the settlement of disputes arising out of the Law of the Sea Convention was – and I quote from a statement I made in Plenary on 6 April 1976:

> We are for an effective, comprehensive, expeditious and viable dispute settlement entailing a binding decision regarding all disputes arising out of the substantive provisions of the Convention. We are convinced that such a system is a necessary corollary to the substantive rules in the Convention and should form an integral part of it. This position is dictated both by reason of our attachment to the general principle of equal justice under the law and by reason of our national self-interest as a small and militarily weak state which needs the protection of the law, impartially and effectively administered, in order to safeguard its legitimate rights under the Law of the Sea Convention.

As we all know, this "purist" approach – some critics of it might describe it as too doctrinaire or too simple – was qualified by a series of exceptions and qualifications, in some cases so complex as to require Ariadne's mite to find one's way out of the resulting labyrinth. Indeed, some cynic might argue that the dispute settlement system under the Convention, coupled with the vague and imprecise wording of some of the substantive provisions (sometimes called misleadingly "constructive ambiguity"), was deliberately designed to ensure to present and future generations of lawyers a busy and presumably lucrative practice – a view to which I, not being a cynic, of course do not subscribe! More correctly, it was the price paid for consensus.

Professor Sohn, in his excellent paper, has rightly described the dispute settlement system under Chapter XV of the Convention as "at the same time simple and complex". The key feature is that the parties to a dispute can by agreement select any dispute settlement method they wish. The parties have a wide variety of tribunals to choose from: the International Court of Justice (which I may observe parenthetically has already been resorted to in several cases involving law of the sea disputes), the newly established Law of the Sea Tribunal and its Sea-Bed Disputes Chamber, arbitration tribunals or special technical commissions. And, failing agreement between the states concerned as to their choice of tribunal, arbitration is provided as the common denominator under Article 287 and Annex VII. My own view was, and still is, that since a special Law of the Sea Tribunal was set up under the Convention, it would have been more logical to give to it the central role in the overall system, since this would ensure uniformity of approach in the interpretation and application of the Convention. However, I have no strong views and, hopefully, in practice this will prove to be less complicated than it looks at first sight.

It is when we come to the exceptions (in Articles 297 and 298) that the real complexities arise. I will not even attempt to enumerate these as Professor Sohn has already simplified them to the extent humanly possible.

I would only say that one of these exceptions, indeed an optional one but nevertheless an exception, is under Article 298 "disputes concerning sea boundary delimitations or involving historic bays or titles" and these are sub-divided into four categories, out of which only one category (i.e. not if the dispute arose before the entry into force of the Convention; not if it is concurrent with a dispute concerning sovereignty over continental or insular land territory; and not if it was settled by an arrangement between the parties or which is to be settled in accordance with an agreement between them) is subject to compulsory conciliation or, put more accurately, to compulsory resort to conciliation, a procedure which leads only to the issue of a report and does not entail a binding decision.

Now, Article 298 (1) (a) which sets out this situation was the result of protracted acrimonious debates and negotiations. It became increasingly clear during the debates in various forums of the Conference (and especially in Negotiating Group 7), that a substantial number of states (including at least one major Power) were unwilling to submit issues touching upon their national sovereignty to a third party settlement entailing a binding decision and this view prevailed in so far as it concerns sea boundary delimitation disputes. The hope has been expressed that, to the extent applicable, the procedure of compulsory conciliation will prove to serve the same purpose in practical terms – but this may be no more than wishful thinking.

The fact is that sea boundary delimitation, because of the high stakes involved due to the increase of the zones of maritime jurisdiction under the present Convention (as compared to the 1958 situation), because of its contentious potential since it touches sensitive nerves of national sovereignty and because of the vagueness of the substantive rules adopted in other parts of the convention – particularly in the case of Articles 74 and 83 on the delimitation of the exclusive economic zone and the continental shelf between states with opposite or adjacent coasts – especially lends itself to third party compulsory settlement if solutions are to be found peacefully and actual or potential disputes are not to escalate into confrontations, including in many instances even armed conflict.

Such a situation – the relative vagueness of the substantive rules on the one hand and the absence of compulsory third party dispute settlement procedures of a binding nature on the other – is bound to create problems and to work an injustice at the expense of smaller and militarily weaker states because larger and stronger states may be tempted to claim the lion's share and are not obliged to accept third party adjudication. I submit that this is one of the more unfortunate compromises reached during the Conference, even though it may prove to be mitigated by the compulsory resort to the conciliation procedure where this is applicable – and whether it is applicable is in itself subject to argument and procrastination if the state concerned chooses to make it so.

I have chosen to concentrate on this issue raised in Article 298 (1) (a) partly because it is one I have been familiar with and I feel strongly about and partly because it illustrates in a vivid way the shortcomings of the dispute settlement system arrived at after so much effort in the Third United Nations Conference on the Law of the Sea.

Other shortcomings on other issues made subject to exceptions, automatic or optional, can no doubt also be pointed out.

By saying this, I do not by any means intend to denigrate or to diminish the importance of the work done and the monumental result achieved. "Politics" it has been said "is the art of the possible" and this is also true of international law-making conferences such as the Law of the Sea Conference. From the point of view of lawyers, expecting the rule of law to prevail at the international as much as at the national level, we have not achieved an ideal solution. But what is ideal is not always feasible and this has been the price that had to be paid in working on a complicated and ambitious undertaking through compromises necessitated by the objective of reaching an overall agreement by consensus.

In my view, while in certain respects the Convention and more particularly its dispute settlement system is not fully satisfactory, not fully streamlined and not always logical or fair, I believe the net result is, on balance, constructive and a significant achievement in multilateral lawmaking. As such it deserves general support.

A Review of the 2004 General Assembly Discussions on the Law of the Sea*

The annual debate on "Oceans and the Law of the Sea" (item 49 (a) and (b) of the Agenda) took place in the General Assembly on November 16 and 17, 2004. It was a joint debate on sub items:

(a) Oceans and the Law of the Sea (i) Reports of the Secretary-General A/59/62, A/59/62/Add. 1, A/59/63 and A/59/126; (ii) Report of the United Nations Open-ended Informal Consultative Process on Oceans and the Law of the Sea at its fifth meeting, A/59/122; and, (iii) the omnibus draft resolution A/59/L.22;

(b) Sustainable fisheries, including through the 1995 Agreement for the Implementation of the Provisions of the United Nations Convention on the Law of the Sea of December 10, 1982 relating to the Conservation and Management of Straddling Fish Stocks and Highly Migratory Fish Stocks and related instruments (i) Report of the Secretary-General, A/59/298 and (ii) draft resolution, A/59/L.23.

The day the debate commenced, November 16, coincided with the 10th anniversary of the entry into force of the 1982 Law of the Sea Convention, an event marked by a ceremonial session in Kingston, Jamaica, ten years earlier where I had the privilege of participating and speaking as the head of the Cyprus delegation (text attached Annex I).

Many of the delegates who participated in the General Assembly's debate highlighted the importance of the anniversary. For example, the delegate from the Netherlands, speaking for the European Union, stressed that the Convention and its implementing Agreement were milestones in the efforts to manage the planet's ocean affairs. Looking back on the achievements of the Third United Nations Conference on the Law of the Sea, he said that not only did the Convention deal with a wide variety of issues, but its text proved flexible enough to address problems that had emerged during the decade since it entered into force. The two integrated documents proved to be useful

---

* Previously published in RECENT DEVELOPMENTS IN THE LAW OF THE SEA AND CHINA, ed. M. Nordquist, BRILL (2006).

tools for the governance of the world oceans, they stood the test of time and there was no need for additional provisions at the time.

The debate, which carried on to a second day, November 17, was entered by some 40 delegations that included the Prime Minister of Norway, the Minister of Fisheries and Oceans of Canada, the representative from Brazil speaking for the Rio Group, the representative from the Netherlands speaking on behalf of the European Union, the representative from Barbados speaking for the Caribbean Community (CARICOM), and the representative from Samoa speaking for the Pacific Islands Forum. Substantive statements were also made by the Secretary-General of the International Seabed Authority, the President of the International Tribunal for the Law of the Sea and the Observer of the International Union for the Conservation of Nature.

The Omnibus Draft Resolution on Oceans and the Law of the Sea (L.22) was introduced by Brazil and the Draft Resolution on Sustainable Fisheries (L.23) was introduced by the United States. Both had been, as customary, negotiated at informal meetings over a period of several weeks prior to their introduction and each had wide co-sponsorship of member States. While one cannot fail to recognize the variety and complexity of the topics covered in each of these resolutions and the fact that this practice has been followed over the preceding years, one must pause and think about the advisability of continuing the practice in light of the current debate on United Nations reform (doc. A/59/565). Resolution L.22 is 17 pages long and includes 103 operative paragraphs in addition to 19 preambular paragraphs, while Resolution L.23 is 16 pages long and has 84 operative paragraphs and 26 preambular paragraphs. For instance, L.23 devotes two preambular and two operative paragraphs (73 and 74) to the protection of sharks ("recognizing further the economic and cultural importance of sharks in many countries, the biological importance of sharks in the marine ecosystem, the vulnerability of some shark species to over-exploitation… and the International Plan of Action for the Conservation and Management of Sharks" adopted by the FAO in 1999, which was implemented by "only a small number of countries"). While one can readily recognize the relevance of preservation of all God's creatures and the desirability of not disturbing the balance of nature, can one not reasonably question the emphasis on the "economic and cultural [sic] importance of sharks" and perhaps be reminded (if I could be permitted the flippancy) of the proverbial joke about lawyers being well treated by sharks out of "professional courtesy"?

Topics dealt with during the debate included navigational rights, territorial sea limits, economic jurisdiction, the legal status of seabed resources beyond national jurisdiction, conservation and limits of living marine resources and the protection of the marine environment.

Main themes included the need to tackle the problem of overfishing through two methods. The first is sustainable resource management and fighting against illegal, unreported and unregulated fishing, especially through the action of the flag States of vessels engaging in such fishing. The second is through an immediate moratorium on bottom trawl fishing in all high sea regions, as well as within the zones of national jurisdiction.

Another major concern was piracy and robbery at sea. Half of the yearly 400 incidents reported worldwide have occurred in the Asian region.

Additionally, maritime transportation of radioactive materials and the transport of weapons of mass destruction on the world's waterways were prominent themes. Support was expressed for Security Council Resolution 1540 (2004) on the prevention of the proliferation of nuclear weapons, a significant recent instance of the exercise of legislative power by the UN Security Council. The Prime Minister of Norway stressed that shipping interests must be weighed against environmental considerations and the legitimate interests of the world's coastal populations, while recognizing them as important for world trade, energy efficiency and as an ecologically sound mode for freight transportation. He noted that there had been several environmental catastrophes caused by shipping accidents and welcomed new measures adopted by the IMO (International Maritime Organization) to prevent oil pollution from vessels, including the decision to speed up the phasing out of single-hull tankers. It was also stressed that shipping security was internationally linked with flag States shouldering their responsibilities and that this could only be done through a genuine link between flag States and the ships flying their flag.

The delegate from Barbados, speaking for the CARICOM, referred to two separate arbitration proceedings currently under way in the Caribbean (between Barbados and Trinidad & Tobago, Guyana and Suriname) in order to settle, amicably and definitely, the respective maritime boundaries of the states concerned and to other bilateral negotiations to conclude delimitation agreements. This topic, alluded to also by other delegations (notably by Mexico), refers to cooperative efforts at the national as well as the regional level for the settlement of boundary and delimitation issues, especially in the Caribbean.

More specific and very useful information on state practice, maritime claims and the delimitation of maritime zones ten years after the entry into force of the Convention is provided in paragraphs 20 to 39 of the Secretary-General's Report (A/59/62) and paragraphs 31 to 40 of its Addendum (A/59/62 Add.1). Included are important recent developments in the area affecting my own country, Cyprus. The Agreement between the Republic of Cyprus and the Arab Republic of Egypt on the Delimitation of the Exclusive Economic Zone, was signed on February 17, 2003, ratified on March 7, 2004 and enacted on April 2, 2004. It provides for the proclamation of the contiguous zone and for the proclamation of the EEZ of the Republic of Cyprus.

Other important developments include the submission of requests to the Commission on the Limits of the Continental Shelf by the Russian Federation, Brazil and Australia. These are to be followed by additional requests currently under preparation, with DOALOS assistance, regarding the limits of the continental shelf beyond 200 miles from the baseline from which the breadth of the territorial sea is measured.

The Minister of Fisheries and Oceans of Canada, after stating that according to FAO estimates, 70 percent of the world's fisheries were depleted or nearly depleted, and that illegal, unreported and unregulated fishing was estimated to represent 30 percent or more of the world's total catch, stressed that now is the time to act before it is too late. The Minister announced that a high seas ministerial task force was being set up, chaired by the U.K.'s Minister of Environment and that Canada would kick start the effort with an international conference on the Governance of High Seas Fisheries from May 1–5, 2005.

The representative from Kenya stressed that a balance must be struck between the need for economic exploitation and the need for conservation. He announced that his Government had established a technical interministerial committee to consider delimitation of his country's maritime zones and, in compliance with the Convention, to carry out a comprehensive review of Kenya's maritime laws and other laws relating to the exploration and exploitation of natural and mineral resources within its maritime zones. This is a good example to follow, especially by developing countries, in light of the frequent call (repeated in paragraph two of L.22) on all states to "harmonize, as a matter of priority, their national legislation with the provisions of the Convention…"

The delegate from Egypt stressed the importance of UNCLOS, called on others to accede, and emphasized the need to protect fisheries from exploitation. The delegate from Indonesia, referring to terrorism at sea, announced that Indonesia has intensified joint patrol activities in the Malacca strait, along with Malaysia and Singapore. The delegate from Tunisia expressed the concern that most Mediterranean countries have of seeing their fauna and flora threatened by pollution originating from both land and sea sources. The delegate from India indicated the importance of navigation, conservation and management of living marine resources and the conservation and management of biological diversity of the seabed in areas beyond national jurisdiction. India was also concerned with piracy an armed robbery against ships and announced its active involvement with Japan in establishing a regional cooperation agreement against piracy.

The delegate from Iceland, as the current chair of the Arctic Council, stated that the Arctic Climate Impact Assessment showed that the warming climate would bring about shifts in ocean ecosystems, including changes in fish populations and the Arctic coastline. With this in mind, a Marine Strategic Plan had been prepared on an integrated ecosystem based approach to sustainable ocean management. Iceland also announced generous financial contributions to Law of the Sea related activities, including the newly established Assistance Fund for the Fish Stocks Agreement.

The representative from the United States introduced the Draft Resolution on Sustainable Fisheries (L.23), stressing that the key element was to protect sensitive underwater features and vulnerable marine ecosystems from destructive fishing practices. Concerning the wider question in the Law of the Sea Resolution, he said that one of the highlights was the group working on the issues of marine biological diversity beyond national jurisdiction, since these presented particular legal and logistical challenges for the international community.

The representative from China expressed his country's position on the Global Marine Assessment mechanism that should operate within the United Nations framework and should make use of existing global and regional assessment mechanisms to avoid overlap. Its activities should be consistent with the Law of the Sea Convention and should respect the sovereign rights and jurisdiction of the coastal States. He also indicated that China actively participated in regional activities of the 1995 Fish Stocks Agreement, which provided the underlying framework for regional fishery management mechanisms.

Uganda, a landlocked developing State, urged that the International Seabed Authority, in partnership with States, investors and the scientific community, explore the potential for cobalt-rich ferromanganese crusts and polymetallic sulphides while being cautious to minimize the environmental impact arising from such exploration. She also suggested that the lessons from UNCLOS could be helpful toward the management of inland bodies of water such as Africa's Lake Victoria, an important source or food, commerce and transport in East Africa.

The representative from Japan made specific reference to the very recent Regional Cooperation Agreement on Combating Piracy and Armed Robbery against ships in Asia that, he hoped, would not only enhance cooperation and information sharing among Asian States, but would also serve as a good example of regional cooperation for other parts of the world. Japan, as a fishing State and a State surrounded by sea, attaches great importance to the preservation of the marine environment. Japan was seriously concerned about illegal, unreported and unregulated fishing, and actively supported the Conventions and initiatives to this end.

Speaking also for the Pacific Islands Forum, the representative from Samoa expressed concern over the length of the two oceans-related draft resolutions and the growing number of issues covered. At the same time, she said this showed the commitment to address these issues and to manage the global marine environment and its resources. She referred to the forthcoming meeting of the Western and Central Pacific Tuna Commission and to the Mauritius International Meeting, stressing that illegal, unreported and unregulated fishing is one of the greatest threats to the sustainability of the marine resources and the environment in the region.

This theme was also stressed by the representative from Chile. He said that in addition to the adverse impact of illegal, unregulated and unreported fishing, practices destructive to vulnerable marine ecosystems and especially high-seas bottom-trawling are also of great concern. He called for urgent action in this regard, including interim prohibitions of such practices and expressed support for the Conference of Maritime Delimitation in the Caribbean.

Fiji also addressed the concerns of illegal, unregulated and unreported fishing and bottom-trawling fishing practices. Stressing that oceans and seas were at the very core of island nations' existences, he stated that protecting the Pacific Ocean had always been central to Fiji's policy making and aimed to ensure that all states of the region got the maximum returns from the important regional tuna fishery. Similar views were expressed by the Federated States of Micronesia. 52

The representative from the Republic of Korea stressed that trafficking in weapons of mass destruction, narcotics and even humans via maritime transport were of grave concern to the international community. Equally stressed were the concerns of piracy, robbery and terrorism at sea. He called for intensified flag and port State cooperation to combat them and noted that his government was implementing measures to ensure the protection of the ocean environment, including phasing out 80 single-hull tankers. The representative called for other flag and port States to take appropriate measures to prevent the operation of sub-standard vessels.

The representative from Bangladesh also stressed his country's commitment to combating illegal fishing, piracy and other crimes at sea. He considered the evolution of the concept of the exclusive economic zone (EEZ) as one of the most significant developments resulting from UNCLOS. Its resources are among the richest in the world in terms of biodiversity and energy potential and yet are threatened by pollution caused by land-based activities and ocean-going vessels. He urged greater international cooperation for the conservation, management and sustainable use of marine living resources.

Ukraine talked about the same themes as a geographically disadvantaged nation bordering a sea poor in living resources and suffering from the depletion of fish stocks in its exclusive economic zone.

The representative from Bolivia concentrated on his country's claim for a free, useful and sovereign outlet on the Pacific Ocean and referred to the 1904 Treaty (now 100 years old) that caused the loss of 400 kilometers of coastline. He complained that Chile had not complied with its commitment to allow free transit to Bolivia. This last point was later disputed by the representative from Chile, who stated that free transit was a daily practice, that his country complied with the 1904 Treaty and that the matter could be discussed bilaterally between Chile and Bolivia. There was also a further exchange between the two delegations through rights of reply. Evidently, this is not a multilateral Law of the Sea issue.

The representative from Nigeria considered the top priority to be the implementation of the plan of action against illegal, unregulated and unreported fishing in areas under national jurisdiction and on the high seas. He called for measures to prevent the reflagging of fishing vessels to states that did not comply with the Fish Stocks Agreement. He also stated that his country would soon present its submission on the outer limit of the continental shelf.

New Zealand's representative also referred to its commitment to address destructive fishing practices and bottom-trawling saying that unsustainable fishing activities should be managed through appropriate fisheries management structures and mechanisms.

The representative from Vietnam commended the positive developments in implementing the Law of the Sea Convention. He stated that the Declaration on the Conduct of Parties in the South China Sea, signed by ASEAN members two years ago, was an important step toward building a Code of Conduct for the South China Sea. He then referred to his country's commitment to implement the Declaration as guided, he said, by its policy of the peaceful settlement of disputes and respect for international law.

Australia's representative announced that his country had just lodged its submission on the continental shelf, the third received by the Commission on the Limits of the Continental Shelf. He also announced that Australia had concluded a maritime delimitation agreement with New Zealand. With regard to fisheries, he welcomed the enforcement of the Convention and Management of Highly Migratory Fishstocks in the Western and the Central Pacific Ocean, with wide participation, including states with distant fishing interest in the Convention Areas, regulating the sustainable exploitation of tuna. He expressed concern that so much attention was devoted to bottom-trawling. Australia recognized that although some practices damage biodiversity, other practices that do not damage such diversity in the high seas might be unduly penalized if too broad of an approach is taken. He differentiated between destructive and non-destructive measures and would allow fishing conducted responsibly and with observer coverage.

This issue was also addressed by Palau which urged urgent action to prevent destruction of the magnificent diversity of the deep seas and stated that it is essential to take immediate and effective action this year to protect the deep sea from destructive fishing practices. The representative expressed the need for an immediate moratorium on bottom-trawl fishing in all high seas regions, as existed in the past (1989 and 1991), and for consensus resolution on large scale pelagic driftnet fishing on the high seas.

In a broad statement, the representative from Poland covered many of the main themes of the debate, including issues of piracy and armed robbery, terrorism, and maritime transport of weapons of mass destruction. He referred also to the activities of the Baltic Marine Environment Protection Commission and supported the establishment of a European coastguard service.

The representative from Uruguay stressed the importance of all states regulating all their activities in the oceans in strict compliance with the Law of the Sea Convention and all of its provisions. He joined the generally expressed concern about bottom trawling, over-fishing and illegal fishing, and trafficking of drugs and people.

During the continuation of the debate on November 17, 2004, the representative from Russia stated that the Convention on the Law of the Sea and its Implementation Agreement was a just and balanced reflection of the interests of all states and called on all states to accede to it as soon as possible. He stressed the need to strengthen state oversight of vessels by the governments whose flags they fly. He recalled that Russia had recently deposited its submission on the continental shelf, and foresaw that 10 or more such submissions would be made in the coming years. Argentina underlined that the Convention provided the legal framework for activities involving the oceans, which are multifaceted, complex and of great interest to his country.

This was echoed by Cuba, which stressed that the Convention was still as relevant and valid as ever and remained the benchmark for global ocean affairs as well as for international peace and security. He called for increasing cooperation from developing countries to ensure that UNCLOS is fully implemented.

The last speaker from a state was the representative from Guyana who said that the major effect of UNCLOS was the more equitable distribution of worldwide maritime resources. He illustrated this by referring to the extension of the territorial sea, the creating of the exclusive economic zone, the codification of the rules governing the continental shelf and the recognition of the existence of the common heritage of mankind beyond the limits of national jurisdictions.

The General Assembly was, as customary, addressed by the Secretary-General of the International Seabed Authority, Satya N. Nandan, who put emphasis on the conduct of the Authority in putting together technical workshops by bringing together internationally recognized scientists, experts, researchers and representatives of the mining industry and of member States. Marine scientific research is an essential tool for ocean governance since, despite progress, the knowledge of the oceans remains insignificant. More is known, he said, about the surface of the moon than about the oceans from which life on earth depends. Turning to fisheries he referred to the review conference for the Fish Stock Agreement scheduled for 2006. He noted that neither the Agreement nor any of the regional fisheries management organizations are equipped to deal with the problem of allocation of high seas resources.

Mr. Nandan was followed by the President of the International Tribunal for the Law of the Sea, Mr. L. Dolliver M. Nelson, who discussed the Tribunal's work in the preceding year. Certain legal and judicial matters were dealt with in the course of two sessions, although no new cases had been submitted. He said that during its eight year existence, the Tribunal dealt with 12 cases in which it delivered six judgments and issued 26 orders. Thus the Tribunal is making its contribution to the development of international law with regard to such issues as the nationality of claims, reparation, use of force in law enforcement, hot pursuit, and the question of the genuine link between vessel and flag State. He acknowledged that the Tribunal has not been put to full use by prospective litigants and has, therefore, not been able to develop its full potential as the specialized organ for the settlement of maritime disputes. (The relationship between the Law of the Sea Tribunal, the International Court of Justice and ad hoc arbitral tribunals is, of course, a much wider question, which is by itself a major topic for discussion.) Mr. Nelson also referred to some administrative and financial aspects affecting the Tribunal, including the question of expenses and arrears.

Earlier, the Observer for the International Union for Conservation of Nature also addressed the General Assembly, providing some weighty observations from IUCN's perspective. She reminded them that 70 percent of harvested fish stocks worldwide were fished at or beyond their sustainable limit. In deep-sea areas, she said, bottom-trawling had destroyed vital coral communities and depleted target fish stocks. Scientific evidence increasingly shows that maritime species do not recover from overfishing once it has stopped. While the General Assembly had implicitly recognized bottom trawling as a destructive fishing practice and a threat to vulnerable marine ecosystems, she said, it was regrettable that more forceful action had not been agreed upon to prohibit it on an interim basis.

This concludes the summary presentation of the views stated during the debate last year. I apologize in advance that because of time constraints, I did not do justice to all of the points expressed during this very full debate.

Commentary

The draft resolutions were adopted by the General Assembly with a recorded vote of 141 in favour, 1 against (Turkey) with two abstentions (Venezuela and Colombia) in the case of A/59/L.22 on Oceans and the Law of the Sea; and without a vote in the case of A/59/L.23, on Sustainable Fisheries.

There were explanations of vote, before the vote, on L.22 by Turkey, which every year has voted against because of objections it always had to UNCLOS (no adequate provision for special geographical situations and no provision for making reservations for specific articles); Venezuela, also every year (because of "historical reservations" about UNCLOS); Chile, even though it voted for the draft resolution; and by Peru, which also voted in favour, each interpreting in their way operative paragraph 66.

There was also an explanation of vote on L.23, after the vote, by Italy (which would have preferred if operative paragraph 7 had contained a reference to UNCLOS and to the UNESCO Convention on Underwater Cultural Heritage); and by Iran (disassociating itself from preambular paragraph 17), although neither asked for a vote or was prepared to block the consensus.

As I earlier indicated, both of the adopted Resolutions (now A/RES/59/24 and A/RES/59/25) consisted of very extensive texts, both preambular and operative, covering in detail all aspects of their respective topics. For full understanding it is necessary to study them paragraph-by paragraph.

For the purposes of this presentation, suffice it to say that the General Assembly, in the omnibus resolution on oceans and the Law of the Sea, called on all states that had not done so to become parties to the 1982 Convention (currently 148). It also called for the harmonization of national legislation with the provisions of the Convention. It also decided to establish an Ad Hoc Open Ended Informal Working Group to study issues relating to the conservation and sustainable use of marine biological diversity beyond the areas of national jurisdiction. And, in the resolution on sustainable fisheries, the General Assembly deplored overfishing of straddling and highly migratory fish stocks in many parts of the world. The Assembly also expressed concern that illegal, unreported and unregulated fishing seriously threatened to deplete certain fish species and to damage marine ecosystems to the detriment of sustainable fisheries, as well as food security and the economies of many states, particularly developing states.

As a footnote, to note in the omnibus resolution, operative paragraph 15 on the Hamilton Shirley Amerasinghe Memorial Fellowship and operative paragraph 33 in reference to the Conference on Legal and Scientific Aspects of Continental Shelf Limits, held in Reykjavik, Iceland, from June 25–27, 2003. United Nations, General Assembly, A/Res/59/24, February 4, 2005.

By and large, the 2004 consideration of the Oceans and the Law of the Sea item was substantive and full. It acquires a broader significance if one considers that in the same session of the General Assembly two other events of major significance in the international legal field also occurred. One was the significant call at the opening of the General Assembly Session in September by the Secretary-General Kofi Annan to all states represented in the General Assembly to strengthen respect for the rule of law. The other was the publication of the Report on UN Reform (A/59/565, December 2, 2004) that addressed many aspects of international law, including the legal regulation of the use of force and international terrorism. These, together with the other international legal activity during the 2004 General Assembly Session, with the Report of the International Court of Justice, with the work of the Sixth Committee and the Meeting of the Legal Advisers to Foreign Ministries, make up an impressive array of activities in the United Nations toward the shared objective to promote and strengthen international law among nations.

Statement at the Inaugural Meeting of the General Assembly of the International Seabed Authority*

Upon the Entry into Force of the 1982 Law of the Sea Convention, Kingston, Jamaica, November 16, 1994

The coming into force today of the 1982 Law of the Sea Convention is an event of historic significance. It marks the fruition of what has been rightly described as the most important multilateral lawmaking undertaking since the Charter of the United Nations and as a veritable constitution for the seas and oceans. All those who value international legal order and who toiled long and hard to bring about this result deserve the satisfaction they justly derive for this major accomplishment.

Cyprus, an island state located in the Mediterranean at the crossroads of three continents, is vitally concerned with the legal regulation of the uses of the sea in a just and orderly manner, ensuring fairness and predictability.

According to legend, it was off the coast of Cyprus that Aphrodite, the Goddess of love and beauty, was born rising from the foam of the glittering sea. According to history, our sea-faring tradition and involvement with the sea go back to more than three thousand years and today shipping is a major industry. Our past, present and future are inexorably meshed with the sea and its uses.

It is right and fitting that this historic occasion takes place in Jamaica, another island state with which we are related by bonds of friendship and cooperation. We take particular satisfaction in the fact that we were among the first to have supported back in 1974 our host country's claim to provide the site of the Seabed Authority. I would like to take this opportunity, in the dual capacity as head of the Cyprus delegation to the law of the Sea Conference from its beginning and as my country's representative to Jamaica since 1973, to say how gratified I am to be here, in the same dual capacity, to congratulate the Government and people of Jamaica at the beginning of

* Previously published in Recent Developments in the Law of the Sea and China, ed. M. Nordquist, BRILL (2006).

this new major chapter and to thank them for their warm hospitality and excellent facilities they provided for our work. While this is not the occasion to attempt even a cursory analysis of the provisions of the Convention which has just entered into force (320 articles and 9 annexes), I might be permitted a brief look back – because of sentiment as well as reason – and to view in broad perspective our aims and objectives twenty years ago when the Conference started and to what extent these have been met, both in terms of substantive provisions on the issues of primary concern to Cyprus and in terms of the peaceful settlement of disputes arising from these provisions. Looking back to these positions, it can be said with conviction, and perhaps with a degree of satisfaction, that these aims and objectives have to a large extent been met, both from the point of view of our national interest and from the broader perspective of the interests of the international community as a whole.

To very briefly indicate some of these aspects of concern to us, I would cite the issue of the extent of territorial waters (which, under Article 3 of the Convention, entrenches the 12-mile general rule, as Cyprus had done already in 1964); the position of islands (which, under Article 121, part VIII, clearly vindicates our strongly held view that islands are fully entitled to all the zones of maritime jurisdiction viz. territorial sea, contiguous zone, exclusive economic zone and continental shelf, no less than other land territory); the question of enclosed and semi enclosed seas, the question of delimitation of zones of maritime jurisdiction between states, the coasts of which are opposite or adjacent to each other; questions of the protection of the environment; and questions of the protection of and the jurisdiction over archaeological and historical objects found at sea. Likewise, the system of the peaceful settlement of disputes – very important, especially for the protection of small states while not as far reaching as we would have preferred, marks a significant advance from the previously existing situation. We look forward to the early establishment of the Law of the Sea Tribunal in the great maritime city of Hamburg and to the major contribution this tribunal is expected to make in interpreting the Convention and further developing its rules.

It is for all those reasons that Cyprus was among the first to sign and ratify the 1982 Law of the Sea Convention and we have signed the recent Agreement on the implementation of Part XI in the hope and expectation that this will make possible the universal participation in the Convention.

We look forward to playing a role in the future activities of the Seabed Authority.

That this universal legal regime for the seas and oceans has been made possible is a tribute to the many dedicated individuals – too many to mention by name, several of whom are present at this historic occasion as is only right and fitting – as much as to the collective wisdom and moderation of the international community. This has been a victory not of individual states or groups of states but of reason, the rule of law and humankind as a whole. It has been demonstrated that, through a process of compromise and consensus, in most instances a judicious balance was reached between the new and revolutionary approach required by the technological, political and economic trends of our times and the retention of those positive rules of traditional international law which have stood the test of time and have served well the needs of the international community. It has also been demonstrated that the newly independent and developing states, in particular, are fully capable of contributing constructively to the development of international law and can show a sense of responsibility and moderation for the wider common good.

To conclude, Mr. President, let me say that, in evaluating the outcome of so many years of work, we must see it in proper perspective. The 1982 Convention and the recent Agreement on Chapter XI could not and do not fully satisfy all delegations in each and every respect. One could point to ambiguities where there should have been clarity, to complexities where there could have been streamlining and to exceptions where there should be a general rule. But it has to be accepted that compromises, necessitated by the objective of reaching an overall agreement by consensus, are the price paid for the successful conclusion of a complicated and ambitious undertaking. By definition, law and order are preferable to chaos and the law of the jungle and, as current events in many parts of the world harshly remind us, there is dire need for the rules of international law to be observed. The Law of the Sea Convention and its dispute settlement system goes a long way, in an imperfect world, in meeting this need. The entry into force of the 1982 Law of the Sea Convention is good for Jamaica, good for Cyprus, good for the United Nations on the eve of its 50th anniversary and good for the world as a whole. It is indeed an important achievement for which we should all be proud.

Some Aspects of the Law of the Sea: Islands, Delimitation, and Dispute Settlement Revisited*

Introduction

A word of explanation as to my own involvement with the topic of this article is in order. Before the commencement of the Law of the Sea Conference (UNCLOS III, 1973–82), I represented Cyprus in the Preparatory Committee (1970–73), where much of the maneuvering took place on the topics of islands and delimitation. After 1982 (and while at the time Ambassador to the United States) I spoke at Kingston in 1994 on the occasion of the coming into force of the Convention. Moreover, I spoke on the topic in the UN General Assembly on a number of occasions (as Permanent Representative of Cyprus in 1992 and as Cyprus Delegate in 1998). In 2002 I was actively involved in the arrangements for the commemoration of the 20th Anniversary of the Convention. I also served in recent years as an unpaid adviser to the Cyprus Attorney General on matters of the law of the sea.[1]

There is a multitude of issues dealt with in and indeed regulated by UNCLOS III, this veritable constitution of the Oceans. Small delegations such as mine, while not totally neglecting issues marginal to their country's interest, such as for instance protection of the environment, scientific research (indeed I had to pay some attention to these as Vice Chairman of the Third Main Committee and Member of the General Committee), archipelagic waters, passage through straits, etc., had of necessity to concentrate on those issues which were vital to them. In addition to strongly supporting the 12-mile territorial sea (Article 3 – Cyprus had already in 1964 proclaimed a 12-mile limit), that enclosed and semi-enclosed seas, such as the Mediterranean, are regulated by the same basic rules as those applicable to

* Previously published in Festschrift to Professor Carl-August Fleischer, eds. O. Fauchald, H. Jakhelln and A. Syse, Oslo University Press (2006).

[1] Reference can also be made to my participation in the 1976 ASIL Annual Meeting Panel (with J.N. Moore, E. Lauterpacht, S. Nandan, L. B. Sohn, and M. Nordquist); 1979 Marine Policy article; 1983 Duke University paper; 1982 ILC Seminar lecture; 1979 Columbia Law School lecture; 1974 (July 8th) and 1976 (April 6th) UNCLOS speeches; Regime of Islands legislative history by Division for Ocean Affairs and the Law of the Sea (DOALOS); etc.

all other seas and oceans subject only to the duty to cooperate in certain areas (Articles 122 and 123 and Part IX), and the protection of archaeological objects (Articles 149 and 303), we concentrated on certain key issues of primary importance to Cyprus. These were, first, the regime of islands and their undiminished entitlement to the zones of maritime jurisdiction (Article 121); secondly, the question of delimitation of those zones of maritime jurisdiction between states the coasts of which are opposite or adjacent to each other (Articles 15, 74, 83); and thirdly, the question of settlement of disputes (Part XV; Articles 279–299 and Annexes VI, VII, VIII).

Cyprus is an island state as, for instance, also is Malta in the Mediterranean and Jamaica in the Caribbean (another semi-enclosed sea). The efforts by some states (notably Turkey) in the course of the early stages of the Conference to differentiate between island states and other islands did not succeed, and all islands, including the Greek islands, are governed by the same basic rule. Cyprus is a small island state surrounded in four directions by states (Turkey to the North; Syria, Lebanon and Israel to the East; Egypt to the South; and Greece's islands, primarily Crete and Rhodes, to the West) in no direction reaching four hundred nautical miles. Therefore, the application of the median line as the basic rule for delimitation, especially of the Exclusive Economic Zone (EEZ), is evidently of primary importance. I shall revert to this later in light of the recent EEZ delimitation agreement with Egypt. Additionally to establishing that an island has no less entitlement to zones of maritime jurisdiction than continental territories and to the median line as the starting point and basic rule of delimitation, it is essential, especially for small states[2] that there be in place an iron-clad system of compulsory settlement of disputes ensuring that these rights are effectively protected.[3]

So, our basic position being what I have just indicated, how did it fare after several years of hard negotiations and tactical alliances with like-minded delegations in the Conference? In addressing these issues, I rely on a lecture I delivered as a member of the International Law Commission at the International Law Seminar in Geneva in May 1982, taking the topics one by one (section 2). I shall thereafter bring the issues up to date by relying on a lecture by Judge Guillaume in the Sixth Committee in 2001 in light of the *Qatar v. Bahrain* and the *Nigeria v. Cameroon* cases, and on the relevant discussions at the 20th Anniversary Commemoration (section 3). And I shall

---

2 See Jacovides, International Tribunals: Do They Really Work for Small States? in *New York University Journal of International Law and Policy*, vol. 34 (2001); and The Future for Small States: Overcoming Vulnerability, *Commonwealth Secretarial publication* (1997), Commonwealth Advisory Group.

3 See Jacovides, Peaceful Settlement of Disputes in Ocean Conflicts: Does UNCLOS III point the way?, in *Essays in Honour of L.B. Sohn*, edited by T. Buergenthal, Duke University (1983).

conclude by briefly touching on some very recent developments with regard to Cyprus (section 4).

The legal regime of islands, the delimitation of zones of maritime jurisdiction between states the coasts of which are opposite or adjacent, and dispute settlement are distinct topics forming different aspects of the law of the sea. However, in particular situations they may, and in practice often do, interact with each other. The topics of islands and delimitation are relatively narrow aspects of the substantive law of the sea. Although dispute settlement is of a much broader nature, it is particularly relevant in solving problems relating to these topics, especially the latter.

The importance of the rules of international law relating to islands and delimitation has grown considerably because of recent developments and current trends. In fact, it has grown in proportion to the increase of size and changes in the types of zones of maritime jurisdiction, as compared to the zones of jurisdiction set out in the 1958 Geneva Conventions on the Law of the Sea. In 1958 there were 3 nautical miles (NM) territorial seas and 12 NM contiguous zones, the concept of the exclusive economic zone (EEZ) was still unknown, and continental shelf zones depended on the relatively modest "depth" and "exploitability" criteria. Now, there are as a rule 12 NM territorial seas, 24 NM contiguous zones, 200 NM EEZs, and 200 NM (in certain cases up to 350 NM) continental shelf zones under the criteria of "distance" and "natural prolongation".

Because of the high stakes involved under these new conditions, new disputes between states over their corresponding rights are bound to arise, multiply and intensify. Existing disputes also have become more acute. Thus, dispute settlement becomes proportionately much more important, the more so since some of the substantive rules adopted are vague and imprecise, thus lending themselves to subjective interpretation by the interested parties. This is especially true in the case of delimitation between opposite or adjacent states and has become evident in a number of situations, some of which have been settled bilaterally through agreements[4] or have been dealt with through third party adjudication. Others are still pending and are acquiring the dimension of political and even military confrontation.

Conceptually, each of the abovementioned issues can be subjected to a fundamental proposition:

---

[4] See relevant DOALOS publications, listed on http://www.un.org/Depts/los/doalos_publications/doalos_publications.htm.

- Proposition 1: There should be no distinction between islands and other land territories in determining zones of maritime jurisdiction.
- Proposition 2: The general rule of delimitation between opposite or adjacent states should be the median or equidistant line.
- Proposition 3: Any dispute arising out of the substantive provisions of the proposed Law of the Sea Convention, and, more specifically, those relating to islands and delimitation, should be subject to compulsory third party settlement entailing a binding decision.

While the merit and basic validity of each of these propositions, in terms of objectivity, orderliness and predictability, are self-evident, each is subject to exceptions and qualifications. The opposing view may be summarized as follows. First, the entitlement of islands to zones of maritime jurisdiction should depend on criteria such as size, population, geographical location and geomorphology. Secondly, "equitable principles" should be applied by agreement between the states concerned in the case of delimitation of maritime zones between opposite or adjacent states. Thirdly, there should be no compulsory third party dispute settlement procedures, especially when it comes to matters of delimitation, because these involve sensitive issues of sovereignty and thus do not lend themselves to third party adjudication.

The Rules of the UNCLOS and Their Background

General Issue

The international law of the sea which existed prior to UNCLOS III consisted of customary rules which evolved over many centuries and were codified and developed in the four Geneva Conventions of 1958. These rules, both customary and conventional, were elaborated further through the practice of states, through judicial decisions, including decisions of the International Court of Justice, and through the writings of publicists. The totality of these rules formed the traditional law of the sea.

The Conference evolved out of the pioneering work of the United Nations Committee on the Peaceful Uses of the Seabed and the Ocean Floor Beyond the Limits of National Jurisdiction (Seabed Committee). It was aimed at reexamining and, where appropriate, recasting virtually all aspects of the law of the sea, and has combined the element of codification with that of progressive development, with emphasis on the latter. It has thus been a lawmaking conference in the full sense of the term.

In significant respects, new and revolutionary concepts have been introduced and elaborated, such as the common heritage of mankind and the

EEZ. On the other hand, it has been found, after extensive examination, that other aspects of the law have stood the test of time and should remain as before, or minor modifications made to adjust them to the overall scheme (e.g. the freedom of the high seas and the regime of islands) thus demonstrating that novelty is not necessarily synonymous with progress. On the whole, the course UNCLOS III took was characterized by a judicious blending of elements of progressive and even revolutionary change in some respects with those of stability and continuity in other respects, thus helping to preserve a balance between conflicting claims and interests.

The Conference commenced in 1973 and was concluded in December 1982. The first session considered procedure, the rest mostly substantive issues. In addition to the actual sessions of the Conference, numerous regional, intergovernmental, and non-governmental meetings took place, parallel to the official meetings and intersessionally. All are indicative of the complexity of the issues involved and the importance which states attached to them. The Conference was convened against the background of the recent transformation of the international community, caused by many new states coming into existence with the end of colonial rule, and by advances in technology which brought opportunities for obtaining new resources from the sea and the seabed. Technological advances profoundly affected the expectations of states in general as to how the international legal system should define, protect and harmonize their interests in the seas. More particularly, newly independent states, which did not have the opportunity of participating in the formulation of the traditional law of the sea, felt that they should play a full role in the process of moulding the contemporary law of the sea in a way which safeguarded and promoted their political and economic viewpoints. Thus UNCLOS III had to reconcile competing economic, political, scientific, strategic and even ideological factors, and acquired dimensions far beyond that of mere lawmaking. The many complex problems with which UNCLOS III was confronted, combined with operating procedures that were unusual for a lawmaking conference, largely explain the slow rate of progress. The procedural aspects and the legislative history of the present text deserve separate examination in their novelty, complexity and ingenuity. Evidently, space does not allow for them to be dealt with now – and so we shall proceed with each of the particular topics mentioned above.

Regime of Islands

Article 121 of UNCLOS states:

1. An island is a naturally formed area of land, surrounded by water, which is above water at high tide.

2. Except as provided for in paragraph 3, the territorial sea, the contiguous zone, the exclusive economic zone and the continental shelf of an island are determined in accordance with the provisions of the present Convention applicable to other land territory.
3. Rocks which cannot sustain human habitation or economic life of their own have no exclusive zone or continental shelf.

The definition of an island is identical with that in Article 10 (1) of the 1958 Geneva Convention on the Territorial Sea and Contiguous Zone, which was elaborated by the International Law Commission and had been framed in accordance with the traditionally held view. This definition marks the rejection of the attempt, systematically pursued by a number of states in the Sea-bed Committee and UNCLOS III, to establish different categories of islands with correspondingly different rights to zones of maritime jurisdiction.[5]

The proposition that the same criteria apply for determining the maritime zones of jurisdiction of islands as for other land territories also follows the traditional line. It had always been considered in customary law that islands generated a territorial sea. This was expressly recognized in Article 10 (1) of the 1958 Convention. With regard to the continental shelf of islands, Article 1 of the 1958 Geneva Convention on the Continental Shelf expressly stated that "for the purpose of this Article the term 'continental shelf' is used as referring to… (a) the seabed and sub-soil of similar submarine areas adjacent to the coasts of islands". This was also recognized to be the customary rule of international law by the International Court of Justice in the North Sea Continental Shelf cases, 1969. Article 121 (2) simply recognizes this rule.

The position stated in Article 121 (2) marks the acceptance of the views of a number of states participating in the Conference, including several island states that no distinction whatsoever should be made between islands irrespective of their size, population or political status, and the continental land masses, and that the criteria for determining maritime zones of jurisdiction must apply to islands in the same way as they apply to continental land. The same states have argued that, if any discrimination was to be made between islands on the one hand and continental land masses on the other, this should be in favour rather than at the expense of islands, because ordinarily the population of the latter is dependent on the resources of the sea for its survival and economic development, whereas the population of continental territories could draw on the resources of the hinterland. The position reflected in paragraph 2 of Article 121 marks the rejection of the view that the maritime spaces of islands should be determined on the basis

[5] See Division for Ocean Affairs and the Law of the Sea, *Legislative history. Regime of Islands*, published by DOALOS.

of the special circumstances of each, such as size, population, contiguity to the principal territory, the physical, geological and geomorphological area involved, the general configuration of the respective coasts, and even whether they were "situated on the continental shelf of another state".

A valid reply is that any apparent or real inequity that might result if such views were not accepted would not be more than other inequities created by nature. Why should the maritime zones of islands of a small size or population be questioned while, for example, the same zones of continental countries consisting largely of deserts or otherwise underpopulated or unpopulated areas have not been open to dispute?

Article 121 (3) gave rise to additional arguments but was left unchanged. Unlike the 1958 Territorial Sea Convention, a distinction is made between "islands" and "rocks", the latter being described as incapable of "sustaining human habitation or economic life of their own". In practical terms, this distinction may give rise to difficulties over interpretation, and borderline cases may occur where there can be room for difference of opinion. In such cases, the dispute settlement system can usefully come into play.

Departure from the traditional position in the case of rocks is, in any case, more apparent than real. First, the exception does not cover the territorial sea or the contiguous zone. Hence, islands which are no more than "rocks" continue to generate these zones of jurisdiction (e.g. Rockall). Also, under the Convention the breadth of the territorial sea over which sovereignty exists extends up to 12 NM, unlike the situation in 1958. Secondly, under the 1958 Convention "rocks" generated continental shelf; the applicable criteria then being depth and exploitability. The criteria of distance and natural prolongation under the present definition are considerably wider. Thus, in practical terms, this solitary exception to the principle in Article 121 (2) should not be considered of major significance. Conversely, to insist on full rights of a 200 NM EEZ and the equivalent continental shelf area on the basis of distance and natural prolongation for rocks might reasonably have been criticized as unduly excessive and indefensible. On the whole, therefore, the exception in Article 121 (3), when properly applied and interpreted, does not materially affect the fundamental principle set out in proposition 2 above.

We now pass on to consider briefly the four zones of maritime jurisdiction (the territorial sea, the contiguous zone, the EEZ, and the continental shelf) and their delimitation between adjacent or opposite states.

Delimitation According to UNCLOS

The Territorial Sea

The juridical status of the territorial sea, the airspace over the territorial sea and its seabed and subsoil, is set out in Article 2 of the Convention. The coastal state exercises sovereignty over this zone which, under Article 3, can be extended to a limit not exceeding 12 nautical miles which is now accepted as the standard rule.

Article 15 provides that:

> Where the coasts of two States are opposite or adjacent to each other, neither of the two states is entitled, failing agreement between them to the contrary, to extend its territorial sea beyond the median line every point of which is equidistant from the nearest points on the baselines from which the breadth of the territorial seas of each of the two States is measured. This article does not apply, however, where it is necessary by reason of historic title or other special circumstances to delimit the territorial seas of the two States in a way which is at variance with this provision.

This Article is identical with the equivalent provision of the earlier negotiating texts and the 1958 Geneva Convention on the Territorial Sea and Contiguous Zone. It states the customary rule evolved through the decisions of tribunals, the writings of publicists and the practice of states as reflected in bilateral agreements and as incorporated in the 1958 Geneva Convention. In essence, it accepts the principle of the median line between opposite or adjacent states, unless modified by agreement between the parties concerned and in the absence of historic title or other special circumstances.

The median line principle as the general rule of delimitation has much to recommend it. In fact, it was argued during the 1958 Conference that qualifying circumstances should be omitted because they introduced an element of uncertainty and would thus give rise to disputes. The same line of reasoning has also been followed during UNCLOS III and earlier, during the Seabed Committee's deliberations. Conversely, it was proposed to delete or downgrade the reference to the median line and substitute a reference to "equitable principles including the presence of islands". As stated above, neither point of view prevailed, and the text remains as in the 1958 Geneva Convention.

What is the exact meaning of "other special circumstances"? Because no two geographical situations in the world can be identical it seems that the term "special circumstances" was intended to be the exception rather than the rule and must therefore be interpreted restrictively. The existence of islands does not per se constitute "special circumstances", because, as stated earlier, islands are in the same position as other land territory. But islands can, of course, come within the rubric of "special circumstances" in the same way as other land territories if it is so alleged by a party to the dispute. This party should presumably have to prove that this is so. If this contention is not accepted on a bilateral basis by the other party through negotiations or otherwise, it follows that the matter should be settled by appropriate third party adjudication. Indeed, additional judicial practice in this regard would provide an authoritative guideline as to what "special circumstances" are, because the law at present is far from certain.

Contiguous Zone

The concept of a contiguous zone within which the coastal state may exercise the control necessary to prevent and punish infringement of its customs, fiscal, immigration or sanitary regulations within its territory or territorial sea is dealt with briefly in Article 33 of the Convention. This provides that the contiguous zone may not extend beyond 24 nautical miles from the baselines. However, it is worth noting that no provision is made in the Convention (or indeed in the earlier Single Negotiating Text or Revised Single Negotiating Text) regarding delimitation of the contiguous zones between opposite or adjacent states. This is in marked contrast to the equivalent provision of the 1958 Geneva Convention which provides for the application of the median line, without any qualifications referring to historic title or special circumstances.

The reasoning behind this omission is not clear. A possible explanation is that, in the light of the new concept of the EEZ, the contiguous zone concept would be submerged in the latter, as some states suggested during UNCLOS III. However, this is an inadequate explanation. As long as the concept remains in the Convention, it should be accompanied by a delimitation provision based on the application of the median line principle, as in the 1958 Convention. This was proposed by a number of states during the debate on the relevant Article. The omission can only be described as a lacuna, especially because no explanation for it is furnished in any official documents of UNCLOS. It can thus be validly argued that the provision of the 1958 Convention continues in effect as between the parties to it and even that it has become part of customary law.

The Exclusive Economic Zone and the Continental Shelf

The new concept of the EEZ is described in Part V of the Convention as an area beyond and adjacent to the territorial sea of a coastal state which does not extend beyond 200 NM from the baselines from which the breadth of the territorial sea is measured. Delimitation of the EEZ between adjacent or opposite states is dealt with in Article 74 of the Convention which states:

1. The delimitation of the exclusive economic zone between states with opposite or adjacent coast shall be effected by agreement on the basis of international law as referred to in Article 38 of the Statute of the International Court of Justice, in order to achieve an equitable solution.
2. If no agreement can be reached within a reasonable period of time, the States concerned shall resort to the procedures provided for in Part XV.

3. Pending agreement, as provided for in paragraph 1, the States concerned, in a spirit of understanding and co-operation, shall make every effort to enter into provisional arrangements of a practical nature and, during this transitional period, not to jeopardize or hamper the reaching of the final agreement. Such arrangements shall be without prejudice to the final delimitation.
4. Where there is an agreement in force between the States concerned, questions relating to the delimitation of the exclusive economic zone shall be determined in accordance with the provisions of that agreement.

The delimitation of the EEZ and of the continental shelf between adjacent or opposite states is, for the purpose of avoiding duplication, taken together since the arguments used during the debates in the Conference and the solutions found have been basically identical. Although the issues in each case have been similar and the same arguments used interchangeably, the assumption that the rules on delimitation of the EEZ and the continental shelf are identical is not entirely correct since, in the case of the EEZ delimitation, the median line principle is easier to apply because the "distance" criterion is the only one applicable, while in the case of the continental shelf delimitation, the matter is more complicated because of the applicability of the "natural prolongation" factor. Be that as it may, for the purpose of simplifying our discussion here, they are being treated together.

Under Article 55 of UNCLOS the EEZ is described as "an area beyond and adjacent to the territorial sea, subject to the specific legal regime established in this Part [Part V], under which the rights and freedoms of other states are governed by the relevant provisions of this Convention". Under Article 57, "the exclusive economic zone shall not extend beyond 200 nautical miles from the baselines from which the breadth of the territorial sea is measured". Since the concept of the EEZ originates from UNCLOS III, no equivalent provision is found in the 1958 Geneva Convention or in customary law.

Under Article 76 of the Convention, the continental shelf is defined as "the sea-bed and sub-soil of the submarine areas that extend beyond its territorial sea throughout the natural prolongation of its land territory to the outer edge of the continental margin, or to a distance of 200 nautical miles from the baselines from which the breadth of the territorial sea is measured where the outer edge of the continental margin does not extend up to that distance". This definition differs from the definition in Article 1 of the 1958 Convention in that, under the latter, the continental shelf extended "to a depth of 200 meters or, beyond that limit, to where the depth of the superjacent waters admits of the exploitation of the natural resources of the said areas".

The questions of the delimitation of the EEZ and of the continental shelf (which is a misnomer because it is as much "insular" as "continental" under Article 121 of the present Convention and Article 1 of the 1958 Conference) gave rise to acute controversy throughout the Conference, both in the Second Committee and in Negotiating Group 7, between two groups of states favouring, respectively, the median line or equidistance approach (including Cyprus, which served as spokesman of this group) as the general though by no means the absolute rule for such delimitation, and those advocating the application of "equitable principles" for this purpose (including Ireland, which acted as spokesman).

The key paragraph of Articles 74 and 83 of the previous draft (and its equivalent in the previous negotiating texts, the SNT and RSNT) was that such delimitation "shall be effected by agreement in accordance with equitable principles, employing, where appropriate, the median or equidistance line, and taking into account all the relevant circumstances".

During the relevant debates, one set of proposals was aimed at strengthening the reference to the median line by making it the general rule, while another set of proposals sought to remove altogether any reference to the median line and to stress "equitable principles" as the basis of the agreement between the states concerned.

The compromise solution reached at the end of the 1981 Tenth Session of the Conference was to replace this text with another which provides for "agreement on the basis of international law, as referred to in Article 38 of the Statute of the International Court of Justice, in order to reach an equitable solution". It was drafted by President T. Koh after efforts by Judge Manner in Negotiating Group 7 were inconclusive.

This compromise intentionally leaves open to the circumstances of each case what is the international law rule applicable. Evidently, each side will argue that the rule which favours its position is applicable (including treaties, customary law, the decisions of tribunals, the teachings of publicists and even the general principles of law recognized by civilized nations, as spelled out in Article 38 of the ICJ Statute). Similarly, each side will argue that the position it favours is aimed at achieving "an equitable solution". Indeed, it has been argued that in many cases equidistance is the basis for an equitable solution. The fact is that this compromise was accepted by the majority and is currently a part of the Convention (even though some of the proponents of the "equitable principles" view, voted against the Convention at least partly because of this delimitation provision).

As with most compromises, this is not an ideal solution. It is bound to leave the issue open, and the only hope to avoid tensions and even conflicts is for the parties to accept the decision of third party adjudication or even the suggestion of the conciliation procedure under the Convention, as indeed provided in Articles 74 (2) and 83 (2). But, as we shall see, the law has been clarified to a large extent by subsequent judicial decisions.

Dispute Settlement

During the 1958 Conference, the suggestion of the International Law Commission to make the whole Convention on the Continental Shelf subject to adjudication by the International Court of Justice was accepted in Committee but not by the Plenary of the Conference and the result was an ineffectual Optional Protocol.

During UNCLOS III, a major effort was mounted, including support by most of the states which advocated the median line principle as the basis for delimitation, to include an effective dispute settlement system as an essential corollary to the substantive rules of the draft Convention. The advantages of such a system are self-evident from the point of view of lawyers. UNCLOS III was broader than the 1958 Convention, and the range of potential disputes increased considerably due to the new topics and rules which had been introduced, many of them ambiguously worded as a price for their acceptability by consensus. It had seemed that the introduction of such a comprehensive dispute settlement system, entailing in all cases a binding decision, would have been easier to achieve both because of this reason and because, unlike the 1958 Convention where such procedures were limited to the ICJ, which was viewed with a certain amount of reserve by third world states, especially after the first Namibia decision, the choice of tribunals was now much wider and included, in addition to the ICJ with its new and more confidence-inspiring composition, also ad hoc arbitration tribunals and, more importantly, the new special International Tribunal on the Law of the Sea (ITLOS).

Under Part XV of the Treaty new and major steps were taken to meet the demand for the settlement of disputes under procedures entailing a binding decision. But after prolonged and often acrimonious arguments, delimitation disputes regarding Articles 15, 74 and 83 (i.e. delimitation of the territorial sea, the exclusive economic zone and the continental shelf respectively) were made subject to an optional exception and limited to the "compulsory conciliation procedure" under Annex V Section 2 of the Convention, viz. Article 298 (1) (a).

This has been the result again of a compromise and the price paid for a generally acceptable formulation. It became increasingly clear during the debates in various forums, and especially in Negotiating Group 7, that many states, including at least one major Power, were unwilling to submit issues touching upon national sovereignty to third party settlement entailing a binding decision. This view prevailed in the end. It could be hoped that the procedure of compulsory conciliation would prove to serve the same purpose in practice, but this did not happen and may be no more than wishful thinking. The fact is that delimitation, because of its contentious potential and because of the vagueness of the substantive rules adopted – particularly in the case of Articles 74 and 83, especially lends itself to third party settlement if solutions are to be found peacefully and disputes are not to escalate into confrontations, including in some cases, even armed conflict.

The vagueness of the substantive rules on the one hand and the absence of compulsory third party dispute settlement procedures of a binding nature on the other are bound to work to the disadvantage of small and militarily weak states because larger and stronger states may be tempted to claim the lion's share and are not obliged to accept binding third party adjudication. While this is one of the less fortunate compromises reached during the Conference, events have shown that the International Court of Justice and other tribunals have had a number of occasions to elaborate on the issue and currently the legal position is clearer.

Some Preliminary Conclusions

As stated above, conceptually, the topics we have examined can be satisfactorily dealt with through the application of three fundamental propositions. The examination of the relevant Articles of the Convention shows that proposition 1, i.e. that islands and other land territories are in the same position in determining zones of maritime jurisdiction has been applied, subject to the qualified exception of "rocks" as distinct from "islands". Proposition 2, i.e. that the general rule of delimitation between adjacent or opposite states is the median line, continues to be the general rule with regard to the territorial sea and the contiguous zone, subject in the former case to the exception of historic title and special circumstances, and in the latter case to the fact that no express reference is made in the text. However, with regard to the delimitation of the economic zone and the continental shelf, the median line principle may or may not be applied, depending on agreement on the basis of international law in order to achieve an equitable solution. This, in my view, is a valid thesis even though it opens the door wide to arguments and counter-arguments as to what the applicable rules of international law and an equitable solution are and thus begs the issue and lacks predictability. As for proposition 3, i.e. that disputes relating to sea boundary delimitations should be subject to third party dispute settlement procedures entailing a binding decision, this is made subject to an optional exception, and can at the discretion of the states involved be dealt with by the non-binding procedure of compulsory conciliation.

From the point of view of lawyers, expecting the rule of law to prevail, this is perhaps not an ideal solution. But this has been the price that had to be paid in working on a complicated and ambitious undertaking through compromises necessitated by the objective of reaching an overall agreement. "Politics", it has been said, "is the art of the possible" and this is also true of international law-making conferences such as the Law of the Sea Conference. In my view, even if in certain respects the Convention is not fully satisfactory, not fully streamlined and not always logical, the net result is on balance constructive and deserves general support.

Developments Subsequent to 1982

Introduction

We now turn the clock 22 years later and revisit these topics in light of the present perspective. Regarding islands, the period since 1982 has not witnessed any major developments. It is interesting to note that the report of the Conciliation Commission concerning the continental shelf of the Jan Mayen Island (1981) regarded Article 121 as "reflecting the present status of international law on the subject". As to the effect of Article 121 (3), it is worth noting that the United Kingdom when it acceded to the 1982 Convention in 1997, gave up the 200 NM fishing zone that it established in 1976 around the minute islet of Rockall and which was protested to by several states. In terms of the EEZ, a number of claims were made by states such as Mexico, France, Fiji and Venezuela around islets which could be regarded as uninhabitable rocks, evoking some protests. Another effect of the wording of Article 121 is that it removed any possible doubt as to whether an island had to be capable of effective occupation. A number of cases before international tribunals, including the International Court of Justice (e.g. *Qatar v. Bahrain*) and the *Yemen/Eritrea* arbitration, dealt with questions concerning which state was entitled to sovereignty and, as far as could be ascertained, did not change the basic rule on islands, as described earlier.

Delimitation

On questions of delimitation, there has been considerable activity since the 1982 Convention, both in terms of the practice of states and through bilateral agreements, as set out in United Nations publications,[6] and in terms of case law, including some significant cases recently decided by the International Court of Justice.

Judge Gilbert Guillaume, as President of the ICJ, delivered an important speech before the UN General Assembly's Sixth Committee on 31 October 2001 primarily on the law of maritime delimitation in the light of the *Qatar/ Bahrain* territorial dispute. In this case, the determining criterion was, as far as the territorial seas were concerned, Article 15 of the 1982 Convention

---

[6] Notably by DOALOS, see http://www.un.org/Depts/los/doalos_publications/doalos_publications.htm.

(equidistance subject to historic title on other special circumstances). In terms of delimitation of the continental shelf and the EEZ, Judge Guillaume made some highly pertinent and important observations. He said:

> In 1969, in the North Sea Continental Shelf case, the Court initially inclined towards a delimitation of that shelf in accordance with equitable principles and taking account of all the relevant circumstances. Next in the case between Tunisia and Libya (1989) concerning a similar delimitation, it recalled that the delimitation must be achieved on the basis of equitable principles. The same approach was adopted in the Gulf of Maine case (1984). These decisions were not without influence on the solution adopted by the Conference as the Law of the Sea. Thus, the Montego Bay Convention [UNCLOS], in Articles 74 and 83, provides for states to effect delimitation by agreement on the basis of international law… in order to achieve an equitable solution. At this stage, case law and treaty had become so unpredictable that there was extensive debate within the doctrine on whether there still existed a law of delimitations or whether, in the name of equity, we were not ending up with arbitrary solutions. Sensitive to these criticisms, in subsequent years the Court proceeded to develop its case law in the direction of greater certainty.

Judge Guillaume then referred to the *Libya v. Malta* case (1985) in which the Court took the equidistance line as the point of departure and stated that "thus, equidistance was reinstated as a provisional line open to possible corrections in order to achieve an equitable result". He went on to state that:

> A new stage was then reached with the Judgment delivered on 14 June 1993 in the case between Denmark and Norway concerning the maritime delimitation in the area between Greenland and Jan Mayen…Thus, the law of maritime delimitations was completely reunified. Whether it be for the territorial sea, the continental shelf on the fishing zone, it is an equitable result that must be achieved. Such a result may be achieved by first identifying the equidistance line, then correcting that line to take into account special circumstances or relevant facts, which are both essentially geographical in nature.

This was the rule the Court applied in the *Qatar/Bahrain* case, even though this was a case of adjacent rather than opposite coasts. And judge Guillaume concluded that:

> …by means of these developments in the Court's case law, the law of maritime delimitations has reached a new level of unity and certainty, while conserving the necessary flexibility…In all cases the Court, as states also do, must first determine provisionally the equidistance line. It must then ask itself whether there are special or relevant circumstances requiring this line to be adjusted with a view to achieve equitable results. The legal rule is now clear.

In a subsequent speech, this time before the UN General Assembly on 29 October 2002 and in reference to the just decided (10th October 2002) *Cameroon/Nigeria* case (Bakassi Peninsula), judge Guillaume stated that "in regard to the maritime boundaries further out to sea, the Court adopted as the delimitation line the equidistance line between Cameroon and Nigeria, which appeared to it in this case to produce equitable results between the two States". The arbitral decision in the *Yemen/Eritrea* case (1999) was taken on the same lines, with appropriate reference to the median line in the context of articles 74 and 83.[7]

During the 20th Anniversary Commemoration panel discussion on "Challenges for the Present and Solutions for the Future", I raised directly this point in the light of the past 20 years and of several cases, such as *Qatar/Bahrain* and *Cameroon/Nigeria*, and asked whether maritime delimitation by agreement on the basis of the median line has taken a more prominent role, having in mind the instances just cited. In response, Mr. Rolf Einar Fife (Norway's Legal Adviser) stated that more clarity and predictability were brought about by the case law, while agreeing with Professor Rosenne that the best delimitation is by agreement or agreed arbitration. Judge Raymond Ranjeva, speaking on behalf of the ICJ, cited the three recent cases on the point (*Jan Mayen, Qatar/Bahrain* and *Cameroon/Nigeria*) as indicative of developments in this area, while Professor Rosenne thought that Articles 74 and 83 "reflect the ambiguity of geography". In his earlier statement, Mr. Fife had stated that "the International Court of Justice has played a key role in developing the law of maritime delimitation...Through the jurisprudence, applicable treaty rules, including articles 74 and 83 of the Convention, have been substantially clarified, thus consolidating the law governing maritime delimitation".

The position, forcefully and authoritatively stated by the President of the International Court of Justice and this last-quoted statement by the distinguished Norwegian jurist summarize the position which I feel represents the current state of international law on maritime delimitation.

Dispute Settlement

My own position on dispute settlement was expressed in very clear terms in the statement I made in Plenary in the Conference as the delegate of Cyprus (on 6 April 1976):

> We are for an effective, comprehensive, expeditious and viable dispute settlement system entailing a binding decision regarding all disputes arising out of the substantive provisions of the Convention. This position is dictated both by reason of our attachment to the general principle of equal justice under the law, and by reason of our national self interest as a small and militarily weak state which needs the protection of the law, impartially and effectively administered, in order to safeguard its right under the Law of the Sea Convention.

[7] Paragraph 132 of the Decision.

To my mind, this position was valid then and is valid now as an objective and a rationale why small states should prefer third-party binding adjudication through arbitration or judicial settlement. New and major steps were taken in the 1982 Convention, through its incorporation of Part XV and various Annexes to meet this demand, but significant areas of potential disputes, including delimitation, were made subject to an optional exception under Article 298(1)(a). Judge Hugo Caminos, in his message to the 20th Commemorative session, rightly stated that:

> The regime of the settlement of disputes in the Convention is not only an innovation. It is also an important step in the development of this area of international law. Many observers have quite correctly noted that the most important contribution of the convention in strengthening the rule of law in international affairs is contained in Article 286. That provision, notwithstanding some limitations and optional exceptions, declares that any dispute where no settlement has been reached by recourse to other peaceful means agreed by the parties shall be submitted, at the request of any party to the dispute, to arbitration or judicial settlement. This means that by becoming a party to the Convention, a state becomes bound by the compulsory procedures laid down in Part XV.

The 20th Anniversary event provided the forum for major and very relevant contributions to the topic of our discussion by Judge R. Ranjeva on behalf of the International Court of Justice, Judge Alexander Yankov on behalf of the Law of the Sea Tribunal as well as by Professor S. Rosenne and others as to how dispute settlement developed since 1982.

It was rightly pointed out by Judge Ranjeva that "matters relating to the law of the Sea constitute a significant proportion of the Court's activity. Since 1946 it has delivered 24 judgments in this field". The Court has dealt and continues to deal with numerous questions relating to the law of the sea and in particular the delimitation of maritime areas and maritime navigation and safety. Echoing Judge Guillaume (as earlier cited), Judge Ranjeva stressed that:

> The maritime delimitation of states with opposite or adjacent coasts is now governed by a unified system of applicable law. For the Court, any delimitation must lead to equitable results. It first determines provisionally the equidistance line and then asks itself whether there are any special circumstances or relevant factors requiring this initial line to be adjusted with a view to achieving equitable results. In this context, it often settles disputes relating to the sovereignty of States over islands or peninsulas.

Judge Ranjeva concluded that the first twenty years of the Convention have proven the correctness of the legislative policy opted by the UNCLOS III in the area of dispute settlement. The Court remains the only court with both universal and general jurisdiction capable of dealing with all disputes relating to the sea and to activities pursued at sea and the Court welcomes the fact that an increasing number of states are bringing their disputes to it.

The activities of the Law of the Sea Tribunal since its creation in 1996 were described at the 20th Anniversary event by Judge Yankov. He outlined the 11 (now 12) cases which have been submitted to the Tribunal, primarily for prompt release of vessels and crews and provisional measures, and indicated the areas where the Tribunal developed the law of the sea, in particular nationality of claims and reparation and the use of force in law enforcement activities. He acknowledged that the Tribunal, in its short life of 6 years, has not yet fully developed its potential as the specialized judicial organ of the international community for the settlement of disputes concerning the interpretation and application of the Convention, and quoted the UN Secretary-General's description of it as "the central forum" available to states, to certain international organisations and even to some corporations for resolving disputes relating to the 1982 Convention.

Besides the International Court of Justice and the Law of the Sea Tribunal there are two more choices for potential dispute settlement under the Convention, Annex VII arbitral tribunals and Annex VIII special arbitral tribunals (the latter for specialized disputes on fisheries, environmental protection, marine scientific research and navigation including pollution and dumping from ships). All these tribunals apply the rules of the 1982 Convention and other rules of international law. Moreover, the disputants may agree to request a decision *ex aequo et bono* (fairness and equity, Article 293).

Through all these processes the law has been developed since 1982 in a number of areas to a considerable extent, especially for the purposes of our topic, in the area of delimitation. Interesting situations have arisen in terms of choice of tribunals (the *Blue Fin Tuna* case readily comes to mind). By and large it can be safely stated that considerable progress has been and is being made in developing the law of the sea in general and the 1982 Convention rules in particular, on the basis of the rules of interpretation in the 1969 Convention on the Law of Treaties.

It should of course be borne in mind that the law of the sea is no more than a part of international law and that other topics of international law such as state responsibility, nationality and international claims are also essential for the proper understanding of the law of the sea.

Recent Developments Regarding Cyprus and the Law of the Sea

It being understood that it is for the purposes of this academic exercise and that my statements are those of a private individual with no present official capacity, it might be of some interest to briefly describe some recent developments regarding Cyprus and the law of the sea. These can be grouped under four headings:

(a) The Cyprus/Egypt EEZ delimitation agreement signed in February 2003 and ratified 7 March 2004;
(b) Recent Cyprus legislation proclaiming EEZ and Contiguous Zone (2 April 2004);
(c) The position regarding the Sovereign British Areas (SBAs) in terms of the law of the sea;
(d) Relevant provisions in the UN plan on a Cyprus settlement and more particularly "Annan V".

Let me recall that the Republic of Cyprus, as of 1964, has claimed a 12 NM territorial sea and has, as of this year, adopted laws proclaiming an EEZ and a contiguous zone. It signed the Law of the Sea Convention in 1982 and ratified it in 1988. The 1964 proclamation was objected to by certain states (including Turkey) but the 12 NM limit was of course accepted generally through the 1982 Convention. In 1993 the low water mark line was replaced by a system of straight base lines and communicated to the United Nations. It was objected to by the United Kingdom in that it affected the territorial waters of the Sovereign Base Areas. The United Kingdom, which adhered for a long time to the 3 NM territorial sea limit, in 1987 claimed a 12 NM zone around the British islands but, as far as I could ascertain, maintains the 3 NM limit for the SBAs. Turkey, a non-party to the 1982 Convention and in fact the only country to vote against the annual omnibus resolution in the UN General Assembly, claims a 12 NM territorial sea in the Black Sea (north) and the Cilician Sea (south), but firmly insists that neither Greece nor Turkey claim more than a 6 NM territorial sea in the Aegean (west) to the point of calling any Greek move in the direction of 12 NM a *casus belli.*

Against this background, let us now take the above topics one by one:

(a) The Agreement between the Republic of Cyprus and the Arab Republic of Egypt on the Delimitation of the Exclusive Economic Zone was signed on 17 February 2003 and ratified on 7 March 2004. For Cyprus, it was a significant event. Apart from its practical aspects (fisheries, potential oil and natural gas deposits, etc.), it is the first such agreement by Cyprus with one of its major neighbours, indeed, I believe the first such agreement in the turbulent Eastern Mediterranean region, on the basis of a pure median line, which had been our position in the Conference all along. Egypt, which in UNCLOS III also supported the median line as the basis for EEZ delimitation, acted consistently with its position and proceeded with the signature and ratification of the Agreement despite representations and protests by Turkey.

Another positive feature of the Agreement is that, under its Article 4, any dispute which might arise and not be settled within a reasonable time by diplomatic means should be resolved by arbitration. It is understood that one of Egypt's motivations was to establish a precedent also in its delimitation arrangements in the Red Sea vis-à-vis Saudi Arabia. This Agreement was notified to the United Nations Secretariat and can serve as a precedent in the region with some of the other neighbouring countries. Indications to this effect, I understand, are positive.

(b) To remove any doubt about the legal position and despite certain earlier hesitation, the Republic of Cyprus, rightly in my view, proceeded on 2 April 2004 to adopt two Laws proclaiming respectively an EEZ and a contiguous zone. In both cases, the laws provide that in case of overlap with the coast of opposite states, the delimitation shall be established by agreement and, in the absence of agreement, the delimitation shall not extend beyond the median line or equidistant line, measured from the respective baselines from which the width of the territorial sea is measured. These laws were also duly notified to the United Nations.

(c) The legal position of the SBAs is *sui generis*. Through the 1960 Treaty of Establishment the British sought to retain sovereignty over two specified areas, Akrotiri/Episkopi and Dhekelia, totaling just under 100 square miles, for military purposes. It was specified for instance, that should minerals be found in the soil of the SBAs, the benefit should accrue to the Republic of Cyprus. Hence, the argument can certainly be made that this applies to any oil or other deposits found in the sea or seabed attached to the SBAs. The British authorities continue to claim no more than 3 NM territorial waters for the SBAs (again, presumably for military purposes only). Moreover, the British authorities maintain their reservation or objection to the straight base line method adopted by the Cyprus authorities for measuring the Cyprus territorial sea (preferring the line of low water mark following the sinuosities of the coast) on the ground that the straight base line method affects the territorial sea of the SBAs. One possible solution in possible future negotiations is to notify the United Nations that as far as the SBAs territorial sea is concerned, the relevant provisions of the 1960 Treaty of Establishment applies.

(d) In the recent now defunct UN Plan ("Annan V", in its latest version of 31 March 2004) it is understood that certain last minute efforts were made by Turkish/Turkish Cypriot negotiators to introduce as part of the Plan their respective positions on law of the sea issues. Turkey aimed at excluding the application of the Montreux Convention of 1936 and thereby excluding Cypriot registered ships from entering Turkish ports, reserved its position vis-à-vis the Cyprus/Egypt EEZ Delimitation Agreement, and insisted that Cyprus was not entitled to continental shelf as such and in any case subject to conditions. The British, who had offered a portion (some 45% of the SBAs) to be returned to Cyprus as their contribution to the UN Plan being adopted, introduced wording amending Section 3 of Annex A to the Treaty of Establishment to the effect of (possibly) limiting the claims of Cyprus to its territorial sea ("waters adjacent to the Sovereign British Areas that the United Cyprus Republic shall not claim as part of its territorial seas"). These were to be specified in "a report to be prepared by a duly qualified person to be designated by the Government of the United Kingdom". It is also stated that "the United Kingdom shall continue to enjoy complete and unimpeded access for any purpose whatsoever to the waters lying between the waters which the United Cyprus Republic shall not claim adjacent to the eastern part of the Dhekelia Sovereign Base Area". Article 9 of the Protocol is also revelatory of the purpose of the UN plan. It provides that "any dispute about the interpretation or application of this Protocol shall be resolved by consultations and shall not be referred to any international tribunal or third party for settlement". I cited these provisions in order to demonstrate the extent to which those at the UN and those dictating to them these terms were willing to go. It is not for the present article to address the UN plan which, by its own terms, is null and void following its overwhelming rejection by 76% for the Greek Cypriot electorate at the 24 April 2004 referendum. This is another issue about which much can be said, including its blatant inconsistency with at least four areas of international law (state responsibility, forcible intervention, settlers in occupied territory, and human rights and property rights).

The Contribution of the International Tribunal for the Law of the Sea to International Law

Remarks at the American Society of International Law, 16 September 2008

I am honoured to be asked to be the moderator of this special event and very pleased to be among old friends and colleagues on a topic which has been very close to my heart and mind for the past several decades.

Allow me to recall that, in the 1976 Annual Meeting of ASIL, I was privileged to participate on a Panel of the Society with the title: "Will there be Law of the Sea?" There has indeed been Law at Sea, the monumental 1982 Law of the Sea Convention. At the risk of being accused of being a name dropper, perhaps I might mention that the other Panel participants were John Norton Moore, Eli Lauterpacht, Myron Nordquist and Satya Nandan!

Presently, I may be a little rusty since I just returned to the United States after several months on the other side of the Atlantic, dealing with such subjects as the ICSID Convention and Bank Corporate Governance but – alas! – not on the Law of the Sea. Much to my regret, because of a conflicting obligation, I was unable this year to update myself on law of the sea matters through participating in the annual session of the Rhodes Academy on Maritime Law, as I did in the past several years. So, I ask for your indulgence if I am not up to speed on very recent developments.

We are honoured and privileged to have with us today my good friend of long standing – in the UN Sixth Committee, in the Washington and Vienna Diplomatic Corps and, more relevantly, in the Law of the Sea Conference – Ambassador Helmut Tuerk, currently a Judge of the Hamburg Law of the Sea Tribunal. I have no doubt that he will expound fully on the role and contribution of ITLOS to the development of International Law, including the two very recent (August 2007) cases between Japan and the Russian Federation (the Hochinmaru and the Tomimaru).

As we all know, the International Court of Justice has had a substantial share of law of the sea adjudications, including, recently the *Qatar/Bahrain* and the *Cameroon/Nigeria* (Bakassi) case and, more recently the *Nicaragua/*

Honduras case, which have clarified the law on the important role of the median or equidistance line in delimitation disputes. Additionally, there have been important cases before arbitral Tribunals, such as *Barbados/Trinidad & Tobago, Guyana/Suriname, Eritrea/Yemen* among others, which also made major contributions to various aspects of the law of the sea and especially the applicable rules on delimitation!

As Judge Alexander Yankov reminded the twentieth anniversary of the Law of the Sea Session in 2002, ITLOS has also made important contributions, primarily for the prompt release of vessels and crews, the nationality of ships and reparation as well as in the use of force in law enforcement. This has been expanded and updated by the current President of ITLOS, Judge Rudiger Wulfrum, before the General Assembly during the annual consideration of the Law of the Sea items in Plenary.

I recall that during the elaboration of the Convention at the 1973–82 Conference, several delegations put great faith in the creation of a new tribunal, tailor-made as a specialized judicial organ of the International Community for the settlement of disputes concerning the interpretation and application of the Convention under elaboration. To quote the UN Secretary-General, this would be "the central forum" available to States, to certain international organizations and even to some corporations for resolving disputes under the 1982 Convention, especially taking into account the scepticism of many third world countries of the ICJ's reliability in light of its decision on the first *Namibia/South West Africa* case – a scepticism since then dispelled.

The present ITLOS, a relatively young institution of some twelve years, has a great potential even if it has not yet been fully developed. I and, no doubt, all of us, look forward to hearing from Judge Tuerk and the other participants about ITLOS's contribution, actual and prospective, in the discharge of its mandate for the development of the Law of the Sea.

It is my great pleasure to request Judge Tuerk to address us.

Current Issues of the Law of the Sea and Their Relevance to Cyprus

Roundtable Presentation at the European Rim Policy and Investment Council, 23 June 2009

Let me start by saying that I am very pleased to be speaking to a knowledgeable and concerned audience on a topic with which I have been dealing, in different capacities, for some four decades – and which is currently of considerable significance in its many facets.

Time does not allow to go into the historical development of the rules of the Law of the Sea, going back to Hugo Grotius and his De Mare Liberum (1648), or, earlier still, the Rhodian Code of the 3rd century B.C. Nor is it possible to deal with the earlier attempts at codification by the United Nations, which were superseded by the much more ambitious undertaking of the Third United Nations Conference of the Law of the Sea (1973–1982). The resulting Convention, this veritable Constitution of the Oceans consisting of 320 Articles and nine Annexes, was signed in Montego Bay, Jamaica on 10 December 1982 and regulated a multitude of issues. Having been ratified by some 160 states (including the EU), its provisions are considered to have become part of customary international law.

These included old traditional concepts, such as the territorial sea and freedom of navigation and new concepts, such as the exclusive economic zone (EEZ), the regime of the deep seabed and archipelagic waters. Small delegations (such as ours) while not totally neglecting issues marginal to the country's interest, such as environmental protection and scientific research (indeed, I had to pay some attention to these as Vice Chairman of the Third Committee and member of the General Committee), archipelagic waters, passage through straits, etc, they of necessity had to concentrate on the issues which were if direct significance to them.

In the case of Cyprus, in addition to strongly supporting the adoption of a 12 mile territorial sea (Art. 3 of the Convention – Cyprus had already in 1964 proclaimed a 12 mile territorial sea zone) and that enclosed and semi enclosed seas, such as the Mediterranean, are regulated by the same basic rules as those applicable to open seas and oceans (e.g. the Pacific or the Atlantic) subject to the acceptable anodyne duty to cooperate with the riparian states (Articles 122 and 123) and for the protection of archaeological objects found in the seabed (Articles 149 and 303), we concentrated on certain key issues of primary importance to Cyprus.

These were, firstly, the regime of islands and their undiminished entitlement to the zones of maritime jurisdiction, i.e. territorial sea, EEZ, continental shelf and contiguous zone (Art. 121): secondly, the question of the delimitation of these zones of maritime jurisdiction between states, the coasts of which are opposite or adjacent to each other (Articles 15, 74, 83); and, thirdly, the question of settlement of disputes (Part XV, Articles 279–299 and Annexes VI, VII, VIII).

I do not think I need to elaborate on why these issues are of primary concern to Cyprus. All you need to do is to have a look at a map of the Eastern Mediterranean to realize why. Cyprus is of course, an island state as, for instance, is Malta in the Mediterranean and Jamaica in the Caribbean (both are located in semi-enclosed seas).

Despite efforts made by some states (notably Turkey) in the Preparatory Committee (1970–73) and in the early stages of the Conference, to differentiate between island states or other islands, this effort faced coordinated opposition and did not succeed. Consequently, all islands (including the Greek islands in the Aegean), other than uninhabited rocks, are governed by the same basic rule, as was our objective. Cyprus is an island surrounded in three directions (north, east, south) by continental states and, to the west, by the Greek islands of Crete, Rhodes and Carpathos (and indeed, Castelorizo), in no direction reaching 400 miles (200 from each side). Therefore, it is self evident that the application of the median or equidistant line as the basic rule for delimitation is of primary importance, especially when it comes to the EEZ (and indeed, to the continental shelf, which are co-extensive in the ordinary situations).

Additionally to establishing that an island has no less entitlement to the zones of maritime jurisdiction than continental territories, and also that the median line is the starting point and basic rule for delimitation, it is essential, especially for small and militarily weak states such as Cyprus, that there be in place an effective system of compulsory settlement of disputes ensuring that the rights of all states are equally protected. Our position on this point was spelled out in a statement we made in the Plenary of the Conference in 1976, and was motivated both by reason of our attachment to the general principle of equal justice under the law and by national self interest as a small and military weak state, which needs the protection of the law, impartially and effectively administered, in order to safeguard its legitimate interests under the Convention. In other words, we were firmly for the rule of law and against the law of the jungle – a point to which I shall revert in light of the current situation regarding the EEZ.

Evidently, time does not allow to develop the arguments used and get into tactics and alliances utilized, or to describe in any detail as to how these basic positions fared in the course of the Conference – the Cyprus delegation was, at different stages, the champion and spokesman of the 'islands' and 'median line' groups. The UN publications on the 'legislative history' of the regime of islands, delimitation and dispute settlement provide ample material to anyone wishing to pursue it. May I also refer you to a 28 page lecture I gave at the Rhodes Academy for Maritime Law and Policy in July 2004 (and its published version in the 2006 Oslo University publication for Professor Carl August Fleischer) for additional material.

For the purposes of today's presentation, suffice it to say that as far as the status of islands is concerned, our position is fully safeguarded through Art. 121, subject to the qualified exception of rocks; as far as the median line is concerned, it continues to be the general rule as far as the territorial sea and the contiguous zone are concerned, but less clear as far as the EEZ and the continental shelf are concerned under Articles 74 and 83. However, in subsequent years, the situation was clarified in the right direction through judicial interpretation in such cases before the international Court of Justice and arbitral tribunals as Libya/Malta, Norway/Denmark (the Jan Mayen case): Qatar/Bahrain; Cameroon/Nigeria (the Bakassi peninsula case); Yemen/Eritrea; Barbados/Trinidad and Tobago, Guyana/Suriname and, most recently, Romania/Ukraine. As far as compulsory third party settlement is concerned the relevant part, XV, of the Convention, represents a significant advance from previous UN codification conferences, but the disputes relating to sea boundary delimitations were made subject to an optional exception as an unavoidable concession to political realities. In subsequent years, many states have by agreement referred their delimitation disputes to the ICJ or to Annex VII arbitral tribunals by mutual consent (some such cases I have already cited). Realistically speaking, because of Turkey's unwillingness to accept third party settlement, it is unlikely that the situation being faced by Cyprus with Turkey in the EEZ will be submitted to such a settlement (and, of course, Turkey is a non party to the 1982 Convention). I shall revert to this later.

Since the topic of today refers to 'current issues' of the Law of the Sea, it may be of interest to you if I cite two or three issues which currently receive much attention. One such 'hot' issue (if you excuse the pun!) is the Arctic, which is thawing as a result of global warming, and the extension of the continental shelf by the riparian states which are the Russian Federation, Canada, Norway, United States through Alaska and Denmark through Greenland. This is a matter where big stakes are involved since it is estimated that 20–25% of the world resources of oil and gas are situated on the Arctic seabed, and may be exploitable in the near future. The allocation of claims to the continental shelf beyond national jurisdiction (up to 350 miles) is the responsibility of one of the main bodies established by the UNCLOS III, the Committee on the Outer Limits of the Continental Shelf, and this applies globally, not just in the Arctic. For this, and the related issue of the revival of interest for commercially exploitable minerals in the deep seabed, much is currently written. Some of you may have seen, for instance, the 16th May 2009 issue of "The Economist" for interesting facts, maps and figures on these current issues.

Another such issue which is currently receiving much attention is that of piracy at sea, especially off the coast of Somalia. Many nations, including those of the EU, deployed warships in the area under enabling Security Council resolutions, and in cooperation with the International Maritime Organization (IMO), in order to combat this phenomenon. While pirates can be prosecuted under the long existing principle that pirates are *hostes humani qeneris* (enemies of the human race), the subject is not free of legal complications.

Returning now closer to home after this brief diversion, let me tell you that in my 2004 Rhodes lecture (to which I referred earlier), there was a postscript of four pages (pp. 25–28) focusing on some developments relative to Cyprus. Those were grouped under four headings:

a) The Cyprus-Egypt EEZ delimitation agreement, signed in February 2003, and ratified in March 2004. To this should be added the subsequent Cyprus-Lebanon EEZ delimitation agreement of 2007, in the same terms based on the median line and including a paragraph on the provision of arbitration regarding any disputes arising from it. I understand that a supplementary agreement was reached recently (2006) with Egypt for joint exploitation of resources which may be found straddling the line of delimitation.
b) Recent Cyprus legislation proclaiming EEZ and Contiguous Zone (April 2004).
c) The position regarding the Sovereign British Areas (SBA), as related to the law of the sea.
d) Relevant provisions in the 2004 UN plan (Annan V) on a Cyprus settlement.

Since we have some way to go this afternoon, I will not tire you by going into these headings, but will be glad to make this material available, and perhaps some of you, more knowledgeable than I am on recent and current developments, can supplement it.

Let me now turn to the current issue of oil/natural gas exploitation by the Republic of Cyprus in its EEZ and Turkey's behaviour in this regard.

For the past few years, periodically reports appear in the Cyprus press, sometimes under sensational headlines, accompanied by maps and pictures of oil platforms, on the oil and natural gas wealth of the region. It is said that the Eastern Mediterranean basin contains some 400 billion dollars' worth of oil and natural gas, that much of it lies in the areas south of Cyprus (between Cyprus and Egypt or Cyprus and Israel, Ghaza and Lebanon) within the Cyprus EEZ. Some such press reports have mentioned that Cyprus will become the new Eldorado, that we shall assume the status of sheiks and emirs with more money than we would know what to do with, and anticipate that Cyprus will join OPEC! No doubt, such talk is exaggerated. There are indeed indications that some oil deposits, and most probably considerable quantities of natural gas, do lie in the seabed in areas to the south, east and west of Cyprus. Foreign companies, including Noble Energy and Shell, have discovered substantial natural gas deposits off the coast of Egypt and off Israel/Ghaza, and chances are that there are deposits in the adjacent Cyprus EEZ, as preliminary research has confirmed. But whether these deposits are in such a quantity and quality as to be commercially exploitable, and whether the depth at which they are found makes exploitation too difficult and expensive, remains to be seen. I say this in order to put the matter in perspective, but I do not claim any scientific expertise on such maters. In fact, this is one of the reasons I suggested that an expert, such as Mr. Solon Kassinis, might be willing to be here and enlighten us.

My own impression is that the Cyprus Government (particularly successive Ministers of Commerce, beginning with Mr. Nicos Rolandis with the valuable help of the Head of the Ministry's Energy section) have taken appropriate steps through the conclusion of delimitation agreements, notably with Egypt and Lebanon so far, and through dividing the EEZ area over which Cyprus has jurisdiction and sovereign rights, into blocks for allocation to oil exploration companies under appropriate procedures, for us to have cautiously optimistic expectations. Legally, but at present theoretically, the Republic of Cyprus has sovereign rights over the whole of Cyprus' EEZ but, under present circumstances where Turkey occupies 37% of the land and considerably more of the coasts of the island, it is prudent not to push this point, at least for now.

These prospects, however, are threatened by the fact that Turkey, and the Turkish Cypriots, are raising political and legal obstacles, which in turn may discourage major oil companies from undertaking commitments in areas the legal status of which is disputed. The Turkish Cypriot argument that "the Greek Cypriots are not to proceed on their own and the Turkish Cypriots are co-owners and they have to participate in the prospective profits", legally speaking, has no leg to stand on. The ownership of such deposits as may be found in the Republic's EEZ is of the Republic of Cyprus which has a Government recognized by all States in the world as such, except for Turkey (under the Ankara Protocol, Turkey has a conventional obligation to recognize the Republic of Cyprus, and to open its ports, airports and air space to it, an obligation which Turkey has so far failed to meet). So, it is not a matter of a national group within Cyprus (be it the Greek and Turkish Cypriots, or indeed, the Armenians, the Maronites and the Latins), but the state of Cyprus and its internationally recognized Government, which is entitled to the living and non living resources of the Cyprus EEZ (incidentally, under the Treaty of Establishment of 1960, Appendix O (3) (10), it was specified that should minerals be found in the soil of the SBAs, the benefit should accrue to the Republic of Cyprus). If and when, hopefully when, there is a solution to the Cyprus problem, the people of the reunited Cyprus will, through such governmental structure as will have been agreed upon, own such wealth of the Cyprus EEZ. I am aware that there has been a suggestion that a portion of the oil/gas wealth to be found (if it is found, and if it is commercially exploitable) be deposited in an account to the benefit of the Turkish Cypriots upon a political solution being achieved. However, this – if it is practicable – would be a political pragmatic accommodation, not a legal obligation, and here we are discussing the legal position.

A more substantial obstacle lies in Turkey's claim to a segment of the EEZ under the Cyprus/Egypt Delimitation Agreement, west of 32, 16, 18 parallel (if I understand it correctly). Turkey also claims not to recognize the Cyprus/Egypt Agreement.

Apparently, this claim is based on the theory, put forward by Turkey during the Law of the Sea Conference, originally to the continental shelf and EEZ of the Aegean purporting to divide it between the continental shores of Greece and of Turkey. This novel, unfounded and arbitrary theory, based on the false assumption that islands have no continental shelf received no support. Since the Conference, as we have already seen, by adopting Article 121 asserted that all islands in the Aegean have their own continental shelf, no more was made of it. Turkey's subsequent attempt to argue that, in enclosed and semi enclosed seas, special rules should apply other than those already adopted (including Article 121) was also rejected after considerable argument and the result was Articles 122, 123 on enclosed and semi-enclosed seas, which were not satisfactory to Turkey.

As a result of losing on these, and other issues (such as the prohibition of reservations to particular Articles, as Turkey wanted), Turkey did not sign or ratify the Law of the Sea Convention. To this day Turkey is the only country in the world to vote against the annual Law of the Sea resolution in the UN

General Assembly. Turkey did so, most recently, in December 2008 as it did in all previous years, a matter which, in my opinion, should have been appropriately raised and highlighted by Cyprus in the General Assembly, the more so since Turkey had proceeded with threats against Cyprus authorized vessels in the Cyprus EEZ two weeks earlier (13 November 2008), a fact which was duly referred to the Security Council, (the same Security Council to which Turkey had just been elected as a non permanent member by 151 votes without Cyprus or Greece lifting a finger to avert such election of a habitual violator of Security Council resolutions on Cyprus since 1974 – but this is another subject).

So Turkey, a non-party to the 1982 Convention, asserts that its EEZ extends half way between the south coast of Anatolia to Egypt's coast in the Mediterranean, encroaching on Cyprus's EEZ, as agreed with Egypt in a valid agreement on the basis of the 1982 Convention to which Cyprus and Egypt are state parties. Turkey has notified its position to the UN Secretariat (which, as is the practice, simply noted it). Cyprus protested repeatedly to the Security Council, as well as to the UN Secretariat, and to the EU. The EU recently included a reference in its report on Turkey's Association Agreement that Turkey should respect the sovereign rights of the EU member states. The UN Security Council (of which, ironically, Turkey is this month's President) took no action.

Turkey continues to harass and threaten Cyprus authorized vessels in the EEZ and Cyprus reiterates its intention to continue exercising its sovereign rights within its EEZ.

Under these circumstances, what are the appropriate steps to be taken by the Republic of Cyprus to safeguard its legitimate sovereign rights? One option would be to meet force with force but Cyprus is one hundred times smaller than Turkey, and has no effective way of meeting the Turkish naval threat, and no realistic prospect that anyone else will do it for her. Not Greece, which has its own situation vis-à-vis Turkey; not the United Kingdom which has shown the value of its 'guarantee' in 1974; not the EU towards one of its members, although she sent warships off Somalia against the pirates; not the US and its Sixth fleet, unless perhaps an American vessel was involved.

Another option would be for Cyprus to play more decisively and effectively its cards in the EU on Turkey's accession process (in this respect the case of Slovenia and Croatia is instructive).

The third option is provided by the indisputable fact that Cyprus has international law on its side. Islands have the same entitlement to the EEZ as continental territories, under the 1982 Convention and customary international law. Cyprus has a valid agreement with Egypt dividing the EEZ between the two countries on the basis of the median line. Cyprus has taken a firm position in the Law of the Sea Conference, and elsewhere, in favour of international disputes being solved peacefully, on the basis of the applicable international law rules through compulsory third party dispute settlement.

Taking all this into account, why not proceed to declare that, while it has no doubt as to its legal rights in the EEZ, Cyprus is willing to test this before the International Court of Justice (as happened in so many recent cases of the ICJ deciding delimitation disputes e.g. Qatar/Bahrain, Norway/Denmark, Cameroon/Nigeria, Romania/Ukraine)? It is of interest to recall that very recently, a senior EU official, Michael Leigh, raised the possibility of third party settlement if the parties are unable to solve the issue by other means.

If we had resorted to the ICJ for an Advisory Opinion on the alleged and unfounded right of forcible intervention by Turkey under the Treaty of Guarantee in March 1964, as suggested by U Thant (see relevant references on this point in the books by Mr. Clerides and Mrs. Soulioti) our legal position would have been incomparably stronger on this point. If we had not resorted to the European Court of Human Rights, we would not have had the significant decision of Loizidou v. Turkey (1996). If we had not resorted to the US Federal Court in Indianapolis, in 1988, we would not have had the Kanakaria mosaics back in Nicosia, to mention a few examples where resort to justice has proven most valuable to the Cyprus cause, the Orams case being the most recent one.

A few days ago, a Cyprus newspaper quoted a "Cypriot diplomatic source" that to go to third party settlement would mean that we would cede away our legal rights. It must have been a misquotation since to go to court to assert your rights is the proper way to safeguard your rights, not to cede them. This is how the rule of law works in the national as well as the international level.

The difficulty with what I just urged is that Turkey would not accept the jurisdiction. But, if we took this initiative, we would at least have the significant advantage of being perceived as relying on international law to assert our strong legitimate rights, and this in itself would be a major gain. If the case were to be adjudicated by an international tribunal, there can be little doubt that the result would be favourable, on the basis of the existing conventional and customary international law.

It is sometimes said that the Cyprus problem is a political one and will not be solved through resort to courts. I do not disagree. The Cyprus problem, if it is to be solved, will be solved politically. But it will strengthen our position enormously, as well as the viability of such agreement, if the political solution was based solidly on the relevant international law rules, and not be incompatible with such rules. Small states have to rely on the rule of law, and this should be obvious even to those who are not knowledgeable on international law.

International Dispute Resolution

International Tribunals: Do They Really Work for Small States?*

Let me start by expressing my pleasure in being here. After thirty-six years of being a diplomat and four years as a practitioner of international law, I have to confess that I am a cryptoacademic at heart and am delighted to participate in exercises such as the present one. I might be allowed to add that I came back a day early from a very interesting fact-finding mission to Prague, on behalf of the Council of Europe Committee for the Protection of Minorities, in order to keep my commitment to appear here today.

A great deal has been said and written of globalization in recent years, both in the Millennium Assembly of the United Nations and elsewhere. James Wolfensohn, the President of the World Bank, in his keynote address at the annual conference of the World Bank Group and the International Monetary Fund (IMF) in Prague at the end of last month, after citing figures on the glaring inequality of global income distribution, which state that three billion people live on two dollars or less a day, stressed that, "[o]ur challenge is to make globalization an instrument of opportunity and inclusion-not of fear and insecurity."[1] Similarly, Kofi Annan, the U.N. Secretary-General, speaking at the Harvard Law School Advisory Board Dinner on September 28, 2000, stated that international law will "have a vital role in establishing the universal framework which is needed if globalization is to become the universal force for progress and prosperity that we would all like it to be."[2] Three years ago, in a conference on globalization in Asilah, Morocco, I had occasion to state my views on international law and globalization, an easy subject to deal with considering that, by definition, international law is global.

---

* Previously published in *New York University Journal of International Law and Politics*, Volume 34, Number 1, Fall 2001.

1 James D. Wolfensohn, Building an Equitable World, Address to the Board of Governors of the IMF and the World Bank Group (Sept. 26, 2000) (transcript available at http://www.worldbank.org/html/extdr/am00/jdwsp/jdwsp–en.pdf).

2 Press Release, United Nations, Secretary-General Asks Harvard jurists to Work for Better Understanding of Benefits of International Criminal Court (Sept. 29, 2000) (U.N. Doc. SG/SM/7565, at http://www.un.org/News/Press/docs/2000/20000929.sgsm7565.doc.html).

While "we need to work towards making globalization benefit all through a cross-cutting approach,"[3] there can be little doubt that the nation-state remains the foundation of the society of nations. While not excluding the evolution of international law norms – indeed we should encourage it – we should not lose sight of this fundamental fact, and this is relevant in assessing the role of international tribunals in the context of globalization.

Besides globalization, the other key component of our topic in this Symposium is the role of small states. In 1997, the dearth of solid analytical work done on the special problems of small states prompted the then Commonwealth Secretary-General Emeka Anyaokou to convene a nine-member Advisory Group of select individuals (and I had the honor of being one of them) who reached certain relevant conclusions, endorsed by the Heads of Government Meeting (GHOGM) later that year. I commend the resultant publication, *A Future for Small States: Overcoming Vulnerability*,[4] published by the Commonwealth Secretariat, for its analysis and its conclusions, which are relevant to the whole range of issues before this Symposium. Particular attention should be given to the chapters on "Enhancing the Role of Small. States in the International System: The Position of Small States in the Global Context."[5] These chapters stress that:

> through developing their expertise small states have already made signal contributions to world order, as in the pivotal role of Malta to the development of the new Law of the Sea, of Cyprus in advancing the adoption of the notion of peremptory norms of international law in the Law of Treaties, and of Trinidad and Tobago in the nascent International Criminal Court. These are areas where the newly created legal regimes can contribute to the welfare of small states, and thus are samples of an enlightened self-interest while serving the international community. Other issues on which small states have been very supportive of measures which build world community and improve welfare are the environment, disarmament, land mines, equality of gender and race, and human rights. By continuing and upgrading their contributions in such areas small states can make a vital contribution to building the sort of world in which their existence and status would not be questioned.[6]

There is much more that is valid and relevant to our topic today in this publication, including the role of small states in the development of international

[3] I borrow this quote from the President of the 55th Session of the United Nations General Assembly in summing up the outcome of the General Debate on this point. See Harri Holkeri, Briefing for the NGO-Community (Sept. 28, 2000) (transcript available at http://www.un.org/ga/president/55/speech/ngo.html).

[4] Commonwealth Advisory Group, A Future For Small States: Overcoming Vulnerability (1997).

[5] *Id.* at 139.

[6] *Id.* at 140.

law, the establishment of regimes within the WTO, reform and revitalization of the United Nations, and support for the Commonwealth.

At the same time it is recognized that the ability of small states to maximize their roles in the international arena is severely limited both by their inability to participate fully at international meetings of importance to them including being elected to and meaningfully participating in the workings of international tribunals, and by their limited capacity in accessing relevant information and data over a wide range of matters.

This leads directly to the focal point of my topic of today, namely the increase in number of international tribunals and how this affects small states.

It is an indisputable fact that the past two decades have seen an explosion of new international courts and tribunals. Indeed, "international adjudication [is] in ascendance."[7]

Moreover, international courts and tribunals are being utilized much more intensively and frequently.

In addition to the International Court of Justice, which has more cases before it than ever before (the ICJ Report was presented by its newly-elected president, Judge Guillaume, to the General Assembly on October 26, 2000),[8] and the International Tribunal for the Law of the Sea (ITLOS),[9] we have the WTO's Dispute Settlement Body in Geneva,[10] the two International Criminal Tribunals on the former Yugoslavia and Rwanda respectively[11] and hopefully soon (once the needed sixty ratifications are obtained), the permanent International Criminal Court.[12] The International Centre for the Settlement

---

[7] This phrase is borrowed from the title of a very good lecture given by Roger P. Alford before the April 2000 Annual Meeting of the American Society of International Law in Washington, D.C. *See* Roger P. Alford, *The Proliferation of International Courts and Tribunals: International Adjudication in Ascendance*, 94 AM. SOC'y INT'L L. PROC. 160 (2000).

[8] For the result of Judge Gilbert Guillaume's report to the General Assembly's Sixth Committee, see Press Release, United Nations, President of World Court Warns of 'Overlapping Jurisdictions' in Proliferation of International Judicial Bodies (Oct. 27, 2000) (U.N. Doc. GA/L/3157, at http://www.un.org/News/Press/docs/2000/20001027.ga13157.doc.html).

[9] The ITLOS was set up under the Law of the Sea Convention of 1982, which entered into force in 1994 and which is functioning in Hamburg. Convention on the Law of the Sea, Dec. 10, 1982, Annex 6, 21 LL.M. 1261, 1345–50.

[10] See Final Act Embodying the Results of the Uruguay Round of Multilateral Trade Negotiations, Apr. 15, 1994, Annex 2, 33 LL.M. 1125 (1994).

[11] Statute of the International Tribunal for Rwanda, Nov. 8, 1994, 33 LL.M. 1598; Security Council Resolution on Establishing an International Tribunal for the Prosecution of Persons Responsible for Serious Violations of International Law Humanitarian Law Committed in the Territory of the Former Yugoslavia, May 25, 1993, 32 LL.M. 1203.

[12] Rome Statute of the International Criminal Court, July 17, 1998, 37 LL.M.999. As of March 12, 2002, fifty-five countries have ratified the treaty. The current number of ratified countries can be found on the Human Rights Watch website at http://www.hrw.org/campaigns/icc/ (last visited March 13, 2002).

of Investment Disputes (ICSID)[13] at the World Bank has had more arbitration cases than ever in the past few years, while arbitral tribunals, be they ad hoc between states such as the Eritrea-Yemen example[14] or international or regional bodies like the International Chamber of Commerce (ICC) in Paris,[15] the London Court of International Arbitration (LCIA),[16] the American Arbitration Association (AAA),[17] and the Swiss Arbitration Association (ASA),[18] also flourish.

An important, relatively recent, development has been the coming into existence of four mass claims tribunals, each one of which has its own history and special features. These are the Iran-United States Claims Tribunal in the Hague,[19] the United Nations Compensation Commission (UNCC) in Geneva,[20] the Claims Resolution Tribunal for Dormant Accounts in Switzerland (CRT) in Zurich,[21] and the Commission for Real Property Claims in Bosnia and Herzegovina (CRPC) in Sarajevo.[22]

Time does not allow me to go into the description of each of these tribunals or to give a detailed account of their functioning. If I am not

---

13 Convention on the Settlement of Investment Disputes Between States and Nationals of Other States, opened for signature March 18, 1965, 4 LL.M. 532.

14 The Eritrea-Yemen arbitration took place under the Permanent Court of Arbitration (PCA). The text of the Eritrea-Yemen arbitration agreement is available at the PCA's official website at http://www.pca–cpa.org/ER–YEarbagree.htm (last visited Feb. 21, 2002).

15 The ICC International Court of Arbitration is the ICC's arbitration body. Information on the ICC International Court of Arbitration can be found on the ICC's official website at http://www.iccwbo.org/court/english/arbitration/introduction.asp (last visited Feb. 21, 2002).

16 The LClA provides service on international dispute resolution. Information on the LClA can be found on the LClA's official website at http://www.lcia–arbitration.com/lcia/.

17 The AAA administers international commercial cases under various arbitration rules in and outside of the United States. Information on the AAA can be found at its official website at http://www.adr.org/index2.1jsp (last visited Feb. 21, 2002).

18 The ASA is a non-profit association of professionals. Information on the ASA can be found on its official website at http://www.arbitration–ch.org/pages/about/ab_eben3/ab_3wh.htm (last visited Feb. 21, 2002).

19 Declaration of the Government of the Democratic and Popular Republic of Algeria Concerning the Settlement of Claims by the Government of the United States of America and the Government of the Islamic Republic of Iran, Jan. 20, 1981, U.S.-Iran, art. 2, 20 I.L.M. 223, 230 (1981).

20 The UNCC is a subsidiary organ of the U.N. Security Council and processes claims and compensation for damages and losses resulting from Iraq's invasion and occupation of Kuwait. The UNCC was established by the adoption of Resolution 692. S.C. Res. 692, U.N. SCOR, 46th Sess., 2987th mtg., U.N. Doc. S/RES/692 (1991).

21 The CRT was established to resolve all claims to dormant accounts opened by non-Swiss customers following the publication of those accounts by the Swiss Bankers Association. A copy of the Rules of Procedure for the Claims Resolution Process, as adopted on Oct. 15, 1997, can be found at http://www.icep–iaep.org/crp/crp_rules.htm (last visited Feb. 21, 2002).

22 The Commission for Real Property Claims of Displaced Persons and Refugees (CRPC) was established under Annex 7 of the Dayton Peace Accord. General Framework Agreement for Peace in Bosnia and Herzegovina, Dec. 14, 1995, Annex 7, 35 I.L.M. 75, 137 (1996).

misinformed, there is a new Project on International Courts and Tribunals at New York University (about which I myself would like to know more),[23] and I might refer you to two recent publications, one by the Permanent Court of Arbitration[24] and the other by the Swiss Arbitration Association,[25] which are self-explanatory, and contain a wealth of very useful material.

So, there is no doubt that with all these new mechanisms for peaceful dispute settlement, the options available are increased. In my view, this is a positive development for the rule of law in international relations and a development which should be seen as positively and beneficially affecting small states.

In taking this view, I may be somewhat prejudiced. In my very first year as a delegate of Cyprus to the Sixth (Legal) Committee of the General Assembly in 1960, at the ripe age of twenty-three, I am on record as having stated that, "[I] viewed with some apprehension… the suggestion that new states need not be bound by rules of international law which they had not helped to create and which ran counter to their interests. National interests," I stressed, "could not be allowed more weight than international legal obligation."[26] Indeed, the newly independent states have proven fully capable of contributing constructively to the progressive development of international law by exhibiting a proper sense of responsibility for the common good, as was demonstrated in a variety of forums and, notably, in the Law of the Sea Conference, which judiciously blended codification with progressive development.

The position on the peaceful settlement of disputes which I consistently advocated in all forums, most recently in the International Law Commission in the context of State Responsibility, is what I stated in the Plenary of the Law of the Sea Conference (on April 6, 1976) as the delegate of Cyprus. I stated that:

> [we are] for an effective, comprehensive, expeditious and viable dispute settlement system entailing a binding decision regarding all disputes arising out of the substantive provisions of the Convention, and [believe] that such a system should form an integral part of it. This position [is] dictated both by [reason of our] attachment to the general principle of equal justice under the law and by reason of our national self-interest as a small and militarily weak state which

[23] For more information on the Project on International Courts and Tribunals, see the PICT website at http://www.pict–pcti.org.

[24] International and procedural aspects of mass claims settlement systems (Int'l Bureau of the Permanent Court of Arbitration ed., 2000).

[25] The claims resolution process on dormant accounts in Switzerland (Pierre A. Karrer ed., 2000).

[26] U.N. GAOR 6th Comm., 15th Sess., Agenda Item 65, at 93, U.N. Doc. A/C.6/SR.668 (1960).

> needs the protection of the law, impartially and effectively administered, in order to safeguard its legitimate rights [under the Law of the Sea Convention].[27]

Whether such a system can be adopted as a general measure in all, or indeed in most, cases, given the present state of evolution of the society of nations, is of course debatable, but the rationale why small states should prefer third-party binding adjudication, whether through arbitration or judicial settlement, to my mind, was valid then and is valid now.

Let me add that this attitude of mind and approach of relying on the law and the impartial administration of justice led my country, Cyprus, to resort to national and regional courts and was vindicated repeatedly, for instance in the Federal Court of Indianapolis with the recovery of the Kanakaria Mosaics,[28] an important precedent-setting case for the protection of cultural property looted and purportedly sold abroad, more recently before the European Court of Justice on the phytosanitary certificates issue,[29] and even more recently before the European Court of Human Rights of the Council of Europe on the Titina Loizidou matter.[30] These adjudications have had far reaching legal and political implications and justified taking the risk of resorting to U.S. and European justice.

Let me also recall that Cyprus is a party to the Optional Protocol accepting the jurisdiction of the International Court of Justice and repeatedly has challenged Turkey, a non-party to the Optional Protocol, to test the key issue of the legality of Turkey's 1974 invasion and continuing occupation of the Republic of Cyprus, as well as the many other issues of international law raised by this invasion and occupation and the 1983 Unilateral Declaration of Independence (UDI), so far to no avail. There can be no doubt that the third-party determination of the legal issues involved in the current Cyprus situation, preferably by the main judicial organ of the United Nations, the International Court of Justice in The Hague, would go a long way towards achieving a just solution of the overall problem through the current negotiations under U.N. auspices, to the benefit of all parties concerned and for

---

27 Third United Nations Conference on the Law of the Sea at 25, U.N. Doc. A/Conf.62/WP.9 and Add.1, U.N. Sales No. E.76.V.8 (1976).

28 Autocephalous Greek-Orthodox Church of Cyprus v. Goldberg & Feldman Fine Arts, Inc., 717 F. Supp. 1374, 1404 (S.D. Ind. 1989) ("the mosaics must be returned to the true and rightful owner, the Church of Cyprus"), aff'd, 917 F.2d 278 (7th Cir. 1990). For a summary and analysis of the case, see Keith Highet & George Kahale III, International Decisions, 86 Am. J. INT'L L. 128 (1992).

29 See, e.g., Case C–432/92, The Queen v. Minister of Agric., Fisheries and Food ex parte S.P. Anastasiou Ltd., 1994 E.C.R. 1–3087, [1995] 1 C.M.L.R. 569 (1994) (holding that any phytosanitary certificate issued by any entity other than the government of Cyprus would not be recognized).

30 See Loizidou v. Turkey, 81 Eur. Ct. H.R. 1807, 1821 (1998) (holding that Loizidou is entitled to compensation from Turkey for losses directly related to the violation of her rights).

peace in that volatile region of the world. One way this could be brought about, in the absence of Turkey's consent to adjudication, would be through a request by the Security Council or by the General Assembly of the United Nations for an Advisory Opinion by the International Court of Justice.

Having declared my thinking on the merits of third-party settlement entailing a binding decision as being to the advantage of small states, let me add that I am not so naïve or so doctrinaire as to take the view that in all cases we can expect a perfect result from the point of view of small states or that in no case do extralegal considerations (political, economic, personal) apply. It also could well be that other factors enter into the picture. Third-party settlement can take a long time and be quite costly, and this gives an advantage to large and wealthy states, which can afford the cost of being involved in prolonged and costly proceedings more easily. Expertise in effectively presenting cases before international tribunals is limited – if I may be allowed the flippancy with no disrespect to the distinguished jurists who belong to this category – to "the usual suspects," mostly but not exclusively from developed and large states. Yet, this is not as much of a problem as may be assumed. After all, one of the more prominent such international advocates remarked, only half in jest, that fees associated with either litigation or arbitration are not nearly as much as the cost of even a small war, and there is the Secretary-General's Trust Fund to help cover expenses of developing countries in order to enable them to resort to the International Court of Justice.[31]

So, on balance, I have no hesitation in maintaining the position that the proliferation of international tribunals ought to and can be to the benefit of small states, and that in solving a dispute through third-party settlement, a small state is at much less of a disadvantage in relation to a large and powerful state in a court of law or an arbitral tribunal than in any other manner of dispute resolution.

And, to quote again from Secretary-General Kofi Annan's statement of September 28, 2000, "the language of global society is international law."[32]

---

[31] For an overview of the Secretary-General's Trust Fund, see Secretary-General's Trust Fund to Assist States in the Settlement of Disputes through the International Court of Justice: Report of the Secretary-General, U.N. GAOR, 56th Sess., Agenda Item 13, at 2, U.N. Doc. A/56/456 (2001), available at http://www.un.org/documents/ga/docs/56/a56456.pdf (last visited Feb. 21, 2002).

[32] See Secretary-General Asks Harvard Jurists to Work for Better Understanding of Benefits of International Criminal Court, supra note 2.

Great Expectations: Where Does the Proliferation of International Dispute Resolution Tribunals Leave International Law?*

Lecture Commentary

We have just been treated to a very fine presentation by our distinguished lecturer, Lucy Reed, with whom I have had the privilege of working in different contexts in the past few years – in Zurich at the Claims Resolution Tribunal for Dormant Accounts in Switzerland and in the Hague with the Steering Committee of the Permanent Court of Arbitration for Mass Claims Processes – and, of course, we are both currently based in New York.

In discussing "Great Expectations: Where does the Proliferation of International Dispute Resolution Tribunals leave International Law?" not surprisingly, she has done a masterful job. My assignment is to comment on this lecture, taking into account I presume also the overall theme of the ASIL's Annual Meeting this year, which of course is "The Legalization of International Relations/The Internationalization of Legal Relations."[1]

This year's theme is well founded and can be substantiated in a number of ways. Much has been said and written in recent years on globalization in different contexts. Some years ago, I had the occasion in Asilah, Morocco, at a conference on globalization, to express my views on "international law and globalization," an easy subject considering that by definition international law – public international law, at any rate – is global. On globalization, I agree in general with James Wolfensohn, president of the World Bank, who stressed that "our challenge is to make globalization an instrument of opportunity

---

* Previously published in *American Society of International Law Proceedings of the 96th Annual Meeting 2002*, pp. 231–237.

[1] All these references to "relations" reminds me of the contrast, until recently, in the United States Congress of the House Foreign Affairs Committee and the Senate Foreign Relations Committee. The reason for the distinction, it was said, was that Senators were too old to have affairs, they only had relations! This, as we well know, in reality has not always been the case.

and inclusion – not of fear and insecurity."[2] This is valid in the context not only of international trade and economics but also of international law.

It is generally true that where you stand depends on where you sit: Besides being a diplomat in the service of my country, Cyprus, for over thirty-six years, I have been, at Cambridge University, Harvard Law School, and the Inns of Court, a student of public international law, an interest which I later pursued in the Sixth (Legal) Committee of the UN General Assembly and related bodies, in major multilateral lawmaking conferences such as on the Law of Treaties (1968–1969) and on the Law of the Sea (1973–1982), and as a three-term elected member of the UN International Law Commission (1981–1996). You might say that I am a public international law person. After leaving the Foreign Service (most recently, as ambassador to the United States), and while continuing with the Sixth Committee, I found myself engaged in a variety of other tasks – perhaps fitting Ruth Wedgwood's description, adopted by Lucy Reed, as "double jointed" – straddling public and private international law and indeed transnational law as an arbitrator (at the International Centre for Settlement of Investment Disputes (ICSID), Claims Resolution Tribunal for Dormant Swiss Bank Accounts in Switzerland I (CRT-I) and the American Arbitration Association), a commissioner (of the UN Compensation Commission), and a senior judge (at CRT-II) while continuing to pursue my long-standing interest in the law of the sea and in international criminal jurisdiction, peremptory norms of international law, and international terrorism.

Perhaps a brief word updating each of these topics would be of general interest: On the law of the sea, December 10, 2002, is the twentieth anniversary of the signing in Montego Bay of that "veritable constitution of the seas and oceans," the Law of the Sea Convention (LOS Convention).[3] Certain activities are being planned in New York and probably in Jamaica not only to celebrate this major achievement in international lawmaking but also to take stock and consolidate its universal acceptance. It is hoped, on the basis of its public positions in the General Assembly (Assembly) last November and other indications, that it will not be long before the United States will accede to the 1982 LOS Convention (as amended in 1995), thus taking a major step forward in completing the goal of universality.

On international criminal jurisdiction, there is good reason to expect that, with so far fifty-five ratifications (one of them Cyprus) and more expected soon, the goal of sixty ratifications will soon be reached. Possibly this year,

[2] James Wolfensohn, Building an Equitable World, at the Annual Meeting of the Board of Governors of the International Monetary Fund and the World Bank (Sept. 26, 2000).

[3] Convention on the Law of the Sea, Dec. 10, 1982, 1833 UNTS 397.

the 1998 Rome Statute for an International Criminal Court (ICC)[4] will come into force and the ICC will be established soon thereafter, albeit not with U.S. participation, despite the eloquent argumentation by, among others, the late Monroe Leigh in the *American Journal of International Law*,[5] This will be a source of great satisfaction to many who, like myself, pioneered the notion of an effective permanent international court – in preference to ad hoc criminal tribunals – as an instrument of deterrence and punishment of international crime in its various manifestations and advocated it in the Sixth Committee, the ILC, the Commonwealth Heads of Government Conference (1993), and such specialized conferences as those in Talloires (1990) and Courmayer (1991) at a time when the very idea was ignored as unrealistic or even scoffed at as inappropriate. The role played to this end by civil society and the nongovernmental organizations (NGOs) in alerting and mobilizing public opinion in individual countries should certainly be recognized and appreciated.

On peremptory norms of international law, or *jus cogens*, a topic of special interest to me over the years,[6] including in particular the prohibition of the use of force in international relations,[7] and the right of self-defense,[8] we have recently witnessed some significant developments. I mention in passing only the debate over "humanitarian intervention," or more appropriately the duty to protect in situations of gross violations of human rights, as articulated in the recent report of the International Commission on Intervention and State Sovereignty,[9] and, of course of more current significance, the debate on legal issues arising out of the atrocious events of September 11, 2001 and the war against international terrorism.

At the United Nations, the response of the Security Council through the unanimous adoption of Resolutions 1368[10] and 1373[11] has been of major significance in effectively combating the financing of terrorism and denying support to its perpetrators. The response of the Assembly, expressed through

---

[4] Rome Statute of the International Criminal Court, July 17, 1998, 37 ILM 999 (1998).

[5] Monroe Leigh, The United States and the Rome Statute, 95 AJIL 124 (2001).

[6] Treaties Conflicting with Peremptory Norms of International Law and the Zurich-London Agreements, Nicosia (1966): Law of Treaties, Official Records of United Nations Conference 1968–89, Jus cogens, Outlines on selected topics of international law, UN Doc. A/CN.4/454, Nov. 9, 1993, at 16–26. See also United Nations, *International Law on the Eve of the Twenty-First Century: Views from the International Law Commission*, 69–78 (1997).

[7] UN Charter Art. 2 (4).

[8] UN Charter Art. 51.

[9] Canadian Department of Foreign Affairs and International Trade, *The Responsibility to Protect: Report of the International Commission on Intervention and State Sovereignty* (2001).

[10] SC Res. 1368 (Sept. 12, 2001).

[11] SC Res. 1373 (Sept. 28, 2001).

adoption of various conventions and resolutions, has fallen short of a comprehensive convention or a definition of the scope of international terrorism. The so far unsuccessful Sixth Committee effort, beginning as early as 1972, to define terrorism continues. Even though the Rome Statute does not place "terrorism" within the jurisdiction of the ICC, I have no doubt that, actions such as those of September 11 would come squarely within the jurisdiction of the ICC under "crimes against humanity." This constitutes one more reason for the ICC to begin operating at the earliest possible time.

More relevant here, the machinery put in place by the Counter Terrorism Committee set up by the Council by Resolution 1373 (under the vigorous leadership of the British delegate, Sir Jeremy Greenstock, assisted by specialized experts in financial, banking, legislative, and other fields) moves beyond public international law into a variety of other fields.

This is an appropriate stage to revert to Lucy Reed's excellent lecture and her references to "mixed" public-private international law institutions, to "great expectations," and to the proliferation of international law courts, tribunals, and commissions. I share her view that this is not a subject that lends itself to clear definition; of necessity its treatment has to be somewhat fragmentary and skeletal. Some of the questions are easier to raise than to answer.

To take one example, the rationale for the 1965 Washington ICSID Convention[12] was to assure potential prospective investors that disputes arising out of investments, primarily in developing countries, could be adjudicated before an international tribunal, rather than before the courts of the country concerned. The existence of such a facility and the assurance of impartiality and predictability also works to the benefit of the country concerned, which has an interest in attracting foreign investment for its economic development. Depending on the circumstances of each case, the law to be applied by the tribunal can well be the law of the country where the investment has been made.

The jurisdiction of ICSID is ever-increasing, because, as stressed in the lecture, foreign investors unwilling to subject themselves to the perceived vagaries of host country courts require binding private international dispute resolution mechanisms before proceeding. This is relevant not only to the 1965 Washington Convention establishing ICSID and the 1958 New York Convention,[13] which allows international enforcement of international

[12] Convention on the Settlement of Investment Disputes Between States and Nationals of Other States, 4 ILM 532 (1965), available at <http://www.worldbank.org/icsid/basicdoc/9.htm>.

[13] Convention on the Recognition and Enforcement of Foreign Arbitral Awards, June 10, 1958, 21 UST 2517, 330 LINTS 38 (1970).

arbitration awards, and to the many bilateral investment treaties (BITs). It is rightly stated that "host state obligations under BITs typically include guarantees of fair and equitable treatment as determined by international law, national treatment and most-favored nation treatment, guarantees of free repatriation of profits and liquidated proceeds; and most significantly, the duty to pay full economic value in the event of expropriation."[14]

Another aspect of topical importance dealt with in Lucy Reed's lecture is the proliferation of international courts, tribunals, and commissions. This is a phenomenon that has attracted attention that brings many interesting issues to the fore in the context of our current topic.[15] Different tribunals might well take different positions on the same issue of international law. Judge Guillaume in his lecture to the Sixth Committee[16] cites *Loizidou v. Turkey*[17] as one case where the European Court of Human Rights (the Strasbourg Court) took a position different from that of the International Court of Justice (ICJ) on the question of territorial reservations in declarations of compulsory jurisdiction. However, as Judge Guillaume acknowledges, this decision of the Strasbourg Court may be regarded as an instance of *lex specialis*, being founded on the specific characteristics of the system of the European Human Rights Convention.

This is a risk that cannot be altogether avoided, as other instances also show (e.g., the recent *Blue Fin Tuna* cases before both the Law of the Sea Tribunal and the Arbitral Tribunal),[18] but I agree with Judge Guillaume that the proliferation of the courts should be a source of enrichment, not of anarchy. There should be no doubt that, especially when it comes to public international law, the ICJ is the principal judicial organ of the United Nations; its decisions are, in the vast majority of cases, cited and followed. And I agree with Lucy Reed when she states that international law remains more decentralized than ever as the number of actors and arbitrators continues to increase. But the gap is not as great as it might appear. For instance, as she pointed out, certain of the

---

[14] Lucy Reed, Great Expectations: *Where Does the Proliferation of International Dispute Resolution Tribunals Leave International Law?* 96 ASIL PROC. 217 (2002).

[15] Judge Gilbert Guillaume, *The Proliferation of International Judicial Bodies: The Outlook for the International Legal Order*, Speech to the Sixth Committee of the General Assembly of the United Nations (2000), available at <http:// www.icj.cij.org/icjwww/ipresscom/SPEECHES/iSpeechPresident Guillaume_SixthCommittee_20001027.htm>. See also, Roger Alford, *The Proliferation of International Courts and Tribunals: International Adjudication in Ascendence*, 94 ASIL PROC. 160 (2000); Cesare P. R. Romano, *The Proliferation of International Judicial Bodies: The Pieces of the Puzzle*, 31 N.Y.U. J. INT'L L & POL. 709 (1999).

[16] Guillaume, supra note 10.

[17] Loizidou v. Turkey, 310 Eur. Ct. H.R. (ser. A) (1995).

[18] Southern Bluefin Tuna Cases (N.Z. v. Japan, Austl. v. Japan), Provisional Measures (1999), available at <http://www.itlos.org>.

same lawyers have served or do serve as counsel and judges in ICJ, ICSID, and private commercial arbitrations, applying a combination of private and public international law. Indeed, the exposure to private international law principles, procedures and substantive legal doctrines has had an effect on the jurisprudence of the ICJ, just as the jurisprudence of the ICJ has had an effect on arbitral decisions.

I mention in passing, in the context of *lex specialis* and the protection of human rights in the Council of Europe, the recent Framework Convention for the Protection of National Minorities (Framework Convention),[19] which goes beyond the protection of individual human rights (as in the United Nations system) and not only protects but also monitors the rights of national minorities on a regional basis in Europe. It is a new (or, more accurately, revived) system that is still being developed under the guidance of the Advisory Committee on the Framework Convention for the Protection of National Minorities (of which I am a member) that monitors the Framework Convention's implementation in each state party.

I also agree with Lucy Reed that international law, public as well as private, is increasingly affecting national law. Courts and litigants are referring to international law standards in domestic cases more than ever before. In this connection two matters came to my mind. One is the outreach program carried out by the ASIL to familiarize American judges with public international law, to my mind a very worthwhile undertaking; the other (from my earlier experience as ambassador of Cyprus to the United States) is the case of the Kanakaria mosaics,[20] brought by the Cyprus Church in federal court in Indianapolis. Among other issues the case involved the UNESCO Convention for the Protection of Cultural Property.[21] It resulted in the restitution of the mosaics to their rightful owners, partly because a domestic U.S. court applied international law.

Lucy Reed stated and I fully agree that "Familiarity with international law as a source of rights and remedies for private actors will become greater, as perhaps will a greater respect for international law as more than an expression of political will." In this connection, Lucy Reed cites a dictum by General de Gaulle, "I am for law as long as it is not contrary to our interests." Other political figures may be inclined to take the same view. When I served in Washington in the 1980s I asked a senior policymaker what role the rules

---

[19] Framework Convention for the Protection of National Minorities, Feb. 1, 1995, 34 ILM 351 (1995).

[20] Autocephalous Greek-Orthodox Church of Cyprus v. Goldberg & Feldman Fine Arts Inc., 717 F. Supp. 1374 (S.D. Ind. 1989).

[21] [UNESCO] Convention on the Means of Prohibiting and Preventing the Illicit Import, Export and Transfer of Ownership of Cultural Property, Nov. 14, 1970, 823 UNTS 231 (1972), reprinted in 10 ILM 289 (1970).

of international law played in formulating a major policy decision; his reply was disarmingly candid: "After we took the decision, we called in the lawyers to give us some arguments in support of the policy we had decided on." Needless to say, my view was different and I have expressed it on a number of occasions.[22] I trust that, in this forum at least, there would be a tendency to support this view – in fact I recall the ASIL producing a very fine study on the role of the Legal Adviser of the State Department in reaching policy decisions, which is on exactly the right lines.

In late 2000 the Secretary-General of the Permanent Court of Arbitration established a steering committee, chaired by Judge Howard Holtzmann, to consider institutional and procedural aspects of mass claims processes. The list of such processes is open-ended; it includes the Iran-United States Claims Tribunal, the UN Compensation Commission, the first and second Claims Resolution Tribunal for Dormant Accounts in Switzerland, the Commission for Real Property Claims of the Displaced Persons and Refugees in Bosnia and Herzegovina, the German Slave Labor Programme, the Eritrea- Ethiopia Claims Commission, the Housing and Property Claims Commission in Kosovo, and the International Commission on Holocaust Era Insurance Claims. Other tribunals (such as the new Austrian tribunal) may be added to this list. It would go far beyond the present statement to attempt even a cursory description of these processes, but I cite them as an example of the variety and number of such tribunals.[23]

Moreover, taking my clue from Lucy Reed's reference to the Korean comfort women bringing charges against the Japanese government in a Tokyo district court in 1994, let me mention in passing that there is no end to class action suits, actual or potential, by groups that rightly or wrongly feel aggrieved and demand justice and compensation; some recent examples are Holocaust victims suing Swiss banks in U.S. courts; Roma groups, also Holocaust victims, suing IBM in a Geneva court under Swiss law; Armenians suing in California for insurance claims for the Armenian Holocaust; Namibians/South West Africans claiming compensation from Germany; and African Americans seeking damages from the U.S. government and companies that profited from slavery. In a recent *New York Times* piece, William Glaberson added to the list:

> Last year, five Chinese natives sued the former Chinese Prime Minister, Li Peng, in an American Court for his role in the Tiananmen Square crackdown that killed hundreds of civilians in Beijing. While visiting the United Nations in

[22] See, e.g., Andrew Jacovides, International Law in International Diplomacy, 77 ASIL PROC. 100–02 (1983).

[23] See, e.g., The Permanent Court of Arbitration, The 1999 PCA Seminar (forthcoming).

> September, President Robert Mugabe of Zimbabwe was served with a civil suit saying he ordered killings, torture, and terrorism in his country and seeking 400 million dollars in damages. In Brooklyn a Federal Judge is considering legal claims of Canadians and Israelis in addition to Americans against a French railroad that transported people to Nazi death camps. These and many other kinds of cases reflect the growing use of the American legal system to judge rights and wrongs all over the globe... Among others who have been sued in this country are the former President Slobodan Milosevic of Yugoslavia, the Islamic Republic of Iran, the Prince of Wales and former Prime Minister Margaret Thatcher.[24]

More recently a February 19, 2002 dispatch from Washington states, "The families of seven victims of the terrorist attack on the World Trade Center filed a class action law suit today against Osama Bin Laden, Al Qaeda and the Taliban as well as Iran and Iraq" seeking more than one hundred billion dollars in compensatory damages and one hundred billion dollars in punitive damages on behalf of all those killed on September 11.[25]

This gives you an idea of the range and variety of possible actions in international tribunals and national courts invoking international and domestic legal norms – great expectations indeed! Returning to Lucy Reed's conclusions, by and large I find myself in agreement with them. Cross-fertilization and proliferation of courts and tribunals can be useful elements in the progressive development of international law, provided they are approached wisely and with caution. It is important to the international lawyer of today to have a grounding in both public and private international law. I hope that practicing and aspiring international lawyers not only found the lecture useful – as they undoubtedly have – but also that the commentary provided them with some useful food for thought.

---

[24] William Glaberson, U.S. Courts Become Arbiters of Global Rights and Wrongs, N.Y. Times, at A I (June 21, 2001).

[25] A Nation Challenged: The Victims; 7 Families Sue bin Laden and Others for Billions, N.Y. Times, at A II (Feb 20, 2002).

U.N. Reform and the International Court of Justice: Introductory Statement*

It is customary during anniversaries to devote some attention to introspection and stock taking. Looking back at my own writings on the subject of U.N. reform (during the fortieth, the fiftieth and now the sixtieth anniversary in 1985, 1995 and this year), I confirmed my long held conviction that the United Nations is indispensable and its Charter, in its basic provisions, has stood the test of time.

All Member States are legally bound by their signature to the United Nations Charter. If its principles and rules are often disregarded in practice, this is not the fault of the Organization but of those Member States who fail to honour their solemn obligations. The Charter is based on sound foundations and has proven sufficiently flexible to allow, through progressive interpretation, substantial adjustments to meet emerging needs: peacekeeping and the limitations to domestic jurisdiction or sovereignty, especially in the protection of human rights, come readily to mind. While there is considerable room for improvement, restructuring and regeneration, the emphasis should not be on tinkering with the Charter but on organizational reforms. Even more importantly, there must be emphasis on implementing, effectively and consistently, its purposes and principles and more specifically the resolutions of its principal organs such as the Security Council and the General Assembly – a sore point, I might add, as a Cypriot who has seen numerous U.N. resolutions on Cyprus remain unimplemented. Obviously, there is considerable room for improvement in the Organization itself and in the Secretariat. Much can be done to eliminate cronyism and deadwood and prevent the erosion of the concept of the international civil servant who owes primary allegiance to the Organization. I refrain from going into specifics for this would go far beyond today's topic and the time available.

Last year and especially this year, on the occasion of the sixtieth anniversary of the U.N., considerable activity has taken place at the United Nations

* Previously published in *ILSA Journal of International and Comparative Law*, Volume 12, Spring 2006, Number 2.

itself, at the U.S. Association for the U.N. (USUN), at learned societies such as the American Society of International Law (ASIL) and such academic/political/diplomatic institutions as the Institute for the Study of Diplomacy (ISD) of Georgetown University, under the generic rubric of "UN Reform." A major study was also commissioned by the U.S. Congress on "American Interests and U.N. Reform" (issued on June 2, 2005 under the names of Newt Gingrich and George Mitchell) which makes several sound proposals.[1]

A major contribution was made by a High-Level Panel of sixteen distinguished panelists – some more distinguished than others – from different countries proposing 101 recommendations on U.N. reform, including defining international terrorism, regulating the use of force, restructuring the Security Council, abolishing the Trusteeship Council, revamping human rights, etc.

Secretary-General Kofi Annan, in turn, came out with his carefully considered report "In Larger Freedom" on March 21, 2005, in a significant effort to effectively respond to the call for adjusting the United Nations to the 21st century needs, the more so in the wake of the debate on the legality of the Iraq war and the "Oil-for-Food" and other controversies currently burdening the Organization.[2]

Following considerable diplomatic activity in the past few months and facing the prospect of collapse because of competing interests and divergent views, especially on the highly controversial issue of the expansion of the Security Council, what could be rescued out of these major reform proposals was what was described as "The 2005 World Summit Outcome" (significantly not called a "Declaration"), adopted on September 15, 2005 by the High Level Plenary Meeting of the General Assembly.[3] Even though falling far short of the earlier targets, it was a considerable achievement under the circumstances and a major effort is under way, spearheaded by President Eliasson, for it to serve as a stepping stone to meaningful reform in the areas it covers. This document was also described as "modest" (and, here, may I remind you of Sir Winston Churchill's saying of his political opponent, "Mr. Attlee is a very modest person – he has so much to be modest about!"

---

1 See generally United States Institute of Peace, American Interests & U.N. Reform: Report of the Task Force on the United Nations (2005), available at http://www.usip.org/un/report/usip_un_report.pdf (last visited March 8, 2006).

2 The Secretary-General, *Report of the Secretary-General – In Larger Freedom: Towards Development, Security and Human Rights For All*, U.N. Doc. AJ5912005 (March 21, 2005, available at http://daccessdds.un.org/doc/UNDOC/GEN/N051270/78/PDF/N0527078.pdf! OpenElement (last visited March 8, 2005) [hereinafter In Larger Freedom].

3 U.N. General Assembly, *2005 World Summit Outcome: Draft Resolution Referred to the High-Level Plenary Meeting of the General Assembly by the General Assembly at its Fifty-Ninth Session*, U.N. Doc. AJ60/LI, available at http://www.unis.unvienna.org/pdf/A60L.pdf (last visited March 8, 2006) [hereinafter Outcome].

Incidentally, Mr. Attlee was also described by Churchill as "a sheep in sheep's clothing"!). However, when it comes to references to international law and the rule of law the Outcome document is not so modest, with a multitude of such references in several parts of the text:

> [W]e emphasize the obligations of States to settle their disputes in accordance with Chapter VI of the Charter, including, when appropriate, by the use of the International Court of Justice. All States should act in accordance with the Declaration on Principles of International Law concerning Friendly Relations and Cooperation Amongst States in accordance with the Charter.[4]

This is an important reminder that the contents of General Assembly Resolution 2625 XXV (1970) – in the adoption of which I played a very modest role – are still valid and relevant in 2005 as they were thirty-five years ago.[5]

More specifically and relevantly regarding today' s topic, in Paragraph 134 of the 2005 World Summit Outcome, under the rubric "Rule of Law," it is stated that

> Recognizing the need for universal adherence to and implementation of the rule of law at both the national and the international levels we... Recognize the important role of the International Court of Justice, the principal judicial organ of the United Nations, in adjudicating disputes among States, and the value of its work, call upon States that have not yet done so to consider accepting the jurisdiction of the Court in accordance with its Statute and consider means of strengthening the Court's work, including by supporting the Secretary-General's Trust Fund to Assist States in the Settlement of Disputes through the International Court of Justice on a voluntary basis.[6]

When compared to the paper adopted, after much activity and debate but also much fanfare, by the High-Level Panel which, inexplicably and somewhat paradoxically, had nothing to say about the International Court of Justice while dealing with all five of the other principal organs of the United Nations (Security Council, General Assembly, Economic & Social Council, Trusteeship Council, Secretariat), this text is substantial.

However, when compared to the equivalent paragraph 139 of the Secretary-General's Report "In Larger Freedom" of March 21, 2005 (inserted after considerable efforts by the Court itself, U.N. Secretariat and others concerned by the evident *lacuna* in the High-Level Panel's text...) it is less far reaching. Paragraph 139 of the Secretary-General's report reads as follows:

> The International Court of Justice lies at the centre of the international system for adjudicating disputes among States. In recent years, the Court's docket has

[4] *Id.* ¶ 73.

[5] G.A. Res. 2625 (XXV), U.N. Doc. A/Res/2625(XXV) (Oct. 24, 1970), available at http://domino.un.org/pdfs/ARES2625XXV.pdf (last visited March 8, 2006).

[6] Outcome, supra note 3, ¶ 134.

> grown significantly and a number of disputes have been settled but resources remain scarce. There is a need to consider means to strengthen the work of the Court. I urge those States that have not yet done so to consider recognizing the compulsory jurisdiction of the Court – generally, if possible or, failing that, at least in specific situations. I also urge all States to bear in mind, and make use of, the Court's advisory powers. Measures should also be taken, with the cooperation of litigating States, to improve the Court's working methods and reduce the length of its proceedings.[7]

When comparing the two texts, it should be noted that the World Summit Outcome document specifically makes reference to the Secretary-General's Trust Fund to Assist States in the Settlement of Disputes through the International Court of Justice (a positive element generally and, I imagine, particularly welcome by the distinguished lawyers who habitually practice before the ICJ, sometimes irreverently referred to as "the usual suspects"!). But, in other respects, it is less precise and specific than the equivalent paragraph 139 of the Secretary-General's report. Most notably, there is no reference to the urging by the Secretary-General of "all parties to bear in mind, and make greater use of, the Court's advisory powers."[8]

I recall that in a well thought out statement before the Sixth Committee of the General Assembly, on November 5, 2004, the President of the ICJ, Judge Shi (following earlier suggestions to the same effect by, for instance, Judge Schwebel when President of the ICJ) made some significant suggestions on the underutilization by States of the ICJ advisory jurisdiction and its potential for expansion. He stated that: "…the advisory procedure provides the Court with a very real way of participating and contributing to the overall objectives of the United Nations. In addition to offering legal guidance to the requesting bodies, it can play a role in international dispute resolution."[9] He also stated that: "the advisory procedure of the Court can also play an 'indirect' part in preventing disputes and conflicts from developing, by clarifying the legal parameters within which a problem may be resolved."

Clarifying authoritatively by the ICJ of the legal aspects of pending international political disputes can go a long way towards lastingly resolving such disputes in a way consistent with the applicable rules of international law. For instance, in my earlier official capacity – and in the absence of a practical possibility for resorting to contentious proceedings – I have for many years advocated resort to the International Court of Justice, through a decision of

[7] In larger Freedom, supra note 2, ¶ 139.

[8] *Id.*

[9] H.E. Judge Shi Jiuyong (President to the International Court of Justice), Speech to the Sixth Committee of the General Assembly of the United Nations (Nov. 5, 2006), available at http://www.icjcij.org/icjwww/ipresscomlSPEECHES/iSpeech_President_Shi_Speeches_Sixth Committee _20041105.htm (last visited March 8, 2006).

the General Assembly or of the Security Council, for an Advisory Opinion clarifying the applicable rules of international law on several aspects of the Cyprus situation, such as the unilateral forcible intervention under Art. IV of the 1960 Treaty of Guarantee; the illegality of the 1983 UDI; the illegality of the establishment of settlers under the 1949 4th Geneva Convention and the 1998 Statute of the International Criminal Court; the applicable rules of State responsibility as, for instance, were applied on Iraq-Kuwait under S.C. Res. 687; violations of human rights etc. If this had been done, the contents of the recent U.N. (Annan V) plan would, I believe, have been drastically different and, quite possibly, it might not have been rejected, thereby becoming defunct and causing a backsliding of the process for a just solution to this long pending but solvable international problem.

I strongly feel that, in a comprehensive plan for a reformed and more effective United Nations, there exists ample room for such proposals for the fuller utilization of the International Court of Justice in general and of its advisory jurisdiction in particular. The recent Advisory Opinion on the *Legal Consequences of the Construction of a Wall in the Occupied Palestinian Territory*, July 9, 2004, furnishes a concrete such example.[10]

In the same lecture Judge Shi, in a commendable attempt to stimulate debate among policymakers, cited a number of other possibilities. One is to broaden the field of application of the Court's advisory jurisdiction to intergovernmental organizations, perhaps through appropriate resolutions of the General Assembly or the Security Council. Another is to empower the Secretary-General on his own initiative to request advisory opinions, as already proposed by Mr. Boutros-Ghali in 1992 in his Agenda for Peace and by Mr. Kofi Annan in 2001.[11] The issue was also raised in 1998 in the Charter Committee Report (U.N. Doc. A/53/33). A third possibility is to authorize national supreme courts as well as international courts and tribunals to request advisory opinions on certain difficult or disputed questions of international law so as to allow for uniform interpretation for such rules and principles.

One other aspect I would very briefly comment on is the Court's composition. We have all witnessed the great interest and acrimony over the expansion of the Security Council in order to meet the realities of power in the

[10] Advisory Opinion No. 131, Legal Consequences of the Construction of a Wall in the Occupied Palestinian Territory, 2004 I.C.J. 131 (July 9), available at http://www.icjcij.org/icjwww/idocket/imwp/imwp_advisory_opinion/imwp_advisory_opinion_20040709.htm (last visited March 8, 2006).

[11] The Secretary-General, *Report of the Secretary-General on the Work of the Organization's Prevention of Armed Conflict*, U.N. Doc. N55/985–SI2001/574. available at http://domino.un.org/unispal.nsf/0/b5bffcd5b649239585256caa006efab6?OpenDocument (last visited March 8, 2006).

21st century, an exercise the outcome of which is far from certain, and, yet, the Security Council was already expanded from eleven to fifteen members in the early sixties. By contrast, (under Art. 3 of its Statute) the ICJ consists of fifteen judges in 2005 when the United Nations has 191 Member States, the same number as it had in 1945 with fifty-one Member States. During the same period other main organs of the U.N. have been expanded in order to meet emerging needs of representation. The ECOSOC expanded from eighteen to fifty-four, the Security Council (as I just said) from eleven to fifteen and now possibly to twenty-four, and the Secretary-General has acquired one Deputy and possibly another. The Law of the Sea Tribunal (set up in 1996 under the 1982 Law of the Sea Convention, currently some 148 States Parties) consists of twenty-one Judges. The International Law Commission was twice expanded from eighteen to twenty-five to the present thirty-four.

I recall that in the U.N. Charter Committee session of 1993, the issue was raised as something worth thinking about though not by a way of a specific proposal.

It would seem appropriate to also do the same in the context of U.N. reform, although I readily concede that, realistically, there is no support for any such initiative, in the ICJ itself or politically among Member States and that different considerations apply to the Court's composition than in the composition of other bodies. But is this not something to reflect upon and, perhaps, after proper reflection, to reject it if it is not so warranted and its minuses outweigh its pluses? It is noteworthy, that in a footnote to his article in the July 2005 American Journal of International Law (at page 637) on Security Council Reform, Professor Yehuda Blum writes: "while the question of the Court's enlargement has not been raised by the [High-Level] panel (or subsequently), in the long term the Security Council enlargement may conceivably trigger demands for the Court's expansion as well."[12]

This concludes my contribution on "U.N. Reform and the ICJ." It is my hope and expectation that, under the firm and able guidance of the General Assembly President, Jan Eliasson, sufficient progress will be made, with the World Summit Outcome 2005 document as a starting point, to meet at least some of the expectations of the international community for U.N. reform in general and more particularly of the International Court of Justice and on the rule of law, nationally and internationally.

[12] Yehuda Z. Blum, *Proposals for U.N.Security Council Reform*, 99 AM.J.INT'l.L. 632, 649 n.45 (2005).

UN Peacekeeping

A View from Within: The Role of Small States and the Cyprus Experience*

I met John McMahon at Cambridge as a fellow law student soon after I went up in 1955. His keen sense of humour, his generosity, his open-mindedness, and his other great human qualities of heart and mind were only too apparent and we were friends throughout the three years of undergraduate work, the year of study for the LL.B. in international law, and later at Harvard and in New York.

The present essay, which was prepared in draft form barely two weeks before his death, was probably the last one that he had the occasion to go through, at my request, for corrections and suggestions. He returned it with a few minor observations and an undue amount of praise. It is almost unbelievable that it should now serve as a contribution to this memorial volume.

I come from a country which, from the beginning of its existence as an independent state, has always attached cardinal importance to its membership of the United Nations, has been dedicated by word and deed to the Charter and its principles and proved by the position it has taken on the variety of issues on which it has been called upon to take a stand, whether in the Organization itself or in the Non-aligned or the Commonwealth Conferences, that it is what one might call 'United Nations-minded'. Being a very small country, unencumbered by exclusive ties to either of the two major blocs in the cold war and having no world-wide military, political, or economic interests of its own to further, Cyprus found it possible to make the United Nations and the principles of its Charter central to its foreign policy,[1] particularly during the years 1960 to 1963 when it did not labour under the

---

* Previously published in INTERNATIONAL ORGANIZATION: LAW IN MOVEMENT, ESSAYS IN HONOUR OF JOHN MCMAHON, eds. J. Fawcett and R. Higgins, Oxford University Press, (1974).

[1] See e.g. General Debate statement by the Chairman of the Cyprus Delegation, Ambassador Z. Rossides, *GAOR*, 15th sess., 906th mtg; address by H. B. Archbishop Makarios, President of the Republic of Cyprus, to the General Assembly, 7 June 1962, *GAOR*, 16th sess., 1107th mtg, and to the Belgrade and Cairo Conferences of Non-aligned States, 1961 and 1964, *The Conference of Heads of States or Government of Non-Aligned Countries* (Belgrade, 1961), pp. 170–5, and *Cyprus Today*, Suppl. 28, 15 Oct. 1964, resp.

strains of a political problem of its own. It never hesitated to take positions dictated primarily, if not solely, by its dedication to the furtherance of the aims of the United Nations. It so happened that this attitude, determined, by its commitment to principle, coincided with the country's enlightened self-interest as a small and militarily weak state depending for its security on the collective security system of the United Nations and, as a developing country, standing to gain through multilateral technical assistance and know-how. Both in the political and the economic fields, the attitude of Cyprus as a small state was conditioned by its understanding of what was in the best interest of the United Nations consistently with what was in the best interest of Cyprus itself.

In saying this, I sincerely hope that I shall not be understood as wishing to portray the country of which I happen to be an official as being always on the side of the angels – indeed, some may hold a very different view – but because this attitude is illustrative of that which many small, newly independent, economically developing countries have towards the United Nations.

No doubt, dedication to the Organization is not limited to this category of states. However, while not wishing in any way to cast aspersions upon the major powers as regards their attitude towards the United Nations – and in fact their respective philosophies vary substantially – I cannot help but recall the picture of Dag Hammarskjöld, who, sitting on the podium of the General Assembly Hall and holding his pencil in his typical way, in 1960, after hearing the then Premier of the Soviet Union denounce him from the very rostrum of the General Assembly, refused to resign and explained his position by stressing that 'It is not the Soviet Union or indeed any other big powers which need the United Nations for their protection. It is all the others. In this sense, the Organization is first of all their Organization…'[2]

It is the nations of the Third World, which now constitute more than two-thirds of the total membership of the Organization, that are the main beneficiaries of the existence of the United Nations and its activities. At the same time their contribution should not be underestimated. 'The new nations', U Thant said in the course of his address at the University of Denver on 3 April 1964, 'have brought new and refreshing perspectives to old controversies and issues. They have shown an independence and common sense which compares very favourably, for example, with the long, arid and vituperative debates of the worst years of the cold war… In fact they have greatly contributed to a more balanced and realistic atmosphere by staying outside of the East-West ideological struggle. They have loyally supported the United Nations in its peace-keeping operations in sensitive parts of the world, and

---

[2] *GAOR*, 15th sess., 883rd mtg, p. 332.

they have often produced useful and constructive initiatives in finding solutions to great political problems.'[3]

While it would be a mistake to carry the generalization too far, it is correct, I believe, to state that there exist certain common characteristics in the attitude of smaller states towards the UN in general and towards peacekeeping in particular to warrant the use of the term 'role of the small states'. While this category is necessarily inexact and it is occasionally used to cover, in this context, the related and overlapping categories of the Third World, newly independent, and non-aligned states – some of which are far from small – the term, as used here, denotes those states manifesting certain common attitudes. In the first place they are the states which have a vital stake in the continuity and strengthening of the United Nations for their security and economic development, and are prepared to use their collective weight to prevent a confrontation of the major powers which might ruin the Organization or even destroy the world. In the second place, they are the states which, when confronted by a real emergency in which their security, independence and territorial integrity are threatened, are prepared to a less or greater extent to place reliance on the United Nations, in preference to other alternatives (such as a military alliance of which they are not parties or regional or quasi-regional arrangements)[4] to the extent of consenting to the limitations of sovereignty which the presence of a UN force necessarily implies. In the third place, these are the states upon which, as a rule, the Organization draws for contributing forces when the need for setting up a peacekeeping force arises. Moreover, it is primarily and perhaps in practice exclusively, in the territories of these states that the United Nations is likely to be called upon, and in fact permitted, to set up peacekeeping operations – as opposed to territories of states which are either major powers themselves or are considered by the major powers to fall under their exclusive sphere of influence, whether for strategic or ideological reasons, as indeed recent events in this hemisphere and in central Europe have reminded us.[5]

At the risk of being accused of flippancy, I would like to recall the saying that whenever a dispute is brought to the United Nations, something will inevitably disappear. If it is a dispute between two small powers, the dispute will disappear; if it is one between a large power and a small one, the small power will disappear; and if it is a dispute between two big powers,

[3] 'The Strengthening of the UN', Press release SG/SM/51.

[4] For these alternatives see generally A. Cox, *Prospects for Peacekeeping* (Washington, DC, Brookings Inst., 1967), pp. 50–72. The Cyprus case presents a clear illustration.

[5] Such as the Dominican Republic (1965) and Czechoslovak (1968) situations. See e.g. the Introduction to the Secretary-General's Annual Report on the Work of the Organization, *GAOR*, 23rd sess., Suppl. IA, A/7201/Add. 1, para. 189.

the United Nations will disappear. If one makes allowances for its cynicism, perhaps the picture is not too far removed from reality.

The Original Charter Scheme for Collective Security and the Present Situation

It was, no doubt, the express first purpose of the United Nations "to maintain international peace and security" and it was stressed in Article 1 of the Charter that to that end it was 'to take effective collective measures for the prevention and removal of threats to the peace, and for the suppression of acts of aggression or other breaches of the peace.' Under Article 24, it was envisaged that the Security Council, upon which the Members of the Organization conferred primary responsibility for the maintenance of international peace and security, would take prompt and effective action in this respect, and, in Chapter VII, a detailed scheme was set out to regulate such action.

It would be belabouring the obvious to discuss at any length the circumstances under which the ostensibly watertight system of collective security – through the Security Council's being able to decide and act – was rendered impotent by the exercise of the veto which in turn was made inevitable through the advent of the cold war. Naturally, stated Mr. Gromyko in 1945, 'the very best and most perfect Charter in itself is not yet a guarantee that its provisions will be carried out and insure the preservation of peace. In order to achieve this important and noble task, it is also necessary, in addition to the existing Charter, to have the unity and co-ordination of members of the International Organization, and first of all the unity and co-ordination of actions between the most powerful military powers of the world.'[6] These essential preconditions were simply not present in the years immediately following the signing of the Charter, for reasons that we need not go into now, and there is no prospect of this situation changing in the immediate future. Whether in the next decade[7] or longer there will have taken place some fundamental realignment, particularly among the two super-powers, any valid expectation of change in this respect can only be a matter of speculation – although there have recently been indications to that effect – and for the purposes of the present essay, we should proceed on the assumption that the

[6] *Documents of the UN Conference on International Organization, San Francisco, Calif.*, vol. 1, doc. 1209, p. 665.

[7] See report of Third Conference on the UN of the Next Decade, held in Dubrovnik, June 1968, under the auspices of the Stanley Foundation (Muscatine, Iowa, 1968).

collective security system, as envisaged in the Charter,[8] will remain in a state of impotence.

In addition to the lack of unanimity among the great powers there has been another fundamental reason for the transition away from the collective security system as envisaged in 1945. Due to the radical changes brought about in the nature and effects of war through the development of atomic and hydrogen weapons of mass destruction by the great powers, it would be unreasonable to expect that military forces of these powers will be employed in practice, as contemplated by the Charter. The mutual balance of terror has precluded any thought of using the forces of great powers against each other – even if there were any possibility of circumventing the exercise of the veto – and, in cases where armed forces through the United Nations have been employed, the tendency has been in practice to rely upon the military resources of the smaller powers. This has had the distinct advantage of avoiding great power confrontation or entangling the United Nations too deeply in the antagonism of the cold war.

It is generally acknowledged that the one collective action undertaken under the aegis of the United Nations – in Korea – was made possible by highly exceptional circumstances. It raised many questions as to whether it was a genuine UN operation and it is not at all likely that anything in a similar form will recur in the future. It can only be a matter of speculation whether operations could be envisaged involving enforcement action within Chapter VII presupposing great-power unanimity. The 1966 decision of the Security Council authorizing Britain to use force in connection with Southern Rhodesia[9] is a possible example. The possibility of a Security Council decision under Chapter VII to take action, e.g. against South Africa in connection with the latter's refusal to implement United Nations decisions in connection with Namibia, cannot be excluded even though at present it does not appear to be a very realistic prospect. But, barring such exceptional cases, where the interests of the great powers and of their 'clients' may happen to coincide, the collective security system of Chapter VII, under present circumstances, does not have a bright future in front of it.

In the light of this situation what then is the prospect for United Nations peacekeeping?

---

[8] It is interesting to note that an offer by Bulgaria and Czechoslovakia in 1964 to provide forces on call by the Security Council under Art. 43 of the Charter has not been taken up in view of the fundamental disagreement on the issue.

[9] In Apr. 1966, authorizing the UK to stop, if necessary by force, ships carrying oil to Southern Rhodesia – res. 221 (1966). Likewise res. 232 (1966) of Dec. 1966 imposing economic sanctions.

Proposals for a Permanent United Nations Peace Force

The proponents of a system of world government give their answer as the creation of a permanent United Nations peace force recruited by and for the United Nations with United Nations allegiance, organized, commanded, and financed by the United Nations.[10] Nor has this line of thought been limited to individuals. A number of states, including Cyprus, have not been shy in advocating the same objective. My own chief, the Chairman of the delegation of Cyprus, for example, had occasion to stress that 'Measures will have to be taken for the establishment and systematic development of a United Nations peace force, recruited by and for the United Nation, which would form the basis of an international security force. The primary allegiance of such a United Nations force would be directly to the United Nations, rendering this force truly international in the service of mankind.'[11] On another occasion, he remarked that 'loaned forces, owing allegiance to the States from which they come, cannot be fully relied upon for United Nations actions. They may, for one thing, be withdrawn at any time – as was the ease in the Congo'.[12] And again, in connection with the financing of future peacekeeping operations, he said that 'there are many ways by which contributions could be obtained from the peoples of the world, as distinct from their Governments, for instance, through a very small special tax or a stamp duty.'[13]

There is no doubt that the idea of projecting the stability and orderliness of a well-governed state onto the plane of relations between states has a lot to commend it. It has long been a noble human aspiration, reflected in many a scheme from ancient times onwards to develop an international order regulated by a system of universal law and backed by an effective international force. The United Nations was seen by many at the time it was set up – and is still seen by some today – as that form of world government, whether with its present or with an improved or otherwise supplemented constitution. But I believe most will agree today that there is a great distance

---

[10] See e.g. W.R. Frye, A UN Peace Force (Dobbs Ferry, NY, Oceana, 1957); *Federal Union's Proposals for a Permanent UN Force* (London, FU, 1957); G. Clark and L.B. Sohn, *Draft of a Proposed Treaty establishing a World Disarmament and World Development Organization within the Framework of the UN* (1962), pp. 78–90.

[11] See Z. Rossides, *Cyprus in the UN* (New York, 1963), p. 12 (General Debate statement, *GAOR*, 17th sess., 1155th mtg, p. 534).

[12] See Z. Rossides, *Cyprus in the UN* (New York, 1962), p. 14 (General Debate statement, *GAOR*, 16th sess., 1039th mtg, pp. 486–7).

[13] Rossides, *Cyprus in the UN* (1963), p. 81 (statement made in 5th Cttee, Dec. 1962). On this aspect see R. and H. Taubenfeld, 'Independent Revenue for the UN', Int. Org., vol. XVIII, no. 2 (1964), 241–68; and see generally J.G. Stoessinger, *Financing the UN System* (Washington, DC, Brookings Inst., 1964).

between the dream and the reality – the need and the fulfillment of the need. This ideal system presupposes an absence of fundamental conflict of interest and a willingness on the part of all states to surrender a very large measure of their sovereignty to a super-state or supranational authority. These essential preconditions simply do not exist at present and they are not likely to exist tomorrow. It will be a long process of evolution before we reach that stage if we ever do. On the opposite side of the spectrum we find the Soviet approach – and not the Soviet alone – to the United Nations as being simply an intergovernmental organization and an institutional form of multilateral co-operation between sovereign states. According to this view the competence and functions of such international institutions are determined by the states members, on the basis of their mutual consent.

U Thant in his address to the Harvard Alumni Association at Cambridge, Massachusetts, on 13 June 1963,[14] put the subject in its proper perspective, with his customary lucidity and with his admirable blending of realism and idealism: 'In my opinion', he said, 'a permanent United Nations force is not a practical proposition at the present time.' He doubted whether many governments in the world would yet be prepared to accept the political implications of such an institution and they would have serious difficulties in accepting the financial implications. 'Personally', he continued,

> I have no doubt that the world should eventually have an international police force which will be accepted as an integral and essential part of life in the same way as national police forces are accepted. Meanwhile, we must be sure that developments are in the right direction and that we can also meet critical situations as and when they occur…
>
> I believe that we need a number of parallel developments before we can evolve such an institution. We have to go further along the road of codification and acceptance of a workable body of international law. We have to develop a more sophisticated public opinion in the world, which can accept the transition from predominantly national thinking to international thinking. We shall have to develop a deeper faith in international institutions as such, and a greater confidence in the possibility of a United Nations Civil service whose international loyalty and objectivity are generally accepted and above suspicion. We shall have to improve the method of financing international organization. Until these conditions are met, a permanent United Nations force may not be a practical proposition.[15]

[14] Press release SG/1520.
[15] Ibid. p. 8.

Development of Ad Hoc Peacekeeping Operations

These words were spoken in 1963. Ten years later, despite the goodwill, imagination and ingenuity shown by many ingenious and internationally minded men and women in many parts of the world,[16] we are not appreciably nearer to the goal of a permanent UN force. But there have been some encouraging developments which, in a practical and piecemeal fashion, have gone a long way towards fulfilling the role which member states permit the United Nations to play in the field of maintenance of peace and security. I am referring to the advent of peacekeeping operations.[17] They are pioneering, improvised, ad hoc, do not fit into any streamlined grand design nor do they fulfill a logician's dream. Not two of them are identical in kind and they present considerable disadvantages as compared to a standing United Nations force. Each is tailored to the particular situation. Yet in a pragmatic unspectacular way, to a greater or less extent, they served the purpose for which each was created. These forces are very different from those envisaged in Chapter VII and yet their existence is not inconsistent with the Charter. As U Thant described them they are 'essentially peace and not fighting forces and they operate with the consent of the parties directly concerned.'[18]

What kind of forces, then, does this category encompass? At the one end of the spectrum we have groups of a few observers keeping watch on a cease-fire line or overseeing the holding of a plebiscite. At the other end we have a sizeable military force of several thousand officers and men undertaking substantial functions in accordance with their respective mandates.

Observer Forces and UNTEA

Under the former category[19] fall such operations as the United Nations Special Committee on the Balkans (UNSCOB), consisting of professional military officers and authorized by the General Assembly after a series of vetoes frustrated an earlier effort in the Security Council, to observe and otherwise

---

[16] See the works cited in n. 10 above.

[17] See generally A. Cox, *Prospects for Peacekeeping* (Washington, DC, Brookings Inst., 1967); R. Higgins, *UN Peacekeeping 1946–1967: Documents and Commentary*, 2 vols. (London, OUP for RITÀ, 1969–70); D.W. Bowett, *UN Forces: a Levi Study of UN Practice* (New York, Praeger for David Davies Memonal Inst., 1964); R.B. Russell, *UN Experience with Military Forces: Political and Legal Aspects* (Washington, DC, Brookings Inst., 1964); R.N. Gardner, 'The Development of the Peacekeeping Capacity of the UN', *Proceed. ASIL* 1963, pp. 224–34. For a comprehensive bibliography see A. Legault (compiler), *Peace-keeping Operations: Bibliography* (Pans, International Information Center on Peacekeeping Operations, 1967).

[18] Press release SG 1520, p. 3.

[19] For a full treatment of the subject, see D.W. Wainhouse and others, *International Peace Observation* (Baltimore, Md. Johns Hopkins Press, 1966).

assist in connection with the border situation of Greece with her northern neighbours; the United Nations Military Observer Group in India and Pakistan (UNMOGIP), set up by the Security Council in 1948–9 to watch over the Kashmir situation and which is still operational; the United Nations Truce Supervision Organization (UNTSO), which since 1949 has played a vital role in the context of keeping the peace in the Middle East and which was preceded by another group that had worked from July 1948 under the United Nations Mediator in supervising the first truce agreements in the Palestine war; the military observers team assisting the United Nations Commission for Indonesia (UNCI) in 1949 during the fighting which preceded Indonesia's independence from the Netherlands; the United Nations Observation Group in Lebanon (UNOGIL), set up by the Security Council in 1958 to ensure that no infiltration was occurring into Lebanon; the United Nations Yemen Observation Mission (UNYOM), created by the Security Council in 1963 to observe whether the UAR-Saudi Arabia disengagement agreement was being implemented; the United Nations India-Pakistan Observation Mission (UNIPOM), to patrol the border between India and Pakistan, created in 1965 by the Secretary-General as part of his action in discharge of the responsibility delegated to him by the Security Council after the outbreak of war between India and Pakistan.

This enumeration, which is not exhaustive, does not cover the unique case of the United Nations Temporary Executive Authority (UNTEA) created in 1962 by the General Assembly, charged with the interim administration of West Iran in implementation of the agreement between Indonesia and the Netherlands for the eventual transfer of administrative authority in 1963 to Indonesia with a plebiscite to take place in 1969 under United Nations supervision. It was a unique case: for the first time – following upon the relinquishing of Dutch sovereignty – control, together with security functions during the interim period, was being exercised by the United Nations as such. The operation was an outstanding success under the brilliant direction of Mr. Rolz-Bennett.

Military Forces – UNEF, ONUC, UNFICYP

I have not so far referred to the United Nations Emergency Force (UNEF), created by the General Assembly in 1956 after the concerted attack on Egypt by Israel, France and Great Britain, and which was given the task of patrolling within Egyptian territory, with the consent of the government of that country, along the Israeli borders in the Gaza strip and in Sinai.[20] These

[20] For the basic documents see e.g. E. Lauterpacht, *The UN Emergency Force* (London, Stevens, 1960). The pertinent UN documents are summarized in Legault (see n. 17 above), pp. 31–137.

forces withdrew in May 1967, after a request to that effect by the government of the United Arab Republic, in circumstances which gave rise to some considerable controversy at the time but which, to my mind, did not provide any valid grounds for criticism of the Secretary-General for his willingness to accede to the request.[21] Nor did I cover the United Nations Operation in the Congo (ONUC),[22] authorized by the Security Council in 1960 to perform difficult functions in a volatile and complicated situation, an operation which put great strains upon the United Nations because of its size (at its peak it numbered over 20,000 personnel contributed by some 35 countries), its cost (over $400 million), and, more significantly, the political, constitutional, legal, and financial controversies which were raised in its wake and which still plague the Organization even though the operation was wound up in the summer of 1964.

These two operations together with the United Nations Force in Cyprus (UNFICYP),[23] fall within the second category to which I referred earlier. Because of their novelty and complexity, but also because of their potential

---

Of these, particular note should be taken of A/3943, 9 Oct. 1958 (*GAOR*, 13th sess., Annexes, agenda item 65), entitled 'Summary Study of the Experience Derived from the Establishment and Operation of the Force: Report of the Secretary-General'. esp. ch. 6 (legal aspects) and ch. 7 (basic principles).

21 See e.g. 'Withdrawal of the UN Emergency Force: Some Questions Answered', *UN Monthly Chronicle*, July 1967, pp. 87–94, and for a full account see the Secretary-General's Report, A/6730 and Add. 1–3 (GAOR, 5th emergency special sess., Annexes, agenda item 5). See also N. El Araby, 'A Case Study of the Withdrawal of UNEF', *New York University Journal of International Law and Politics*, vol. 1, no. 1968.

22 For a full treatment of the subject see E.W. Lefever, *Crisis in the Congo: A UN Force in Action* (Washington, DC, Brookings last, 1965). See also R. Bunche, 'The UN Operation in the Congo', in J. Larus, ed. *From Collective Security to Preventive Diplomacy* (New York, Wiley, 1965). The pertinent UN documents are summarized in Legault (see n. 17 above), pp. 118–27. For legal aspects of the operation see E.M. Miller [pseud.], Legal aspects of the UN Action in the Congo, 55 AM, (Jan. 1961); O. Schachter. 'Preventing the Internationalization of Internal Conflict: a Legal Analysis of the UN Congo Experience', *Proceed. ASIL*. 1963; Thomas M. Franck and John Carey, Working Paper: the Role of the UN in the Congo', in Assn of the Bar of the City of New York, Cttce on Lawyer's Role in Search for Peace (2nd Hammarskjöld Forum. 1962). *Legal Aspects of UN Action in the Congo* (Dobbs Ferry, NY, Oceana, 1963); Bowett, pp. 153–261. See also C. Cruise O'Brien, *To Katanga and Back* (New York, Simon & Schuster, 1962).

23 The bibliography on UNFICYP includes: Andrestinos N. Papadopoulos, *Peace-making and Peace-keeping by the UN: Cyprus, a Case Study* (Nicosia, 1969): J.A. Stegenga, *The UN Force in Cyprus* (Columbus. Ohio State UP, 1968): T. Ehrlich, '*Cyprus, the Warlike Isle; Origins and Elements of the Current Crisis', 18 Stanford Law Review* (May, 1966); T.M. Boyd, 'Cyprus, Episode in Peacekeeping', International Journal, summer 1964: Bowett, pp. 552–60; R. Stephens, *Cyprus: a Place of Arms* (London. Pall Mall Press, 1966): L.B. Miller, *World Order and Local Disorder: the UN and Internal Conflicts* (Princeton UP, 1967), pp. 116–48, and *Cyprus: the Law and Politics of Civil Strife* (Cambridge, Mass., Harvard Univ. Center for International Affairs, 1968); C. Foley, *Legacy of Strife: Cyprus from Rebellion to Civil War* (Harmondsworth, Penguin Books, 1964). The earlier relevant UN documents are summarized in Legault, pp. 138–44. See also *The Function of the UN Force in Cyprus – an Assessment* (Nicosia, Public Inf. Off. 1967).

significance, each of them was accompanied by a host of problems – as is indeed reflected in the abundance of writings upon them.[24] It would therefore seem advisable, bearing in mind the limitations of time and space, to concentrate upon the Cyprus operation, of which I have had some experience, and which is the major operation that is still in existence and for which it can rightly be claimed that it has been successful and useful.

Background to the Creation of UNFICYP

A great deal has been said and even more has been written about the background[25] of the Cyprus crisis as well as about the legal[26] and political[27] factors that were involved, but this is not the place for a recapitulation. It was undoubtedly against a background of great complexity that the first shots were fired on the night of 20–21 December 1963 which marked the beginning of the crisis.

Following the aggravation of the crisis and the first manifestations of overt intervention by Turkey on Christmas day 1963, and after the failure of a number of efforts to arrange local cease-fires, the Cyprus government – from which, by then, the Turkish Cypriot members had withdrawn – had no alternative but to accept a British government offer that the British, Greek, and Turkish troops stationed in Cyprus under the 1960 arrangement be placed under British command to help restore order. In fact this 'tripartite' force, which became operational on 27 December 1963, was essentially British and, irrespective of the motives which prompted its involvement, it was a factor in avoiding further exacerbation of the situation.

[24] See works cited in nn. 20, 22, 23, and Legault (n. 17) above.

[25] See e.g. *Cyprus: the Problem in Perspective* (Nicosia, Public Inf. Off., 1967); H.J. Psomiadcs, 'The Cyprus Dispute', Current History, May 1965. pp. 269–76 and 305–6; Stegenga; Ehrlich; Stephens; L.B. Muller; Foley; RITA Inf. Dept. *Cyprus: the Dispute and the Settlement* (London, OUP, 1959); S.G. Xydis, *Cyprus: Conflict and Conciliation*, 1954–58 (Columbus, Ohio State UP, 1967).

[26] See GB, *Colonial Off. and others, Cyprus,* Cmnd 1093 (London, HMSO, 1960) for the basic documents, and *Cyprus: the Problem in perspective* (cited fully in n. 25 above) for the proposals of 30 Nov. 1963 (13 points); also C. Tornaritis, *The Legal Aspects of the Question of Cyprus* (Nicosia, 1965); G. Zotiades, *The Treaty of Guarantee and the Principle of Non-intervention* (1965); T. Zoupanos, *The Invalidity and the Inapplicability of the Treaty of Guarantee in Cyprus*, Conf. 1964 (in Greek); A.J. Jacovides, *Treaties Conflicting with Peremptory Norms of International Law and the Zurich-London 'Agreements'* (Nicosia, 1966); C. Tornaritis and others, Cyprus Today, vol. II, no. 3 (1964); A. Chayes and others, compilers, *International Legal Process*, vol. 2 (Boston, Little, Brown, 1969), pp. 1234–312. See also the Security Council and General Assembly debates on Cyprus and esp. statement of the Foreign Minister of Cyprus at the 1098th mtg of the Security Council (SCOR, 19th yr).

[27] See works cited in n. 25 above.

From the very beginning of the internationalization of the conflict the Cyprus government resorted to the United Nations. On 25 December 1963 it instructed its Permanent Representative in New York to lodge a complaint with the Security Council against Turkey's acts and threats of use of force in violation of its obligations under the Charter.[28] The Permanent Representative of Cyprus discussed the situation with the Secretary-General on 26 December 1963 and, on the next day, an emergency meeting of the Security Council was held at the urgent request of the Cyprus government.[29] The meeting was inconclusive and no decision was taken pending the clarification of the situation. Meanwhile in Nicosia, bowing to the pressure of events, the Cyprus government agreed to participate in a conference with the other signatories of the Nicosia Agreements, i.e. Great Britain, Greece, and Turkey, to be held in London in January 1964. Consequently the effort in New York was suspended, though not abandoned, while for most of January the effort was on in London. Nevertheless the Cyprus government was quick to accept the suggestion that the UN be further involved through the appointment by the Secretary-General on 16 January of a Personal Representative in the island.[30] After the failure of the London Conference, successive proposals of the British government and subsequently of the British and United States governments were put forward, in a rather pressing manner,[31] for a peacekeeping force drawn from NATO countries with inexact terms of reference and for a mediator drawn also from a NATO country. These proposals were firmly rejected by the Cypriot leadership which insisted that, should there be the need for a peacekeeping force in the island, it would have to be a United Nations force under the authority of the Security Council. Those of us in New York in that tense month heard other ideas – such as a Commonwealth or Nordic force – being mooted as alternatives. Quite apart from the other factors which may have dictated the clear preference for a United Nations peacekeeping force (such as the predictable attitude of the Afro-Asian members and of the Soviet Union, not to mention the fact that apart from the proponents of the scheme and one or two other willing NATO members, the idea of expanding the area of responsibilities of this alliance was not at all enthusiastically received by the other members), I suggest that this

[28] S/5488 (SCOR, 18th yr, Suppl. Oct.–Dec. 1963).

[29] The 1085th mtg (SCOR, 18th yr).

[30] S/5514 (SCOR, 19th yr, Suppl. Jan.–March 1964), and S/5516 (ibid.). Gen. Gyani of India, former commander of UNEF and UNYOM was appointed; he was later to become the first commander of UNFICYP.

[31] For a not unbiased account of the surrounding circumstances, see E. Weinthal and C. Bartlett, *Facing the Brink: an Intimate Study of Crisis Diplomacy*/ New York, Scribner, 1967), pp. 16–36. See also P. Windsor, *Nato and the Cyprus Crisis* (London, ISS, 1964, Adelphi Paper no. 14).

attitude is fully consistent with the overall philosophy of the foreign policy of Cyprus, as a small non-aligned country, depending for its security on, and having confidence in, not military alliances such as NATO, of which it is not a member, but the United Nations. It neatly illustrates the problem of what alternatives there are to United Nations peacekeeping.

By the middle of February 1964 the idea had ripened that, having exhausted the possibilities available through direct negotiations or through the quasi-regional forum provided by the London Conference, the problem should be tackled squarely by the Security Council. A firm decision was taken in Nicosia to this effect and it was announced that the Minister for Foreign Affairs, Mr. Kyprianou, and the President of the House of Representatives, Mr. Clerides, were leaving for New York to present the case for Cyprus to the Council. At that particular moment the British Mission to the United Nations thought it advisable to steal a march by submitting its own request to the Council first, with the resultant advantage that it would not appear as having been 'dragged' before the Council, and also of speaking first. This it did at 3 p.m. on 15 February and informed the Cyprus Mission a few minutes later. I will not recount the procedural moves and debates which followed, and the only reason why I have entered into this amount of detail is that an attempt was made to capitalize on the fact that it was Britain that wanted the Security Council to be seized of the subject[32] – a case of making virtue out of necessity.

In the long debates which followed, the various – aspects of the Cyprus problem were fully set out and divergent points of view were expressed.[33] Obviously the priorities of the parties were not identical but it soon emerged that the result of the deliberations would be, on the one hand, an affirmation of the basic principle of the Charter in Article 2 (4) prohibiting the use of force by one state against another,[34] and on the other, the authorization of the setting-up of a UN force to be present in Cyprus for a fixed period. At the same time the Security Council recommended that the Secretary-General designate a mediator in an effort to promote a peaceful solution. I do not propose at present to examine which side gained more out of the Security Council resolution, but, to my mind, there is no room for doubt that the Cyprus government emerged far stronger as a result.[35]

---

[32] A letter of 26 Dec. 1963 (S/5488, SCOR, 18th yr, Suppl. Oct.–Dec. 1963) from the Cyprus Permanent Representative had already been inscribed on the Security Council agenda.

[33] See *SCOR*, 1964, 1095th mtg and following.

[34] And thus, indirectly, precluding Turkey from using her alleged right of forcible intervention against Cyprus.

[35] On the issue of the validity of the Nicosia Treaties of Aug. 1960, the Council, rightly, did not adopt a position but simply look into consideration in the preamble the position of the parties. See Jacovides, as cited in it 26 above, pp. 25–6.

The resolution, eventually adopted on 4 March 1964, was the result of hard bargaining and compromise at every point, and, as is customary in documents of this nature, certain intentional ambiguities were inserted for the sake of general acceptance. The relevant paragraphs for the present discussion are 4, 5, and 6.[36]

UNFICYP

Setting-Up, Composition, Size, Direction, and Control by the Security Council

Under paragraph 4, the Security Council recommended the creation, with the consent of the government of Cyprus, of a United Nations peacekeeping force in Cyprus. The composition and size of the Force was to be established by the Secretary-General, in consultation with the governments of Cyprus, Greece, Turkey, and the United Kingdom. The commander of the Force was to be appointed by the Secretary-General and was to report to him. It was further provided that the Secretary-General, who was to keep the governments providing the Force fully informed, would report periodically to the Security Council on its operations.

Perhaps a few brief observations at this stage will be relevant. Consistently with the legal foundation of the resolution, it was expressly stated that the consent of the host country was essential. This consent was given promptly by the Cyprus government.[37] No provisions of the Charter, other than Article 2 (4), were expressly mentioned in the resolution – it is believed, intentionally – but it is beyond doubt that its constitutional basis is to be found within the general terms of Chapter VI of the Charter and is within the general framework of the principles originally enunciated by Mr. Hammarskjöld in connection with UNEF.[38]

The wording used regarding the composition of UNFICYP was such as to leave the ultimate decision for the Secretary-General but the opinion of each of the four governments mentioned therein was also made relevant. In practice this has meant a composition reflecting the minimum common denominator of forces from countries to which none of the four governments objected.[39] Countries known to be leaning exclusively towards Turkey or Cyprus were also excluded. The question of finance was also pertinent

---

[36] SC res. 186 (1964).

[37] S/5578 (*SCOR*, 19th yr, Suppl. Jan.–March 1964).

[38] A/3943 (*GAOR*, 13th secs., Annexes, agenda item 65).

[39] E.g. while a certain Eastern European country is said to have offered to participate, this offer was not taken up, presumably because it did not fit within this area of the common denominator.

and this may well explain the absence of African or other Third World participation.[40] On the other hand, it is noteworthy that, for the first time (as far as is known) it was made the practice for a UN Secretariat official from Eastern Europe to be included in the civilian side of UNFICYP.[41] In general, the result has been that UNFICYP has been composed of contingents contributed by Canada, Sweden, Finland, Denmark, Ireland, and the United Kingdom; and units of civilian police from Australia. New Zealand, and Austria together with an Austrian medical unit and field hospital.

The only unorthodoxy and an exception from the Hammarskjöld principles in so far as composition is concerned is the participation of the United Kingdom in that (a) it is a permanent member of the Security Council and (b) it has a special interest in the situation (as a signatory of the Treaty of Guarantee and as having the Sovereign Base Areas in the island). It is explained in terms of purely practical considerations, viz. the fact that UK forces were already present as part of the 'tripartite' force prior to the existence of the UNFICYP, the fact that the British sovereign bases in the island were the backbone of the logistical support for UNFICYP, etc. In practice, this matter has not given rise to difficulties and on the whole, British troops wearing the blue berets of the United Nations, have demonstrated that, where the circumstances require it, the armed forces even of great powers under the proper command can and do behave in accordance with United Nations standards.

It is also significant that the enabling resolution expressly provided that the commander of the force would be appointed by the Secretary-General and would report to him. This is indicative of the wide margin left to the Secretary-General in this operation and evidence of the confidence that was in fact reposed in U Thant by all shades of opinion, especially bearing in mind the doctrinal positions of the Soviet Union and France in this respect. Although both of these powers abstained on a separate vote on this paragraph because of these very doctrinal differences of view, the fact that they voted for the resolution as a whole lends substance to the view that, irrespective of positions of principle, whenever the political conditions exist – as indeed they did in the case under examination – United Nations forces will be authorized by the Security Council and neither the USSR nor France will be unduly inhibited by their doctrinal positions (as indeed was the case with other situations, e.g. UNEF, UNTEA, UNIPOM).

---

[40] See Cyprus Mission press release No. 6 in reply to Max Frankel's *New York Times* article, 8 July 1964.

[41] There have been one Hungarian, one Bulgarian, and several Czechoslovak officials, all of whom, it is the general view, have behaved impartially and conscientiously as UN officials within the letter and the spirit of the Charter.

The Secretary-General originally appointed his former Personal Representative, General Gyani, as commander of the force, and later General Thimayya, who had not only a fine record in the Indian army but also experience in Korea, then, after his unfortunate death in December 1965, General A.E. Martola, a distinguished Finnish military man whose experience included advising the former Secretary-General Dag Hammarskjöld in 1956 and 1957 on UNEF. The deputy commander and, subsequently, the chief of staff was originally a British officer and is now a Canadian. The system appears to work well and there have been no cases, as far as is known, either of insubordination of contingent commanders or other officers to the Force Commander, or of the Commander to instructions from UN Headquarters in New York.[42]

It is noteworthy that, unlike the Congo operation, this one has no institutional advisory committee to limit in any way the Secretary-General's freedom of action, but in the present operation the Secretary-General is required to keep the governments providing the Force fully informed. This the Secretary-General has done. He has likewise been careful to report on all significant developments to the Security Council, especially when potentially controversial matters arise, thus giving to the Council members the opportunity of airing, if they so wish, their views in the Council, which remains constantly seized of the subject. So far, however, no extraordinary Security Council meeting has been held as a result of an initiative by a Council member, though a number of meetings, emergency and other, have been convened at the request of interested parties.[43]

Mandate

Under paragraph 5 the Security Council recommended that the function of the Force should be, in the interest of preserving international peace and security, to use its best efforts to prevent a recurrence of fighting, and, as necessary to contribute to the maintenance and restoration of law and order and a return to normal conditions.

It will be noted that, particularly in the complicated Cyprus situation, this formulation left something to be desired in terms of clarity and precision, but that is the price that had to be paid for a generally acceptable text. It is not therefore surprising that it was the object of diverse interpretations. The

[42] In fact the Secretary-General in S/5671, 29 Apr. 1964 (*SCOR*, 19th yr, Suppl. Apr.–June) set out objectives and interim aims of the Force. The instructions in detail which are being constantly sent, whenever the occasion requires them, from UN Headquarters have not been published.

[43] By Cyprus in March 1964; by Cyprus and Turkey in Aug. 1964; by Turkey and Cyprus in Aug. 1965; by Turkey in Nov. 1965; by Cyprus in Nov. 1967.

Secretary-General stated what he understood by the mandate in an aide-memoire issued on 11 April 1964[44] and elaborated it further in his reports to the Security Council of June 1964[45] and September 1964[46] subsequently reaffirmed. The Cyprus government's view was expressed by the Minister of Foreign Affairs particularly in his statement before the Council in September 1964. All in all, the Secretary-General's interpretation has been one the Cyprus government has been content to live with and be satisfied with. Furthermore it was made clear, fairly early in 1964, that it was not the mandate of the force, nor was it equipped or willing,[47] to fight off an external invasion of the island but rather, through its very presence and calming effect, to discourage and take away the pretext for one.

The only subsequent occasion when there was a serious effort to enlarge UNFICYP's mandate was in September 1964, through the indirect device of saying that the Secretary-General would assume that renewal of the Force would imply enlargement of its mandate in the three specified areas stated therein (wider freedom of movement, creation of buffer zones, defortifications).[48] This effort foundered on the firm opposition of the Soviet Union and France against any enlargement of the mandate (the Cyprus Foreign Minister had expressed mixed views thereon) and was not further pursued. Since that time there has been no effort either to widen or narrow the terms of reference and those concerned have reconciled themselves to,

[44] S/5653 (*SCOR*, 19th yr, Suppl. Apr.–June 1964); also S/5671 (ibid.).

[45] S/5764 (ibid.).

[46] S/5950 (*SCOR*, 19th yr, Suppl. July–Sept. 1964, pp. 280 fr.). In para. 220 the Secretary-General stated that 'UNFICYP was not established by the Security Council as an arm of the Government of Cyprus... It respects at all times the sovereignty and independence of Cyprus and the authority of the Government but it acts independently in the discharge of its mandate, in accordance with the resolutions of the Security Council.' In the same report (paras 218 and 219), U Thant said '...there has been all along and continues to be what I consider to be a misunderstanding on the part of the Turkish community of Cyprus and of the Turkish Government as to the function and duty of the United Nations Force in Cyprus... in their eyes, UNFICYP should have been employing force, wherever and whenever necessary to restore, over the opposition of the Cypriot Government, the constitutional situation relating to the privileges, rights and immunities of the Turkish community in Cyprus... I have not, of course, accepted these positions...'

[47] Cf. in this connection the correspondence between Mr. Aiken, Irish Minister for External Affairs, and the Secretary-General as regards the Irish government's understandings prior to agreeing to participate in the Force, notably that 'an assurance will be forthcoming from the Governments of Great Britain, Greece and Turkey, that, during the presence of the force in Cyprus, they will not intervene or attempt to intervene by force, or by threat of force, to impose a solution of the problem and, particularly, a solution by partition.' (Letter of 13 March 1964.) See also Mr. Aiken's subsequent letter (24 Mar 1964) in which he stressed that 'if during the presence of the United Nations force in Cyprus the Governments of Great Britain, Greece and Turkey or any of them, should intervene, or attempt to impose by force or by threat of force a solution of the problem, and particularly a solution by partition, immediate steps will be taken to withdraw the Irish contingent from Cyprus.' UN Press release, CYP14, 13 March 1964.

[48] S/5950, para. 232.

the original form, as interpreted by the Secretary-General and as applied in practice in the field. The emphasis has been a practical one for stability rather than for strict legalism. The fact is that there was no major need to alter the mandate and in any case it was most unlikely that any effort to do so would succeed without opening a Pandora's box in the process.[49]

Duration and Financing

Finally, the Security Council recommended in paragraph 6 that the stationing of the Force should be for a period of three months, all costs pertaining to it being met in a manner to be agreed upon between them, by the governments providing the contingents and by the government of Cyprus. It was further stated that the Secretary-General might also accept voluntary contributions for that purpose.

As regards the time factor, the underlying thought in the Security Council was that in the three-month period, during which UNFICYP would 'hold the ring', sufficient progress would have been made towards a political solution through the United Nations mediator[50] to warrant the termination of the Force. This, of course, proved to be a far too optimistic assumption and it became necessary again and again to renew the mandate of the Force.[51]

While, understandably, impatience has occasionally been expressed by the Secretary-General, as well as by Council members and by contributing countries, that this state of affairs cannot continue indefinitely, it is at the same time generally recognized that the alternative would be infinitely worse and renewal has on each occasion been forthcoming. Certain developments in 1968 raised hopes that the Force could soon be terminated; however, more recent events have once again made that hope appear unlikely to be realized for some time. In any case, in practice the size of the Force has been reduced from some 7,000 at its peak to nearly half that number.

The financial aspect of the Force is yet another story to which justice cannot be done here. As a reflection of political and constitutional differences, the financial aspect of peacekeeping operations has since 1956 – beginning with UNEF – put the Organization into a state of near-bankruptcy and threatened its collapse politically. The confrontation over Article 19 of the

[49] One such occasion arose in Dec. 1967 over implementation of the Athens – Ankara agreement of 27 Nov. 1967 in conjunction with the Secretary-General's appeal (S/8248/Add. 6 (*SCOR*, 22nd yr, Suppl. Oct.–Dec. 1967). For reasons that cannot be fully explained here it did not result in any change of UNFICYP's mandate.

[50] Under para. 7 of SC res. 186 (1964).

[51] Such renewals took place in June, Sept. and Dec. 1964 (SC res 192, 194 and 198, resp.); in March, June and Dec. 1965 (SC res. 206, 207 and 219); in March, June and Dec. 1966 (SC res. 220, 222 and 231); in June and Dec. 1967 (SC res. 238 and 244); and in March, June and Dec. 1968 (SC res. 247, 254 and 261).

Charter, which was but a reflection of fundamental constitutional[52] and political differences, frustrated the whole nineteenth session of the General Assembly, put serious strains upon the International Court of Justice in its effort to produce the requested advisory opinion on the *Expenses* Case,[53] was the subject of acute controversy not only among the great powers but also among such individuals as the Foreign Minister of Ireland, Mr. F. Aiken, and the then Senator, Mr. P. Trudeau of Canada, in the Twenty-first session of the Assembly, and is now in a state of semi-hibernation in the Special Committee of 33 with no immediate prospects for a solution.[54]

To return to the financing of UNFICYP, no similar 'mistake' as that in the case of UNEF and ONUC was to be committed – in fact there would have been no UNFICYP if there had been such an effort – and, while most recognized the fragile and unsatisfactory nature of voluntary contributions, this was the line of least resistance and was adopted.

By the end of 1968, as it appears from the Secretary-General's report of December 1968,[55] the situation was as follows: the deficit was calculated to be approximately $8 million with an additional $8 million required to cover the period to 15 June 1969. However unsatisfactory this may appear to be,

[52] The main trends were aptly summarized in the statement of the Representative of India in the Special Committee on Peace-Keeping Operations as reflected in A/AC. 121/WGA/SRI: 'There appeared now to he universal agreement that the Security Council had the primary responsibility... for the establishment of peace-keeping operations. That was not to deny such authority as the General Assembly had in that field. The differences that existed arose out of the attempts to define the exact authority of the Security Council and the General Assembly respectively. There was sizable support for the view that the General Assembly was vested with considerable residual authority, particularly in situations in which the Security Council failed to act. There was the opposite view, however, that, while the General Assembly had the right, the authority and, indeed, the responsibility to discuss any question, it could not under any circumstances take action within the meaning of Article 11 (2) of the Charter. The proponents of that view extended their definition of "action" to cover even the dispatch of a single soldier to a trouble spot in the world. There was also a third point of view... in the French Government's view, the apportionment of functions between the Security Council and the General Assembly was based primarily on Article 11 (2) of the Charter; that provision could not be limited to the measures provided for in Articles 41 and 42, but also covered any measures involving the creation of a military force, even if the force was created with the agreement of the states covered and even if the actual use of armed force was theoretically limited to certain exceptional cases. Within those limits, the French Government maintained, the Security Council had exclusive authority; the General Assembly could undertake such operations as observation, surveillance or investigation, provided that those operations were not carried out by units placed under military command and that the units were not responsible for their own security...'

[53] *Certain Expenses of the United Nations* (1962), ICI Rep. 1962.

[54] In fact the opinion prevailed in the Special Cttee that it would he futile to try to resolve the basic constitutional issue, and, instead, the emphasis is currently being placed on less controversial and more practical steps in the implementation of the Cttee's mandate. See e.g. *GAOR*. 23rd sess., Suppl. 1 (A/7201), p. 76; and A/7455 (*GAOR*, 23rd sess., Annexes, agenda item 32).

[55] S/8914 (*SCOR*, 23rd yr, Suppl. Oct.–Dec. 1968).

it is the general belief that, given all the factors involved, UNFICYP will not collapse through lack of financial support.

At the same time, the government of Cyprus met its responsibilities under Article 19 of the Status of the Force Agreement – even though, as one would expect from Ministries of Finance everywhere, not without some haggling – and has made sizeable contributions to the financing of the Force.

This then was the framework of UNFICYP: a peacekeeping force authorized by the Security Council, with the consent of the government of Cyprus, set up by the Secretary-General, operating under a commander appointed by and responsible to the Secretary-General, functioning on the basis of a vaguely worded mandate, composed of national contingents having international status, financed primarily through voluntary contributions under the overall direction of the Secretary-General who in turn has to report and is accountable to the Security Council.

Legal Framework

As I have already remarked, the Security Council in its enabling resolution avoided reference to any particular provisions of the Charter, other than Article 2 (4) in the preamble. However, I am much afraid that this does not absolve me from the responsibility of at least touching upon this subject.[56]

It seems fairly clear that, in terms of Charter provisions, UNFICYP is a subsidiary organ of the Security Council within the meaning of Article 29.[57] In fact, the Security Council did not make a determination of the 'existence of any threat to the peace, breach of the peace or act of aggression' within Article 39 and it is beyond doubt that the operation does not amount to enforcement action within Articles 41 and 42 of Chapter VII. The wording used in the resolution ('situation likely to threaten international peace and security', the repeated use of the term 'recommends' rather than 'decides', the provision of 'mediation' machinery, and the express requirement of the 'consent of the Government of Cyprus')[58] distinctly to Chapter VI and more particularly to Articles 33, 36, 37, and 38.

What is less clear is the applicability of Article 40. The argument might be put forward (on the analogy of that of Mr. Schachter in his now celebrated

---

[56] On the role of the law in the context of peacekeeping operations see generally O. Schachter, 'The Uses of Law in International Peace-keeping', *Virginia Law Review*, vol. 50, no. 6 (1964).

[57] This is also the view set out in *Repertoire of the Practice of the Security Council*, Suppl. 1964–5, pp. 67 ff. Art. 29 reads: 'The Security Council may establish such subsidiary organs as it deems necessary for the performance of its functions.'

[58] See generally Bowett, *UN Forces*, p. 553; Higgins, *World Today*, vol. 20, no. 8 (1964) pp. 347–50; Papadopoulos, *Peace-making and Peace-keeping by the UN*, pp. 27–8.

article, under the name of E.M. Miller, on the Legal Aspects of the United Nations Action in the Congo)[59] that the wording 'call upon' all member-states in operative paragraph 1 of the resolution 'in conformity with their obligations under the Charter to refrain from any action', etc. may have been based on Article 40 and have constituted a 'provisional measure' within the meaning of that article.

Indeed, it might be said that operative paragraph 1, combined with the express reference in the preamble of the resolution to Article 2 (4), amounted to a call upon all member-states not to violate the express prohibition in Article 2 (4) against the use of force by one state against another, and, in practical terms, it could be interpreted as a call upon Turkey to refrain from taking forcible action against Cyprus. In any case, the invoking of Article 40 expressly does not prejudice the rights or position of the parties nor does it bring into play the enforcement provisions of Chapter VII; and consequently, it does not constitute an exception to Article 2 (7) of the Charter.[60]

In addition to the enabling resolution, three other legal documents had to be employed in order to complete the legal framework of the Force. The first was the Agreement on the Status of the Force,[61] concluded on 31 March 1964 by exchange of letters between the Secretary-General of the United Nations on the one hand and the Minister of Foreign Affairs of Cyprus on the other. It covered such diverse matters as respect for local law, jurisdiction, premises, uniforms, flags, arms, freedom of movement, use of roads, settlements of claims, etc. It followed closely the pattern of the equivalent ONUC and UNEF Agreements. The second was a model Participating State Agreement,[62] used, with appropriate variations, for each of the contributing states. The third was the Force Regulations.[63]

These problems had already been encountered and tackled in connection with the previous major peacekeeping operations and all they required was adaptation to the particular circumstances of UNFICYP.

Political Basis

Perhaps I should also say a few words about the political basis for the March 1964 resolution. Once it became commonly accepted (given the delicate balance of power between the opposing sides, both inside and outside Cyprus, the potential danger to international peace that would be created by a possible

---

59 55 *AJIL* (Jan. 1961).

60 See e.g. L.M. Goodrich and E. Hambro, Charter of the UN: Commentary and Documents (Boston, World Peace Federation, 1949), pp. 273–6.

61 492 UNTS 58–87: also S/563.4 (SCOR, 19th yr, Suppl. Jan.–March 1964).

62 E.g. Exchange of Letters between the UN and Sweden, 21 Feb. 1966, 555 UNTS 170–5.

63 ST/SGB/UNFICYP I, issued 25 Apr. 1964, 555 UNTS 132–49.

conflict between Greece and Turkey, both NATO members, as well as the threat to world peace generally, given the proximity of the Soviet Union and its stand in support of an independent Cyprus) that an international peacekeeping force would have to be sent to the island, the question left was what force and drawn from where.

What were the options? A 'tripartite' force – of the United Kingdom, Greece, and Turkey – was not practicable in the circumstances (apart from other considerations); a British force except as an immediate measure, was unpalatable to the Cypriots and would have been a heavy burden to the British; a NATO force was unacceptable to the Cyprus government (apart from other considerations). Consequently, a United Nations force was the obvious answer and one which the Cypriot side had preferred all along. Once the British and United States governments bowed to this necessity and the Secretary-General and his collaborators, with their usual dedication, appeared prepared to accept this additional burden; the problem remaining was primarily the constitutional-economic one which is familiar to those who know something of the previous peacekeeping operations – authorization, composition, command, financing. As we have seen above, all these were solved in a way reconciling doctrinal positions with practical political interests. Since the authorization was by the Security Council and the financing on a voluntary basis, the Soviet Union and France found it possible to accommodate their doctrinal position by simply abstaining on the operative paragraph dealing with the role of the Secretary-General. Neither wanted to demonstrate strongly any lack of confidence in U Thant, and the Russians in particular took into account – and said so publicly – the fact that the Cyprus government had indicated its willingness to receive the UN force. The alternative, possibly of a NATO force, may have been another factor in the Soviet Union's attitude, for by going along with the creation of UNFICYP, it retained a voice through its vote in the Council. Indeed, this is a case of 'when there is the will, there is the way'.

I now intend to touch very cursorily upon some of the aspects of the operation of UNFICYP.

Operation

As far as the military side is concerned, I have already alluded to the mandate and its application. By and large it has worked out well and it has been substantially assisted by the civilian police units which proved their value as, gradually and for most of the time, the situation has become one which calls less and less for a military approach. Ascertaining facts, reporting on incidents, calming down tense situations, calls for police methods and for diplomatic tact rather than military methods.

The civilian side of UNFICYP, which consists of the Secretary-General's Special Representative,[64] the Senior Legal and Political Adviser,[65] the UNFICYP Information Officer[66] and the Political Officer[67] and some financial, administrative and other officials, has done an excellent job in inspiring confidence and promoting the objectives of UNFICYP towards a return to normality and also in such diverse ways as offering their good offices, operating the Political Liaison Committee, and carrying out a variety of activities for a return to normal conditions with tact and impartiality. They deserve a great deal of credit for the success of the operation as also those high officials in the Secretariat[68] dealing with the operation for proving their dedication to the ideals of the Organization by their impartiality, competence, integrity, and sheer hard work in often critical and dramatic circumstances.

It would clearly be going beyond the scope of the present paper to examine in any detail the practical workings of UNFICYP. There have been surprisingly few major causes of friction or embarrassment. The latter did occur, only once but in a glaring way, when two UNFICYP Swedish armoured cars, commanded by officers, were apprehended and forcibly stopped by the Cyprus National Guard in *flagrante delicto* – smuggling large quantities of arms to the Turkish Cypriots. There were a few red faces in Stockholm and in New York and the two officers were tried (as provided for in the relevant regulations) by their national courts and sentenced to cashiering and imprisonment. Such incidents, however, perhaps unavoidable in the circumstances of Cyprus, have been rare and there have been no others of this magnitude, and such as have occurred are certainly not attributable to laxity on the part of UNFICYP authorities.

Another area in which there was some dispute, especially in the summer of 1964, related to the question of freedom of movement of UNFICYP as set out in Article 32 of the Status of the Force Agreement. As interpreted by the government, this meant what it said, viz. free and unimpeded movement along the roads of the Republic, not the right to go into buildings or customs-houses or docks and to inspect what was being loaded or unloaded. After some exchange of correspondence, the matter was amicably settled in a practical – as distinct from a strictly legal – way, by UNFICYP's agreeing

64 Originally Mr. Galo Plaza of Ecuador (who in 1968 became Secretary-General of the OAS), later Mr. C. Bernardes of Brazil, and then Mr. B. Osorio–Taffal of Mexico.

65 A post admirably filled by a meticulously impartial and cautious Swiss, Dr. R. Gorge.

66 Mr. C. Ortiz and subsequently Mr. L. Moreno, both Mexican, who left behind them the best possible impressions.

67 Up till now a post filled by a national of an Eastern European state.

68 Besides the Secretary-General U Thant, these are Under-Secretary-Generals R. Bunche, J. Rolz-Bennett and (as Legal Counsel) C. Stavropoulos, Mr. B. Urquhart, Mr. G. Sherry, Mr. F.T. Liu, and, I am sure, others.

to respect certain sensitive 'restricted areas' (camps, fortifications, etc. of the National Guard), which only the Commander of UNFICYP might visit after consultation with the Commander of the National Guard.[69]

Another difference of interpretation of a legal provision occurred with regard to Article 19 of the Status of the Force Agreement, dealing with the financial obligations of the government in respect of UNFICYP. This, again, was settled amicably in a non-legalistic way by the government's making an ex gratia payment and UNFICYP's writing-off a part of what is claimed was owed to it.

The same approach was followed with regard to claims for compensation by private individuals against UNFICYP. Instead of setting up the cumbersome machinery of the claims commission as in Article 38 of the Status of the Force Agreement such claim settled by a claims officer of UNFICYP in an equitable and expedient way.

Assessment of UNFICYP

To sum up, UNFICYP furnishes an excellent illustration of successful and effective United Nations peacekeeping operation with a proper role of insulating a crisis and filling a power vacuum when processes of peacemaking are under way with the ultimate goal of making its presence no longer necessary. In the case of Cyprus political, constitutional, and financial obstacles were overcome and the necessary conditions were present for the setting up and successful operation of a United Nations peacekeeping operation.[70]

General Conclusions in the Light of Recent Developments

From this often superficial examination what general conclusions can we draw and what are the prospects and the pointers for the future?

As U Thant said in his address to the Joint Meeting of both – of the Canadian Parliament on 26 May 1964,[71] the Organisation is facing a basic dilemma as regards its role in the problem of peacekeeping. On the one hand governments and peoples by and large accept the need for the United Nations

---

[69] S/6102 (SCOR, 19th yr, Suppl. Oct.–Dec. 1964).

[70] Hopefully we can see the light of a peaceful solution at the end of the tunnel. What exact form this solution will take can only be the object of speculation, but it is relevant to mention the suggestion by Mr. Stephens (*Cyprus: a Place of Arms*, pp. 216–18) to the effect that British bases in Cyprus, or at least that of Dhekeleia (which, by most accounts, is redundant), be used for UN forces: that would both assure a tangible UN presence in the island and help to develop the peacekeeping capacity of the UN for future operations elsewhere.

[71] Press release SG/SM/76.

and its central role as keeper of the peace. The Organization is entrusted, especially in times of crisis, with great problems of incalculable importance. On the other hand, the stage has not yet been reached where the necessary material and political support is forthcoming, as a matter of course, to enable the United Nations to meet these problems with the adequacy with which an effective national government accepts similar responsibilities on the national level. This results in considerable strain upon the Organization and exposes it on occasion to serious criticism and hostility. The political, economic, constitutional and even psychological conditions cannot be changed overnight, but they can only be changed gradually as a result of a conscious effort by all to put to good use the lessons of the past and with a view to strengthening the Organization and making it better equipped effectively to meet the challenge in the future.

Barring for the foreseeable future the ideal solution of peacekeeping United Nations forces, there are still several marginal steps to be taken to this end within the framework of existing political and constitutional realities.

By far the most significant of these is the practice of earmarking stand-by national contingents by individual governments for future use by the United Nations as and when required. Even though the original proposal can be traced to the Uniting for Peace resolution, in 1950,[72] it has in fact developed on a different basis, especially since 1963, and today the United Nations can count on substantial forces in this respect.

Canada[73] deserves a good deal of credit for taking practical steps in this direction as early as 1957, and it was followed closely by Sweden,[74] Norway,[75] Denmark,[76] Finland,[77] the Netherlands,[78] and Austria.[79] Iran has made an offer to earmark forces, and others may do likewise. The United Kingdom[80] offered formally to provide, subject to certain conditions, logistical support of a substantial nature. Several other countries are regular contributors to United Nations operations, for example India, Yugoslavia, Brazil, Ireland,

72 Res. 377 A (V), para. C.8.
73 See e.g. Lester Pearson's Dag Hammarskjöld Memorial Lecture 'Keeping the Peace', given at Carleton Univ., Ottawa, 7 May 1964, printed in A.W. Cordier and W. Foote, eds, *The Quest for Peace* (New York, Columbia UP, 1965): and P. Martin's Jacob Blaustein Lecture 'Canada's Role in Supporting UN Peacekeeping Efforts', given at Columbia Univ., 26 Apr. 1967, printed in his *Canada and the Quest for Peace* (New York, Columbia UP, 19671; see also A/AC. 121/17, 19 June 1968.
74 See A/AC. 21/11, 20 March 1968.
75 See A/AC. 21/14, 28 March 1968.
76 See A/AC. 21/12, 29 March 1968.
77 See A/AC. 21/13, 29 March 1968.
78 See A/AC. 21/18, 26 June 1968.
79 See A/AC. 21/19, 9 July 1968.
80 See A/AC. 21/16, 29 May 1968.

Ethiopia – even though, for a variety of reasons, they have not taken the formal step of earmarking. The United States has been a major contributor of logistical support.[81] The various aspects of administration, logistics, training, operational techniques, composition, recruitment, standardization of weapons, equality of pay, etc. involved have been the object of extensive consultation between governments and interested individuals[82] even though the United Nations as such could participate only through an observer (in fact General Rikhye, the Secretary-General's Military Adviser), it being precluded by political considerations from appearing as directly involved. But the Secretary-General has referred with obvious approval e.g. to Mr. Pearson's constructive suggestions for the further development and co-ordination of such stand-by forces and expressed the belief that consultation and cooperation among interested governments can be of much value in contributing to the improvement of the peacekeeping effectiveness of the United Nations.[83]

Earmarking, while not involving the obligation of automatically acceding to a potential request by the Secretary-General,[84] enables the Secretary-General to know in advance what he can rely on. It also has the merit of permitting some advance planning of how to mesh these potentially available forces into one force and facilitates the provision of likely equipment (communications, etc.), the creation of uniform operating procedures and so on.[85] It has likewise had the beneficial effect of making possible the use of United Nations indoctrination material in national military training. All in all, it has constituted an encouraging and significant step in the right direction.

Other such steps that have been suggested are the creation of field manuals and standard operating procedures and the strengthening of the staff of the senior Secretariat officials dealing with peacekeeping.

The former has already been done and it is doubtful whether the latter represents an urgent need in present circumstances. Although these officials can be counted on the fingers of one or, at the most, two hands, they have never the less shown an admirable capacity to respond to challenges in time of pressure; and when multiple crises do not occur simultaneously, they are

[81] See A/AC. 21/15, 21 May 1968.

[82] See generally, P. Frydenberg, *Peace-keeping: Experience and Evaluation* (Oslo, Norwegian Inst. of Int. Affairs, 1964); World Veterans Federation, *The Functioning of Ad Hoc UN Emergency Forces* (Paris, 1963); I.J. Rikhye, UN *Peace-keeping Operations – Higher Conduct* (Paris, Int. Inf. Center on Peace-keeping Operations, 1967); A.J. Wilson, *Some Principles for Peace-keeping Operations – a Guide for Senior Officers* (Paris, Int. Inf. Center on Peace-keeping Operations, 1967); B. Egge, 'The Ottawa Conference on UN Peace-keeping Forces', *Disarmament.* (Paris), Dec. 1965, pp. 210–26.

[83] E.g. SG/SM/76, p. 9.

[84] E.g. see P. Haekkerup, 'Scandinavia's Peace-keeping Forces for UN', *For. Aff,* July 1964, pp. 675–82.

[85] E.g. see the UK paper (A/AC. 121/16, 29 May 1968) for specific suggestions to that end.

adequate to cover the field, even though no one can accuse them of being underworked at any time.

An important factor in the same direction is the creation of conditions whereby East European forces could be employed, in the same way as forces from Western countries, under United Nations command to participate in peacekeeping operations. If this proves feasible it might well be the turning point in the direction of creating confidence among that important section of United Nations membership. For instance, if it proved possible for the UNFICYP Commander to rely upon his deputy who was a British officer why should not, in appropriate circumstances, a commander of a future UN force rely, say, upon a Czech or a Pole as his second-in-command? I have already referred to the creditable participation in UNFICYP of East European Secretariat officials. Indeed, Yugoslavia has participated with distinction in past peacekeeping operations. At present the East European attitude on the surface remains one of strict adherence to the original Charter scheme and is reflected in the Soviet Union's memoranda of 10 July 1964 and 16 March 1967,[86] as well as such documents as the letter of the Permanent Representative of Czechoslovakia addressed to the President of the Security Council offering to conclude an agreement in accordance with the forms of Article 43 for action under Chapter VII of the Charter.[87] However, there are indications that, assuming Security Council authorization of the operation, this attitude might well prove more flexible in specific cases where political considerations so dictated.

There might be the possibility, which should be seriously borne in mind, that – especially if the next few years witness a significant degree of rapprochement between the two super-powers – two other measures might be taken which, though falling short of the scheme envisaged by the Charter, would nevertheless constitute gestures in that direction. The one is to make agreements under Article 43 (i.e. between individual states and the Security Council) not for enforcement action – such would be unrealistic, as we have seen – but for peacekeeping by consent. The other is to utilize the Military Staff Committee, perhaps with an enlarged membership, for purposes of the planning, co-ordination, etc. of peacekeeping operations. This in turn might open the door to other possibilities, but, in the long term, it all depends on political developments.

---

[86] A/5721 (*GAOR*, 19th seas., Annex no. 21) and A/6641, which has also been issued under S/7841 (*SCOR*, 22nd yr, Suppl. Apr.–June 1967). See also N.A. Pitersky, 'On the Establishment of International UN Forces', Disarmament (Paris) March 1965, pp. 5–8.

[87] S/7852 (SCOR, 2nd yr, Suppl. Apr.–June 1967), 13 Apr. 1967, reflecting the earlier offer of 26 Nov. 1964 (S/6070, mimeo.).

Another suggestion which is frequently put forward is the strengthening of the office of the Military Adviser of the Secretary-General. While different views may be taken regarding the advisability of such a step, the fact is that the Secretary-General dispensed with the office altogether (after the retirement of General Rikhye) although undoubtedly, he could, whenever the need arises draw upon the available talent. Such functions as require military advice are being performed in the Secretary-General's office by Colonel Koho, whose title is that of military liaison officer.

It is sometimes suggested that the United Nations should also engage upon advance contingency planning for possible future peace-keeping operations in different parts of the world. However harmless and innocuous this may appear on the surface, I am not convinced that the existing political climate can bear such an activity; in fact, a premature leak of such action taken by the Secretariat, apart from raising a political storm, might well ruin in advance the likelihood of any particular peacekeeping operation materializing in the future. However, these considerations would not preclude the Secretary-General's office from being apprized, through the various offices of the United Nations around the globe and otherwise, of such developments on the international scene and such straws in the wind as might be relevant and significant in this context, but the utmost discretion and tact would be essential.

What then is a realistic assessment of the operations by reference to the present position, and the foreseeable outlook for peacekeeping operations by the United Nations?

These operations are a hopeful and significant factor in the effort to keep the peace in various parts of the world, particularly in areas where the process of decolonization or other circumstances have left a power vacuum. Subject to what has already been said as to the direction in which institutional improvement should be aimed and to the continuing effort at educating world public opinion,[88] which is perhaps the most significant area of potential improvement, the margin for more to be done at present is necessarily narrow. It is clear that, ultimately, all suggestions will be considered to have merit only to the extent that they reflect a realistic assessment of what states – and especially the great powers – are at a given time prepared to accept.

The main effort should be to exploit the ad hoc approach to the limit of the available political consensus in each case, particularly in so far as the vital interests of the super-powers are concerned, so as not to risk ruining the Organization by stretching things too far and being conscious of the fact

[88] E.g. the apparent slowness on the part of Third World countries to participate more actively in the ear-marking process, for example, is due largely to a lack of wide awareness of the problems involved in addition to their financial and technical limitations.

that for better or worse the Organization is based on the sovereign equality of all its members (Article 2 (I)). The know-how, military and administrative, exists and the legal wrappings can easily be adapted from existing precedents.

The direction in which things have been going recently, points steadily to accepting that in practice future peacekeeping operations, as a rule, will be authorized by the Security Council, that executive responsibility will rest with the Secretary-General, subject to stricter or looser control by the Council, and that they will be financed on a consensual basis (whether by the interested parties or through voluntary contributions or a combination of arrangements). This is not as pessimistic an outlook as it might appear at first sight and in fact the experience of the past few years leaves some room for optimism. This may fall far short of the dreams and expectations of those wedded to the idea of the United Nations as a form of world government, but it goes a good deal beyond the image of the United Nations as an impotent debating society or a static conference machinery. Politics, after all, is the art of the possible, and, short of the collective security system envisaged in 1945 or of a permanent United Nations peacekeeping force – both of which are at present unattainable – the picture suggested by the present peacekeeping potential of the United Nations is by no means bleak. In a troubled world beset by conflict and the far too frequent use of armed force, United Nations peacekeeping, even within these limits, presents an acceptable alternative and is likely to lead to a more peaceful world.

It would clearly go beyond the scope of this paper to talk of the necessary corollary of peacekeeping which is peacemaking. But, as the experience of Cyprus[89] as well as of so many other situations has demonstrated, it is only

[89] The case of Cyprus furnishes a remarkable illustration of the variety of methods for peaceful settlement employed in the effort to find a solution: the attempt to forestall the explosion through the offer to negotiate on the local level through the 'thirteen points' proposals of 30 Nov. 1963; the effort to negotiate on the quasi-regional level provided by the London Conference in Jan. 1964; the reference to the Security Council and acceptance of UN mediation in March 1964; the initiative of Mr. Acheson acting under the umbrella of, but in fact substituting, the first UN mediator, Mr. Tuomioja, to secure an agreement between Greece and Turkey in Geneva in the summer of 1964; there followed the renewed UN mediation effort under Dr. Plaza resulting in his report of March 1965; subsequently the General Assembly, called upon to pronounce on the merits of the case, passed the resolution of 18 Dec. 1965; there followed in the spring of 1966 the enlargement of the functions of the Special Representative of the Secretary-General in Cyprus, Mr. Bernardes, to include quasi-mediational functions; the next step was the initiating of the secret 'dialogue' between Athens and Ankara which ended abruptly in failure in Sept. 1967; after the crisis of Nov.–Dec. 1967, the Security Council urged that the parties avail themselves of the good offices of the Secretary-General which they did early in 1968. The effort is carried out in Cyprus itself through the 'local talks' to be followed, if they succeed, by a wider round in which the three outside signatories of the 1959–60 accords would also participate. It thus appears that, short of arbitration and judicial settlement, the full range of possibilities has been used in

when the one is supplemented by the other that the circle is completed, a solution to problems is reached, and the United Nations has, *pro tanto*, discharged its responsibilities and fulfilled, even to that modest limited extent, the expectations of the majority of mankind as an instrument of peace in the world.

---

the effort to find a solution, with special reliance upon the possibilities available through the UN and more particularly the Secretary-General's office. On these, see the views expressed by the Representative of Cyprus, GAOR, 18th sess., 6th Cttee, 824th mtg, pp. 246–8, and Jacovides, *Treaties Conflicting with Peremptory Norms of international Law and the Zurich-London 'Agreements'*, pp. 24–7.

The Cyprus Problem and United Nations Peace-Keeping

Lecture at Harvard University, 15 December 1988

I am pleased and honoured to have this opportunity to address a knowledgeable and concerned audience such as you on "The Cyprus Problem and U.N. Peace-Keeping". I appreciate the presence of all of you here this afternoon. It is a special pleasure for a cryptoacademic like myself to be back in this great place of learning and I recall with some nostalgia the year I spent, nearly three decades ago, as a Henry Fellow at the Harvard Law School's International Legal Studies programme.

The all-embracing concern for us in Cyprus over the past several decades has been the Cyprus problem. It has gone through many phases over the years, from the pre-independence anti-colonial struggle for self-determination in the nineteen fifties, to its present grave dimensions of foreign invasion, occupation and massive violation of human rights since the Turkish invasion of 1974. Currently we are engaged, with constructive good will and determination, in high level inter-communal talks, under the auspices and in pursuance of the good offices of the United Nations Secretary-General, in an effort to reach an overall agreement within a target frame, June 1989.

What I propose to do is to give you an overview of the historical background of the Cyprus Problem and its present dimensions; touch on some other aspects of our present situation and policies; deal briefly with United Nations peace-keeping in relation to Cyprus; update you on current developments and prospects; and try to cover the rest of the topic in response to your questions.

Let me remind you that Cyprus, an island in the Eastern Mediterranean with a land area of 3,572 square miles and a population of 685,000 (of whom 80 per cent are Greek Cypriots, 18 per cent Turkish Cypriots, and the remainder small other minorities of Maronites, Armenians, and Latins), became independent on 16 August 1960, after 82 years of British colonial rule.

During our long, proud and turbulent history, stretching back to 6,000 B.C. – as part of the Hellenic world of antiquity, referred to in Homer as the birthplace of Aphrodite, the goddess of love and beauty – conquerors came and went, leaving behind some traces and monuments to mark their passing and adding to our already rich cultural heritage, but never altering the basic ethnological character or the unity of the island.

The Turkish Cypriots arrived after Cyprus became, as was the case with all other countries in the region, part of the Ottoman Empire, following its conquest from the Venetians in 1571. They were interspersed throughout the island, living peacefully side by side with the majority Greek Cypriot community. With independence achieved in 1960, within the framework of the Nicosia Treaties (the Treaties of Establishment, Guarantee and Alliance), the Republic of Cyprus became an equal member of the United Nations, of the Commonwealth and of the Council of Europe and also joined several other international organisations.

At the end of 1963, internal constitutional difficulties arose and, following a proposal to amend some of the provisions of the 1960 Constitution and threats and acts of intervention by Turkey, the Cyprus Government applied to the U.N. Security Council seeking protection under the fundamental principle in article 2 (4) of the Charter which prohibits the threat or use of armed force by one State against another.

By March 1964, a U.N. peace-keeping force was dispatched, with the consent of the Cyprus Government, and a U.N. mediator was appointed to deal with the dispute which arose. The mediator (whom some of you may remember since he served as Ambassador to the United States and O.A.S. Secretary-General), Dr. Galo Plaza, former President of Ecuador, presented a judicious and balanced report in 1965. His recommendations were accepted by the Government of Cyprus but were rejected by Turkey. These included the maintenance of an independent unitary state, with appropriate guarantees for the human rights of the minorities and he described the compulsory shifting of populations as "a desperate step in the wrong direction".

Time does not allow to go into details regarding the development of events prior to the 1974 invasion even though some of these events, such as the 1964 Johnson letter to Prime Minister Inonou and the Cyrus Vance Mission, would be of particular interest to you.

Suffice it to say that since the 1974 invasion, which was carried out through the use of American-supplied arms in violation of American laws and bilateral U.S.-Turkish agreements, Turkey has illegally maintained its occupation over nearly 40 per cent of the territory of Cyprus which contained some 70 per cent of the economic resources of the island. Through the forcible expulsion of two hundred thousand Greek Cypriots and the implantation into their homes and lands of Turkish Cypriots and of tens of thousands of colonizers from Anatolia (the figure of some 65,000 is our current estimate), Turkey has attempted to alter the age long demography of the island and to impose by force its own arbitrary prescription for a solution.

All Greek Cypriot vestiges are being systematically obliterated, including the turning of ancient churches into mosques and destroying or selling illegally in the black market icons and other priceless antiquities. The Turkish lira has been introduced as legal tender. And, through the presence of some 35,000 Turkish troops, with recently increased fire-power and modernised heavy weapons and through supervisory administration arrangements in the Turkish Prime Minister's office, Turkey has for most practical purposes turned the occupied areas of Cyprus into a Turkish colony under Ankara's effective control, contrary to the true interests of the Turkish Cypriots themselves.

Turkey's illegal actions and atrocities in Cyprus have received universal condemnation from the United Nations Security Council and General Assembly, the Council of Europe, the Commonwealth, and virtually all other international forums.

The U.N. Security Council, through mandatory resolutions, has repeatedly called for the withdrawal of all foreign troops from Cyprus, the voluntary return of the refugees to their homes, for the cessation of all interference in the internal affairs of Cyprus, and respect for its sovereignty, independence, territorial integrity and non-aligned status.

Turkey has chosen to ignore the decisions of the international community and has done so with impunity. This is a sad commentary on the state of international legal order in the world.

The Cyprus Government, although it had every right to refuse to enter into any negotiations until the Turkish occupation troops left Cyprus, nonetheless showed its goodwill and genuine wish for a solution by entering into negotiations with the other side under the auspices of the United Nations Secretary-General. These negotiations on the internal aspect of the Cyprus problem, i.e, the territorial and constitutional questions, were between the Greek and Turkish Cypriot Communities but, in effect because of the dominant role of Turkey over the Turkish Cypriots, the interlocutors were the Cyprus Government on the one hand and the Ankara Government on the other. Because of the oppressive presence of the Turkish troops of occupation they never were, as they were stipulated under the U.N. resolutions, "free" negotiations.

These negotiations went on and off since 1975 but until now yielded no substantive results, even though a basis has existed under the United Nations resolutions and the 1977 and 1979 high level agreements.

The Cyprus Government and the Greek Cypriot side bent over backwards and made a number of significant concessions in the hope that the Turkish side would respond with reasonable proposals for a solution. Regrettably, what the record shows is that the Turkish objective was all along the legitimisation of the results of the 1974 invasion and occupation.

Let me illustrate the extent of these concessions.

The Cyprus Government and the Greek Cypriot side accepted a federal solution to the problem when no geographical basis for it existed in Cyprus prior to 1974; they have presented the other side with a map (in 1977) which delineates a land area in Cyprus (larger than the Turkish Cypriots' 18% of the population) to be under Turkish Cypriot control in a federal administration; they have also accepted that such sensitive issues as internal security and protection of human rights be under international supervision and control for as long as necessary; and they proposed the total demilitarisation of the Republic of Cyprus to alleviate any real or imaginary fears of Turkish Cypriot security, (a proposal recently brought to the foreground, a subject to which I shall revert later).

Basically, what we have asked for is the establishment of a viable and genuine federation based on democratic principles, as in the case in all other federal states (such as the United States but also Canada, Switzerland, Yugoslavia) and with special provision (of "affirmative action") to meet the particular circumstance of Cyprus.

The demand from the other side has been all along the establishment of, in effect, two separate states with separate armies, separate treaty-making capacity, separate economies. In short, while paying lip service to a federal system, the Turkish objective was a partitionist solution through the legitimisation of the results of the internationally condemned invasion. While appearing to negotiate, they were systematically consolidating their position in the occupied areas in preparation for partition.

Hence, the resulting deadlock, which the U.N. Secretary-General was attempting to-break through the exercise of his good offices, as mandated under the Security Council's resolutions. In the summer of 1983, Secretary-General Perez de Cuellar tried his personal initiative on the basis of "soundings" presented to the two sides in an attempt to narrow the existing wide gap. This was derailed when Mr. Denktash sprang his so-called "declaration of independence" on an outraged world. This attempted secession, which could not have taken place without Ankara's knowledge and approval as confirmed by subsequent information and the fact that there was immediate recognition of the pseudo-state by Turkey, drew immediate condemnation from the international community which demanded its reversal.

This attempt to dismember Cyprus was in flagrant violation of the U.N. Charter, of international law and, more specifically, of the 1960 Nicosia Treaties which guarantee that the territory of the Republic of Cyprus shall remain "one and indivisible", expressly exclude "separatist independence" and prohibit "any activity aimed at promoting, directly or indirectly... partition". By promptly recognising the newly declared pseudo-state (the only country in the world to do so), Turkey violated its treaty obligations and confirmed its long-standing partitionist designs over Cyprus.

This flagrant act of illegality has been denounced by most states in the world, including the other two signatories of the 1960 Treaties, Greece and Great Britain. In the United States, the Administration at the highest level and the two Houses of Congress deplored and condemned it and called for its non-recognition and reversal. The Security Council of the United Nations, in its Resolution 541 and subsequently Resolution 550, similarly deplored this "legally invalid" act, called for its non-recognition and reversal and renewed the call for the Secretary-General's exercise of good offices towards a just and lasting solution. Similar decisions were made by the Council of Europe, the European Community as well as the Commonwealth Conference.

The complete isolation of Turkey in its recognition of its illegitimate offspring, which was born in aggression and occupation, is an encouraging sign. Our declared policy has been not to be anything which, directly or indirectly, would amount to recognising the legally invalid pseudo-state and our determination is to pursue all available peaceful means to ensure compliance of Turkey with the Security Council resolutions and the dictates of the international community.

While we count on the support of all fair-minded people and of all Governments which value international legal order, we have looked particularly for support from the United States as a superpower, as the leader of the West and as the country which is in a unique position to assist towards a just and lasting solution to the Cyprus problem.

The United States voted in the United Nations in favour of the key resolutions demanding the withdrawal of the Turkish forces of occupation and the return of the refugees to their homes in safety. The United States is a member of NATO and as such has a particular reason to see the rift between two other members – Turkey and Greece – healed so as to enhance the solidarity of the NATO Alliance. The United States is a major source of foreign military and economic aid to Turkey and therefore is in a position of carrying much weight with the recipient of such aid. The U.S. has declared its dedication to, the application of human rights and of the principles of international law in all parts of the world. Therefore, we feel that the role of the U.S. can be very considerable in bringing the weight of its diplomacy to bear towards a just and lasting solution of the Cyprus problem.

The U.S. has repeatedly stated that there is no question of recognition of the pseudo-state and has also made representations in all capitals and especially of Islamic countries, for its non-recognition by others (most recently, in the context of the Amman Islamic Conference earlier his year). As regards the more general problem, the U.S. has assured us that it strongly supports the good offices effort of the U.N. Secretary-General. The Administration has followed with close interest the efforts of the Secretary-General and supported them in their various stages (including dispatching a letter by President Reagan to President Evren in November 1984). In Congress, both the Senate and the House, there exists much sympathy and support for our position and this has been manifested in a variety of ways (increasing humanitarian aid to Cyprus, cutting down drastically aid to Turkey, imposing conditions on military aid to Turkey and in particular prohibiting U.S. supplied material from being used in the occupation of Cyprus etc.). This was done again this year through the Foreign Aid Bill.

These are positive steps in so far as they go. But we strongly feel that more can and should be done in influencing Ankara to withdraw its troops and to moderate its position and, in turn, influence the Turkish Cypriot leadership in the right direction. Eleven years ago, Lawrence Stern in his book "The Wrong Horse", described how the United States under the direction of the then Secretary of State, through a series of missteps and misguided tiltings in the 1974 crisis and subsequently, antagonised all three countries involved in the Cyprus-Greece-Turkey triangle. The opportunity now exists where, through principled, enlightened and effective diplomacy, the United States can help undo some of the damage and secure the friendship and appreciation of all three countries involved since a fair and lasting solution, on the lines which I indicated, is indisputably to the benefit of all concerned, including Turkey and the United States itself.

Let me stress, as President Vassiliou has recently done, that we cannot accept the permanent military presence of the Turkish Army in Cyprus. There are several other ways to deal with the real or imaginary "security concerns" of Turkey and of the Turkish Cypriots. Following earlier suggestions on the same lines since 1964, during the U.N. Special session on disarmament in 1978 we proposed the total demilitarisation of the Republic of Cyprus (not including, for the present, the Sovereign Base Areas). Mr. Denktash is on record as having agreed in principle to the demilitarisation of Cyprus (in point 7 of the 1979 high level agreement). Demilitarisation was an element in the 1978 U.S.-British-Canadian plan and also in the two subsequent General Assembly Resolutions.

Demilitarisation can meet the security concerns of all Cypriots and, if accepted by Turkey, can be the catalyst for everything else to fit into place.

"*Turkey wants to be the master in the North and partner in the South*" is the epigrammatic phrase of Lord Caradon, the last British Governor of Cyprus, which aptly describes the situation we have been faced with. We do not know whether Ankara and Mr. Denktash have had a change of heart. But, on the basis of bitter experience and present indications, we may be forgiven for suppressing any tendency to excessive optimism.

The situation can be summed up as follows:

The Government of Cyprus and the Greek Cypriot side, which have made serious concessions in their effort to bring about an honourable compromise based on genuine federation, support the efforts of the Secretary-General and want to co-operate with him towards such a solution. The basic elements for such a viable solution, are the termination of the occupation and the withdrawal of the Turkish troops from Cyprus, the safeguarding and implementation of the three fundamental freedoms – freedom of movement, freedom of settlement, and the right to property – and generally of all internationally recognised human rights, as well as effective international guarantees for such settlement. The Anatolian settlers will have to leave, as the majority of the Turkish Cypriots also want.

A just and lasting solution along these lines would be to the benefit of all parties concerned; for peace and stability in the volatile Eastern Mediterranean region; and, in the long term, to the benefit of Turkey itself.

There is much more that unites all Cypriots than the differences that at present divide them. Unlike other international problems in the region, the framework for a solution exists and a negotiating channel is provided for through the UN Secretary-General. What is required for progress to be made is for a drastic change in the Turkish policy away from divisiveness and partitionism. This is not an easy undertaking. But there is ample room for principled and effective diplomacy so that Turkey and the Turkish Cypriot leadership be persuaded and, if need be, be pressured to act in accordance with the dictates of the international community and of international law.

What Cyprus is striving for is justice and fairness and for the application of the rules of international law which are applicable everywhere else in the world.

Beside the political problem, which is our overriding and all embracing concern, there are other aspects of the Cyprus situation which would be of interest to you. There is room not only for frustration and disappointment but also for much pride and satisfaction in what this young and small state, despite all the setbacks, has managed through the native skills, resilience and energies of its people to achieve.

Certainly, the most impressive of those achievements, and the most important in human terms, was the success of the Cyprus Government in meeting the desperate human, social and economic needs of the huge population of 200,000 refugees driven from their homes and deprived of their worldly goods in 1974.

It was a gigantic effort which owed its success on a skilled and intensive organisational feat in the areas of humanitarian aid and crash programs in housing and social services. This was certainly facilitated through hundreds of millions of dollars in humanitarian aid provided through the United States Congress and through such major financial institutions such as the World Bank. But no effort, however skillful and determined, could have succeeded except in the context of an expanding economy capable of absorbing the sudden influx of refugees numbering more than one-third of the Greek Cypriot population, especially considering that 70% of the economic resources of the island came tinder the control of the Attila invader. "Attila" incidentally, was the code name given by the Turkish military to the 1974 invasion.

Of course, as in all countries, we have problems and areas of concern, in fact, we are more vulnerable than most and certainly the need for refugee aid continues. I will not bore you with statistics. The fact is, however, that in the past twenty eight years, the economy of Cyprus has been transformed from that of a colonial backwater, with low per capita income and high emigration, to a bustling, vibrant free market economy with results for everyone to see. Now, 14 years after the invasion per capita income is at a very satisfactory-level, inflation is low, unemployment is negligible, foreign exchange reserves are healthy and our standard of living and quality of life compare favourably with that of most third world and even several developed countries. Tourism is booming with over 1 million visitors last year (despite the loss, temporary we hope, of the best known resorts such as Kyrenia and Famagusta) and a substantial number of offshore companies are currently based in Cyprus and doing business elsewhere in the region. Cypriot businessmen and entrepreneurs have expanded their range of operations to many neighbouring countries; not only do they build bridges, as well as airports and roads – and whole towns in these countries; they also project the good name of Cyprus, build bridges of friendship between us and the respective peoples of these countries, and earn hundreds of million of dollars in foreign exchange.

Our creditworthiness and integrity are well established with the World Bank and other international financial institutions and we have earned a reputation for putting development loans to good use for the betterment of the conditions of living of the people and the economic development of the country.

The level of education, health care, social services, agricultural production are at record highs. Since independence, more water irrigation dams, more schools, more roads and more hospitals have been built than at any other time in our long history.

I said earlier that I would not get into statistics. But you would be interested to know, for example, that Cyprus is one of the top countries in the world in the ratio of university graduates to population; that we are the third country in the world in telecommunication facilities (next to the United States and Sweden); and that we are the seventh country in the world as a maritime nation.

We have a flourishing cultural life and we are, of course, intensely proud of our long history, culture and tradition; some even claim that the Cypriot dialect of today is the most closely linked in vocabulary and syntax to Homeric Greek.

At the same time, we have benefited from the British tradition of a sound civil service, independent judiciary and freedom of speech and of the press.

Overall, we enjoy a democratic system of government, a free enterprise economic system and have an outstanding record in the observance of international standards of human rights.

Yes, indeed, there is a silver lining in the heavy clouds above us. On occasions for stocktaking, while not forgetting our problems and the need to struggle to overcome them, we should also count our blessings for the sake of balance and objectivity.

These encouraging achievements, made in circumstances of the continued dismemberment of the island and constant anxiety over its political future, have been reflected in the respect and esteem which Cyprus has attracted throughout the world. Respect and esteem which may not yet have been translated into effective international action to help resolve its national problem, but which has certainly given Cyprus a standing of influence in the community of nations out of all proportion to its size and resources. For example, in September this year, Cyprus hosted two major conferences, that of the Non-Aligned Movement's Foreign Ministers and that of the Finance Ministers of the Commonwealth.

In its turn, the Government of Cyprus has consistently attempted to employ that influence and good repute in the best interests of peace and to promote humanitarian concerns.

A small state with a huge national problem on its hands, Cyprus must inevitably cultivate an independent stance on the international stage, pursuing relations of co-operation and friendship with all countries and avoiding identification with the conflicting interests of the super-powers. That has not meant, however, that Cyprus has needed to conceal its dedication to the same democratic ideals which inspire this country and which indeed are the foundation of our own free democratic system.

Our affinity and friendship with the United States, and our concern to contribute what small assistance we can to the cause of humanitarianism and peace was demonstrated during the recent years of upheaval and terrorism in Lebanon, years during which we have often and willingly provided logistical and humanitarian help to United States civilians and servicemen and though close co-operation in combating terrorism and drug trafficking and in other ways. These gestures have been appreciated at the highest level of the United States Government. President Reagan and Secretary of State Shultz repeatedly referred to the "excellent relations" between the U.S. and Cyprus on the bilateral level – a fact which is particularly gratifying to me as the Ambassador of Cyprus to this great country in the past nine years – and, last August, we witnessed a highly successful visit by President Vassiliou to Washington. The expression of friendship has also been manifested by the attitude of our numerous friends in the U.S. Congress, both in real terms of economic aid for the refugees and in terms of other expressions of sympathy, concern and support.

Let me now turn to U.N. peace-keeping in relation to Cyprus. I come from a country which, from the beginning of its existence as an independent state, has always attached cardinal importance to its membership of the United Nations, has been dedicated by word and deed to the Charter and its principles and has proved by the position it has taken on the variety of issues on which it has had to take a stand, at the U.N. itself or in Conferences such as of the Non-Aligned and the Commonwealth, that it is what one might call "United Nations-minded". Cyprus found it possible to make the United Nations and the principles of its Charter central to its foreign policy, particularly during the years 1960 to 1963 when it did not labour under the strains of apolitical problem of its own. It so happened, that this attitude, determined by its commitment to principle, also coincided with the country's self-interest as a small non-aligned and militarily weak state depending for its security on the collective security system of the United Nations, an attitude shared by other small states in analogous situations.

It was therefore logical and natural that when, at the end of 1963, Cyprus found itself threatened by an incomparatively larger and militarily stronger state. Turkey, it would turn to the United Nations – in preference to other international organisations or alliances – for protection. It was a dramatic and significant experience to have lived through the Security Council debates and backstage negotiating which resulted in the creation of UNFICYP, with the full consent of the Cyprus Government, in March 1964.

Much has been said and even more written regarding the political and legal factors involved in this recourse. The background for UNFICYP's creation, its setting-up, composition, size, direction and control its mandate; its duration and financing; its legal framework; its political basis; and its operation. Back in 1969, I myself wrote a lengthy paper on these and other aspects for an American Society of International Law symposium entitled "Towards a More Effective U.N.: Prospects for Peace-keeping" (which was subsequently published by the Oxford University Press for the Royal Institute of International Affairs). Time does not allow to go into any of these aspects in detail. Suffice it to say that UNFICYP furnishes an excellent illustration of an effective and successful United Nations peace-keeping operation in its proper role of insulating a crisis and filling a power vacuum, while the processes of peacemaking are under way for the purpose of making its continued presence no longer necessary.

Those associated with UNFICYP and indeed with the other U.N. peace-keeping operations, present and future, can justly take pride in last week's award of the Nobel Peace Prize to the U.N. peacekeeping forces.

Having said this, let me qualify it in certain aspects not so as to diminish its importance but so as to illustrate some of the limitations involved. Thus, in the case of UNFICYP, (a) while it was originally authorised for a period of three months, in March 1964, it is still in operation more that 24 years later (and by coincidence, it is being renewed by the Security Council on this very day, for another six-month period); (b) while, under its original system of financing, it was to be financed primarily through voluntary contributions, in practice this has resulted in an accumulated deficit of some 165 million dollars and has put an unfair burden on those public-minded states which make contributions (such as the United States) and those troop-contributing countries which have had to bear the bulk of the cost; and (c) while set up with a certain mandate in 1964, (viz. in the interest of preserving international peace and security, to use its best efforts to prevent a recurrence of fighting and, as necessary, to contribute to the maintenance and restoration of law and order and a return to normal conditions), since the 1974 Turkish invasion, it operates under very different circumstances, although its original mandate from the Security Council proved to be sufficiently broad and flexible to be adjusted to these very different circumstances and to man the buffer zone between the Turkish occupied and the free areas of the Republic of Cyprus.

Let me make a few brief comments on each of these three aspects.

On (a), UNFICYP's length of stay illustrates the need for peace-keeping to be accompanied by peace-making which should be based, on this and in other cases, in the implementation of the relevant U.N. resolutions. It will be relevant to recall that the 1965 recommendations of the U.N. mediator Dr. Galo Plaza (appointed under the same Security Council resolution which set up UNFICYP, Resolution 186 of 4 March 1964), were accepted by the Cyprus Government but rejected by the Government of Turkey, resulting in the forced resignation of Dr. Plaza and in effect the termination of the U.N. mediation in that form. Since that time, a number of other peace-making efforts have yielded no final result even though, since the 1974 invasion, the U.N. Secretary-General's involvement resulted in the 1977 and 1979 high-level agreements. It is on these agreements and the relevant U.N. resolutions that current efforts at peace-making are based and continued U.N. presence is being envisaged as part of the proposal for the demilitarisation of the Republic of Cyprus. While these peace-making efforts are under way, UNFICYP continues creditably to perform an essential role. The lesson to be drawn from the Cyprus peace-keeping efforts of the United Nations is that as long. as one or more of the parties concerned is unwilling to comply with the dictates of the international community, as spelled out in unanimously adopted and legally binding U.N. resolutions and as long as the international community and more particularly the major powers are not ready to act effectively to implement the resolutions for which they voted and which are binding on them as well as on the parties directly involved, peace-making, which should go step in step with peace-keeping, is lagging behind resulting in the indefinite continuation if not the actual perpetuation of the problem. This is an evidently unsatisfactory situation but the answer lies not in abandoning the peace-keeping effort (thereby leaving the weak at the mercy of the strong) but in pressing on with effective peace-making through the implementation of the relevant U.N. resolutions which are binding on all. The possibilities offered by the International Court of Justice can also be usefully borne in mind in the light of the recent positive trends for the greater utilisation of the judicial arm of the United Nations.

On (b), the question of financing the situation as it now exists is evidently unsatisfactory. The answer lies, as has been the case with other U.N. operations set-up since UNFICYP and as suggested by the U.N. Secretary-General, in making the cost of the force part of the U.N. budget as with the other expenses of the Organisation and to be paid through assessed contributions by all U.N. Member States. This poses legal, as well as political and financial questions but it is to be hoped that under the improved international climate and the increased recognition of the importance of U.N. peace-keeping the obstacles will not prove to be insuperable.

On (c), the question of mandate it illustrates, on the one hand, the flexibility of the concept and the ability to adjust to changing circumstances when the political will is present (as has been the case with UNFICYP) and, on the other hand, the serious constraints in what a U.N. peace-keeping force, such as UNFICYP, labours under in going beyond a limited role and defending a helpless small country against a determined attack by an infinitely stronger neighbour. The unfortunate fact in this case has been that UNFICYP was neither equipped nor authorised to stand in the way of the Turkish invasion troops in July and August 1974. Having themselves suffered some casualties as a result of indiscriminate napalm bombing by the Turkish Air Force and having played some limited role when the conditions permitted it (as, for instance, in preventing the Turkish occupation of the Nicosia airport), the men in UNFICYP redeployed and, in effect, stayed out of the fighting.

Evidently, the result is highly unsatisfactory but this is due to the much broader issue of the absence of an effective U.N. collective security system and is not to be blamed on UNFICYP since this was not its mandate under the Security Council authorising resolution.

Thus UNFICYP continues to perform a valuable, though limited role in Cyprus in assisting towards insulating the opposing forces and filling a vacuum while efforts at peace-making are underway.

In a broader sense, the prospects for U.N. peace-keeping under present circumstances in the world are good. With the new recognition of their importance and worth, as symbolised by the award of the Nobel Peace Prize, the political support broadly expressed to a lesser or greater extent by all sides of the ideological spectrum, the newly found willingness to provide financial support, the potential for additional major operations in the solution of key regional issues, the improved East-West climate and the continued interest of the Non-Aligned countries, the time is ripe for a more meaningful exploration of ways to improve and strengthen U.N. peace-keeping as an essential function of the United Nations in its key objective to maintain and restore peace in an imperfect world.

Before concluding these remarks, let me update you on the important developments of the past several months.

On the first of this year, the Customs Union Agreement of Cyprus with the European Community came into effect. It provides for a period of transition of 15 years before it is fully implemented and, in our view, has far-reaching economic and political implications, tying Cyprus firmly with Europe and the West while retaining our Non-Aligned foreign policy.

At the end of January, the Prime Ministers of Greece and Turkey met in Davos, Switzerland, and agreed on a policy of "no war" between the two countries, and on the setting up of committees to deal with political problems and economic relations between them. It is followed by another meeting between the two Prime Ministers in Brussels and, in June, Prime Minister Ozal visited Athens. The Cyprus issue – quite properly – was not a topic of negotiation but Prime Minister Papandreou, at our suggestion, put to Prime Minister Ozal our proposal for demilitarisation. Mr. Ozal, we were told, neither accepted nor rejected it and this was taken as an encouraging sign.

In February, following two rounds of elections conducted in an exemplary democratic manner, Mr. George Vassiliou, a successful economist and businessman and a newcomer to politics who ran as a progressive independent, was elected as President of the Republic. He has set out his positions in his inaugural address on 28 February and has since articulated and developed these positions in visits to Athens, London, New York, Washington and elsewhere. President Vassiliou has consistently maintained the basic objectives of our position as I outlined earlier, stressing the importance of the demilitarisation proposal; declared the need and his intention to put forward good will and confidence building measures in Cyprus; proposed a meeting with Prime Minister Ozal primarily on the issue of the Turkish troop withdrawal; and has taken the initiative in accepting the Secretary-General's proposal for a meeting with Mr. Denktash (it took place in Geneva on 24 August) and, since 15 September he has been holding an intensive series of meetings with Mr. Denktash in Nicosia in a determined effort at break-through for a comprehensive overall solution. On November 23, after meeting in New York with the U.N. Secretary-General, it was agreed to hold a second round of talks beginning on 19 December in order to explore a wide range of options for each of the issues involved and to meet again with the Secretary-General in March 1989 prior to the next phase.

In a wider context, let me also recall the mellowing of the East-West relations with the I.N.F. Agreement and the Reagan-Gorbachev Summit, the signature of the Afghanistan accords (which have quite a few parallels that could provide useful precedents for a Cyprus accord) and other signs in the international horizon for peaceful solution (the Arias plan in Nicaragua, the cease-fire and peace negotiations in the Gulf, progress in negotiations on Namibia and Angola, Western Sahara, Kampuchea, New Caledonia and so on) – even on such intractable problems as the Middle East we are currently witnessing signs of progress as providing a better international climate which could – I do not say necessarily will but could – affect positively Cyprus also. We have also very recently noted from the significant speech of the Soviet leader M. Gorbachev at the United Nations, his emphasis on enhancing the role of the United Nations in general and of U.N. peace-keeping in particular; the need for co-operation among the super-powers in resolving regional conflicts; the greater reliance on international law and the augmenting of the jurisdiction of the International Court of Justice; and his declaration that "*the use or threat of force no longer can or must be an instrument of foreign policy*". It is to be hoped that these positions will be shared and reciprocated since they do point the direction to a better and more just era in international relations. In this context, there certainly exists enough room for U.S.-Soviet co-operation in helping to resolve the international aspects of the Cyprus problem on the lines I earlier indicated, through meaningful and effective support of the U.N. Secretary-General's efforts and through an international conference.

And, of course, there is the declared objective of the Turkish Government for Turkey to become a full member of the European Community, which also provides a certain leverage for moderating Turkey's positions on Cyprus as it is – or at least to our mind should be – inconceivable for Turkey to be accepted as a full partner in Europe while several of the most basic tenets of European behaviour as spelled out in the Rome Convention are being violated by Turkey in its occupation of Cyprus. Greece has made it clear that the key to Turkey's entering the European Community passes through a Cyprus solution and stressed the importance of the withdrawal of Turkish troops.

What is the cumulative effect of these factors for a just and lasting solution to the Cyprus problem? We would like to hope, and want to believe, that it will be positive. But it is too early to tell and we have been disappointed in the past. President Vassiliou has recently declared our objective as follows:

> We are aiming at a settlement of the Cyprus problem which would secure the real independence, unity, sovereignty, territorial integrity and demilitarisation of Cyprus under a democratic and federal system of government in which all basic human rights and fundamental freedoms of all Cypriots are safeguarded and protected. In the solution we are seeking there is no place for occupation troops or settlers or unilateral rights of intervention.

While there is ample room for hope, the fact is that it takes more than good intentions and determination by one side to get real progress. The key to the solution lies largely in Ankara and we have yet to see concrete indications of a meaningful change of its position. We are convinced that at present there exists an opportunity which should not be missed. There exists in the world a peace epidemic and Cyprus should not be left out of it. In the improved international climate, foreign troops are withdrawing from a number of countries where regional conflicts exist (such as Afghanistan, Angola, Kampuchea) and Cyprus should be no exception. There is much that outside powers, and especially the United States, can do through principled and enlightened diplomacy to help in the road to a peaceful and just solution. When this is achieved, it will be to the benefit of all parties involved – the Greek and Turkish Cypriots, Greece, Turkey – as well as for the United States and the world at large and for peace in our sensitive region.

A prosperous and reunited Cyprus, with a viable constitution and free of foreign troops, can be abridge of peace instead of a bone of contention and can play in the region the role Switzerland and Austria play in central Europe. In the improved international climate and with the proper spirit, reconciliation can come about and this is an objective well worth pursuing, the more so when one considers the awesome alternative.

Thank you for your attention and patience, and I shall be glad to try to answer your questions.

The United Nations Peacekeeping: A View of the First 50 Years at the Brink of a New Century*

The merits and demerits of United Nations peace-keeping are widely debated in various contexts, in the United Nations itself, in the U.S. Congress and in the press, by the likes of Brian Urquhart, Henry Kissinger, Madeleine Albright, Cyrus Vance, Bill Maynes, and John Bolton to mention just a few. Numerous seminars, symposia and conferences on the subject have been organized at major institutions and universities with a high level of participation. To cite one instance, the latest issue of *The Brown Journal of World Affairs*[1] is, in large part, dedicated to U.N. Peacekeeping with contributions by the Secretary-General himself, the representatives of most of the members of the Security Council, Brian Urquhart, Yasushi Akashi, and others.

The debate on U.N. peacekeeping is also timely for another reason since it comes at the fiftieth anniversary of the founding of the United Nations. The various events which took place last year and continue this year to mark this anniversary, provide the opportunity for stocktaking, and for examining the new challenges and new opportunities facing the U.N. after half a century of its existence. Peacekeeping is, indeed, one of the focal points of this wide-ranging debate.

Having myself served at the U.N. on and off since 1960, and having studied it for five years before that, let me state my conviction that the U.N. is indispensable and its Charter has stood the test of time. It is based on sound principles and has proven sufficiently flexible to allow, through progressive interpretation, substantial adjustments to meet emerging needs; peacekeeping, the limitations to domestic jurisdiction or sovereignty, especially in the protection of human rights, come readily to mind. While there is considerable room for improvement, restructuring and regeneration in the organization itself, the emphasis should be not on tinkering with the Charter but on organizational reforms. Even more importantly, there must be emphasis

* Previously published in *Towson State Journal of International Affairs*, Volume XXXII, Number 1, Fall 1996.

[1] Winter/Spring 1996, Volume III, Issue 1.

on implementing effectively and consistently its purposes, principles, and the resolutions of its principal organs; such as the Security Council and the General Assembly.

U.N. peacekeeping has expanded enormously in recent years. Last year, there were 16 instead of the 5 operations in 1989, involving over 62,000 instead of less than 10,000 men, and costing 3.6 billion instead of 230 million dollars. This mushrooming of U.N. peacekeeping operations has paralleled the marked increase in regional and internal conflicts around the world in recent years. As highlighted by the recent U.S. Government report, "Global Humanitarian Emergencies 1996," there are currently more than 20 active conflicts, compared with 4 in 1985: putting at immediate and grave risk more than 42 million people, a 60 per cent increase from 1985. And this may, in fact, be an underestimate, since the report does not even include some unresolved conflicts where U.N. peacekeeping is involved, such as in Cyprus, where the threat to peace and the risk to people is no less real.

I recently reread the latest Report of the Secretary-General on the work of the organization in order to get updated on the long litany of situations under the heading "Current activities in preventive diplomacy, peace-making and peace-keeping", ranging, alphabetically, from Afghanistan to former Yugoslavia. It is a mind-boggling set of problems, and one cannot help but admire those who deal with their complexities and vicissitudes on a daily basis and are still able to sleep at night without nightmares. Indeed, we owe a debt of gratitude to Secretary-General Boutros-Ghali for his thoughtful and wide-ranging "Agenda for Peace" of 1992, which may have been somewhat overambitious, but gave rise to a constructive debate and led to several improvements in the field not only of peace-keeping but also of preventive diplomacy, peace-making and peace-building. In the intervening period, there has been a cessation of the U.N. operation in Somalia, which had given rise to much controversy, but new responsibilities were undertaken by the U.N. in Angola and Haiti.

In 1988, the U.N. peacekeeping was the recipient of the Nobel Peace Prize. By contrast, recently there has been much criticism, not so much of peacekeeping in the classical or traditional sense as such, but of failed attempts at "peace enforcement" and "nation-building". The current and foreseeable U.N. operations deal primarily with situations of civil war caused by ethnic strife.

Henry Kissinger, in the Washington Post, wrote: "What produced a congressional backlash was the shift from 'peace-keeping' to 'peace-making'; that is from protecting an already achieved agreement to using international forces to bring one about. Not to put too fine a point on it, peacemaking spells war." I am afraid Dr. Kissinger committed a terminological inexactitude, or at least made an inaccurate statement. What he evidently must have meant is not "peacemaking," through the accepted methods of dispute settlement set out in

Art. 33 of the Charter, which should always go step-in-step with peacekeeping, but "peace-enforcement" or "nation-building." In that case, he might have a point as to what produced congressional reaction although, in my view, peace enforcement can also have its application in the appropriate circumstances.

The success or failure of the United Nations in this area should be judged against the range and magnitude of the challenges, and the availability or absence of alternative means. We are all aware, I am sure, of the intensity of the debate going on in the U.S. Congress, and elsewhere in the United States on the role of U.N. peacekeeping and the financial and other contributions of the United States to multilateral operations. Hopefully, there will be a constructive outcome to this debate; one which will take into account the need for the U.N. to operate satisfactorily in meeting the challenges that constantly confront it, and for the U.S. to continue to play its important role in light of its legal obligations as a member of the Organization with a special position of power, and also responsibility, in the contemporary international order.

In recent years, peacekeeping by the United Nations has not only been expanded on an enormous scale in numbers and costs, but has also acquired different dimensions in order to meet the new circumstances caused by the recent developments in the world; primarily, though not exclusively, by the consequences of the end of the Cold War, and the ethnic and other conflicts created as a result of the fragmentation of multiethnic states such as Yugoslavia and the Soviet Union.

As Dr. Boutros-Ghali emphasized in the previously mentioned issue of *World Affairs*, "A sober and comprehensive assessment of U.N. peacekeeping as it stands today is urgently needed," since "the future viability of the United Nations as the world's primary vehicle for advancing the project of peace may be at stake." While, as he points out, "traditional peacekeeping, as developed and practiced between 1948 and 1989, has proved largely effective in stabilizing conflict situations between states to facilitate their search for a political settlement." The new "second generation" of peacekeeping since the end of the Cold War, is more multifunctional as it addresses a wider range of challenges, aiming "to help societies move from violent conflict toward peace, national reconciliation, reconstruction and democratic consolidation," thus involving more than the traditional Blue Helmets role. It is, as Boutros-Ghali recognizes, "an approach more farreaching and expensive than traditional peacekeeping," but one that may be necessary and might prove as effective in the future, "if the international, community is willing to commit its energy and resources" towards this end.

I intend to share with you the Cypriot experience with U.N. peacekeeping, in order to outline briefly the key aspects of the United Nations Operation in Cyprus (UNFICYP) as a case-study of what has been termed "classical" or "traditional" U.N. peacekeeping, and, furthermore, to draw some lessons of wider application. In so doing, I shall endeavour to be objective, though naturally I cannot be expected to be completely impartial.

During, a recent seminar on the "United Nations at 50" held at Meridian House in Washington D.C., in which I was a panelist, the case of Cyprus and peacekeeping was discussed. Ambassador Don McHenry remarked that there existed situations, and Cyprus was one of them, which needed to be "managed" while they ripen towards a solution. U.N. Under Secretary-General Marrack Goulding commented that in Cyprus the U.N. has been "successful in peace-keeping but, so far, unsuccessful in peace-making". I believe both of these observations were correct and aptly summarize the situation.

UNFICYP was established by the Security Council in its Resolution 186 (1964) of 4 March 1964, following a substantive debate on the international and intercommunal aspects of the Cyprus situation. This situation was in the first instance brought to the attention of the Security Council by the Cyprus Government on 26 December 1963 (S/5488), in order to consider threats and acts of intervention by Turkey, in the wake of the intercommunal violence which broke out on the island.

Resolution 186 was a balanced resolution and was unanimously adopted. It referred to Art. 2 (4) of the Charter prohibiting the threat or use of force in international relations, and called on all Member States "to refrain from any action or threat of action to worsen the situation in the sovereign Republic of Cyprus, or to endanger international peace," and also recommended the creation of UNFICYP. While at the same time, it recommended the appointment of a U.N. mediator to work for an agreed settlement "in accordance with the Charter of the United Nations, having in mind the well-being of the people of Cyprus as a whole and the preservation of international peace and security".

I cited these provisions regarding Article 2 (4) of the Charter, the sovereign Republic of Cyprus and the need to preserve "international peace," in order to dispel the impression which is sometimes created that the Cyprus problem is an intercommunal one between the Greek Cypriot and Turkish Cypriot communities in the island. While the Cyprus problem has its intercommunal, internal, and constitutional aspects, there can be no doubt that it is primarily an international problem. It was so in 1963–4, which is why the Cyprus Government referred it to the Security Council. It became even more manifestly so in 1974 with the Turkish invasion and its disastrous consequences.

Let me point out that, in legal terms, Resolution 186 was adopted under Chapter VI of the Charter. UNFICYP is a peacekeeping force authorized by the Security Council, with the consent of the Government of Cyprus. It is set up by, and serves under the overall direction of the Secretary-General who, in turn, is accountable to the Security-Council. The commander of UNFICYP is appointed by, and responsible to the Secretary-General. The Force functions on the basis of a vaguely worded mandate, is composed of national contingents having international status, and is financed primarily through voluntary contributions. At its heyday it consisted of national contingents (mostly drawn from Europe, including the United Kingdom, and Canada) totaling 7000 men. Now it consists of some 1200 men, mostly from the United Kingdom, Austria and Argentina, with token numbers from other nations.

Two features are particularly interesting to point out: the UNFICYP's duration and financing. The Force was originally authorized for a period of three months and its costs would have been met by the governments providing the contingents, by the Government of Cyprus and through voluntary contributions.

Thus, UNFICYP was established for the purpose of keeping the lid down on the crisis, internally and internationally, while the U.N. mediator would work out an agreed settlement, thus solving the problem and making the Force no longer necessary.

This was the theory. What happened in practice? As far as its various peacekeeping aspects are concerned, UNFICYP has (by and large, with a few minor problems: during the 1974 Turkish invasion, UNFICYP redeployed and took no part in the fighting, even though it suffered some casualties as a result of the indiscriminate Turkish Air Force napalm bombing. This does raise some serious fundamental questions regarding the efficacy of the mandate of a U.N. peacekeeping force, as it again did more recently in former Yugoslavia, when one side is bent on breaking the peace in an overwhelmingly aggressive manner) provided a very good illustration of an effective and successful U.N. peace-keeping operation in its proper role of insulating a crisis and filling a power vacuum while the process of peace-making is under way. Credit and appreciation is due to all concerned on this count.

Moreover, the UNFICYP's mandate proved sufficiently flexible to be adjusted to the new and infinitely graver situation created on the ground by the 1974 Turkish invasion, which resulted in the *de facto* partition of the island, with 37% of its territory under Turkish military occupation and other serious consequences which followed. Currently, the primary function of UNFICYP is to supervise the ceasefire between the Turkish army of occupation and the Cyprus National Guard, and to man the buffer zone across the island. It does so creditably, even though in much reduced numbers on the basis of the mandate in S.C. Resolution 186. It also carries out certain important humanitarian and civil functions.

The limitations of UNFICYP and the concomitant problems arose in connection with its duration, its financing and, most importantly, in terms of the failure of the peace-making leg of Resolution 186 – and, therein, lies the broader lessons.

Let me take them one at a time. As I stated earlier, the Security Council originally authorized UNFICYP for a period of three months. It is still there, thirty-two years later. This is evidently a very long time and an unsatisfactory situation – not least so to the host country. It is being renewed in six-month intervals by the Security Council and, under present conditions, its presence, regrettably, is still essential to prevent the situation from flaring up and endangering international peace. As the Secretary-General pointed out in one of his most recent reports on the U.N. operation in Cyprus,

> ...this continuing quiet should not obscure the fact that there is only a cease-fire in Cyprus, not peace. The Security Council has repeatedly declared that the status quo is not an acceptable option. It holds dangers that do not diminish with the passage of time. In the absence of progress towards an agreed overall settlement the situation remains subject to sudden tensions, generated by events outside the island as well as within Cyprus.[2]

The financing of UNFICYP, based essentially on voluntary contributions, also proved unsatisfactory, resulting in a massive deficit of over 200 million dollars to the United Nations and unfairness to the troop contributing countries; a state of affairs that, regrettably, holds for U.N. peacekeeping costs worldwide. According to a *Washington Times report*, the U.N. now owes an unprecedented $1 billion to member states for their peacekeeping troops and equipment.[3] This situation came to a head in the first half of 1993, when the Security Council reexamined the issue of financing and the related issue of whether UNFICYP should continue as is, be converted to an observer force, or even ended completely. After intensive diplomatic efforts which lasted for several months, and which involved a very rare veto by Russia in the Security Council, a pragmatic solution was worked out. The Cyprus Government, which already had been contributing substantially to the cost of UNFICYP, made a commitment, on a continuing basis, of a voluntary annual contribution of 18.5 million dollars (on top of its other contributions in terms of facilities, etc.). The Greek Government made a similar pledge of 6.5 million dollars. Thus, the balance of the annual cost of some 47 million dollars was put under assessed contributions, as is the case with all other U.N. peacekeeping operations. As I stated, this was a pragmatic solution (which has subsequently also been applied to the Kuwaiti and Angolan situations) dictated by necessity. And as Secretary-General Boutros-Ghali pointed out, this solution is in a sense "cost-effective" if one takes into account the cost, financial and other, of actual

---

[2] S/1996/488, 15 June 1995.

[3] "U.N. $1 billion Behind in Peacekeepers Pay," 22 April 1996.

armed conflict that might have otherwise erupted in the absence of UNFICYP. Whether it is just is more debatable.

Let me also draw attention to the fact that, under the farreaching and constructive proposal for the demilitarization of Cyprus, put forward by the President of Cyprus Mr. Glafcos Clerides in December 1993, the Cyprus Government offered to meet all the costs of an expanded U.N. Force with broader mandate in a demilitarized and disarmed Republic of Cyprus, if the Turkish forces were to withdraw from the island as numerous U.N. resolutions have called for since 1974. A concurrent resolution, supporting the concept of demilitarization of Cyprus, was overwhelmingly adopted by the House of Representatives of the United States September 1995, and has also attracted wider international support such as in the European Parliament and elsewhere.

Beyond its own catalytic effects for enhancing the prospects of a viable resolution of problems such as that of Cyprus, demilitarization (and not just balance of opposing forces) offers the best prospects for an effective and successful peacekeeping (and not just ceasefire monitoring) operation. In a demilitarized context, the threats posed to peace and to U.N. peacekeeping would be much reduced and of a qualitatively different nature. Such threats, and even violations, can be far more readily met by classical peacekeeping operations; particularly if the U.N. force is the only armed force in a completely demilitarized context. In addition, as Senator Lugar observed in the context of the debate on the wisdom of arming up one faction in Bosnia rather than drawing down on all sides, the commitment to reduce and finally disband the armed forces on all sides is the best, most genuine and credible demonstration of all parties to peace and reconciliation. It is, therefore, the most effective precondition for achieving a just and viable solution to a conflict, i.e. making real, lasting peace which is, or should be after all, the ultimate objective of any peacekeeping operation.

Finally, my last point is the aspect of peace-making which is directly related to the unprecedented length of UNFICYP's stay. As I stated earlier, under Resolution 186 (1964) it was envisaged that UN mediation would solve the problem within a short period of time. Indeed, a UN mediator was appointed, originally Mr. Tuomioja of Finland who died soon afterwards and later Mr. Galo Plaza of Ecuador. Mr. Plaza worked diligently, and in early 1965 produced what was generally considered as a balanced and judicious report, with recommendations for a fair and lasting solution in accordance with his Security Council mandate. These recommendations were accepted by the Cyprus Government but were rejected by the Turkish Government. The Security Council and its members (especially its Permanent Members) did nothing to ensure that its own mediator's recommendations were accepted by the recalcitrant party, or that the problem would be solved in accordance with the principles laid down in its own resolutions. Thus, the result was the forced resignation of Dr. Plaza and, in effect, the termination of the U.N. mediation in the form laid out in Resolution 186.

This was the turning point where matters went wrong in terms of peace-making being in-step with peace-keeping. Since 1965 a number of other peace-making efforts have been resorted to, including the good offices mission of the Secretary-General currently under way (under S.C. Resolution 367 [1975]). On a number of occasions, progress appeared to be made but, in fact, no breakthrough has yet been achieved. Evidently, I have my views as to why a solvable problem like the one in Cyprus is not being solved while many other, seemingly much more intractable international problems (the reunification of Germany, the dismantling of apartheid in South Africa, the Middle East and now Bosnia and Northern Ireland to cite a few), have been or are being solved, but this would go beyond the present subject. Hopefully, recent developments connected with Turkey's Customs Union with the European Union and Cyprus's accession course towards full membership in the European Union, together with upgraded U.S. engagement and bold and constructive ideas such as the demilitarization of Cyprus, can lead to positive developments soon.

The broader lesson to be drawn is this: As long as one or more of the parties to a dispute lacks the political will for a solution (as the Turkish side does, in the present case), and as long as the international community and more particularly the major powers, are not willing to act decisively and effectively in order to implement the resolutions for which they voted, peace-making, which should go step-in-step with peace-keeping, lags behind. The lag, eventually, resulting in the indefinite continuation if not the perpetuation of the problem. This is an evidently unsatisfactory situation. The indefinite freezing of an unjust situation is well exemplified in the case of Cyprus, but also parallels other cases, such as Croatia. Precisely because of fears of this kind of "Cyprusization" of the situation in Croatia, a very different approach was adopted, with advantageous results from its point of view. The answer, in the case of Cyprus as well as in other cases, lies not in abandoning the peace-keeping effort, thereby abdicating responsibility and leaving the weak at the mercy of the strong and risking wider confrontation, but in pressing on with effective peace-making through the decisive implementation of the relevant U.N. Resolutions which provide the guidelines and framework for a solution. The possibilities provided by the International Court of Justice may also be useful in regard to clarifying the legal components of political disputes, as we have repeatedly offered to do.

Before concluding, it is pertinent to mention, in a broader sense, that all U.N. Member States and especially those which, for reasons of principle as well as self-interest, are what one might call "United Nations minded," should demonstrate in every way possible their support for U.N. peacekeeping. Furnishing troops and equipment is one such way. Another way is financing. Interestingly, two years ago the President of Cyprus agreed, on a voluntary basis, to double Cyprus's assessment to the U.N. peacekeeping operations as a practical way of demonstrating support for the U.N. and of encouraging others to do the same; an important objective since, as I noted before, the U.N. currently owes an unprecedented $1 billion to member states for their peacekeeping contributions of troops and equipment.

We should never forget that whatever the shortcomings are of some U.N. peacekeeping operations, they are not really the problem. They can be modified and adjusted to improve their efficiency and effectiveness. The real problem remains in the causes and circumstances that necessitated a peacekeeping operation in the first place and which, if unaddressed, maintain the need for its continuation. As the experience of Cyprus demonstrates, it is toward the resolution of underlying conflicts, on the basis of international law and the applicable U.N. resolutions, that international efforts should be concentrated in order to achieve real and viable peace and, indeed, peace with justice.

The Security Council should be prepared in all cases, (not selectively, as for instance in the case of Iraq's invasion of Kuwait) to take "all measures necessary" to implement its own resolutions. If it did, it would serve the purpose for which it was created and would not be open to accusations of double standards and political expediency; and, furthermore, the prospects for effective U.N. peacekeeping and world peace based on freedom, justice and the rule of law, would be much brighter.

Remarks at the Ceremony to Honour the Canadian Armed Forces for Their Contribution to UNFICYP

Toronto, 30 April 1996

It gives me great pleasure to be here in Toronto this evening, at the home of the Cypriot Community and it is an even greater pleasure to be here considering the lofty purpose of this distinguished gathering.

The purpose of this gathering is to honour the contribution of the Canadian Armed Forces to the United Nations Peacekeeping Force in Cyprus. There is no doubt that this contribution has been substantial and it is my pleasant duty to express to you Mr. Minister of National Defense of Canada and to the Officers and Servicemen who represented Canada for almost 30 years on the Force, my country's great appreciation for Canada's most commendable role in helping keep the peace in Cyprus, internally and internationally.

We remember well that the Canadian contingent was the first to arrive in Cyprus in March 1964, in response to an appeal by Secretary-General U Thant to the then Minister of Foreign Affairs Mr. Paul Martin, the father of the present Finance Minister.

It was an earnest and appropriate response by a country which has impeccable credentials in the area of international peacekeeping, and a country which fought in two World Wars on the side of principle, on the side of freedom and justice.

Putting, very briefly, into context the beginning of UNFICYP will give us a better appreciation for the work that has been done over the years by one of the longest serving peace-keeping forces in the world.

The enabling resolution, S.C. 186 of 4 March 1964, was unanimously approved by the Security Council and defined the mandate of the Force as follows:

> In the interest of preserving international peace and security, to use its best efforts to prevent the recurrence of fighting and, as necessary, to contribute to the maintenance and restoration of law and order and a return to normal conditions.

The Force was set up for an initial period of three months with the consent of the Cyprus Government and it was meant to help contain the crisis by keeping the lid down and to avoid a major international conflict from erupting.

Thirty two years later the Force is still on the island, although with an adjusted mandate, since the Turkish invasion of 1974, namely to maintain and supervise the cease-fire line between the Turkish occupation Forces and the Cyprus National Guard and to carry out certain important humanitarian functions.

It is indeed regrettable that the presence of the peacekeeping Force is still necessary. After so many years and after so many efforts at resolving the Cyprus conflict, peace and security have not yet arrived, and no solution has yet been achieved. We have a cease-fire, not peace and security. This cannot be attributed to our lack of trying. The Cyprus government has diligently supported all efforts of the United Nations and the international community to resolve our long and seemingly intractable problem. We have endeavoured to find a reasonable and workable solution, that would re-unify our island and restore human rights to all its people under conditions of security for all. It is in this context that the President of the Republic, Mr. Glafcos Clerides, has made his comprehensive proposal on demilitarization. A bold and constructive proposal that would guarantee security for both communities, promote mutual confidence and form the cornerstone of a political settlement.

The response of the Turkish side to this proposal so far, as well as to other efforts – beginning with the rejection of the Galo Plaza report in 1965 – has been disappointing, not only to us but to the Secretary-General himself who, in his report of May 30, 1994, pointed the finger directly at the Turkish side for lack of political will to proceed to serious negotiations. We hope that, with enhanced American involvement and the European Union factor, the prospects will become brighter in the not distant future.

However, the disappointment Cyprus feels at the lack of progress, stemming from Turkish intransigence but also from the inability of the international community to enforce its own binding decisions, taken by the Security Council, does not reflect negatively on the contribution of UNFICYP to the maintenance of peace in Cyprus. UNFICYP has proven to be a successful and effective peace-keeping force.

The Force has certainly undergone substantial changes in its history. Not only its composition, but also to some degree its structure and its size have changed. Quite significantly, the method of its financing has been altered since June 1993 to that of assessed rather than voluntary contributions, a system much fairer to the troop-contributing countries. This is in addition to the very substantial voluntary contributions by the Governments of Cyprus and Greece.

To our regret, this came a bit too late for Canada and some other troop-contributing countries. It is no secret that we would have preferred Canada to continue its participation in UNFICYP. However, we are not unaware of the reasons that led to this decision and we are certainly grateful for the nearly 30 years of Canadian contribution to the Force.

At the same time perhaps I could say that Canada's experience with Cyprus has also been a positive one. Canada is itself a bi-communal albeit multicultural country. Some similarities between Cyprus and Canada do exist and as Jean-Luc Pepin once remarked, the more I heard about Cyprus and its problem, the more I learned about Canada. It has been estimated that over 40,000 Canadian soldiers served in UNFICYP and they, with their families, even though saddened by the experience of the division of Cyprus and inevitably made certain comparisons, they maintained a constant interest in our island. A simple indication of this is that tourism to Cyprus from Canada is on a steadily increasing trend, despite the distance and relatively high cost. This is a trend that speaks well for the future of the friendly relations and cooperation already existing between Canada and Cyprus in several other fields.

In concluding, I believe it is quite appropriate to salute Canada's involvement in Cyprus not only in peace-keeping but also in peace-making, remembering that Canada was one of the sponsors of the 1978 Anglo-American-Canadian proposal, and that Joe Clark, a distinguished Canadian, served as the U.N. Special Representative. As a fellow Commonwealth member Canada shares with Cyprus elements of a common governmental heritage and experience which can prove useful in the efforts to find the appropriate governmental structures for a federal Cyprus. Moreover, Canada has over the years subscribed to the Commonwealth position on Cyprus (most recently in the 1995 New Zealand CHOGM), including the proposal for the demilitarization of Cyprus.

As a member of NATO, Canada shares with Greece and Turkey common interests and has every reason to help in the resolution of the Cyprus problem, thus helping to eliminate a source of conflict between NATO members and restore stability in the strategically significant but volatile Eastern Mediterranean region.

Considering Canada's record on the world stage we would expect nothing less. Because we have come to understand Canada as a country in which working for international peace is a basic national value. Its own national experience has developed its ability to mediate, to compromise, to find the middle ground. It is this ability articulated by statesmen like Lester Pearson that has given Canada the title of one of the most experienced and public-minded peace-keeping nations in the world.

Cyprus has been fortunate to be a beneficiary of this and we express to you Mr. Minister, to the Canadian government and to the members of the Canadian Armed Forces, our most profound appreciation.

As a concrete token of this appreciation permit me to present to you this plaque.

Terrorism

International Law Aspects of Combating Terrorism

Opening Statement at Pepperdine University School of Law, Malibu/Los Angeles, 15 April 2005

It is a pleasure for me to be visiting again Pepperdine University's School of Law and to address Professor Roger Alford's class, the more so since this time I am joined by my good friend, and outstanding international lawyer, Pieter Bekker.

International terrorism and the international law aspects of combating it is not a subject that lends itself to easy treatment. But it is important and topical enough to deserve close attention.

I share the view that achieving a comprehensive convention on terrorism, including a clear definition if at all possible, is a political imperative.

I recall that, back in 1972, the Sixth (Legal) Committee of the U.N. General Assembly attempted and failed to achieve an agreed definition of terrorism. As the Vice-Chairman of the Committee at the time, I had the unenviable task of explaining, in a lecture to the Council on Foreign Relations in New York, the circumstances which prevented agreement. There was much argument over the root causes of terrorism, the right of liberation movements of people under foreign occupation or alien domination to use force to achieve freedom and of State terrorism. The basic difficulty was then and continues to be that one's terrorist is someone else's freedom fighter (including – perish the thought – even George Washington and Archbishop Makarios).

In the wake of the universal condemnation of the atrocious terrorist acts of September 11, 2001 and following the unanimous adoption by the Security Council of the United Nations of S.C. Resolution 1373 (2001) – to which I shall revert – there was a new impetus in the Sixth Committee to get over the hurdle with substantial input of Secretary-General Kofi Annan and the then Legal Counsel, Hans Corell, in which I tried to play my modest role as the Cyprus delegate.

Speaking on 19 October 2001 in the Committee I said and I quote:

> We have had so far a constructive and full debate on the basis of the Indian draft comprehensive Convention. We have heard an eloquent appeal by the Legal Counsel, echoing the Secretary-General's principled position, stated on a number of occasions in the aftermath of the atrocious crime of the 11th of September. We join in this appeal. It is time for the Sixth Committee to act so as to meet the expectations of the international community and get over the remaining hurdles in concluding successfully this major piece of international law making. If we hold back, as we have done for too long, we shall not live up to our responsibilities. This will not be good for the Sixth Committee, or for the United Nations or for the world at large in its fight against international terrorism. It has been said that the better is the enemy of the good. It is equally true that international law making, as indeed politics, is the art of the possible. We should, indeed we must, rise to the occasion and take the steps necessary to conclude the comprehensive convention at this session, even if it falls short of fully satisfying everybody. I believe there exist ways of meeting the concerns – and indeed there are legitimate concerns to be met – in ways other than by holding back the adoption of the Convention… If this year, in the wake of current circumstances and atmosphere, we cannot rise to the occasion and make a breakthrough we may never do – and everyone will be worse off except international terrorism.

I cited this brief statement because it encapsulates my genuinely held views on this subject. Regrettably, the opportunity was again missed since the Islamic Group at the U.N. took a firm stand which prevented consensus and the utilization of the then existing momentum.

Some argue that a formal definition is not really necessary since, like other such terms of legal nomenclature as "pornography", "investment", "aggression" (some might also add "sin" to this list but this is a moral rather than a legal term!) are recognizable when you see them, even in the absence of an agreed definition. Not to elaborate on these other terms but it might interest you to be reminded that Justice Potter Stewart was the one who said of pornography that "I recognize it when I see it"; that the ICSID Convention (International Centre for Settlement of Investment Disputes), despite its title, nowhere provides a definition of what an "investment" is and cases involving many millions of dollars are decided upon by ICSID tribunals on a case by case basis on the question of whether a situation merits or not the description of an investment; and the crime of aggression (as distinct from the political concept of aggression, which was settled in G.A. Resolution 3314 (1974)) is still undefined in the context of the International Criminal Court!

A brave effort was made in the recent (2 December 2004) Report of the High Level Panel on Threats, Challenges and Change (paras 157 to 164) to provide a definition to which, significantly, all of its 16 members agreed (including General Scowroft, the U.S. member and Amre Mussa, the Secretary-General of the Arab League). This in terms was commented upon in a variety of forums (among others, the United Nations Association of the United States and WFUNA; the Georgetown University's Institute for the Study of Diplomacy, the Stanley Foundation etc.) and, more relevantly to our own discussion, by members of the ASIL Executive Council, including Roger Alford (as set out in the January–February Newsletter of ASIL). Significantly, Secretary-General Kofi Annan, in his own far-ranging Report "In Larger Freedom" (A/59/2005) of 21 March 2005, fully endorsed "the Panel's call for a definition of terrorism, which would make it clear that, in addition to actions already proscribed by existing conventions, any action constitutes terrorism if it is intended to cause death or serious bodily harm to civilians or non-combatants with the purpose of intimidating a population or compelling a Government or an international organization to do or abstain from doing any act" (para. 91). The Secretary-General goes on to express his belief that this proposal has a clear moral force and strongly urges world leaders to unite behind it and conclude a comprehensive convention on terrorism before the end of the sixtieth session of the General Assembly.

In the same section of his Report the Secretary-General makes some other significant points.

One, that terrorism is a threat to everything the United Nations stands for; respect for human rights, the rule of law, the protection of civilians, tolerance among peoples and nations and the peaceful resolution of conflicts.

Two, that the strategy against terrorism should be comprehensive and should be based on five pillars; dissuading people from resorting to terrorism or supporting it; denying terrorist access to funds and materials; deterring States from sponsoring terrorism; developing State capacity to defeat terrorism; but also defending human rights (stressing the need for counter-terrorism measures to be compatible with international human rights laws).

Three, that it is vital to deny terrorists access to nuclear materials and urging Member States to complete, without delay, an international convention for the suppression of nuclear terrorism (also pending for some time now).

Four, that the debate on so-called "State terrorism" be set aside on the rationale that the use of force by States is already regulated thoroughly under conventional and customary international law. And that the right to resist occupation must be understood in its proper meaning which cannot include the right to kill or maim civilians.

The Secretary-General in introducing his report, forcefully and with conviction, expressed the hope that all of his proposals (including several others evidently to the benefit of the Third World States, such as those on combating poverty and HIV/AIDS) would be taken as a package and be approved of as a whole. Whether this will happen of course depends on States but, in my view, there is much which is meritorious in the Secretary-General's package.

I said earlier in referring to the unanimous adoption by the Security Council of S.C. Resolution 1373 (2001) that I would revert to it. Indeed this decision of the Security Council, taken under Chapter VII of the UN Charter and therefore legally binding, was followed by other far-reaching steps and decisions, with the aim to combat international terrorism. It set up machinery under the Counter Terrorism Committee, intended to monitor the implementation of the measures it provided for and it was followed, last October, by the adoption of S.C. Resolution 1565 (2004) envisaging additional measures of implementation and intensified cooperation against terrorism (sending visiting missions to oversee national action, exploring the possibility of an international fund to compensate the victims of terrorism etc.). Recently the Counter Terrorism Directorate was set up, under a senior former Spanish Ambassador to Washington who himself experienced the ills of terrorism.

From the legal point of view it is interesting to observe that Resolutions 1373 (2001) and 1566 (2004) on Counter Terrorism and S.C. Resolution 1540 (2004), mandating (also under Chapter VII) States not to provide non-State actors with weapons of mass destruction or aid them to produce such weapons are the clearer instances so far of the exercise of the Security Council of legislative power – itself a matter of some controversy but of undoubted validity in the specific areas which these Resolutions cover.

The topic of the exercise of legislative power by the Security Council has been extensively debated recently (including chapters in David Malone's recent book on the Security Council, in the last issue of the American Journal of International Law, and in an article due for publication very soon by Axel Marschik, in a new book by Professor Ronald MacDonald (at which I also had a small role)).

Additionally to the comprehensive convention on international terrorism, hopefully with an agreed definition as already explained and the two major legally binding Security Council Resolutions 1373 and 1566, the UN arsenal includes twelve conventions aimed at fighting international terrorism and beginning with the 1963 Convention on Offences and certain other Acts committed on Board Aircraft and including the 1999 convention on the Suppression of the Financing of Terrorism.

The Group of Eight Major Industrialized Countries (G-8) have also taken important steps to deny terrorists access to nuclear materials, through eliminating hazardous materials and implementing effective export controls and of course in major developed countries, such as the United States far reaching steps have been taken, and constantly improved, to fight effectively the war against terrorists, with the support and cooperation of the large majority of the members of the world community.

Whether these will prove effective is a big question but, at least in the area of international law which is our area of expertise, important steps have been and hopefully will continue to be taken to effectively combat international terrorism wherever possible.

International Law and Diplomacy

The Role and Work of the Diplomatic Corps in Washington[◊]

Introductory Statement at the Brookings Institution Conference on Federal Government Operations, 10 November 1982

It has been said that diplomacy is the application of intelligence and tact to the conduct of foreign relations. Of course, other things have also been said about diplomacy and diplomats. You may well have heard the description of a diplomat as "an honest man who has been sent abroad to lie for his country". Let me hasten to establish my credentials, so to speak, at least on this count and let me, at the very outset, frankly disabuse you of any notion that I can speak authoritatively on the role and the work of the Diplomatic Corps in Washington. In all honesty, I can only speak in terms of my own perception of what this role is, on the basis of my experience of over three years as the Ambassador of the Republic of Cyprus here, and to talk to you about my work in the hope that it can help you draw conclusions of a broader nature.

I should also like to make two other disclaimers. The one is that I am speaking here in my personal capacity and not as the representative of my country. And the other is that, of course, I am not authorized to speak on behalf of my colleagues stationed in Washington (some 150 of them). Indeed, it would have been presumptuous of me to do so. If anyone could speak on behalf of the Washington Diplomatic Corps this is the Dean of the Diplomatic Corps and at present this, on the basis of seniority, is none other than the Ambassador of the Soviet Union, the very distinguished, charming and able Anatoliy Dobrynin – and you wouldn't want me, and I wouldn't want, to be on the wrong side of him by encroaching on his turf!

To start from the beginning, an Ambassador to Washington to the Government of the United States of America (and I say this because as you may know, there is also, for example, the United States of Mexico). His basic

[◊] For other materials by Andrew Jacovides on International Law and Diplomacy see: Statement before the International Law Commission, Congressional Record, Extension of Remarks, Congressional Record, Vol. 133, 8 June 1987, p. 2274.

objective, as customarily stated during the ceremony for the presentation of credentials to the President, is to use his (or her) best endeavours in order to maintain and improve the relations between the two countries.

Now, these relations cover a wide variety of subjects in the political, the economic, the commercial, the cultural and, where applicable, the military and other fields and vary greatly depending on the country concerned.

They are conducted primarily with the Executive Branch of the United States Government. This includes, first and foremost, the State Department, starting from the Desk Officer for the country concerned and going up the ladder to the Regional Director, the Assistant Secretary in charge of the geographical bureau – in this case, Europe –, the Under-Secretaries for Political, Economic, and Security Assistance Affairs, and the Deputy Secretary to the Secretary of State, but also various other officials within the Department such as in our case, Policy Planning, Protocol, Congressional Liaison, International Organizations, Public Affairs, Human Rights, Refugee Affairs, AID, Legal Affairs, etc. It also includes of course the White House, and especially the National Security Council officials dealing, in our case, with Europe including the National Security Adviser and his Deputy and also the senior officials round the President as well as the Office of Management and Budget, the Commerce Department, to the extent applicable the Pentagon, the Department of Agriculture, Transportation, Energy, etc., as well as the various Federal Government Agencies.

The Legislative Branch of Government provides another broad range of necessary and, in our case, very important contacts. In addition to the leadership of the House of Representatives and of the Senate, both majority and minority in each case, of primary interest and importance is maintaining contact and informing of our particular situation and developments affecting Cyprus are the House Foreign Affairs Committee – and especially its Sub-Committee on Europe and the Middle East – and the Senate Foreign Relations Committee – and especially its Sub-Committee on Europe. It also includes, in our particular case, the House and Senate Appropriations Committees and, more specifically, the Sub-Committee of each on Foreign Operations. Very important and not to be under-estimated in this regard are not only the Senators and Congressmen involved and the Chairman of each of these Committees and Sub-Committees, but also the staff members of each and the staff members of individual Senators and Congressmen.

Contacts are also maintained with the Judicial Branch of the United States Government, and primarily with the President and Members of the Supreme Court, but these, as a rule, are of a protocol nature.

But this is by no means the end of the story. In the particular circumstances of the United States, an Ambassador, to be effectively representing his country, has to establish and cultivate a variety of other contacts by way of receiving and imparting information and influencing developments affecting his country's interests. These include the leading representatives of the Press (including television and radio), of Business, of the Universities, of the Arts, of the Foundations, and other influential policy makers, including the "Think Tanks," of which Brookings is of course such an outstanding example. Also, in our case as indeed in the case of several other Embassies, it includes the leaders of the ethnic communities, in our case the Cypriot and Greek American community, and of the Greek Orthodox Church and this involves a great deal of travelling around the country to attend and speak at various functions. And, of course, it includes many of the other Ambassadors and some of their staff members.

Moreover, in addition to those who are presently in authority, there are many others who are no longer holding office but who continue to be influential and therefore important. Such persons (former Cabinet officers, Senators, Ambassadors and other senior officials) as well as other opinion makers, who collectively form what is called the Foreign Policy Establishment, can be of great assistance in terms of helping an Ambassador see past events of topical interest in perspective, understanding current events better and facilitating access to those who are now in authority.

I have mentioned travelling around the country in the context of keeping in touch with ethnic communities, which in turn are very important in influencing Congressmen and Senators on matters of primary concern to our representation in Washington. Travelling is also important to establish and maintain contact with leaders of State and Municipal government affairs and, more generally, in the political, economic, commercial and cultural fields outside Washington.

And, of course, being in Washington, we maintain close contact and conduct negotiations with the appropriate officials of the World Bank (IBRD) and the International Monetary Fund (IMF) and other international financial institutions and attend their Annual and other Conferences. Naturally, we also maintain contact with the Mayor of Washington, D.C.

To complete the picture perhaps I should mention that, in my particular case (as indeed with several other small countries which have reason to maintain good relations with as many countries in the world as possible but do not have the means to maintain more than a certain number of Embassies), I am non-resident Ambassador of Brazil and Ecuador and non-resident High Commissioner (the reason for the distinction, which does not make much practical difference, is common membership in the Commonwealth) to Canada, Jamaica and the Bahamas. This involves following developments in each, dealing with matters within our competence which may arise and visiting once or twice a year each capital in order to meet with the senior officials; in each country and to conduct any outstanding business which cannot be dealt with by correspondence or by telephone.

In addition I may mention parenthetically that, since happen to be an international lawyer by training and to have served many years at the United Nations, I continue to serve on an *ad hoc* basis as a member of the Cyprus delegation to the United Nations General Assembly and to represent Cyprus on its Legal Committee and also, since this year, I have been elected as a member of the U.N. International Law Commission. Additionally, I have been actively involved with the American Society of International Law and with the U.N. Law of the Sea Conference to which, thank God, comes to the conclusion early next month with the scheduled signature of the Law of the Sea Convention in Jamaica.

Now, if you are wondering how all this can be done and if I am not bragging, at least a bit, you would be right, on both counts! Admittedly, not all is done as thoroughly as it should and it means working an awful lot of long hours, including starting very early in the morning and going into holidays, week-ends and evenings, especially since a great deal of social events are also involved and most of these are of a representational nature and therefore should not be missed. But there is also the satisfaction that, to the extent possible, the challenge is met and the work is important for the country as well as for the individual concerned.

I said at the beginning that it would be presumptuous and unwise of me to speak as to the role and the work of the other Embassies in Washington. The work is heterogeneous, priorities differ greatly, the means (both in terms of personnel and financially) vary enormously from Embassy to Embassy. Obviously, the work of the Embassy of a major NATO country, for example Great Britain, is very different from that of the Embassy of the Soviet Union and the same is true of a large third world country such as India as compared, for instance to a small Central American country which in many respects depends on the United States. But there are also several common denominators.

It is generally acknowledged that, because of the importance of the United States as a Super Power and because of the openness of the society and the multiplicity of contacts that can and should be maintained (especially as contrasted to other capitals where contacts available to diplomats are limited and the decision-making on matters which concern them is more clearly defined and limited to certain officials), the importance of the post is correspondingly high and the calibre of the personnel posted here is generally well above average. For certain foreign countries, their Washington Embassy is indisputably their number one post and the Ambassador's position is reserved for influential appointees, some of whom are on their way to become, or have just ceased being, the foreign minister of the country concerned – this is especially true of Latin American countries and there is even the case of an incumbent Ambassador from this region who is concurrently the Vice-

President of his country and a former Foreign Minister and Prime Minister. This, of course, is not the rule and each country applies its own criteria for instance, in my case, I am only a foreign service officer but with twenty two years experience and therefore with some seniority in our service.

Despite the evident inequalities between states in terms of size, population, wealth, etc., since international relations are based on the principle of sovereign equality, in terms of protocol all Ambassadors are treated equally. The determining factor is seniority, based on the date of their presentation of credentials, the most senior being the Dean of the Diplomatic Corps who speaks on behalf of all at ceremonial occasions.

Most, if not all, Embassies have political and economic officers and many have consular, press/information, commercial and cultural sections, carrying out the respective functions under the Ambassador's direction. Several also have defence attaché's offices who, in certain cases, number in the dozens and even hundreds. Moreover, most Embassies have career and/or honorary consuls, in several key Cities and States within the United States. In many cases, the work of the Embassy is supplemented by hiring public relations firms, law firms and lobbyists (who have to register as foreign agents disclosing their clients and the amounts of money involved).

An Ambassador stationed in Washington is expected to absorb each day an enormous amount of information in order to keep pace with developments in the United States, in his home country and in the world at large. In a typical case – if there is such a thing – in addition to receiving and sending secret and confidential information by coded telex, diplomatic pouch, telephone and personal contacts, either directly or through his staff or officials he meets, he is exposed – and he is expected to be exposed – to the news and commentaries of radio and television, daily newspapers and weekly, monthly and quarterly publications in this country and his own. Out of all this only a certain amount would be of direct importance to his daily work but he cannot afford to lose sight of the broader picture and this, in turn, makes him more interesting to those he comes in contact with. Naturally, discretion has to be exercised and shortcuts devised for otherwise there is the danger of being swamped.

As Ambassadors sooner or later find out, the decision making process in the United States is complicated and often shifts from one branch of Government to another depending on a variety of factors and differing from Administration to Administration, depending on the personalities and other factors involved. To be effective in his job, an Ambassador has to have a keen sense of awareness of what goes on, a sound sense of perspective and priorities; good sources of information, access to the decision-makers and the ability to put his case persuasively. Two other important elements, of more general application, are also very relevant. The one is the ability to create and maintain a relationship of trust with those the Ambassador comes into contact with. And the other is to be, and to be perceived to be, a person well attuned to what the policy makers at his home capital think and that therefore speaks with authority on any given issue. To this end he needs to have good channels of communication with and the confidence and backing of the authorities in his home capital at the highest possible level. It should be a cardinal rule that he should not tell lies or intentionally mislead because, even if there is a short term advantage, in the long term his credibility is lost and his usefulness diminishes.

If the full truth cannot be told or if one does not know the answer to a question, there are ways of maintaining discreet silence or tactfully changing the subject.

Nonetheless, it has to be frankly acknowledged that when it comes to certain important issues, constant overriding interests and larger factors enter the decision-making process and, no matter how able the Ambassador or hard working the Embassy staff may be, the most one can hope for, realistically, is to have a marginal effect in influencing developments. Thus, in addition to the satisfaction and the sense of achievement in certain areas, it should be remembered that there are also many causes of frustration and disappointment. Results are of course important but, where the desirable results are not achievable, one has to be content with having made the best possible case under the circumstances – and to hope that his authorities at home also see it this way!

It would be an unforgivable omission not to say at least a few words about the role of the Ambassador's wife – assuming, as in fact is the case, that most of the Ambassadors are married and that they are male, although there have been some notable exceptions to this rule. Usually, husband and wife work as a team and there is generally an unwritten rule regarding allocation of work. Ambassadors' wives – and especially those who are attractive, intelligent, charming, sophisticated and accomplished as all Ambassadors wives are by definition! – can be an enormous asset to their husbands' work. It is not only that they run the Embassy Residence (which in itself requires many more qualities than the five epithets I have already used) and arrange for dinner and cocktail parties which hopefully make the invited guests to want to be invited again; they also can be active participants in the cultural and artistic life of Washington and play an important role in fundraising for charitable purposes; moreover, they often speak out in their own right to suitable audiences, projecting their country in the appropriate light and, through some very influential ladies clubs to which they belong, they can help substantially their husbands meet and become friends with Cabinet members, Senators, Congressmen, other Ambassadors and important personalities who happen to be married to the ladies belonging to the same clubs or associations.

Washington is by definition a Government City and people in Government (often changing with each new administration or even during mid-term congressional elections) are anxious to meet and become friends with foreign Ambassadors and their wives no less than foreign Ambassadors and their wives are anxious to become friends with them.

Thus, there is a two-way traffic, a mutuality of interest, which is part of the Washington scene and occurs naturally and effortlessly – after all, as I mentioned earlier, diplomacy is the application of intelligence and tact in the conduct of foreign relations and the wives are very much part of this process.

In this introductory statement, I did not go into our particular concerns as the Ambassador of Cyprus. As you know, Cyprus is a small country with a big problem as a result of the fact that since the 1974 Turkish invasion part of its territory has been under foreign occupation and many of its inhabitants were forcibly uprooted and rendered refugees in their own country. The question and answer period can give us the opportunity, if you so wish, to go into our specific concerns and objectives in so the United States is concerned. I shall also be glad to answer any questions you may have regarding my own routine as an illustration of how the Diplomatic Corps in Washington works – subject, of course, to what I have said at the beginning about the inappropriateness of over generalizing or speaking on behalf of others.

I thank you for your attention and would be glad to try and answer your questions.

Recent Trends towards International Legal Order

Commencement Address at the University of Indianapolis, 20 May 1989

You do a great honor to my country as well as to myself by your invitation to join you here today.

This is a truly auspicious and unforgettable day for this year's class of graduates. I feel privileged to participate in it, particularly since I happen to be a crypto-academic at heart and I very much enjoy being in an academic environment.

The University of Indianapolis can be justly proud for its achievements in the area of international education. We in Cyprus are fortunate in our close association with you through intercollege. The pursuit of higher education and academic excellence are indeed characteristics of the youth also of my country and we highly appreciate the opportunity provided to them to achieve both through this great university and other institutions of learning throughout the United States. It is no coincidence that Cyprus ranks among the highest in the world in the ratio of university graduates to population.

Since my own student days and throughout my thirty year long service representing my country in the United Nations and, for the past ten years in the United States, one topic has attracted a great deal of my time and attention, and this by choice. It is international law and the vision of a peaceful world where the rule of law is applied equally to all nations, great and small. If I may volunteer a piece of my personal philosophy, when I was once asked some years ago if I was an idealist or a pragmatist, I thought for a moment and answered: "a pragmatic idealist". And since I have today the welcome opportunity of addressing you, the hope of tomorrow – from among your ranks, there could well be future law-makers in Congress, cabinet members, a member of the Supreme Court or even a President of the United States – I think it is fitting that I should speak to you about the role of international law in the world today, in the context of the United Nations and by reference to my own country.

Let me start on a somewhat pessimistic note. In the recent and not so recent past, too often the realities of power relations and the vagaries of international politics have taken the upper hand and resulted in double standards in the application of international law. Too often we have seen the law of the jungle prevail over the principles of international law, even though these principles are solemnly embodied most comprehensively in the United Nations Charter, and binding on all states of the world. To give you one obvious example, under Article 2 paragraph 4 of the UN Charter, the threat or use of armed force by one state against the territorial integrity or political independence of another is prohibited; and under Article 2 paragraph 3, all member states have pledged to "settle their international disputes by peaceful means in such a manner that international peace and security and justice are not endangered". One does not have to be an expert in international affairs to know that – not always but too often – these basic binding and solemnly proclaimed legal obligations have been honored more in breach than in observance. The fact is that, unlike what is sometimes assumed, the United Nations is not a world government nor a superstate nor a court of law in the national sense which passes judgment and relies upon the executive organs of the state to enforce these judgments. It is only an association of sovereign states and, because of this, it is no more than a reflection of the national positions of these sovereign states which, collectively, constitute the United Nations organization. While in theory, the Charter has a foolproof scheme for prompt and effective action in order to ensure compliance with binding decisions taken by the Security Council, and by the International Court of Justice the practice is considerably different. Because of political considerations and the existence of the veto, the effective application of this fool-proof scheme has so far been prevented. Political considerations and narrow national interests too often combine to render inoperative in practice the theoretically binding principles of international law embodied in the United Nations Charter.

At the risk of being accused of flippancy, let me relate to you the story I heard, when I first went to the United Nations in 1960, as to what happens when there is a dispute between two states and the matter is referred to the United Nations: If it is a dispute between two small states, the dispute disappears; if it is a dispute between a large state and a small state, the small state disappears; and if it is a dispute between two super powers, the UN disappears! Well this is not, of course, quite true and yet there is a sufficient element of truth in it, to make us disquiet as to the state of present-day international organization.

That is why your own role, as the coming generation of Americans, is so vital and even determining. Remember, the alternative to international violence, terrorism and anarchy is international law. And remember that fairness, social justice and the rule of law are not empty slogans but essential components of a world system based on peace and justice.

I can understand and even share the logic behind such slogans as "my country, right or wrong" and "extremism in the pursuit of virtue is no vice". Obviously, there are situations where there is no choice but to draw a line beyond which no retreat can be tolerated. But I would also suggest that, in the interdependent world of today, where the rapid strides of technology have reduced distances and brought about the threat of nuclear holocaust for everyone on this globe, there exist additional reasons to exhibit reasonableness, moderation and recognition of the fact that there may be other, also valid, points of view and different legitimate interests that may need to be accommodated in any particular situation. It is rare that things are black and white; the world is full of diversity and in the majority of situations, there are varying shades of gray.

Patriotism and the determination to fight for one's convictions is one thing. Unbridled nationalism and irrational fanaticism is another thing. The former is commendable, the latter is condemnable.

Principles such as justice and peace are indivisible and their gross violation in one part of the world affects all states; for, in the long term, it destroys the fibre of the whole international system. But it so happens that this is an imperfect world and the United Nations is but a reflection of it.

But it should also be remembered, for the sake of balance and objectivity, that while the United Nations is not a world government and not offering a panacea to all of the world's problems, as its more enthusiastic supporters claim, neither is it a mere debating society or worse, as its detractors allege. In the field of the elaboration of rules of international law, through such major law-making conferences as the Law of Treaties and the Law of the Sea, as well as in the field of human rights, the United Nations has made enormous contributions to developing and codifying these rules; and this also has to be acknowledged. It might also interest you to know that the UN International Law Commission (from which in fact I just returned) has been currently working on a number of important and topical projects in this direction, including the elaboration of a code of crimes against the peace and security of mankind, as an instrument of deterrence and punishment of present and future violators of its provisions.

There are the cynics who say that "might is right"; that international law is to be invoked when it is convenient and to be ignored when it is not; that international organizations are useless debating societies or worse; and there are those who employ double standards and apply selectively norms which ought to be of universal application.

Representing a small country which has suffered from grave injustice and having been trained in international law and the workings of international organizations, let me tell you that I do not share these views. And I hope that you, the new generation upon whom so much depends, are idealistic enough not to share them either. At the same time, we should be realistic enough to know that international law and diplomacy are not a panacea to cure all the world's ills; that international organizations are mere reflections of their member states and therefore no better and no more effective that the attitudes and policies of their member states. But, if I may repeat the often quoted saying, "you see things and say why. But I dream of things that never were and say why not".

The grave situation my own country has been confronted with since the Turkish invasion in 1974 and its tragic consequences since that time, including the destruction and looting of the age-long cultural heritage of the areas under occupation, has indeed been a test case of the ability of the world community and of the United Nations to meet a challenge to its most fundamental tenets. At the risk of oversimplifying, let me say with conviction that the Cyprus problem in its real dimensions of invasion, continuing occupation, massive violation of human rights and attempted secession, would not have arisen if the relevant rules of international law had been applied. It can be solved, in a way which would be fair to all Cypriots and consistent with the legitimate interests of all states in the region, if the way could be found to apply these principles and rules. No doubt, the Cyprus problem as is the case with most other current international problems, involves a number of elements and an inter-play of several factors – political, strategic, economic, historical, psychological – of which the legal aspect is one. But I am convinced that the relevant rules of international law are a very important and relevant element, and should be recognized as such. It is no coincidence that recently my government accepted the compulsory jurisdiction of the International Court of Justice nor that we systematically pursue all legal avenues open to us in order to assert the justice of our cause before international and national tribunals.

Mr. President, I said earlier that I would sound a pessimistic note in terms of the observance of the rules of international law in the world during the recent past. I am pleased to say that there are now signs in the international horizon to justify a more optimistic outlook for the future. We can say that we now live in a more peaceful world than was the case some years ago. There has been the mellowing of the east-west relations and the historic agreement on nuclear missiles between the United States and the Soviet Union with prospects for further substantial reduction in armaments and improvement of the international climate. A number of burning regional issues have been or are in the process of being resolved. There have been declarations that the use or threat of force no longer can or must be an instrument of foreign policy; the prestige and influence of the United Nations have been recently enhanced; there is greater reliance on UN peace-keeping as exemplified also by the recent award of the Nobel Peace Prize while peace-making has increased; there has been greater reliance on international law and the jurisdiction of the International Court of Justice has been recently augmented; and prospects are good for cooperation among the superpowers not only in their bilateral relations but also towards greater application of human rights, for resolving regional issues and for combating the global issues of drug trafficking and terrorism, and protecting the environment.

All these are healthy and welcome signs since they point the direction to a better and more just era in international relations.

We in Cyprus certainly share this hope and trust that the improved international climate will affect positively the prospects for the just and lasting solution of the grave problem we have been confronted with. Foreign troops withdraw from several areas of regional conflict. Cyprus should be no exception. We are aiming at a solution which would secure the real independence, unity, sovereignty, territorial integrity and demilitarization of Cyprus under a democratic and federal system of government in which all basic human rights and fundamental freedoms of all Cypriots are safeguarded and protected. In the solution we are seeking, there is no place for occupation troops or settlers nor for unilateral rights of intervention. It is important to remember that not many countries have, as we do, made a standing offer to completely demilitarize and disarm themselves for the sake of peace and this gives a measure of our determination to find a solution taking into account the concerns of both sides and a proof that we do not only talk in the abstract, we are also prepared and committed to act constructively.

A prosperous and reunited Cyprus, with a viable constitution and free of foreign troops, can be a bridge of peace instead of a bone of contention and can play in the region the role Switzerland and Austria play in Central Europe. In the improved international climate and with the proper spirit, reconciliation can come about to the benefit of all concerned and peace in the region and this is an objective well worth pursuing, the more so when one considers the awesome alternative.

Let me conclude by reminding one and all and by quoting from the Bible that precious vision of peace: "They shall beat their swords into plowshares and their spears into pruning hooks; nation shall not lift up sword against nation, neither shall they learn war any more".

This is the message, this is the thought, I would like to leave with you today. As you embark on your careers, remember that international legal order is better than international anarchy, that peace is better than war, that justice is better than injustice and that, in our interdependent world, no man is an island. How much of this is an unrealizable dream and how much can be achieved? There you could be reminded of the medieval theologian whose prayer to God was "Good Lord, give me the courage to change the things which I can change, the serenity to accept the things I cannot change and the wisdom to know the difference between the two". The future is yours. Make good decisions.

And thank you again for the privilege of letting me join your commencement and for sharing with me this very special day.

The Role of International Law in Diplomacy*

It is both appropriate and timely that we should reflect on the role of international law in diplomacy. Not only is this the United Nations Decade of International Law, but it also so happens that, in the wake of the revolutions in the East, of the Gulf war, and of the Balkan Crisis, high-sounding declarations have been made by world leaders proclaiming the value and relevance of international law in today's world and in resolving crises. And it can be legitimately asked whether these declarations will prove to be of lasting value, intended to govern relations between nations in the "new world order" and to be applied universally or only convenient slogans to be applied selectively and according to temporary expediencies. Only time will supply the answer. There is certainly room for hope but, on the basis of past experience, for example similar declarations made during the Falklands/Malvinas situation, there exists also room for scepticism.

Let me set the ball rolling, as it were, by relating to two anecdotes from my personal experience.

When I was a law student at the University of Cambridge some thirty-five years ago, one of our respected and experienced Professors, Dr. Clive Parry, was fond of relating the story of when he was acting as a supervisor at a university examination in international law. While all of those taking the examination, as soon as they got the paper with the questions started writing their answers furiously, there was one who looked and looked at the questions, frowned, thought and wrote nothing for almost the whole allotted time. At the end he scribbled something very brief in answer to all of the questions. Dr. Parry was mystified and intrigued and he could not resist the temptation of looking over the student's shoulder to see what he had written. And what did he see? To everyone of the questions of this international law examination the answer the student had given was: "It all depends!" And Dr. Parry's inimitable comment was "I, of course, agreed with him that when it comes to international law it all depends. But I wish he had written on what!"

* Previously published in Das Neue Europa, Ein europaisch-amerikanischer Dialog, ed. M. Mathiopoulos, Bouvier (1992).

A quarter of a century later, when I was my country's Ambassador in Washington, we were informally discussing with a senior State Department official the Administration's action taken in a given international situation and I inquired as to how much weight was given to the international law aspect, in formulating that policy. The answer was disarmingly frank: "After we decided what the policy was going to be and what action we were going to take, we then called in the lawyers to provide us with some legal arguments to be used in justifying this policy."

In any given situation, there may indeed be room for bona fide argument, different interpretations and lack of clarity and certainly so in international law, as indeed in many other fields of the law. But if the rule of law is to have real meaning in international relations, as indeed in domestic situations, such rules as are clearly discernible and objectively valid need to be observed in practice in all situations. And, before a decision is taken on policy regarding any given situation which is covered by international law rules, the considered view of the legal aspect needs to be asked for, formulated, communicated and be given due weight by the policy makers before deciding on the policy in that situation. This is true everywhere and particularly true in countries which proudly proclaim that they are nations of laws and not of men. The rule of law in international affairs means that narrow national interests are subordinated to international law, especially where the relevant rules of international law are clear and unambiguous.

As a general proposition, it can be said without much fear of contradiction that, by and large, States abide by their treaty obligations, despite the lack of an international legislature with binding powers or an international peace force or even a compulsory third-party adjudication system. Ultimately, the viability of any system of law depends upon the will of the community it seeks to regulate. The vast majority of States ordinarily observe their obligations under international law, even if motivated only by enlightened self-interest. And even when they do not observe such obligations, they tend to attempt to justify their actions or omissions by invoking legal arguments, however contrived, rather than admit their such actions or omissions violate the relevant rules of international law.

The question of what is the practical relevance of international law in international affairs was the subject of examination at the Annual Meeting of the American Society of International Law in 1983 before a panel of international lawyers who were, or had been, Ambassadors of their respective countries. Several points were made and conclusions reached by these experienced practitioners of both international law and international diplomacy.

One of the points raised was the role of the State Department's Legal Adviser in delineating international policies, a point to which I alluded earlier, and it is interesting that several years later, in 1990, the American Society of International Law produced an important report,[1] in which, after extensive discussion, the Joint Committee accepted the proposition that as a general matter it was in the national interest of the United States to support international law and that "it was a specific responsibility of the Legal Adviser to promote respect for and observance of international law by the United States by assuring that decision makers within the Government are made aware of its requirements whenever applicable". It was also found that if legal advisers did no more than provide legal rationalizations of their Government's political actions, the international legal system would be the elaborate charade that some detractors of international law consider it to be, despite recognizing the fact that "since foreign policy decisions are often highly political and policy makers are often sceptical concerning the relevance of international law, pressures on the legal adviser to bend or ignore international law in order to support policy decisions may be intense". And it was stressed that the Legal Adviser's first responsibility is to tell the Secretary of State and the Administration candidly and objectively what existing law is or requires in a given situation. And the Joint Committee recommended, among other things, that "the Secretary should ensure within the Department of State that the Legal Adviser shall participate at an early stage regarding the making of all policy decisions that involve a question of international law".

I have quoted from this document extensively because I believe it touches on the very core of our present subject and, mutatis mutandis, the conclusions reached apply to the role of the legal advisers in the Foreign Ministries of all countries – and, incidentally, supplies the correct answer to the anecdote I cited earlier.

Going back to the 1983 panel discussion, several instructive instances were given by the Ambassador of Canada and the Ambassador of Venezuela of how international law played an important role in diplomacy, ranging from practical day to day matters like consular and diplomatic law, issues relating to privileges and immunities to couriers and communications between the sending and receiving states, to broader observations regarding the need to anchor the conduct of diplomacy in international law, and the need to develop further this body of law. They concluded that international law did play an important role in the conduct of international diplomacy and that the need for an international framework of order was clear given the rapid increase in international political and economic conflicts.

---

1 Report of the Joint Committee established by the American Society of International Law and the American Branch of the International Law Association on the Role of the Legal Adviser of the Department of State, October 1, 1990.

For my part, as a panel participant, I stressed that in my own experience the rules of international law played a very substantial role, that the principles and rules of international law frequently provided the framework in which diplomatic negotiations, arguments and positions were formulated and gave as an example the question of Cyprus in its various phases which involved many issues of international law including the prohibition of the threat or use of force in international relations, the question of unequal and imposed treaties, the legally binding effect of United Nations Resolutions, protection of human rights, protection of national cultural heritage, aggression and peremptory norms of international law (*jus cogens*). I stressed that the Government of Cyprus, in formulating its positions before all available forums, including the General Assembly, the Security Council, the Human Rights Commission, heavily relied on the rules of international law and the results obtained from these and other forums and in particular the key Resolutions on the solution of the Cyprus problem were fully consistent with these legal positions. I also gave several other instances in bilateral relations as well as in terms of my participation in the Sixth Committee and the International Law Commission, the Conferences on the Law of Treaties and the Law of the Sea, as evidence of the importance of international law in diplomacy. My conclusion was – and certainly continues to be – that, while the role of international law in international diplomacy is often limited, yet it is not insignificant. In certain cases where law coincides with power, law is determining – as we have witnessed in the very recent case of the Gulf Crisis. In other cases, where this is not the case, international law at least serves as a restraint on power by providing the weak with arguments to buttress their position and international standards for third parties not directly involved to support these positions. Contemporary international law, as developed in the era of the United Nations with the participation of all members of the international community and particularly the newly independent states which brought some new perspectives to bear to the law-making process, has increasingly tended to sustain those who have justice on their side, particularly in such areas as decolonization, the protection of human rights, the law of treaties and the law of the sea.

As recently as October this year, a two-day meeting of legal advisers to Foreign Ministries from all geographical regions of the world was informally held at the United Nations at the initiative of the Legal Advisers of Canada, India, Mexico, Poland and Sweden. Ambassador Hans Corell, the Swedish Legal Adviser, in his opening statement and in answering the basic question "how can we contribute to a better observance of international law" stressed that "in our opinion there is most certainly room for improvement here; international law should always be taken into consideration in the decision-making in foreign policy matters". He also urged that there should be "a network between the Legal Advisers with the purpose of cooperation in order to strengthen our role" and to "work together for the enhancement of international law and the strengthening of the rule of law in the international community".

How much a role international law is allowed to play of course varies from State to State. It reflects an attitude of mind and much also depends on the individuals who at a given moment or period of time are in the position of decision makers. No general rule can necessarily apply but, on the whole, it is small and weaker States which have more reason to rely on the law rather than on power in defending their sovereignty, independence and territorial integrity and, more generally, projecting their policies. Even though all States are supposed to be equal, some States are more "international law-minded" than others.

My own country, Cyprus, is one of these "international law-minded" and indeed "United Nations-minded" States. Cyprus has endeavoured in its modest way through its 31-year existence as an independent State to abide by the rules of international law, to participate constructively in the major law-making Conferences and to make its contribution in such areas as developing compulsory third-party dispute settlement procedures and the adoption of such progressive notions as *jus cogens*. It is a party to most international Conventions, universal as well as regional, for the protection of human rights. Also, in other small ways such as being the first to contribute to the U.N. Secretary-General's Trust Fund to cover expenses of developing countries in order to enable them to resort to the International Court of Justice and through token voluntary contributions to finance such worthy causes in holding of the International Law Commission's Seminar, UNCITRAL Symposia and the Amerasinghe Memorial Scholarship, Cyprus has endeavoured to play its modest role in this regard.

Cyprus has accepted the compulsory jurisdiction of the International Court of Justice and is on record as having declared its willingness to have the highest judicial organ of the United Nations adjudicate on the legal aspects of the Cyprus problem and, in particular, the key question of the legality of the use of force under the proper interpretation of the 1960 Treaty of Guarantee on the basis of Article 2 (4) of the U.N. Charter, Article 103 of the Charter and the rules of *jus cogens*. The key issue is whether the Turkish military invasion of July–August 1974 was legally justified under Article 4 of the 1960 Treaty of Guarantee. We are convinced that the clear answer is that this invasion, from which many other illegal and disastrous consequences followed, was legally unjustified both in terms of Article 4 and in terms of the peremptory norm in Article 2 (4) of the U.N. Charter. *Ex injuria non oritur jus* aptly states the situation. Article 4 of the Treaty of Guarantee did not and could not authorize the use of armed force by Turkey against Cyprus but, if it were so interpreted, it would conflict with Article 2 (4) under Article 103 of the Charter and would be null and void under *jus cogens*, as accepted in the 1969 Vienna Convention on the Law of Treaties.

Similarly Cyprus did not hesitate to resort even to national Courts abroad and was vindicated as happened recently before the Federal Court of Indianapolis with the recovery of the Kanakaria Mosaics, an important precedent-creating case for the protection of cultural property looted and purportedly sold abroad. A useful note of this topic will soon appear in the next issue of the *American Journal of International Law.*

It is our conviction that if the rules of international law had been applied, the Cyprus problem would not have arisen. And, if these rules were to be applied, I believe the problem we have been confronted with can be solved, in conformity with the relevant U.N. Resolutions, fairly for all parties concerned and in the interest of international peace in our volatile region.

Particularly relevant to our subject are the topics of "State Responsibility" and the "Code of Crimes against the Peace and Security of Mankind", which includes the question of the establishment of an international criminal court.

Regarding the topic of "State Responsibility", even though it has to be admitted that it has been on the International Law Commission's (ILC) agenda for far too long (and this because of reasons largely beyond the Commission's control), it is important to observe that it has gone through considerable progressive development. Gone are the days when state responsibility concentrated in remedying injury to aliens and, in effect, catered to the needs and requirements of a small number of powerful developed states, often at the expense of weaker and less developed states. With the development of the notion of *jus cogens*, even though as yet undefined, and its acceptance in the 1969 Vienna Convention on the Law of Treaties, and the existence of hierarchically higher rules as set out in the United Nations Charter, the topic of state responsibility is put on a much broader foundation and it is now recognized, also by the International Court of Justice, that there exist obligations *erga omnes* and that the interest of the whole international community and of international public order need to be duly taken into account. State responsibility has thus been transformed as a proper expression of the application of progressive development. The Commission must ensure that the expectations of the international community and of the new states in particular, which came into existence after the classical rules of international law on this topic were formulated, are not disappointed. The Commission must also keep pace with contemporary notions of international law such as international crimes. It must keep pace with current developments in the international scene and not be slow in recognizing the opportunities provided by recent shifts of attitude in the right direction by major powers in accepting the notion of compulsory third party dispute settlement. The effective and expeditious third party disputes settlement procedure which eluded the international community for unavoidable reasons of political reality in past major projects, including the Law of Treaties and the Law of the Sea, is – thanks to these developments – within reach and, in my view, we should certainly aim at including such a system in the draft on state responsibility currently under elaboration as an integral part of the draft Convention. Indeed an effective and expeditious third party dispute settlement system should be included in all future multilateral law-making treaties.

The "Code of Crimes against the Peace and Security of Mankind", is a topic which has acquired additional importance and topicality in the light of recent and current developments in the world scene and one to which my country has consistently placed high priority over the years. Let me stress that it has been my firm conviction that the Code of Crimes against the Peace and Security of Mankind deserves its rightful place in the corpus of current-day international law and that its existence as a complete legal instrument, encompassing the three essential elements of crimes, penalties and jurisdiction, can and should serve the important purpose of deterrence and punishment against present and future violators of its provisions. My country's position in the General Assembly in advocating the adoption of such a legal instrument was dictated by reasons of principle, long before recent and current developments in the world gave additional impetus to this endeavour. It is certainly a welcome development that, in light of current events, some of those who viewed the Code of Crimes against the Peace and Security of Mankind with scepticism have had second thoughts and have come forward to the vanguard in proposing the establishment of international criminal jurisdiction. The Vice Chancellor and Minister for Foreign Affairs of Germany, Mr. Hans-Dietrich Genscher, for example, in his address before the U.N. General Assembly on 25 September this year, stated "we call for an international Court of Justice of the United Nations where crimes against humanity, crimes against peace, genocide, war crimes and environmental criminality can be prosecuted and punished". Similarly the Prime Minister of Trinidad and Tobago, Mr. Robinson, has called for the creation of an international criminal tribunal against international drug trafficking. Irrespective of the feasibility or appropriateness of specific initiatives directed at particular situations (something which needs to be very carefully weighed, even though the notion itself appears to have much merit), the conclusion can only be that the overall effect of the Gulf Crisis and its aftermath, by highlighting the necessity of observing the relevant rules of international law and the implementation of the United Nations Resolutions, is conducive to promoting international legal order. It is awelcome development that the Commission, well in tune with political developments and other trends in the world, this year made major progress towards the fruition of this major undertaking. Once it is completed and in place I am convinced it will constitute a most significant contribution by the Commission to the progressive development of international law and a highlight of the U.N. Decade of International Law.

Once these topics are brought to a satisfactory conclusion, it is important in terms of our subject, for the Commission and the Sixth Committee of the U.N. General Assembly to choose wisely the topics which the ILC should deal with in the years ahead. Environment and economic relations are obvious priorities and other topics such as Implementation of United Nations Resolutions, and the Binding Nature of Security Council Resolutions also merit examination, codification and progressive development by the Commission as international legal tools of contemporary diplomacy. So does a more comprehensive and binding system of peaceful settlement of disputes through third-party settlement, perhaps the legal aspects of United Nations peacekeeping which is becoming of evergrowing relevance and importance and the defining of the exact legal content of *jus cogens*.

The International Law Commission quite properly maintains a close relationship with regional bodies such as the Asian-African Legal Consultative Committee, the Interamerican Juridical Committee, the European Commission of Legal Cooperation and the Arab Commission of International Law. These learned bodies make a major contribution to the work of the Commission through their input of regional perspectives into general international law and such cooperation is certainly mutually beneficial in developing international law in its proper role in diplomacy. I mention particularly the Asian-African Legal Committee, as providing a very useful way for the topics of primary interest to these regions of the Third World being properly projected into the mainstream of international law. Furthermore, ways should be found for the Commonwealth, representing as it does a principal legal system in the world based on the common law, also to make its constructive input into the work of the International Law Commission and public international law in general. Similarly, one can think that the Non Aligned Movement, which let me say parenthetically had the initiative of proposing that the decade of the nineteen nineties be declared as the U.N. Decade of International Law, can also make a substantial contribution to the development of international law as part of the process of the evolution of the Movement in the light of current developments. Its input in this respect carries additional weight considering that it represents a majority of the U.N. Member States. It may well prove that focusing on international law development and implementation may provide the Non Aligned Movement with a fruitful area on which to concentrate some of its attention now that developments on the world scene and more particularly the disappearance of the East-West confrontation, caused a vacuum in some of its priorities of earlier years. To quote again from Mr. Genscher's address to the General Assembly "as before we regard the Non-Aligned Movement as an indispensable source of global stability".

We are living through interesting and challenging times, times full of opportunities but also pitfalls, in terms of politics and economics as well as in terms of the development and the role of international law.

We have witnessed and we are witnessing developments of historic importance all over the world. Global interdependence and the need to protect the environment and to ensure economic development are increasingly recognized as priority areas in the post cold-war era and there has been progress towards solution of several, but certainly not all, regional problems. The Charter of Paris of November 1990 has been the culmination of the CSCE process in Europe, (and potentially opens the way to a similar process in the Mediterranean). Africa can be described as a continent in transition, with hopeful though as yet inconclusive steps towards the abolition of the obnoxious doctrine of apartheid. We have recently seen the declaration by the leadership of two key powers, the Soviet Union and China, regarding the need for the peaceful solution of international disputes. And in the wake of the Gulf Crisis and the series of Resolutions adopted by the Security Council with the concurrence of all its Permanent Members (including resolution 688 where, for the first time in the history of the United Nations, contempt for human rights was recognized as constituting a threat to international peace and security), new possibilities open for a revitalized United Nations under its newly elected Secretary-General (who, incidentally, is an expert in international law and a long-time member of the International Law Commission) and the further development of international law. While the recent unanimity of the Permanent Members of the Security Council making possible enforcement action under the original Charter design is a welcome development (whether it will continue and in which situations is less than certain), care should be taken so as not to lead to abusive interpretations of the law prejudicial to the rights and legitimate interests of the rank and file of the U.N. Member States. *Pax Romana* was based, after all, on the existence of Roman imperium while the era of the United Nations should be based on the democratic exercise of rights by all Member States under the rules of international law and in particular those of *jus cogens*. What we need is a "Pax United Nations" or "*Pax Unitarum Nationum*".

There is indeed much to be said in favour of the recent emphasis on effectively protecting human rights, as stressed more recently in the Moscow CSCE Meeting and as expected to be further developed in the World Conference on Human Rights due to take place in 1993. As Mr. Genscher stressed, "the violation of human rights must no longer be a domestic concern of individual states but a domestic concern of the community of nations as a whole". But, at the same time, a case can and should be made for not impinging on the sovereignty, territorial integrity and political independence of States. To quote from the thoughtful and wise last report of the present UN Secretary-General:

> It seems to be beyond question that violations of human rights imperil peace, while disregard of the sovereignty of States would spell chaos. The maximum caution needs to be exercised lest the defence of human rights becomes a platform for encroaching on the essential domestic jurisdiction of States and eroding their sovereignty. Nothing would be a surer prescription for anarchy and an abuse of this principle.

Some caveats are, therefore, more necessary at this point. First like all other basic principles, the principle of protection of human rights cannot be invoked in a particular situation and disregarded in a similar one. To apply it selectively is to debase it. Governments can, and do, expose themselves to charges of deliberate bias; the United Nations cannot. Second, any international action for protecting human rights must be based on a decision taken in accordance with the Charter of the United Nations. It must not be a unilateral act. Third, and relatedly, the consideration of proportionality is of the utmost importance in this respect.

Will the "new world order" acquire proper legal meaning and lead to international legal order? Will this happen, if it does, not through a directorate of the powerful but through equal justice for all? Will the United Nations be sufficiently revitalized in the right direction and take on additional responsibilities in effective peace-keeping and peace-making, protection of human rights and saving the environment? Will unity and cooperation, as we are witnessing in Europe with German reunification and the process of European integration through the European Community, prevail over disintegration and conflict as we are witnessing in other parts of the world as in the Soviet Union and indeed in some parts of Europe as in Yugoslavia? Will disputes, which inevitably will continue to arise, be solved peacefully in accordance with the law or shall we witness more instances of the application of the law of the jungle? Will major law-making Conventions such as on the Law of the Sea, laboriously and successfully negotiated over the years, be ratified by a sufficient number of States so as to come into force and will more States have recourse to the International Court of Justice?

These and other relevant questions ought to be very much on our mind if the dream of a more just and peaceful world is not to prove utopian. They should be very much on the mind of my generation and I hope also on the mind of the younger generation of up and coming international lawyers, the future members of the International Law Commission, of the International

Court of Justice, of the International Criminal Court and the Law of the Sea Tribunal when they hopefully will come into being and on the mind of those who will be the next generation of decision makers in the top levels of national governments and in the international bureaucracy.

The best formula is idealism tempered with realism. There is much that international law can do for contemporary diplomacy if the emphasis is put where it should and if the natural desire to move forward fast is tempered with wisdom. The well-known prayer of the medieval theologian has relevance in many situations including the creation and application of international law. It is: "Good Lord, give me the courage to change the things that can be changed, the patience to tolerate the things that cannot be changed and the wisdom to know the difference between the two".

I shall add a quotation from a recent speech of the present U.N. Secretary-General given at the University of Bordeaux, on 24 April 1991:

> We can thus see the emergence of some of the basic requirements for international law, to become more effective in governing international relations. First, it must not stagnate but must keep pace with change in the conditions of international life. Second, it must evoke a shared understanding and it must be seen to derive from the morality of international behaviour. Third, it must not be applied selectively.

A principle invoked in a particular situation but disregarded in a similar one, is as good as no principle at all. Indeed, its application elicits suspicion and contempt as far as the swelling ranks of law-minded world opinion are concerned. There are other requirements too, which present themselves in different contexts but, at this stage we have now reached in international relations, these three, it seems are paramount.

These are valid propositions. International law does play an important role in international diplomacy.

State practice shows that, even when government policies are not on solid legal ground, the attempt at justification in terms of international law is invariably made. The role of the Foreign Ministry legal adviser is important and should be maximized. Whether States are more or less sensitive to international law compliance is, to a certain extent, a matter of attitude. The power and the size of the State concerned and the personality of the decision makers are often, though not always, relevant.

The present world situation is conducive to enhancing the role of international law and maximizing its effectiveness.

Attention should focus on areas of the law reflecting present needs and these should be progressively developed accordingly.

The role of the International Law Commission and of regional bodies are important in achieving this objective.

International Law must keep pace with the conditions of international life, it must be based on international morality and must be applied not selectively but universally.

We should all try our best, from our respective vantage points, to see that these noble objectives are met during this, the United Nations Decade of International Law.

(gehalten am 2. Dezember 1991)

The UN Decade on International Law: Progress and Promises*

Remarks by Ambassador Andreas J. Jacovides

It has long been my conviction that international law should and does play an important role in diplomacy and international affairs. How much a role it is allowed to play varies from state to state. It reflects an attitude of mind. Much also depends upon the individual officials who, at a given period of time, are in a position to take decisions on a particular situation. No general rule necessarily applies but, on the whole, it is small and weaker states that have more reason to rely on the law rather than on power in defending their sovereignty, independence and territorial integrity and, more generally, in promoting their policies in the international field. Although all states are supposed to be equal in law, some states are more "international law-minded" than others.

My own country, Cyprus, is one of these "international law-minded" and, indeed, "United Nations-minded" states. Cyprus, in its modest way, has endeavored throughout its thirty-five year existence as an independent state to participate constructively in the major law-making conferences held under UN auspices, and to make its contribution in such areas as developing compulsory third-party dispute-settlement procedures (notably in the UN Conference on the Law of the Sea) and the adoption of important notions as *jus cogens* (notably in the Vienna Conference on the Law of Treaties). Cyprus is a party to most international conventions, universal as well as regional, for the protection of human rights. Cyprus has accepted the compulsory jurisdiction of the International Court of Justice (ICJ) and has declared its willingness to have the highest judicial organ of the United Nations adjudicate on the legal aspects of the long-standing Cyprus problem, whether through contentious proceedings if Turkey were to accept the ICJ's jurisdiction, or through an Advisory Opinion of the Court as a result of a decision of the General Assembly or the Security Council to that end. Moreover, we have

---

* Previously published in *American Society of International Law Proceedings of the 89th Annual Meeting 1995*, pp. 172–177 and 189.

supported the UN Secretary-General's right to seek advisory opinions from the ICJ in appropriate circumstances.

Similarly, Cyprus did not hesitate to resort also to national and regional courts abroad and was vindicated, for instance, in the federal court of Indianapolis with the recovery of the cultural property in the Kanakaria Mosaics case, an important precedent-setting case for the protection of cultural property looted and purportedly sold abroad; and, very recently, before the European Court of Justice of the European Union and currently before the European Court of Human Rights – of which I shall say no more in the presence of one of the outstanding judges of this latter Court who happens to be our Chair for this panel.

Also in other small ways, such as being the first to contribute to the UN Secretary-General's Trust Fund to cover expenses of developing countries in order to enable them to resort to the International Court of Justice and through voluntary – albeit token – contributions to finance such worthy causes as holding the International Law Commission's Annual Seminar, UNCITRAL symposia and the Shirley Amerasinghe memorial scholarship, Cyprus has endeavored to play its modest role in this regard. Since 1961, Cyprus served on the UN Advisory Committee on the Teaching, Study, Dissemination and Wider Appreciation of International Law.

As a student of international law, as a delegate to the Sixth Committee since 1960, and as a member of the International Law Commission since 1981, I can say that if the rules of international law had been applied, the Cyprus problem would not have arisen. And if these rules are applied today, the international aspects of this problem can be solved fairly for all parties concerned and in the interest of international peace in our volatile region.

I hope you will excuse this diversion, but what I have said serves as an introduction and an illustration of the attitude that dictated the proposal, originally made at the Non-Aligned Foreign Ministers Conference in Nicosia, Cyprus, in September 1988, subsequently elaborated on in the Declaration adopted by the NAM Meeting on Peace and International Law in 1989 and endorsed by the NAM Summit later the same year, to declare the 1990s the UN Decade of International Law.

Since we are currently at the halfway point of the Decade, it is indeed appropriate that we should pause and take stock as to the progress made, and whether the promises and expectations have been fulfilled. It is also timely that we should do so, this being the 50th anniversary of the United Nations, when much thinking and soul-searching is going on at various forums, national and international, as to where the United Nations stands and where it is going after fifty years in existence. All the more appropriate since the United Nations and its Charter have provided the forum and the guiding principles for much of the activity in codifying and progressively developing international law during the past half-century. Indeed, some of us who are over this mark like to think that life begins at fifty!

The main objectives of the Decade were spelled out in General Assembly Resolution 44/23 of 17 November 1989:

(1) To promote acceptance of and respect for the principles of international law;
(2) To promote means and methods for the peaceful settlement of disputes between States, including resort to and full respect for the International Court of Justice;
(3) To encourage the progressive development of international law and its codification;
(4) To encourage the teaching, study, dissemination and wider appreciation of international law.

In short, the purpose of the Decade is to enhance and solidify respect for international law. It should also serve the purpose of popularizing it.

So where do we stand on the Decade of International Law? Much work has been done, as detailed in the Secretary-General's reports, the work of the relevant Working Group and the relevant General Assembly resolutions.[1] I do not propose to comment on the International Court of Justice, other than to express satisfaction at its recently increased jurisdiction – a reflection of the confidence that the Court currently enjoys. I would only like to echo the suggestion put forward by its former President, Sir Robert Jennings, that the ICJ can perform a very useful role in clarifying the legal aspects of political disputes when such aspects are referred to it for an Advisory Opinion.

Let me make some observations from a broader perspective.

Within the context of the Decade, recently we have witnessed the holding in New York of the Congress on Public International Law. It was an impressive event, both in terms of attendance and of content. Due recognition and appreciation is offered to all concerned: the Secretariat under Hans Corell and his able colleagues, the moderators and other speakers, and the international legal community at large, who demonstrated their interest and concern through their participation. I believe the Congress met the objectives that it set, and I, for one, look forward to having its Proceedings published as a rich source of valuable material and for future reference.

Another event of particular interest and, I believe, importance, considering the pivotal role of its participants, is the new informal institution (which developed not expressly within the purview of the Decade but is very much related to it) of annual meetings of the Legal Advisers of Foreign Ministries, on the sidelines of the annual debate of the ILC report in late October in

[1] Most recently, see UN Doc. A/49/737, A/C.6/48/L.9.

New York. It is a non-institutional forum that provides the opportunity for the practitioners, who can really make a difference through the exercise of their respective functions; to compare notes on issues of mutual concern and – also important – to get to know one another. It certainly contributes to the objectives of the Decade. Let me here remind you of the important debate: the need for legal advice to be sought and to be followed by policy makers before, not after, making decisions on matters of policy that include international legal elements.

I remember some years ago talking with a top policy maker at the State Department as to what went into the making of a major decision involving the use of force. I asked if the State Department's Legal Adviser was consulted and if he was in agreement with the decision taken. His answer was disarmingly, and revealingly, frank: "Well, after we took the decision to act we called in the lawyers to provide us with some legal arguments to justify it." I certainly hope that this is the exception and not the rule, and that what the law is plays a major, in fact a determining, role in the actions of all foreign ministries rather than serving as ex post facto justification of such actions.

In the same context I would also like to mention the very useful practice of such regional organizations as the Asian African Legal Consultative Committee (AALCC) to hold meetings of their respective countries' representatives in New York, at the same time as the ILC debate in the Sixth Committee. These meetings are often addressed by personalities visiting New York at the same time, such as the President and other members of the International Court of Justice. This practice, in addition to the annual sessions of the AALCC and other regional organizations, such as the European Committee on Legal Cooperation and the Inter-American Juridical Committee, certainly contributes positively to the objectives of the Decade.

In this regard let me repeat my often stated conviction that not only these regional institutions but also such major bodies as the Non-Aligned Movement and the Commonwealth are fertile grounds for pursuing international law activities. I already referred to NAM's initiative that resulted in the idea of the Decade. Especially in light of the transformation of the international community with the end of the Cold War, increased activity in the international legal field certainly offers itself as providing a focal point of the NAM within the broad framework of the principles that dictated its existence. Similarly, the Commonwealth, representing as it does nearly a third of the total membership of the United Nations and based on the common law, constitutes a principal legal system in the world (in the meaning of the ICJ Statute), and should be encouraged to play more of a role in the international legal field than before; I advocated this approach when I served in 1990–1991 on a "think tank" appointed by the Secretary-General of the

Commonwealth, Chief Emeka Anyaokou, to look into the future activities of the Commonwealth. During the 1993 Summit held in Cyprus, our President was the proponent of the International Criminal Court item on the Summit agenda, which received a positive and favorable reference in the conclusion of the Conference.

Another important landmark was the coming into force last November, after obtaining the requisite sixty ratifications, of the Law of the Sea Treaty, following the painstaking modification of its Chapter XI by the July 29, 1994 Agreement, which removed the primary concerns of most of the developed industrialized countries. This compromise incidentally was made possible through the moderation, realism and sense of responsibility demonstrated by all concerned, but primarily by the developing countries, which made major concessions to political and economic realities. It was a repeat performance of the same attitude during the Conference itself (1973–1982), whereby the newly independent states participated constructively in shaping new rules, where necessary, and retaining old rules where appropriate.

This is not the time to go into specifics on the cardinal importance of this major law-making treaty covering the activities of three-fourths of the globe; this was done at the Inaugural Session held in Kingston, Jamaica, on 16 November 1994, and in which I had the privilege of participating. There is one point, however, particularly relevant to our topic here: the dispute-settlement system of the Law of the Sea Convention which, in certain respects, is more advanced than that under previous law-making conventions (although it falls short in certain important respects, e.g., those of delimitation disputes, from compulsory third-party settlement procedure). The Law of the Sea Tribunal under the Convention, to be located in Hamburg, Germany, is due to be created in August of 1996. This will open a new and promising chapter, parallel with that of the International Court of Justice. It deserves every possible support in developing its jurisdiction and jurisprudence in this fertile area of disputes, particularly considering the vagueness and imprecision of Articles 74 and 83 of the Law of the Sea Convention on delimitation of the economic zone and the continental shelf between opposite or adjacent states.

Speaking of new institutions of this kind naturally brings to attention the recent important developments in international criminal jurisdiction. Some of us have for decades advocated an international criminal court as a permanent institution and as an instrument of punishment and deterrence to current and future aggressors and violators of international criminal law. Considerable momentum has been created for the setting up of such a permanent international criminal court. The ILC did an outstanding job in producing a draft statute for it, as called for by the General Assembly, and later this month a Committee of the Whole in the General Assembly will be considering ways of removing the remaining difficulties. While I and others would have preferred a less minimalist approach than the ILC adopted, that was inevitable considering the political realities. If and when (and I prefer to think not of "if" but of "when") such a Tribunal is set up, one hopes during the Decade, it will be a major step forward and a fitting contribution by the international community to the Decade.

This leads me to addressing, very briefly, the work of the International Law Commission and its contribution to the objectives of the Decade. In specific terms, the ILC has agreed to produce a volume, entitled "International Law on the Eve of the Twenty-First Century", with articles contributed by virtually all members of the Commission. In broader terms the Commission has, through its regular work, already contributed substantially to the objectives of the Decade. I refer particularly to the adoption on first reading of the Draft Code of Crimes against the Peace and Security of Mankind (due to be taken up on second reading this May), Watercourses, Diplomatic Immunities, and substantial progress on State Responsibility and Liability, among others.

It should be noted, in particular, that State Responsibility has been transformed over the years from the traditional narrow notion primarily covering protection of aliens to a much broader topic including such progressive key elements as international crimes and *jus cogens*. In my view, these elements need to be retained and elaborated on in the future work of the ILC.

It is understandable that the Commission, in examining its future work, has opted for two items that are more manageable (reservations to treaties, and state succession and its impact on nationality). Nonetheless, since the notion of *jus cogens* (peremptory norms of international law from which no state may derogate by agreement or otherwise) was incorporated into international law in the 1969 Convention on the Law of Treaties, it has been referred to in debates at the United Nations, including the Security Council, has been the subject of in-depth studies by scholars, has been raised in the proceedings of learned societies, has been alluded to by the International Court of Justice and is often referred to in debates and documents of the International Law Commission (particularly the Code of Crimes and State Responsibility items). Yet there exists no authoritative statement of what the peremptory norms are or where they may be found. It is frequently said – and correctly in my view – that the principle of the prohibition of the use of force in international relations contained in Article 2 (4) of the UN Charter is *jus cogens*. Undoubtedly other principles and rules of international law exist for which the same status may be claimed. Evidently the exact parameters of what comes under the rubric of *jus cogens* need defining, since the situation as it now stands is not conducive to the objectivity, transparency and predictability that should characterize a legal principle, especially one so solemnly incorporated in such landmark treaties as the 1969 Vienna

Convention on the Law of Treaties and the 1986 Vienna Convention on the Law of Treaties between States and International Organizations. As it stands, *jus cogens* can mean a great deal to some and very little to others. It is important that this concept be considered by the ILC, a highly qualified authoritative body of experts (which codified it in the first place in the 1960s) with a view to establishing which rules of international law are indeed peremptory.[2]

I hope that a way will be found to do this during the Decade of International Law as an important contribution to the Decade, whether by the ILC or otherwise.

Finally, let me mention the very interesting and well-presented proposal by Professor Sohn for the adaptation of the Hague Conventions on the Pacific Settlement of International Disputes to the needs of the twenty-first century, as yet another possible contribution to the UN Decade of International Law. It certainly is an idea worth considering.

By way of tentative assessment, I would say that much has already been achieved in the past five years to promote the objectives of the Decade in a variety of areas I touched on and, no doubt, many others. Much more remains to be done during the remaining five years and beyond, and we should rededicate ourselves to achieving that. In this area, as in so many others, the relevance of the medieval theologian's prayer is ever present: Good Lord, give me the courage to change the things that can be changed, the patience to tolerate the things that cannot be changed and the wisdom to know the difference between the two.

[2] UN Doc. A/CN.4/454 of 9 November 1993 contains a further elaboration.

UN Reform Forum, America's Interests in the United Nations

Notes for a Statement at Georgetown University, Institute for the Study of Diplomacy, 14 February 2005

As a person who has been associated in different capacities with the United Nations (including a 3-term member of the U.N. International Law Commission) for the past forty-five years, and as a former longtime Ambassador of my country to the United States (1979–89 and 1993–96) I am very pleased to participate in this conference on "America's Interests in the United Nations", in the wake of the Report of the UN Secretary-General's High Level Panel (HLP) on Threats, Challenges and Changes or, more simply, on UN Reform.

Others are much better positioned to address the subject from the point of view of the interests of the United States in the United Nations. Indeed a very distinguished panel of former U.S. representatives to the United Nations, under the chairmanship of our own Chairman in the Institute for the Study of Diplomacy, Tom Pickering, have already been grappling with the subject in its various manifestations earlier today and we just had the benefit of hearing their views. We also heard from the Executive Office representative of the UN Secretary-General and the Director of the ISD and I want to thank Tom Weston for all his efforts in organizing this conference.

What I would like to do, taking into account the time constraint, is to make a few observations on the Report itself. I do so as a private individual and in the conviction, that, to a very considerable extent, the interests of the United States can and very often do coincide with those of the United Nations.

The Panel's Report (A/59/565, 99 pages with 101 recommendations, handsomely printed and widely distributed by the United Nations Foundation) released on December 2, 2004, was generally well received by the UN Member States, with some notable exceptions, e.g. by North Korea (People's Republic of Korea).

There is much worth noting in the Report on poverty reduction, environmental protection, nuclear non proliferation, steps to be taken for a better

United Nations etc. including the expansion of the Security Council so as to reflect the realities of 2005 and not of 1945. For example – in my view at least – the European Union should be represented on the Council.

Of these, I shall comment briefly on the aspect of international terrorism and the question of the legality of the use of force. Subsequently I will comment on what the Report, somewhat surprisingly, does not say on the International Court of Justice. In doing so I would emphasize the importance of the strengthening of the rule of law, as Secretary-General Kofi Annan rightly emphasized in his significant Address to the General Assembly last September.

International terrorism indeed attacks the values that lie at the heart of the Charter of the United Nations: respect for human rights; the rule of law; rules of war that protect civilians; tolerance among peoples and nations; and the peaceful resolution of conflict. share the view that achieving a comprehensive convention on terrorism, including a clear definition, is a political imperative. I recall that, back in 1972, the Sixth (Legal) Committee attempted and failed to achieve an agreed definition of terrorism. As the Vice-Chairman of the Committee at that time I had the unenviable task of explaining, in a lecture to the Council on Foreign Relations in New York, the circumstances which prevented agreement. The basic difficulty was that one's terrorist is someone else's freedom fighter. In the wake of the universal condemnation of the atrocious terrorist act of September 11, there was a new impetus in the Sixth Committee to get over the hurdle with substantial input by Secretary-General Kofi Annan, in which I tried to play my modest role as the Cyprus delegate. Regrettably, that opportunity was again missed since the Organization of the Islamic States took a firm stand which prevented the utilization of the momentum then existing and this persists today. Some argue that a formal definition is not really necessary since, like other such terms in legal nomenclature as "pornography", "investment", "aggression", are recognizable when you see them even in the absence of an agreed definition. I believe the Report performs a useful service to the international community in attempting such a definition (Para 164) and in indicating the other recommended steps to effectively combat international terrorism, although the definition proposed falls short of curing the key outstanding problems (military forces and liberation movements).

On collective security and the use of force, I am reminded, if I am permitted the flippancy, of the saying that when a dispute is taken to the United Nations something always disappears. If it is a dispute between two small States the dispute disappears; if it is a dispute between a large State and a small State the small State disappears; and if it is a dispute between two large States the United Nations disappears! It has to be recognized that effective collective security may require the backing of military force. But, if anarchy is not to prevail, any such decision for the use of force must be governed by international law. President Truman had it right when he stated that "we all have to recognize – no matter how great our strength – that we must deny ourselves the license to do always as we please".

The Panel is correct in stating that, in all cases, the Charter of the United Nations, properly understood and applied, is equal to the task: Article 51 (on self-defense) needs neither extension nor restriction of its long understood scope, and Chapter VII fully empowers the Security Council to deal with every kind of threat that States may confront. Indeed the task is not to find alternatives to the Security Council as a source of authority but to make it work better than it has. In this connection recent instances of the exercise of legislative power by the Security Council in combating international terrorism and nuclear proliferation deserve close attention.

There has been an evolution from the time of the adoption of the Declaration on Friendly Relations and Cooperation in Accordance with the Charter of the United Nations (GA Res. 2625 XXV) of 1970. In my view, these principles (sovereign equality, prohibition of the use of force, non intervention, peaceful settlement of disputes) remain valid but, in the light of subsequent experience including the humanitarian disasters in Somalia, Bosnia/Herzegovina, Rwanda, Kosovo and now Darfur, there is room for an emerging norm for a collective international responsibility to protect. This, however, must be exercised by the Security Council authorizing military intervention, as a last resort, in the event of genocide and other large-scale killing, ethnic cleansing or serious violations of international humanitarian law which sovereign governments are powerless or unwilling to prevent. The five basic criteria of legitimacy cited in the Report (Para. 207) are indeed relevant in authorizing the use of force.

Much thought has evidently been given by the Panel and its supporting personnel in setting out constructive suggestions regarding a more effective United Nations for the twenty-first century regarding all major United Nations organs, namely the Security Council, the General Assembly, the Economic and Social Council, the Trusteeship Council and the Secretariat. However, there is no mention of the sixth principal organ of the United Nations (as listed in Art. 7 of the Charter), the International Court of Justice which is (Art 1 of its Statute)" "the principal judicial organ of the United Nations". If there is an explanation for this evident omission I would appreciate hearing it.

This is not the occasion to expound on the very useful role the ICJ has and continues to play in the UN system and how it can be further improved. I would, however, like to be allowed to make two relevant observations.

The one is that the ICJ consists of 15 judges in 2005 when the United Nations consists of 191 Member States, the same number as it did in 1945 with 51 Member States. During the same period other main organs have been expanded in order to meet emerging needs. The ECOSOC from 18 to 54, the Security Council from 11 to 15 and now perhaps to 24 and the Secretary-General has acquired one Deputy and now possibly another under the proposed reform. Is this not something to reflect upon and, perhaps, after proper reflection, to reject only if it is not so warranted?

The other observation concerns the advisory function of the International Court of Justice. In a statement before the Sixth Committee of the General Assembly, on 5 November 2004, the President of the ICJ, Judge Shi, made some significant and thoughtful suggestions on the underutilization by States of the ICJ advisory procedure and its potential for expansion. He stressed that "in addition to offering legal guidance… the Court can play a role in international dispute resolution and prevention by providing legal guidance in order to facilitate the finding of a solution to actual international disputes".

For instance, I have for many years advocated resort to the International Court of Justice, through a decision of the General Assembly or of the Security Council for an Advisory Opinion clarifying the applicable rules of international law on several aspects of the Cyprus situation such as the disputed right of unilateral forcible intervention under Act IV of the 1960 Treaty of Guarantee; the illegality of the 1983 UDI; the illegality of the establishment of settlers in occupied territory, under the 1949 Geneva Conventions and the 1998 Statute of the International Court; the applicable rules of State responsibility, as for instance, occurred on Iraq-Kuwait under S.C. Res. 687; human rights etc.

I strongly feel that, in a comprehensive plan for a more effective United Nations, there exists room for such suggestions as the fuller utilization of the International Court of Justice in general and its advisory jurisdiction in particular. Clarifying authoritatively by the ICJ of the legal aspects of pending international political disputes, such as on Cyprus, can go a long way towards lastingly resolving such disputes in a way consistent with the applicable rules of international law.

International Law and Diplomacy, Some Reflections

C.V. Starr Lecture, New York Law School Center for International Law, October 25, 2006

When a well known and articulate American Ambassador finished his speech, an enthusiastic lady in the audience walked up to him to congratulate him and said: "Oh Mr. Ambassador, this speech was superfluous!" Realising her mistake, he replied tongue in cheek, "Perhaps I should publish it posthumously," to which she immediately responded "Oh yes! The sooner the better."

It is a great pleasure for me to be addressing a concerned and knowledgeable audience such as you. I realise that the topic I selected is very broad, but I hope it will give me the opportunity of summarising certain views – of necessity, not in depth – distilled over several decades, on a number of subjects of international law of topical importance.

While in my professional life I have been primarily a diplomat, and less so an arbitrator and a banker, I have over the years been, by conviction and training, an international lawyer, genuinely concerned with the need and desirability of the observance of the rules of international law, and have done – if I may say – my modest best to contribute to this end.

Allow me to recall, as an illustration of this position, that in my first statement in the Sixth Committee as a very green 23 year old delegate of Cyprus (Cyprus became independent in 1960 and was admitted to the United Nations in September of that year), I said that I "viewed with some apprehension… the suggestion that new States need not be bound by rules of international law which they had not helped to create and which ran counter to their interests" and stressed that the right view is that "national interests could not be allowed more weight than international legal obligations."

Perhaps before I go any further, I should caution you on a couple of points. I was once described as a "warm" speaker and I was pleased to hear it until the awful truth dawned on me that what was meant by "warm" was "not too hot!" The other is that currently I am in this country as a visitor, or non-resident alien, and I would not want to, and I presume you would not want me to, say or do anything that would make me an undesirable alien… There is another saying – attributed to a Japanese Ambassador – that a diplomat is someone who thinks twice before saying nothing. But if I applied this here literally it would not help much for, if it were so, what business do I have to be giving the C.V. Starr Lecture today?

So I shall proceed with the subject which, let me remind you, is Some Reflections on International Law in Diplomacy.

The old fashioned definition of international law is "the body of rules and principles of action which are binding upon civilised States in their relations with each other." Diplomacy has been described as "the application of intelligence and tact to the conduct of foreign relations." Indeed, other definitions exist, and other epithets have been applied to diplomats and to lawyers, but this may not be the appropriate time or occasion to go into...

What role does international law play in the conduct of diplomacy? This was one of the main subjects of the 1983 Annual Meeting of The American Society of International Law (ASIL), to which I, as the Ambassador of Cyprus to the United States at the time, participated as a panellist, together with the Ambassadors of Canada and of Venezuela, who were prominent international lawyers. The discussion elicited the conclusion that international law rules were invoked and relied upon in a great variety of situations, especially in negotiations which were juridical in nature. For my part I observed that, in my experience, international law principles and rules played a substantial role in my diplomatic work, more particularly in presenting, bilaterally and in international forums, aspects of the Cyprus question, couched in legal terms. It would go beyond the time limit of this lecture to expand, but this might be pursued in the Q and A period.

In subsequent years I had the occasion, time and again, to invoke rules such as diplomatic and consular privileges and immunities and the observance of the provisions of the United Nations Headquarters Agreement of 1947, as the Deputy Dean and later the Dean of the Diplomatic Corps in Washington, and as Chairman of the lost Country Relations Committee at the United Nations in New York. Each case provided many instances where diplomacy was exercised on the basis of the applicable international law rules.

It would perhaps be relevant to remind you of the very recent publication of ASIL "International Law: 100 Ways it Shapes Our Lives," which lists 100 tangible examples to demonstrate that "international law not only exists, but also penetrates much more deeply and broadly into every life than the people it affects may generally appreciate," ranging from health, to telecommunications, to labour relations, etc, etc. This goes way beyond the normal range of diplomacy. ASIL's activities in educating federal and other national judges on international law through its programme of judicial outreach, could be usefully supplemented by similar outreach exercises by foreign diplomats in national capitals, as we did in Washington, through an informal group of

Ambassadors who had previously served at the United Nations, on such topics as the U.S. ratification of the 1982 Law of the Sea Convention or the U.S. contribution to U.N. financing.

Now, going into the main part of my presentation, international terrorism, and international law aspects of combating it, is not a subject that lends itself to easy treatment. I recall that, back in 1972, the Sixth (Legal) Committee of the U.N. General Assembly attempted and failed to achieve an agreed definition of terrorism. As the Vice-Chairman of the Committee at the time, I had the unenviable task of explaining, in a lecture at the Council on Foreign Relations in New York, the circumstances which prevented agreement. There was much argument over the root causes of terrorism, the right of liberation movements and of people under foreign occupation or alien domination to use force to achieve freedom, and also of State terrorism. The basic difficulty was then, and continues to be now, that one's terrorist is someone else's freedom fighter (including, perish the thought, George Washington and Archbishop Makarios!)

In the wake of the universal condemnation of the atrocious attacks of 11 September, 2001, and following the unanimous adoption by the Security Council of S.C. Resolution 1373 (2001), there was a new impetus in the Sixth Committee to get over the hurdle of the definition, with substantial input by Secretary-General Kofi Annan, in which I tried to play my modest best as the Cyprus delegate. Alas, the opportunity was again missed, primarily because the Islamic group at the U.N. took a firm stand which prevented consensus and the utilisation of the existing momentum. A contributory factor to the lack of progress was also the divergence of positions on activities of military forces of a State during peacetime. Thus, there has yet to be achieved a universal convention against terrorism, including an acceptable definition, despite intensive efforts in various forums, including the High Level Panel on Threats, Challenges, and Change (paras. 157 to 164), and the Secretary-General's far reaching report "In Larger Freedom" (A/59/2005) of 21 March, 2005 (as well as other efforts at various forums, among other WFUNA, ASIL, the Stanley Foundation, and Georgetown University's Institute for the Study of Diplomacy, etc.).

In his most recent Report on the Work of the Organisation (A/61/1), the Secretary-General underlines that in the past 10 years, the threat of terrorism to international peace, security and development, has taken on new importance. The international community has taken a number of important steps to provide a solid legal basis for common action against terrorism, including the adoption of 13 universal instruments, the latest of which – the Convention for the Suppression of Acts of Nuclear Terrorism – was opened for signature at the 2005 World Summit. At the summit, world leaders resolved to take concerted action and strongly condemned, for the first time, terrorism in all its forms and manifestations, committed by whomever, wherever, and for whatever purpose.

United Nations counterterrorism activities expanded dramatically through the adoption of the milestone Security Council resolutions 1267 (1997), 1373 (2001), 1540 (2004), 1624 (2005), and through the setting up of three counterterrorism subsidiary bodies, making States more responsible for taking practical measures to prevent terrorist financing, travel, and access to weapons of mass destruction, as well as incitement to terrorism – remarkable instances of the exercise of legislative power by the Security Council. Additionally, many departments and agencies of the United Nations system are actively involved in their respective areas of competence.

In his latest report, the Secretary-General specifies additional steps he proposed based on the conviction that no cause, no matter how just, can excuse terrorism. The last chapter of this systematic effort is the adoption by the General Assembly (A/Res/60/288) on 8 Sept, 2006, of the "United Nations Global Counterterrorism Strategy" and its annexed Plan of Action. It was ceremoniously launched on 19 September, 2006, by the President of the General Assembly and the Secretary-General, with the participation of many foreign ministers. The Foreign Minister of Finland, speaking for the European Union, stressed that for the first time, the efforts of Member States, the United Nations system, and other relevant actors in the field of counterterrorism were highlighted in a single document, and urged all Member States to ratify or accede to all counterterrorism conventions and protocols, which formed – as he rightly stressed – the solid legal basis of the counterterrorism measures.

It remains to be seen whether the comprehensive convention of international terrorism will be achieved in light of all this.

It also remains a big question to what extent all this activity will achieve its purpose. But I believe it is correct to say that, in the area of international law, very important steps have been taken to effectively combat international terrorism to the extent political realities allow.

Passing on now to international criminal jurisdiction, perhaps I might be allowed some satisfaction by the fact that in the Sixth Committee, in the International Law Commission (ILC), and in the 1993 Commonwealth Heads of Government Conference (CHOGM), Cyprus, and if may say so, I personally, were among the pioneers favouring the establishment of an international criminal code and an international criminal tribunal as an instrument of deterrence and punishment, long before it became fashionable and acquired momentum through its espousal by the NGOs and was established in its present form, through the 1998 Rome Statute (with currently 102 Member State Parties). I realise this is a politically sensitive subject, especially in the United States but also in Russia and China, and perhaps I should hasten to add that the ICC and its Statute might have been different and more effective than in its present form in meeting the objective requirements of justice in any given situation. As to how effective the ICC as it is under the Rome Statute will prove to be, the jury is till out but some positive steps have already been taken.

Let me add parenthetically that, even though the Rome Statute does not place "terrorism" within the jurisdiction of the ICC, I have no doubt that actions such as those of September 11 would come squarely within the jurisdiction of the ICC under "crimes against humanity." Also that an agreed definition of the crime of aggression is still pending (as distinct from the definition in GA Resolution 3314, 1974).

I would also suggest that international criminal jurisdiction, as we originally proposed it in the ILC ("Code of Crimes Against the Peace and Security of Mankind"), in such conferences as at Talloires (1990) and Courmayeur (1991) and in the 1993 CHOGM, serves the requirements of justice in preference to ad hoc tribunals, in that it was not based on victors' law as in the Nuremberg and Tokyo tribunals or tailored to the occasion as in the former Yugoslavia and Rwanda tribunals. This does not mean that these tribunals have not served a useful purpose, only that a standing tribunal, based on objective notions of justice and of universal individual criminal liability, is preferable.

International criminal liability of individuals is the other side of the coin of the much wider concept of State Responsibility. Under customary international law, as articulated in the landmark case of the *Factory at Chorzow* (Germany v. Poland) by the Permanent Court of International Justice (1928), holding States responsible for damages caused by their unlawful actions, the governing principle is that damages should be awarded that are sufficient to wipe out the consequences of the illegal act and re-establish the situation that would, in all probability, have existed if that act had not have been committed. This was the principle on which the U.N. Compensation Commission (on which I served as a Commissioner for four years) operated in awarding to the government of Kuwait and other claimants, many billions of dollars as compensation for Iraq's illegal invasion and occupation of Kuwait in 1990, under S.C. Resolution 687 (1991).

Perhaps I could parenthetically observe that one can envisage many other situations in which unlawful acts generally, and unlawful invasion and occupation in particular, have occurred without the victim State obtaining any remedy. Indeed, it was a rare convergence when unanimous support in the Security Council for the adoption of Chapter VII binding resolutions occurred simultaneously with the availability of resources, in this case Iraqi oil, to satisfy the resultant claims. In a world where the rule of law applies, this exceptional situation ought to be the rule rather than the exception.

State Responsibility, this major topic of international law, was examined for many years by the ILC (of which I was a member for 15 years), having been progressively developed from a relatively narrow base of remedying injury to aliens. With the development of the notion of *jus cogens* and its acceptance in the 1969 Vienna Convention of the Law of Treaties, and the existence of hierarchically higher rules as set out in the U.N. Charter (articles 2 (4), 51, 103 and also 2 (6)) the topic of State Responsibility was put on a much broader foundation. It was also recognised by the International Court of Justice, that there exist obligations *erga omnes*, and that the interests of the whole international community, and of international public order, need to be taken into account. My own view, in the ILC and in the Sixth Committee, was strongly in favour of this transformation of State Responsibility as a proper expression of the application of progressive development. I urged that the Commission must ensure that the expectations of the international community, and of the new States in particular which came into existence after the classical rules of international law on this topic were formulated, not be disappointed. I also urged that the Commission must keep up with contemporary notions of international law such as international crimes, and not shirk from providing an effective and expeditious third-party dispute settlement system in the convention under elaboration. The Commission did produce a draft convention on State Responsibility in 2001, as a result primarily of the efforts of Professor James Crawford – the last of a long series of Special Rapporteurs – and this was noted and approved in principle by the General Assembly and will be taken up for further consideration and decision in 2007. It was a fine effort to finalise the project by the ILC but, perhaps unavoidably in order to reach consensus, it involved substantial surgery on some of the long-standing points of his agreement, and thus fell short of an ideal solution. But it did rely, in several respects, on the recognition of the validity of *jus cogens*, and in my view, this was a very positive contribution.

This leads me to a brief examination of the legal issues involved in this important topic of *jus cogens*, or peremptory norms of international law. This is a topic to which, over the years, I devoted a considerable amount of work, beginning in 1966 with a major paper at the Dag Hammarskjöld Seminar in Uppsala, continuing in the Vienna Convention on the Law of Treaties 1968–69, and in the Sixth Committee, including a paper submitted to the ILC proposing that it be taken up by the Commission (A/CN4/454, 9 November, 1993). Very briefly, *jus cogens* or peremptory norms of international law are rules from which the law does not permit any derogation by agreement between the parties *inter se* as distinct from *jus dispositivum*, i.e., rules which the parties may freely regulate by such agreement. First incorporated into international law by the Vienna Convention on the Law of Treaties in 1969 (articles 53, 64, and 66), it has had considerable historical background and was preceded by substantial preparatory work in the ILC and the Sixth Committee. While it has been frequently referred to in debates in the United Nations, including in the Security Council (e.g. on Cyprus in 1964), has been the subject of in-depth studies by scholars, has been raised in the proceedings of learned societies, has been alluded to by the International Court of Justice (with explicit reference most recently in its judgment of 3 February, 2006, *Judgment on Preliminary Objections in Armed Activities on the Territory of the Congo*, DR Congo/Rwanda on genocide), and is often referred to in debates and documents of the ILC (particularly in relation to the topic of State Responsibility as I indicated earlier), there exists no definitive statement of what norms are peremptory, or where they may be found.

It is frequently said, in my view correctly, that the principle against the use of force in international relations as set out in Article 2 (4) of the U.N. Charter, is *jus cogens*. Other principles and rules of international law exist for which the same status may be claimed (genocide, now recognised to be so by the ICJ, and slave trade, among others). Evidently there is need to define the content, i.e., the exact parameters of what comes under the rubric of *jus cogens* since the situation as it now stands is not conducive to the objectivity, transparency, and predictability which should characterise a legal principle. As it now stands, *jus cogens* can mean a great deal to some, and very little to others.

As I indicated earlier, during the 1993 session of the ILC, I took the initiative to propose that the selection of topics for inclusion in the Commissions long-term programme of work should include *jus cogens*. This would have given the opportunity to this highly qualified body of experts (which can be credited with progressively developing and codifying the concept in the first place, prior to the 1968–9 Vienna Conference) to study the subject, with a view of establishing which rules of international law are indeed peremptory. On the basis of the ILC's findings, States would then have the opportunity, through their representatives in the Sixth Committee and through written comments, to express their views, thereby carrying forward the process of giving exact legal meaning to *jus cogens* and filling in the legal vacuum on this topic. There was some support expressed in the Commission for the proposal, but not sufficient for its adoption, for reasons which are understandable, but, to me at least, not entirely convincing.

The current topic on the ILC's agenda of "Fragmentation of International Law" could have provided another channel to confront the problem, together with the notion of *erga omnes* and Article 103 of the Charter, but it appears from its latest reports that this was a challenge not taken up by the present membership of the ILC, and so the situation remains far from satisfactory.

This leads me to the next stage of our inquiry, which is the relationship between Article 2 (4) and Article 51 of the U.N. Charter, and their application to recent trouble spots in the world.

Article 2 (4) reads that "All Members shall refrain in their international relations from the threat or use of force against the territorial integrity or political independence of any State, or in any other manner inconsistent with the Purposes of the United Nations."

Article 51 states, in part that "Nothing in the present Charter shall impair the inherent right of individual or collective self-defence if an armed attack occurs against a Member of the United Nations, until the Security Council has taken measures necessary to maintain international peace and security. Measures taken by Members in the exercise of this right of self-defence shall be immediately reported to the Security Council…"

All Member States are legally bound by their signature to the United Nations Charter. This having been said, as in most legal situations, much depends on the interpretation of the law, as well as on the facts. Justice Sandra O'Connor once told me, only half in jest: "If you are strong on the law, argue the law; if you are strong on the facts, argue the facts; and if you are weak on both the law and the facts, cry a lot…"! Coming from a small State which has been the object of invasion and occupation by a much bigger and militarily stronger neighbour, my own inclination has been to interpret strictly Articles 2 (4) and 51 and state, in the words of Sir Humphrey Waldock, the British member of the ILC, soon after the Charter was adopted:

> The net result is that Article 2 (4) prohibits entirely any threat or use of force between independent States except in individual or collective self-defence under Article 51 or in execution of collective measures under the Charter for maintaining or restoring peace. Armed reprisals to obtain satisfaction for an injury, or armed intervention as an instrument of national policy otherwise than for self-defence, is illegal under the Charter.

The ICJ also tended toward a strict interpretation (in cases such as Nicaragua/US (1976); Iran/USA (2004); the Wall Advisory Opinion (2004); and most recently Congo/Uganda (2006) and so did the General Assembly of the U.N. (through its Resolutions 2625 (1970) on Friendly Relations, and 3314 (1974) on the Definition of Aggression).

However, there have been other interpretations supported by not inconsiderable arguments that, for instance, "if an armed attack occurs" is broad enough under the evolving rules of warfare, or in the new circumstances brought about by international terrorism, that a strict interpretation is no longer applicable, thus allowing for preventive or pre-emptive action, even before "an armed attack" occurs; and there has long been the concept of anticipatory self-defence under The Caroline doctrine (in the words of Secretary of State Daniel Webster: "necessity of self-defence instant, overwhelming and leaving no choice of means and no moment for deliberation").

The facts of the first Gulf War (1990–91) were such that there was no doubt as to the illegality of the Iraqi invasion and occupation of Kuwait, hence, the Security Council's unanimous reaction. The 2003 action against Iraq was supported by legal arguments based on the non-implementation by Iraq of existing Security Council Resolutions; the 1998 Kosovo military action was rationalised by the emergent doctrine of "responsibility to protect" (the scope of which remains disputed and controversial); while the recent involvement of Israel in Lebanon, which invoked self-defence against Hezbollah, was questioned as disproportionate. It is not my intention to go into the merits of these disputed arguments which are predicated on the distinction between what is new but permitted, and what has to be deemed unlawful, except to underline that the rule of law is essential for international legal order. In case of a disputed rule, the machinery provided first and foremost by the UN principal judicial organ, the International Court of Justice, but also by other means of third-party dispute settlement, including the Secretary-General's good offices should be resorted to, if we are to apply the rule of law and not the law of the jungle. Clarifying authoritatively by the ICJ, by its advisory jurisdiction, of the legal aspects of pending international political disputes – as proposed by successive Presidents of the ICJ Jennings, Schwebel and Shi – can go a long way towards lastingly resolving such disputes in a way consistent with the applicable rules of international law. Cyprus is one instance in point.

In the distant past, the world experienced *Pax Romana*, more recently it experienced *Pax Britannica*, currently there is talk of *Pax Americana*. Perhaps, to coin a phrase, what we should look for is *Pax Unitarum Nationum* based on the democratic exercise of rights and duties, equally by all Member States, under the principles and rules of the U.N. Charter, a treaty binding on all 192 Member States (and which indeed under Article 2(6), goes beyond the U.N. membership "so far as may be necessary for the maintenance of international peace and security"). Whether this is a realistic expectation, under the presently existing conditions in the world, is of course open to doubt – one could even describe it as mere wishful thinking.

On occasion, one can notice a tendency, even from unexpected quarters, of downgrading or even completely ignoring the relevance and applicability of international law rules. Perhaps I might cite the case of an article by a prominent personality in international affairs, who, in advocating a diplomatic solution to the current Iran situation (Financial Times, 12 April, 2006) cited a number of cogent relevant arguments in support of his position, but was totally silent on the applicable rules of international law. This was criticised in a letter published on the 17 April, 2006 in the same newspaper by Mr. Howard Mayer of New York, who considered it "striking, dismaying, and, sadly, not surprising that this failure even to consider the law that forbids such threats, agreed upon by our nation in the U.N. Charter, comes from the President of the Council on Foreign Relations, whose membership must be more familiar with our treaty obligations than the average American."

There is indeed another school of thought which proclaims that decisions involving the use of force in international relations are taken by politicians on political grounds and the function of the lawyers is "to be called in afterwards to provide arguments to justify these decisions." I recall that private admission of a very prominent British international lawyer who, in the context of the action taken by British Prime Minister Margaret Thatcher on the Falklands/Malvinas in 1982, said to her: "Prime Minister, you do what you think is right and international law will provide the arguments to support it." It so happens that, in this case, there were substantial legal arguments supporting the British use of military force. I would submit however, that the proper role of the legal adviser to a Foreign Ministry is to be consulted in advance and for the decisions, especially those involving the use of armed force, to be made taking fully into account the legal advice received before such decisions are taken, not afterward. Here, I am reminded that when a Cambridge don, lecturer in law died, they found in the margin of his lecture text, the notation "Argument weak. Raise voice!" Also of the reply of Senator Dirksen when accused of being unprincipled: "Me, unprincipled? Why, I am firmly wedded to the principle of utter flexibility."

We now pass to another field to which I have been exposed since leaving the Foreign Service. It involves such areas as arbitration, mass claims processes and corporate governance.

My experience with arbitration has been partly as an arbitrator at the International Centre for the Settlement of Investment Disputes (ICSID) at the World Bank in Washington, D.C.

The rationale behind the 1965 ICSID Convention was to provide potential prospective investors with the assurance that legal disputes arising out of investments, primarily in developing countries, could be adjudicated before an international tribunal rather than the courts of country of the State concerned, as an incentive for making such an investment. The existence of such a facility, and the assurance of predictability and impartiality, equally in relation to both parties, works correspondingly also to the benefit of the State concerned since it can thereby attract foreign investment needed for its economic development.

It is a key element in international arbitrations in general, and ICSID arbitrations no less, that, short of deciding *ex aequo et bono*, there is a greater latitude than in proceedings before national or international courts, enabling the tribunal to look at the broad picture in order to reach a just and fair result, beyond narrow legalism and technicalities – whether this is always observed in practice is another matter.

The role of ICSID and of bilateral investment treaties – many of which incorporate the "fair and equitable" standard – have lately become more significant and the Centre's jurisdiction substantially expanded, taking also into account its role under NAFTA. While it is essential for all of the players to have confidence in the fairness of any decision, unavoidably there is an element of subjectivity and unpredictability in international arbitral awards, depending on the tribunal making the decision. In my view, it would help to reduce this element of unpredictability if the critical element of "investment" were clarified. It was not defined, intentionally, in the ICSID Convention although, admittedly, there exist several other terms in legal nomenclature such as "terrorism" – as we have already seen –, "aggression" and "pornography" (not to mention also "sin" which mayor may not be a legal term…) which do not readily lend themselves to definition and yet are recognised and given legal effect when they occur.

Besides ICSID at the World Bank, international arbitrations are being carried out under the auspices of the Permanent Court of Arbitration (The Hague) and by other international, regional or national bodies such as the International Chamber of Commerce (ICC, in Paris), the London Court of International Arbitration (LCIA), the American Arbitration Association (AAA), and the Swiss Arbitration Association (ASA), among others, which also flourish.

An important, relatively recent, development has been the coming into existence of several mass claims tribunals. These include the Iran – United States Tribunal in The Hague, the United Nations Compensation Commission (UNCC) in Geneva – to which I alluded earlier in the context of State Responsibility –, the Claims Resolution Tribunal for Dormant Accounts in Switzerland (CRT I, II in Zurich), the Commission for Real Property Claims in Bosnia and Herzegovina (CRPC) in Sarajevo, the German Slave Labour programme, the Eritrea-Ethiopia Claims Commission, the Housing and Property Claims Commission in Kosovo, and the International Commission on Holocaust Era Insurance Claims. For those who are interested to pursue the subject there have been several publications and a new major book is coming out very soon under the auspices of the Permanent Court of Arbitration, through a steering committee appointed by its Secretary-General, in which I participated.

I have already referred to the workings of the United Nations Compensation Commission, a subsidiary organ of the U.N. Security Council established by Security Council Resolution 692 (1991) which, through Panels of Commissioners processed claims for compensation for damages resulting from Iraq's invasion and occupation of Kuwait. I was with the F-3 Panel dealing with the Kuwait Government claims and we recommended the award of 8.5 billion dollars after thorough examination of claims amounting to over 100 billion dollars.

I also had the unique experience of serving for four years under the Volcker Process with the Claims Resolution Tribunal for Dormant Accounts in Switzerland as an Arbitrator for CRT I, and as a senior judge with CRT II (one of sixteen, the others being Americans, Israelis, Swiss, one Canadian and one British). It was a challenging and daunting assignment to resolve all claims to dormant accounts opened by non-Swiss nationals in Swiss banks in the period prior to and during the Second World War, many of them holocaust-related. The tribunal completed its work, using relaxed rules of evidence and other rules adjusted to the uniqueness of the situation, in a way which satisfied, by and large, both the account holders and their heirs and also the Swiss Banks, the reputation of which was in jeopardy as a result of negative publicity internationally.

It is a fact that in recent years there has been a proliferation (my friend, Judge Rosalyn Higgins prefers to call it "burgeoning") of international courts, tribunals, and commissions. This in general is good news for the profession, but there are risks. For instance, different tribunals might take different positions on the same issue of international law. For example, the Strasbourg European Court of Human Rights took a position different from that of the International Court of Justice on the question of territorial reservations in declarations of compulsory jurisdiction in the *Loizidou v. Turkey* case before ECHR – a case which can be explained as due to *lex specialis*. There should be no doubt that, especially when it comes to questions of public international law, the ICJ is the principal judicial organ of the United Nations and its decisions are, in the vast majority of cases, cited and followed. While international law remains more centralised than ever, the number of actors and arbitrators continues to increase. But the gap is not as great as it might appear. For instance, some of the same lawyers serve as counsel and judges in ICJ, ICSID and private commercial arbitrations, applying a combination of public and private international law. Indeed, the exposure to private international law principles, procedures and substantive legal doctrines has had an effect on the jurisprudence of the ICJ, just as the jurisprudence of the ICJ has had an effect on arbitral decisions. Cross fertilisation and proliferation of courts and tribunals can be useful elements in the progressive development of international law, provided they are approached wisely and with caution.

In my most recent incarnation, that of a banker back home on the Board of the Bank of Cyprus (in Cyprus itself and also in the United Kingdom and in Australia), I have been exposed to the current notions of corporate governance, of which there is awareness of, and compliance with, as much as in the United States. There is enhanced recognition that the Board of Directors, particularly its independent non-executive members, are under the obligation to effectively exercise checks and balances and to question the actions and proposals of the executives, bearing in mind primarily the interests of the shareholders, and also of the need and the responsibility to guide management on matters involving general policy and direction. Cyprus having become a European Union member as of 1 May, 2004, the boards of public companies are subject to the regulation not only of the Central Bank of Cyprus, but also of the European Central Bank. Our bank retained McKinsey and Co. to advise on restructuring so as to comply fully with current notions of corporate governance and have not been insensitive to the concerns of corporate abuse, which led to the adoption in the United States of the Sarbanes-Oxley Act. While I think that the corporate regulation under the Act, brought about after the Enron, WorldCom and other scandals, was necessary, it may well be that there is some room for reform so as to lighten the burden, especially for smaller companies, and to avoid the emigration of American corporations to other jurisdictions, such as in the United Kingdom, which have less stringent requirements. While it seems there is an emerging consensus in the United States that the law needs some change in this direction, a full-scale repeal is quite unlikely since it is recognised that its adoption resulted in improvement in corporate accounting and control.

This leads me to the last part of my presentation, dealing very briefly with some aspects of the Law of the Sea.

This is a very broad subject, developed over centuries as customary law, since the time of Grotius (and earlier, in the Rhodian Code) and codified with new features such as the Exclusive Economic Zone (EEZ), and the common heritage of mankind, in the landmark 1982 U.N. Convention of the Law of the Sea, the veritable constitution of the oceans (which I had the honour to sign in Montego Bay in Dec 1982 having participated in its various phases since 1973, and earlier in the Preparatory Committee). The large majority of the international community (149, as of now) are States Parties to the convention, and it is expected that the United States will do likewise as soon as it is ratified by the U.S. Senate which hopefully will happen soon (successive administrations, including the present one, are in favour of the convention, and it has been approved by the Senate's Foreign Relations Committee.)

During the Conference, the Cyprus delegation strongly supported the 12-mile limit for the territorial sea and advocated that enclosed or semi-enclosed seas, such as the Mediterranean, should be regulated by the same basic rules as those applicable to other seas and oceans, and also for the protection of archaeological objects found at sea. Beyond these, we concentrated on certain key issues of primary concern to Cyprus. These were first, the Regime of Islands and their undiminished entitlement to the zones of maritime jurisdiction (territorial sea, contiguous zone, exclusive economic zone, and continental shelf) which was achieved through the adoption of Article 121; secondly, the question of the delimitation of these zones of maritime jurisdiction between States the coasts of which are opposite or adjacent to each other on the basis of the median or equidistance line, to some extent achieved, but in some other respects left ambiguous (Articles

15, 74, 83); and thirdly, the question of settlement of disputes (Part XV Articles 274–99 and Annexes VI, VII, VIII). During the intervening years, as a result of decisions of the ICJ in the *Libya v. Malta* case (1985), the *Jan Mayen* case (Denmark/Norway, 1993); the *Qatar/Bahrain* case (2001); and, most recently, the *Bakassi Peninsula* (Cameroon/Nigeria, 2002) and also as a result of decisions of arbitral tribunals in the *Eritrea/Yemen* (1999) and *Barbados/Trinidad and Tobago* (2006) cases, the court "first determines provisionally the equidistance/median line and then asks itself whether there are any special circumstances or relevant factors requiring this initial line to be adjusted with a view to achieving equitable results" (Judge R. Ranjeva on behalf of the ICJ, in the 1982 Convention's 20th anniversary event). This is a fair and reasonable solution, clarifying the vagueness in the wording of Articles 74 and 83 of the Convention.

It might interest you to know that very recently, Cyprus concluded an agreement with Egypt on the delimitation of the EEZ between the two countries (signed in 2003 and ratified in 2004), a significant event in that, apart from its practical aspects (fisheries, potential oil and natural gas deposits, etc.) it is the first such agreement by Cyprus with one of its major neighbours on the basis of thc pure median line, which had been our position in the Conference all along, hopefully to be followed by other such agreements with other neighbours in the eastern Mediterranean. Another positive feature of this agreement is that, under its Article IV, any dispute which might arise and not be settled within a reasonable time with diplomatic means, should be referred to arbitration.

Indeed, the consistently held position, which I articulated since 1976 in the Law of the Sea Conference and which, in my opinion, is applicable also to the dispute settlement systems of all other multilateral law-making treaties, is that the substantive provisions of each such treaty (be it the Law of the Sea, State Responsibility, or any other) ought to be accompanied by "an effective, comprehensive, expeditious and viable dispute settlement system entailing a binding decision regarding all disputes arising out of all substantive provisions of the Convention." This position was dictated both by reason of attachment to the general principle of equal justice under the law, and by national self-interest, as representing a small and militarily weak State, which needs the protection of the law, impartially and effectively administered, in order to safeguard its legitimate rights under the convention.

I still maintain this is a right and defensible position, but whether it is achievable in practice is another question. Progress has been made in this direction during the Law of the Sea Conference, and there is currently a wide variety of tribunals, the Law of the Sea Tribunal (which has just celebrated the 10th anniversary of its establishment in Hamburg), the International Court of Justice, which over several years has dealt with several aspects of Law of the Sea, and *ad hoc* arbitral tribunals, some of which have made major contributions to the development of the subjects they dealt with (*Barbados/ Trinidad & Tobago* of April 2006 being the most recent example).

This concludes my reflections on International Law in Diplomacy. If I tired you, I apologise, but the intention was to try to educate rather than to entertain.

It was said, at a time when it was safe to make such observations without being considered a sexist, that a speech should be like a lady's skirt: long enough to cover all the essential parts, and short enough to be interesting… In this case, I am afraid the skirt may have gone all the way to the floor! So let me finish where I began: if you feel that my lecture was superfluous, shall I consider publishing it posthumously?

Part B

Cyprus

The Cyprus Problem and the United Nations*◊

When I was first approached with the request that I participate in this Seminar to present a paper on the Cyprus problem and the United Nations, my first question was how long that paper was expected to be. A conscientious researcher, in order to do justice to the subject, could easily fill many bulky volumes on the basis of the available material. To give just two examples, the late Professor Xydis produced two books of over one thousand pages (entitled *Cyprus: Conflict and Conciliation and Cyprus: The Reluctant Republic*) to cover solely the early stage of the subject and I myself remember writing a never-published more than a hundred-page confidential memorandum, for the purposes of the Ministry of Foreign Affairs of the Republic, with the Cyprus recourse to the General Assembly in 1965 alone. The unquestionable fact is that the Cyprus problem, in its various aspects and phases of evolution, has been inextricably linked with the history and evolution of the United Nations over the past twenty-three year period.

What I propose to do, for the purposes of today's presentation, is to identify four phases corresponding, respectively, to (i) the period before the independence of Cyprus; (ii) the period of 16 August 1960 to December 1962; (iii) the period of December 1963 to July 1974; and (iv) the period from July 1974 to the present date. In view of the limitation of time, I will not even attempt to deal now with the first period and I shall briefly touch upon the second, thus making it possible to concentrate more on the remaining two periods.

When Cyprus, as an independent state, was unanimously admitted to membership of the United Nations on 20 September 1960, it started with a clean slate. It was hoped that the traumatic experiences of the years

* Previously published in CYPRUS REVIEWED, ed. M. Attalides, Jus Cypri Association (1977).

◊ For other selected writings by Andrew Jacovides on Cyprus *see*: Cyprus: international law and the prospects for settlement, Opening Statement 78th Annual Meeting of ASIL, Washington, 12–14 April 1984; International Law and Diplomacy: The Case of Cyprus, *Los Angeles World Affairs Council World Affairs Journal*, Winter 1985, pp. 42–52; Ask the International Court of Justice to assist in Cyprus Settlement, Letter to *Cyprus Weekly*, 20–26 January 2006.

immediately preceding would be forgotten and that, despite its small size and population, it would be able to play a modest but constructive role in international affairs by taking positions on issues before the Organization not mechanically and on the basis of allegiance to military alliances but on the merits of each issue in relation to the principles of the Charter. More specifically, in its geographical region and being located between three continents, it aspired to transform its role from being a bone of contention and a source of discord to serving as a bridge of peace and cooperation among its immediate neighbours. This position was authoritatively stated by H.B. Archbishop Makarios, President of the Republic, in his address to the General Assembly on 7 June 1962.

The international climate of the time was conducive to that end. It will be recalled that this was the time of the emergence from colonial rule of many new states, mainly in Africa, which upon independence joined the United Nations thus transforming its composition and voting patterns. It was the time when the concept of Non-Alignment was first elaborated upon through the Belgrade Conference of 1961 and became a sizable moral and political force in world affairs. And it was the time when, under President Kennedy and Chairman Kruschev, respectively, the United States and the Soviet Union were eagerly competing for influence among the non-aligned and newly independent states, In short, the circumstances were propitious and the delegation of Cyprus had the opportunity, through active participation on issues before the various United Nations organs, of effectively playing a role considerably exceeding that which would be expected if one only took into account the country's size and population. Whatever the issue, be it disarmament, decolonization, international law matters or, more specifically, questions such as that of Algeria, Palestine, South Tyrol, Korea, Cuba or the India-China situation, the Cyprus delegation was consulted, its assistance was sought and its positions, which were dictated by the basic considerations indicated earlier as a small, non-aligned, developing state, newly independent and having just emerged from colonial rule after a liberation struggle, were carefully listened to and given considerable weight. Put differently, even though somewhat immodestly, Cyprus was a factor to be reckoned with in United Nations affairs.

It should be remembered that the period of 1960 to the end of 1963, was the time, in fact the only time, when Cyprus was not labouring under a problem of its own.

During this formative period, Cyprus made the United Nations and the principles of the Charter central to its foreign policy and this had a significant and direct effect upon subsequent developments. In December 1963 when, following serious internal difficulties the Republic of Cyprus was confronted by serious threats and acts of aggression by Turkey, it was natural that it should turn for protection to the United Nations in preference to other international Organizations or Alliances, and seek the application to its case also of the Charter principles for the application of which it has struggled in the cases of others. Correspondingly, the Organization through its political organs, notably the Security Council and the General Assembly, as well as the Secretariat, responded positively to this appeal. Thus, the good standing of Cyprus in the United Nations and its policy of commitment to the Charter principles, had a direct effect upon the positive response which was given by the Organizations to the plea for protection and support against the actions in violation of these same Chatter principles.

It would be relevant to make clear that from 1964 onwards, and even more so since July/August 1974, the primary consideration determining the position of the Cyprus delegation on issues before the United Nations has been, of course, the Cyprus problem in its various facets. Nevertheless, both as a matter of principle and as a matter of national self-interest, every effort is being made consistently to continue playing an active role on as many other issues as possible and through active participation in as many United Nations bodies as are available, on the basis of the same considerations which guided our stand during these first four years.

The Cyprus problem was formally placed before the United Nations, for the first time since the pre-independence events, on 26 December 1963. On that day, the Cyprus Government, through a letter of its Permanent Representative in New York (S/5488) lodged a complaint to the Security Council charging Turkey with acts of aggression and intervention against the Republic in violation of Turkey's obligations under the Charter. This was inscribed on the Council's agenda and, as subsequently supplemented, has been the basis of the item during the whole of this period of 1963–1974 to which I would now turn.

As stated earlier, it would be beyond the pale of practical possibility to give a detailed chronological account of all the developments concerning the examination of the Cyprus problem by the United Nations and, still less, of the corresponding actions taken and resolutions adopted by other international forums such as the Commonwealth and Non-Aligned Conferences, although it is significant to bear in mind that, in view of the overlapping involved, the United Nations developments directly affect such other actions and resolutions and vice versa. Nor will it be possible to deal with developments concerning the Cyprus problem in the UNDP or in such Specialized Agencies of the United Nations as UNESCO, ILO, WHO, etc., even though they too had an involvement directly or indirectly with it regarding matters falling within their range of activities.

What I intend to do is to provide an account, in general terms, of the main developments and to refer, for additional background and details, those who are particularly interested to such useful reference material as the publications of the Public Information Office (*Cyprus – The Problem in Perspective*, 1967 and subsequent editions; *The Function of the United Nations Force in Cyprus*, 1967 – with both of which I am not entirely unrelated – *The Cyprus Problem*, 1975) other books and publications and, of course, the relevant United Nations records.

The Cyprus Government's complaint was examined in an emergency session of the Security Council on 27 December 1963, in the light of information received of naval movements and other preparations for a Turkish invasion in the context of the intercommunal troubles. This meeting was adjourned after a debate which served its purpose but without a formal conclusion and, after the failure of the London Conference and certain NATO initiatives and the further aggravation of the situation, the question was considered by the Council extensively during its meetings of February and March 1964, convened also at the request of the Cyprus Government (even though the British delegation, in an effort to preempt the field, also made a request for a meeting). Meanwhile, the United Nations Secretary-General with the willing consent of the Government of Cyprus, had appointed, on 16 January 1964, General Gyani (India) as his Personal Representative in order to follow developments on the Island. The result of the Security Council's deliberations was the unanimous adoption on 4 March 1964, after protracted negotiations of its landmark Resolution 186 (1964), which has since been repeatedly reaffirmed and which throughout the period under review has provided the basic framework of the Security Council's action. Resolution 186 (1964) was based on the premise that, under Article 2 (4) of the Charter,

> all Members of the United Nations shall refrain in their international relations from the threat or use of force against the territorial integrity or political independence of any state.

In its three main elements, it provided (i) that the above principle should be respected with regard to Cyprus; (ii) that a United Nations Peace-Keeping Force in Cyprus (UNFICYP) be set up, with the consent of the Government of Cyprus, and laid down its mandate land modalities; and (iii) that a United Nations mediator be appointed for the purpose of promoting a peaceful solution and an agreed settlement of the problem confronting Cyprus in accordance with the Charter. While the Council took no clear position as to the validity or invalidity of the Treaty of Guarantee, by calling for the respect of the principle cited in Article 2 (4) above, it indirectly vindicated the Cyprus Government's claim that the Treaty conferred no right to use military force against Cyprus in violation of this peremptory norm (*jus cogens*) of international law which prevails over any treaty which is in conflict with it.

Let us now consider how this Resolution was implemented. In so far as element (i) was concerned, Turkey continued the threat and use of force against Cyprus and this necessitated additional Security Council emergency sessions, such as that in August 1964. Regarding element (ii), UNFICYP was set up and it is generally acknowledged that it has been discharging its functions, as set out in the Resolution and interpreted from time to time in the light of factual developments by the Secretary-General, in a commendable manner. While it was set up originally for three months only, it has proven necessary for the Security Council on the recommendation of the Secretary-General, to renew its mandate time and again in six-monthly intervals as its presence is still considered indispensable. As for element (iii) in Resolution 186, the Secretary-General designated as United Nations Mediator originally Mr. Tuomioja (Finland) and after his sudden death in August 1964, Dr. Galo Plaza (Ecuador). Dr. Plaza's Report, which he submitted to the Secretary-General on 26 March 1965, was a closely reasoned and constructive document which was fully consistent with his mandate under para. 7 of the Resolution 186 and, in the opinion of all impartial observers, both at the time of its issue and in retrospect, could have formed the basis of a fair, just and viable solution to the Cyprus problem.

In some of his observations, Dr. Plaza proved prophetic when one looks at his Report now in the light of the intervening developments and with the benefit of hindsight. Thus, referring to the Turkish proposals for federation, he wrote "it seems to require a compulsory movement of the people concerned – many thousands on both sides – contrary to all enlightened principles of the present time, including those set forth in the Universal Declaration of Human Rights." He also wrote:

> In fact, the arguments for the geographical separation of the two communities under a federal system of government have not convinced me that lit would not inevitably lead to partition;

and further that the physical division of the minority from the majority should be "considered a desperate step in the wrong direction". Despite the fact that the Secretary-General supported Dr. Plaza's interpretation of his mandate, his Report was flatly rejected by Turkey on the spurious ground that he exceeded his mandate, and this caused the subsequent resignation of the mediator. Even though certain quasi-mediational functions were conferred by the Secretary-General upon his Special Representative in Cyprus in 1966 and the latter exercised his good offices in this regard, the United Nations mediation system under para. 7 of Resolution 186 has remained dormant since that time.

The Security Council continued to be seized of the item on Cyprus throughout the period under review, to receive the Reports of the Secretary-General and communications from the parties concerned regarding the situation, to hold periodic debates on the occasion of the renewal of UNFICYP's mandate as well as emergency sessions such as those during the November–December 1967 crisis, in which the Secretary-General also played a very active and constructive role, and to re-affirm its basic Resolution 186 and subsequent resolutions. But, for a variety of reasons about which I shall say more later, it did not find it possible to proceed to more drastic action.

During the same period, the General Assembly was also seized of the situation in Cyprus at the initiative of the Cyprus Government. As a result of a request originally submitted to its Nineteenth Session (1964) and which was pursued during the Twentieth Session, the General Assembly, after fully debating all the aspects of the matter in the First Political Committee, adopted on 18 December 1965 its Resolution 2077 (XX), which amounted to a full vindication of the Cyprus Government's position for the full sovereignty, complete independence, unity and territorial integrity of Cyprus and thus considerably strengthened our position. It included a reference not only to the Report of the United Nations Mediator (*A/6017*) but also to the *Declaration of Intent and Memorandum of the Cyprus Government (A/6039)*, whereby it committed itself to the full application of human rights to all citizens of Cyprus, irrespective of race and religion, and to the ensuring of minority rights and in which the Government offered to adopt any appropriate machinery that the Secretary-General, on the advice of the Human Rights Commission, might recommend in order to ensure the practical observance of these rights.

This Resolution was also brusquely rejected by Turkey which totally ignored its provisions. It was followed by the Greek-Turkish dialogue and was left largely unutilized for reasons which go beyond the scope of this paper.

In subsequent sessions of the General Assembly, the Question of Cyprus though not placed as such on the agenda, was raised and briefly discussed both in the course of the General Debate on the overall international situation which takes place every year, and in the context of specific items before the Main Committees of the General Assembly but was not actively pursued.

You will have noted that the 6-year period of 1968 to 1974 was one of relative quiet in so far as the Cyprus problem before the United Nations was concerned. The explanation lies of course in the fact that from June 1968, the local intercommunal talks on the constitutional aspect of the Cyprus problem were being held in Nicosia. These were initiated following a series of unilateral normalization measures carried out by the Cyprus Government and as a result of certain diplomatic initiatives. These talks were held within the framework of the good offices of the Secretary-General and, as was made clear by him and accepted by the Turkish side, on the basis of a unitary, independent and sovereign state in Cyprus. As you are also aware, these talks did not result in agreement and by early 1974, when rumblings were heard from the new Ankara Government which were inconsistent with this agreed basis of the talks, and due to certain other developments in Cyprus and Greece, prospects for an agreement were further dimmed. Nevertheless, this procedure was still in existence until it was brought to an abrupt end by, the events of the summer of 1974.

This brings us to the last, and more current period under review, which is the Cyprus problem before the United Nations from the Turkish invasion of July/August 1974 until today.

I will not take your time by recapitulating the chronology of events which are well established and known to all.

The Turkish invasion, which began on 20 July 1974, using the criminal coup d'état of five days earlier as a pretext, led, through a combination of brute force, blackmail and deception to the completion of the Attila II operation in August 1974, with the tragic results in terms of human suffering and material destruction of which we are all too aware, to the aggressive occupation by Turkey of a large part of the territory of Cyprus and the uprooting of nearly two hundred thousand Greek Cypriots. This blatant aggression, and its sequel, the attempt to alter by force the demographic character of Cyprus by the massive importation of alien population from Turkey, coupled with the inhuman policy of expulsions of the remaining Greek Cypriots in the occupied areas, have combined to give the Cyprus problem infinitely more serious dimensions. In relation to the United Nations it has become a test case of the ability of the Organization to meet a challenge to its most basic tenets. The Turkish aggression in Cyprus has raised fundamental questions for the United Nations which affect not only Cyprus, which is the immediate victim, but also the very ability of the United Nations itself to survive after such gross violation of its principles.

In so far as the Cyprus Government is concerned, it has multiplied and intensified its efforts to project the problem in the international field and to obtain the maximum political and diplomatic support for its case. This effort has been particularly pursued before all available appropriate organs of the United Nations. In practical terms, this means the Security Council, the General Assembly, and its various Main Committees (especially the Third Committee which deals with humanitarian matters), the Commission on Human Rights, the Committee on the Elimination of Racial Discrimination (CERD) but also, whenever the opportunity arises, before such bodies as the Economic and Social Council, the Committee on the Review of the Charter, etc. Appropriate representations are also made whenever necessary and contacts are maintained with the United Nations Secretariat, The importance of the role played by the Secretary-General should not be underestimated, and his overall contribution and efforts should be duly appreciated. In addition, the United Nations provides the possibility for many contacts with the 144 Member States represented at the United Nations. These contacts are carried out both collectively, such as with the Coordinating Committee of 17 of the Non-Aligned and individually, especially bearing in mind our minimal possibilities of diplomatic representation on the bilateral level. In short, much of our diplomatic activity in projecting the Cyprus cause is performed through the United Nations. While the details of this activity do not, and ought not, as a rule become public knowledge, I believe it is right and fair that it should not be assumed that these possibilities are neglected.

I shall now proceed to give, as dispassionately and objectively as I can, a brief account of the main decisions taken by the United Nations regarding the Cyprus problem since the Turkish invasion. (Regarding the texts and other details I would again refer those interested to the Public Information Office Publication *The Cyprus Problem*, December 1975 edition, and to the relevant United Nations records.)

During the early stages of the invasion and throughout the critical months of July and August 1974, the Security Council which was already in session on the Cyprus situation immediately following the coup at the instance both of the Permanent Representative of Cyprus and of the Secretary-General of the United Nations, passed a series of resolutions beginning with Resolution 353 (1974) adopted on 20 July 1974 in which *inter alia*, it called for a ceasefire and demanded an immediate end to foreign military intervention and followed this up by Resolutions 354 (1974), 355 (1974), 357 (1974), 358 (1974), 359 (1974), 360 (1974) and 361 (1974). By December 13 of the same year, the Security Council, in addition to renewing UNFICYP's mandate (Resolution 364 (1974)), unanimously adopted the important Resolution 365 (1974) by which it endorsed General Assembly Resolution 3212, adopted earlier by the General Assembly, thus vesting its provisions with the authority of the Security Council.

Following the unilateral declaration of 13 February 1975, purporting to create a so-called "federated Turkish state" in Cyprus, the matter was again referred to the Security Council by the Cyprus Government. After protracted deliberations, the Council adopted on 12 March 1975 Resolution 367 (1975) by which *inter alia*, it "regretted" the purported declaration, affirmed that such a declaration does not prejudge the final political settlement, called for the urgent and effective implementation of Resolution 3212 (XXIX) endorsed by its Resolution 365 (1974) and requested the Secretary-General to undertake a new mission of good offices under his personal auspices and direction towards comprehensive negotiations. In June and December 1975, the Security Council held two more debates on the Cyprus situation and passed two resolutions (*S/RES/370* of 13 June 1975 and *S/RES/383* of 13 December

1975 respectively) renewing UNFICYP's mandate and re-affirming its earlier resolutions and, in the latter case, making reference also to General Assembly Resolution 3395 adopted on 20 November 1975.

During all this period, numerous letters from the Permanent Mission of Cyprus containing protests and denunciations against the Turkish actions and furnishing evidence of violations by Turkey of the principles of the Charter, the United Nations resolutions on Cyprus and the rules of international law, were submitted and circulated to all Members of the United Nations as Security Council documents, most recently *S/12077* dated 17 May 1976, regarding the expulsions of the Greek Cypriots.

As far as the General Assembly's action is concerned, every effort was also made to inform its members of the true facts in Cyprus and to enlist its support for a just solution. The President of Cyprus Archbishop Makarios himself delivered two major addresses as Head of State (the one on October 1, 1974 and the other on October 7, 1975 – *A/PV.2251* and *A/PV.2378*) and major debates were held during the twenty-ninth and thirtieth sessions in 1974 and 1975 in the Plenary itself as well as in the Special Political Committee. After considerable preparatory work, in which the Non-Aligned played a major part, these debates resulted in General Assembly Resolution 3212 (XXIX) adopted unanimously on 1 November 1974 and of General Assembly Resolution 3395 (XXX) adopted on 20 November 1975, by a vote of 117 in favour with only Turkey voting against.

These can only be regarded as major diplomatic successes, both in terms of the overwhelming support they received and in terms of their provisions, which called *inter alia* for the respect of the sovereignty, independence, territorial integrity and non-alignment of the Republic of Cyprus; for the withdrawal without further delay of all foreign forces from it; for the voluntary return of all refugees to their homes, as well as for meaningful and constructive negotiations.

The adoption of Resolution 3212 (XXIX), endorsed by Resolution 365 (1974) of the Security Council, was in turn helpful for the adoption by the Non-Aligned Coordinating Committee meeting at Ministerial Level in Havana in March 1975 of the declaration on Cyprus pledging in addition "full support to the Government of Cyprus" and declaring that "aggression against it constitutes an aggression against the whole body of non-aligned countries and a menace against their independence...". In turn, the Lima Declaration of the Non-Aligned Foreign Ministers Meeting in September 1975, inter alia, also called for the "immediate and unconditional withdrawal of foreign troops", for the "immediate return of the refugees" and condemned the purported declaration regarding the so-called "Turkish federated state". The same can be said of the Kingston Commonwealth Heads of Government Meeting of May 1975 which, in addition to expressing its solidarity with the Government and people of Cyprus and reiterating the call for the implementation of the provisions of the United Nations Resolution on Cyprus, decided also the setting-up of a Commonwealth Committee of 7 members in order to assist in every possible way to that end. In addition, several communications were circulated to all United Nations members as General Assembly documents putting forward our case.

During the thirtieth session of the General Assembly, as a result of our delegation's efforts and despite the strenuous opposition of Turkey, a separate resolution (*A/RES/3450 (XXX)*) was adopted on 9 December 1975 requesting the Secretary-General to exert every effort in assisting the tracing and accounting of missing persons as a result of armed conflict in Cyprus and also to provide relevant information to the Human Rights Commission. In turn the Commission at its 32nd Session adopted on 27 February 1976 Resolution 4 (XXXIX) by which it referred to the General Assembly resolutions and stressed the humanitarian aspects of the return of all refugees and of the missing persons. This was considered by the ECOSOC which, on 12 May 1976 (*E/SR 2002*), noted with approval the Report of the Commission. The consideration of these items before these bodies also gave to our delegation the opportunity to stress the principles upon which the solution of the Cyprus problem should be based.

I have said earlier that I would give a brief factual account of the consideration of the Cyprus problem before the United Nations and in doing so I hope I did not bore you too much by the enumeration of the relevant resolutions and their provisions.

After all this is said, however, the question arises, and it is a legitimate question, where is all this leading to? Unanimous or near-unanimous resolutions are adopted by the General Assembly and are endorsed by the Security Council calling for the withdrawal of the Turkish troops, for the return of the refugees, for the respect of the sovereignty, independence, and territorial integrity of Cyprus, for the cessation of all foreign interference in its affairs and for refraining from changing the demographic structure of Cyprus. And yet, nearly two years after the invasion, there has been no withdrawal of foreign troops, no return of the refugees, no cessation of foreign interference, no respect for the sovereignty, independence or territorial integrity of Cyprus. In fact, the colonization by alien population continues and more Greek Cypriots from occupied areas are daily rendered refugees despite not only these resolutions but also in flagrant violation of the specific humanitarian Vienna agreement of 2 August 1974 concluded under the auspices of the Secretary-General while the intercommunal talks have so far led nowhere owing to Turkish recalcitrance. Why is nothing effective being done by the United Nations in all these regards in order to restore justice as well as in order to see to its own resolutions being implemented?

These are in fact questions that we persistently also ask, orally and in writing, formally and informally, in urging effective United Nations action and not mere repetition of exhortations. By any criterion of justice and legality there is no justification for such lack of effective action. And I for one certainly do not see any justification.

However, what I believe I should do, in a scientific seminar intended to provide a better understanding of the situation, is to attempt to provide some explanation, as distinct from justification, for this apparent and real inaction.

In the first place, what appears on the face of it, and certainly to us, to be clear and unambiguous injunctions are interpreted by others as no more than conditional recommendations. Conditional in the sense that their implementation is tied to other provisions and recommendations in the sense that they are not considered as obligatory but as mere exhortations. Thus, the representatives of Turkey allege that they have no objection to the eventual withdrawal of the Turkish forces in Cyprus but this can only take place after a solution acceptable to them is reached through "agreement" as a result of the intercommunal negotiations or otherwise. And in any case, it is said, resolutions of the General Assembly and even of the Security Council so long as they do not come under Chapter VII of the Charter, are mere recommendations which they may or may not heed at their discretion. There exist of course strong legal and political arguments against such interpretations but those who wish to believe them, whether in good faith or out of a sense of loyalty and friendship towards Turkey, do accept them on their face value.

What is true is that in diplomacy some vagueness in wording is often intentionally employed so as to allow different parties to give different interpretations in order to save face and thus appear to reach a consensus upon which all can agree. In order to illustrate this point by a classic case in recent United Nations history, under Resolution 242 (1967) of the Security Council, Israel has been called upon to withdraw its armed forces from "territories occupied in the recent conflict" meaning the 1967 war. The word "the" does not appear in the English text of the Resolution which was at the time accepted by all and gave rise to great hopes for a solution of the Middle East problem. But these hopes, as we all know, did not materialize since there has since been interminable argument as to whether the wording used meant *all* the territories or *some* territories occupied by Israel. Irrespective of the merits of the argument, and we have our own view of them, the fact is that no implementation has taken place and the situation in the Middle East remains, as it does in Cyprus, stalemated.

Why then, it may again be legitimately asked, cannot the United Nations give an authoritative and definitive interpretation as to what these resolutions mean and, once this is done, why does not the United Nations take prompt and effective action to enforce compliance?

The answer to this lies in the understanding of the nature and composition of the United Nations. I trust that those among you who have United Nations experience or have been associated with it will bear me out: Unlike what is sometimes generally assumed, the United Nations is not a world government nor a superstate nor a court of law in the national sense which passes judgement and relies upon the executive organs of the state to enforce these judgements. It is an association of sovereign states and because of that it is no more than a reflection of the national positions of these sovereign states which, collectively, constitute the Organization. While in theory, the Charter has a fool-proof scheme for prompt and effective action in order to ensure compliance of decisions taken by the Security Council under Chapter VII, as well as the International Court of Justice whose decisions can also be enforced, due to political considerations to which I have alluded, the practice is considerably different and the existence of the veto provision, whether it is actually used or only threatened as a deterrent against a resolution directed against one of the Permanent Members of the Council or one of its allies or friends, has so far prevented the effective application of this theoretically fool-proof scheme. Suffice it to say that, with the exception of the Korean case (where there was no Soviet veto only due to the absence at the time when the vote was taken of the Soviet delegation from the Security Council) and the very limited, and inadequately enforced, case of sanctions against Rhodesia, no enforcement action involving sanctions has ever been taken in the history of the United Nations against any state. This includes two evident cases which are apartheid in South Africa, and the Middle East. In both of these cases, the overwhelming majority of member states strongly align themselves on one side and yet, due to the existence of the veto and the other political considerations involved, no enforcement action and no sanctions have been taken against South Africa or Israel for persistent non-compliance with General Assembly and Security Council resolutions overwhelmingly adopted.

In the second place, it has been correctly pointed out that often there is a great gap between declarations of principles and their implementation in practice, not only in the United Nations, but also in other forums where solemn declarations have been adopted. Political expediencies and narrow national interests too often combine to render inoperative in practice the theoretically accepted principles. This of course is not right but, however unsavoury it may be, it is a political reality which cannot be ignored.

It is also a fact that many states, though by no means all, tend to concentrate on issues of immediate concern to themselves and, while paying lip service or even if they have some genuine sympathy for evident cases of injustice, such as the case of Cyprus, are basically indifferent or at most only theoretically interested in ensuring the application of the Charter principles to others, especially if they are geographically located far away. Even we ourselves, can we in good conscience say that, when approached by other countries with their problems and preoccupations, which they consider just as serious, important and meritorious as we consider ours, we have invariably shown the degree of understanding, interest and support which we expect of others?

This, of course, is a short-sighted attitude for in our interdependent world there is no room for narrow national interests and boundaries. Principles such as justice and peace are indivisible and their gross violation in one part of the world in the long term affects all in that it destroys the fibre of the whole international system. But this is an imperfect world and the United Nations is but a reflection of it.

In the third place, we cannot overlook the fact that Turkey is a comparatively large country, a member of military alliances such as NATO and CENTO, geographically located in a sensitive part of the world (being close to the Middle East, bordering on the Soviet Union and controlling the Dardanelles). In the past several years, in fact since the outbreak of the Cyprus crisis in 1963–4, she has been making a systematic, if opportunistic, effort through its large and well endowed Foreign Services to get herself outside isolation and to cultivate relations with several groups of states and bilaterally, making use among other things of the fact that, as she has somehow belatedly discovered, she is an Islamic country. In the light of all this what is remarkable is more the fact that on the Cyprus problem Turkey found herself so isolated so often than anything she has achieved through these efforts. But these are factors which should also be taken into account in explaining why she has been able to defy the United Nations resolutions so far with impunity.

Well then, it might be asked, in the light of these facts are we to fold our arms, confess our impotence and capitulate in desperation? Certainly not. With initiative, imagination and systematic work in the international field, with perseverance and faith in our leadership, we can struggle to improve the odds especially since, we do have, on merit, a very good case and ask for no more than what is self-evidently warranted by even the most elementary principles of international justice and morality. Politics, as the saying goes, is the art of the possible. But if what is possible today is not acceptable because it is unjust and nonviable, we have no option but to strive in order to make possible tomorrow what is not possible today.

To this end, the United Nations, despite its limitations has an important role to play. Through its Charter principles and resolutions on Cyprus, it provides the framework for the solution of the Cyprus problem. If we get away from these, there is no alternative but total defeat and complete capitulation.

The United Nations is still the conscience of mankind and an important forum in which our case is heard and through which international public opinion can be mobilized further. Even though not a world government nor offering a panacea to all of the world's problems, as its more enthusiastic supporters claim, neither is it a mere debating society or worse as its detractors allege. Within its limitations and potentialities it can be of considerable importance and this, in my view, is the only way to approach the matter if we are going to be neither disillusioned nor unduly pessimistic.

While free from illusions as to what we can realistically achieve, there is a very substantial scope for making the best use of the possibilities offered by the United Nations in internationally projecting our case in the appropriate light and dimensions. Much can be done through the Organization for obtaining essential diplomatic, political and moral support and sustenance to our just cause. We do have genuine friends and supporters in the international field and of course we always count upon the solidarity and support of Greece and its democratic Government in this field also. For the Cyprus problem, the United Nations within its limitations and potentialities has always been and can still be of considerable importance to Cyprus. For there is a great range of possibilities which can be usefully explored as to ways in which the United Nations can help us, and help itself, in promoting the implementation of its resolutions on Cyprus.

I would like to quote a brief passage from an interview given by the President of the Republic Archbishop Makarios to the Athens newspaper VRADYNI as recently as 6 May 1975, which aptly if cautiously indicates the correct attitude. I quote:

> And if the talks are not resumed or if they fail after resumption, I consider imperative a new recourse to the United Nations. I will not argue that the international Organization will definitely give a solution to the problem. It can, however contribute to a solution and, if nothing else, it can help keep the Cyprus problem on the international scene and give it international dimensions.

Allow me to conclude on a slightly personal note. I have had the honour and the privilege to be associated with the representation of Cyprus to the United Nations in one capacity or another since 1960 when I was a member of the first delegation of independent Cyprus upon joining the United Nations and, during almost all of my working life, I happened to have been involved, not necessarily always by choice, with the United Nations and with the Cyprus problem. There is a lot of drama involved in this kind of work, a great deal of pressures and anxieties – the midnight overseas calls, the convening of and participating in emergency sessions of the Security Council the all-night meetings in caucuses and Committees, the anticipation of procedural problems, the often rushed drafting of speeches and alternative texts of resolutions are all aspects of this work and a serious drain on any person. But there is also the very considerable satisfaction of doing work which you feel is important for more than just yourself and when the results are successful, this more than compensates for all the pressures and anxieties.

In addition, I have had the satisfaction of working under or with many distinguished, dedicated and brilliant persons who earned my affection and respect and to have enjoyed their friendship is also a great and lasting reward and source of satisfaction. Bearing in mind the old legal maxim *expressio unius est exclusio alterius* I will not mention any names since there are so many. In this paper I deliberately chose not to make the narration a personal one, even though it might have bored you less, as I felt that it would be more appropriate and useful to you to concentrate on giving the full picture by putting the emphasis on the facts rather than on personalities or value judgements. A future historian or a current politician might feel more at liberty to state his analysis of motives and policies, to highlight or downgrade the role played by individuals and to express conclusions as to whether things were handled well or badly at particular phases and generally. By contrast, a member of the Foreign Service (who is not planning on retiring in the immediate future) might be better advised to refrain from expressing in public such opinions and value judgments as long as the problem is alive and he continues to be involved with it.

The Cyprus Question: Its Dimensions, Implications, and Prospects for a Solution*

It is good to be speaking to you this evening. It is good to have this opportunity to share my thoughts with a distinguished audience of Americans seriously interested in the country which I represent and in the Mediterranean region of which it is a part.

At the same time, I am deeply distressed by the situation in which my country finds itself. I am distressed by the artificial division imposed on Cyprus by the Turkish invader; at the suffering imposed upon the Cypriot people, both Greek and Turkish Cypriots; at the huge losses, in lives and property, inflicted on my homeland; and by the fact that, more than five years after the invasion and occupation, the situation remains basically unremedied.

One of your great orators, Daniel Webster, more than a hundred years ago, said that justice "is the ligament which holds civilized beings and civilized nation together." Justice is what Cyprus is pleading for. What I intend to do this evening is to bring you up to date on the Cyprus situation to outline how the problem evolved; touch upon its present dimensions and its implications for the United Nations and the United States; and consider with you the prospects for its just and lasting solution and, more particularly, the role which the United States can play to this end.

I am certain that, to a knowledgeable audience such as you, there is no need to go into the geography, demography, and history of Cyprus. Let me simply remind you that Cyprus is an island of some 3,600 square miles and a population of some 650,000 (with a ratio of about 80 percent Greek Cypriots, 18 percent Turkish Cypriots, and the remainder Armenians, Maronites, Latins and others). Our recorded history goes back to 6000 B.C. Because of its location at the cross-roads of three continents (Europe, Asia, and Africa) and its natural wealth, Cyprus has been the object of foreign occupation through much of its long history. But throughout these years, it has retained its basic character and unity. It has often been a bone of contention and is now going

---

* Previously published in *Occasional Papers Series*, #1, American University Center for Mediterranean Studies (1980).

through a very critical stage of its history. But I sincerely believe that it has the full potential to become a bridge of peace and cooperation in the region. Those of us who love Cyprus and care deeply for its present and future are determined to work ceaselessly for this to happen. For this, however, we need sympathetic understanding and effective support, and your great country is uniquely placed to provide both of these.

Before I proceed further, it would be useful to define what is meant by the "Cyprus Question." As an international problem, the question of Cyprus has been through various phases. In the fifties, it meant the Greek Cypriot struggle against the colonial power (Great Britain) for self-determination, and it was examined as such in successive sessions of the United Nations General Assembly. It acquired an additional international dimension when Britain, through the London Conference of 1955, sought to enlist the support of Turkey (which had renounced all rights to Cyprus through the Treaty of Lausanne in 1923) in order to avert the union of Cyprus with Greece. At the same time, under the old principle of *divide et impera*, Britain instigated and encouraged the Turkish Cypriot minority to assert itself and advocate in the first stage, the continuation of British rule and, in a later stage, the partition of the island and its annexation to Turkey. This phase ended with the Zurich-London Agreements of 1959 which established the independence of Cyprus within a rigid and inflexible framework of a Constitution and Treaties (the "Treaty of Establishment," the "Treaty of Guarantee," and the "Treaty of Alliance") which were worked out by the Governments of Greece, Turkey, and the United Kingdom and which the leaders of the people of Cyprus had no choice but to accept without any modification. Following the completion of the transitional arrangements, the Republic of Cyprus was declared an independent state in August 1960 and, in September of the same year, was admitted to membership of the United Nations.

The second phase of the Cyprus Question was the period from December 1963 to July 1974. The complicated and rigid Constitution proved unworkable in certain important respects, and *bona fide* efforts for amending it were made on the basis of the 13-point proposals put forward by President Makarios. However, the attempted negotiations between the two Cypriot communities were frustrated through the outright rejection of these proposals by the Turkish Government. As a result, intercommunal violence broke out in December 1963. Amid threats and acts of intervention by Turkey, the Cyprus Government appealed to the Security Council of the United Nations seeking protection under the Charter against outside interference. Following the abortive London Conference in January 1964, the Security Council considered the issue in depth and adopted the landmark resolution 186 in March 1964. This resolution, which was adopted by consensus, was based on the premise that under the Charter, the use and the threat of force in international relations was prohibited. It took a two-pronged approach aimed at remedying the situation through peace-keeping and peace-making measures. On the one hand, it provided, with the consent of the Government of Cyprus, for the setting up of a United Nations peace-keeping force (known as UNFICYP) to ensure the cessation of fighting, and on the other hand, it provided for the appointment of a United Nations mediator to promote a peaceful solution and an agreed settlement in accordance with the U.N. Charter. While UNFICYP continues to exercise its peace-keeping functions in Cyprus in a commendable manner, the peace-making effort, under resolution 186, has remained dormant following Turkey's flat rejection in 1965 of the report of the mediator, Dr. Galo Plaza, on the spurious ground that he exceeded his mandate. In the opinion of all impartial observers (both at the time and in retrospect), the Plaza report contained closely reasoned and constructive recommendations, and had it been accepted, it could have provided the basis for a fair, just, and viable solution to the Cyprus problem. Thus, the tragic events that followed could have been avoided.

The main developments during this period included: 1) the adoption by the General Assembly of the important resolution 2077 in 1965; 2) the crises of 1964 and 1967, in which a threatened Turkish invasion was narrowly averted through effective diplomatic action by the United Nations and the United States (on the first occasion, through the so-called "Johnson letter" and, on the second, through the constructive and effective efforts of Cyrus Vance); and 3) beginning in 1968, the intermittent holding of intercommunal talks on constitutional arrangements and the issue of regional autonomy for the Turkish Cypriots in a unitary system of government. The intercommunal talks made good progress until they were abruptly brought to an end by the events of July and August 1974.

By the middle of 1974, and despite the anomaly of the situation, compounded by the harmful activities of EOKA B extremists (who were directed, instigated, and supported by the anti-Makarios dictatorship that ruled Greece from April 1967 to July 1974), Cyprus continued to have a democratic government, to flourish economically, and to maintain good relations with all countries in the region and in the world – with the exception, of course, of Turkey.

This brings us to the current, and infinitely more grave, phase of the Cyprus Question. The facts are well established, and there is no need to recapitulate the chronology of events or refute again the untenable legal arguments used in a vain attempt to justify the Turkish action. General international law and, more particularly, United Nations law and the Law of Treaties are conclusive in this regard.

Using as pretext the criminal and despicable *coup d'état* against the democratically elected President of Cyprus, Archbishop Makarios, by the dictatorship then ruling Greece, Turkey seized the long-sought opportunity to invade defenseless Cyprus in order to impose its will by the force of arms. In July and August 1974, the Turkish army, using some 45,000 men and hundreds of jet airplanes, tanks, heavy artillery, and napalm bombs, completed (and in fact exceeded) its stated objective and established the infamous "Attila" line across Cyprus. This blatant act of aggression, unprecedented in the era of the United Nations, brought under Turkish military occupation nearly 40 percent of the territory of the Republic, including some 70 percent of it economic resources. It forcibly uprooted some 200,000 Greek Cypriots from their ancestral homes and turned them into destitute refugees. It left several thousand dead and more than 2,000 missing. It made havoc of the economy of Cyprus, which had been prospering until that time. And it entailed massive violations of human rights by the Turkish army (amply documented in the report by the European Commission on Human Rights released in August 1979).

The outcome of this invasion has been tragic in terms of human suffering and material destruction. Its sequel – the systematic attempt to alter arbitrarily the demographic character of the occupied part of the island through the massive importation of alien population from Turkey, coupled with the inhuman policy of the expulsion of the remaining Greek Cypriots from the occupied area – has given to the Cyprus problem an infinitely more serious dimension.

As I said earlier, because of its geographical position and its natural wealth, Cyprus, through its long history, has often been the object of foreign invasion. Ever since the Achaean immigration (which was intensified shortly after the Trojan War and saw the establishment of such city states as Salamis by Teucer, the brother of Ajax, son of the King of Salamis, and Nea Paphos by Agapenor, King of Arcadia), Cyprus has retained intact its ethnological character, language, and civilization as well as its territorial integrity. From the Assyrians, Egyptians, Persians, Romans, Byzantines, Arabs, Franks, Venetians, and Ottomans to the British, conquerors came and went-leaving behind some traces and monuments to bear witness to their passing but never altering the unity and basic ethnological character of Cyprus. The native population assimilated the foreign influences but retained intact its language, religion, culture, and traditions. This allowed, at the same time, the existence of minorities, the largest of which was the Turkish Cypriots who arrived after the conquest of Cyprus by Ottoman Turkey in 1571. Now, for the first time in 3,000 years, the spectre of reshaping the map of Cyprus and forcibly shifting its population looms large and real. That this should be allowed to happen in the second half of the twentieth century and in the era of the United Nations, raises fundamental questions which far transcend the narrow geographical limits of Cyprus itself.

The Cyprus problem, in its present dimensions of unremedied aggression against a small defenseless country and massive and continuing violations of the basic human rights of its population, has global implications and ought to be of grave concern to all who want to see such principles as the rule of law, majority rule, and respect for human rights applied everywhere in the world. The issues involved pose a challenge to the most fundamental tenets of the United Nations and, indeed, its very ability to survive following such gross violation of its principles. They also pose a challenge for the United States as a global power and leader of the western alliance.

The United Nations has responded to our plea through the adoption unanimously or by overwhelming majority of a series of resolutions, both in the General Assembly and Security Council (as well as in other bodies dealing with human rights). These resolutions, reaffirmed time and again, lay down the principles and the framework within which a just and lasting solution can be found. The most recent (General Assembly Res. A/RES/34/30) was adopted on the 19th of this month by overwhelming majority of 101 to 4. The resolutions provide for the withdrawal of all foreign troops; the voluntary return of all refugees to their homes; the cessation of all foreign intervention and interference in the affairs of Cyprus; respect of the sovereignty, independence, territorial integrity, and non-alignment of the Republic of Cyprus; the refraining from measures changing the demographic character of the island; the effective tracing of the missing persons; and respect for the human rights of all Cypriots. They also provide for freely conducted negotiations under the auspices of the Secretary-General of the United Nations in order to arrive at an agreed settlement of the Cyprus problem.

These injunctions of the international community (and I say *injunctions* because even though General Assembly resolutions are recommendatory in legal character, the fact of their endorsement by the Security Council renders them mandatory and legally binding under Article 25 of the Charter) have remained unimplemented and continue to be contemptuously disregarded by Turkey with impunity. More than five years later there has been no meaningful withdrawal of Turkish occupation troops; not a single refugee has been allowed to return home (and, in fact, gradually but systematically, the few remaining enclaved persons are being squeezed out); the machinery for tracing the missing persons remains inoperative because of Turkish lack of cooperation; and alien settlers from Turkey continue to arrive and not only occupy the houses and lands of the expelled Greek Cypriots but also pose serious problems for the Turkish Cypriots themselves. Likewise, there has been no respect for the sovereignty and independence of Cyprus and no cessation of Turkey's interference.

Since 1975, there have been six rounds of intercommunal talks (which, of course, are not "freely conducted," as stipulated under the U.N. resolutions, since the oppressive presence of the Turkish forces of occupation makes a mockery of any claim to the contrary). Despite ephemeral hopes raised from time to time, no substantive progress has been made in these negotiations. The obstacle to progress is the intransigence and lack of political will of the Turkish side, which has the upper hand under the present *status quo* and which will be fully satisfied only through a solution legalizing the *faits accomplis* (the so-called "new realities") brought about by the invasion. Moreover, it is a well-known fact that Ankara calls the tune and that the Turkish Cypriot leadership is totally dependent on Turkey for military, economic, diplomatic, and political support. Thus, in effect, these negotiations are with Ankara.

In contrast, the Cyprus government (and the Greek Cypriot side) has every reason to bring about, at the earliest possible time, a just and peaceful solution within the framework of the U.N. resolutions in order to alter the present unfair and intolerable status quo. In a genuine effort to foster positive negotiations, it has made considerable substantive concessions (apart from agreeing to negotiate before the withdrawal of the Turkish troops), including the acceptance in 1977 of a bicommunal federation and the submission for negotiation of a map showing a region of some 20 percent of the island to be under Turkish Cypriot administration. (And may I remind you that the ratio of population in Cyprus is 80 percent Greek Cypriots and 18 percent Turkish Cypriots.)

Moreover, in 1978 President Spyros Kyprianou proposed two significant measures designed to meet the alleged Turkish Cypriot concern about their security and human rights. His proposal has no precedent in modern international relations. As part of a comprehensive solution of the Cyprus problem, President Kyprianou proposed the total disarmament and demilitarization of the Republic of Cyprus, with only a police force (consisting of Greek and Turkish Cypriots, according to the population ratio) to keep internal law and order, under the supervision of the U.N. so as to ensure its impartiality. Under an effective system of international guarantees, Cyprus would not need to maintain military forces against external danger. President Kyprianou also proposed the setting up of an international body that would report to the Security Councilor any other appropriate U.N. organ to ensure the highest level of protection of human rights and fundamental freedoms for all citizens of Cyprus. I may also add that Cyprus (unlike Turkey) was among the first of the signatories of the U.N. Covenants of Human Rights and the U.N. Convention on the Elimination of All Forms of Racial Discrimination; it is also a party to the European Convention on Human Rights. The availability of legal remedies under such instruments in itself furnishes a silencing reply to the complaints now being voiced by Turkish spokesmen about alleged violations of the human rights of the Turkish Cypriots during the period prior to the 1974 invasion, by way of justifying such invasion. Had there been valid complaints, the appropriate way to pursue them would have been to raise and substantiate them before such impartial bodies and not through invasion and tactics of massive destruction.

On the other hand, the Turkish side, while paying lip-service to a "federal" solution, insists on what in fact (and in law) amounts to a confederation with two separate states, each having separate borders, separate armies, separate treaty-making capacity, passports, etc. In other words, the Turkish model for a settlement is a blue-print for partition. The result would be a politically and economically unworkable and moribund system of two states within a small island which is bound to break down and lead to a bigger crisis with incalculable consequences to peace in the region.

The most recent phase in this chapter has been the agreement concluded under the auspices of the Secretary-General of the United Nations in Nicosia on 19 May 1979, between President Kyprianou and the Turkish Cypriot leader, Rauf Denktash, consisting of ten points. The Cyprus Government considers this agreement, which was widely hailed at the time as a breakthrough and a major achievement, to be a valid basis for the intercommunal negotiations, Soon after this agreement was reached, however, the Turkish side, as has invariably happened in the course of the intercommunal negotiations since early 1975, gave indications of reneging. More specifically, Denktash put forward certain preconditions which, if accepted, would have proven grossly prejudicial to the outcome. As a result of this attitude, the negotiations were adjourned by the Special Representative of the Secretary-General, and despite subsequent efforts, they have not been resumed.

As I said earlier, the Cyprus Government continues to consider the 19 May 1979 agreement as the agreed basis for intercommunal negotiations and would be willing and anxious to have such negotiations resume without any preconditions or misinterpretations. Some reasonable assurance should be offered, however, that such negotiations would be meaningful and not merely a dialogue for the sake of dialogue, or for other tactical considerations related to Turkey's need for foreign aid, or to avoid public debate and condemnation in international forums. Negotiations, in other words, should not be used to deceive international public opinion into thinking that progress is being made toward a settlement while, in fact, none is. It is expected that in the wake of the adoption of the 19 November 1979 resolution, efforts to resume these negotiations will be made again.

The question may be legitimately asked why is it that the United Nations, in the face of Turkey's non-compliance with its resolutions, does not take the steps prescribed by the Charter in order to compel compliance? This is indeed a legitimate question, and the answer lies in the much wider issue of the effectiveness of the world organization. The fact is that the Charter system falls far too short of expectations in terms of law and logic because of political realities which prevent it from being fully applied. This has been true not only in the case of Cyprus but also in several other cases, of which the question of apartheid is the most obvious.

Still, the United Nations, through its peace-keeping force and its peace-making machinery – recently reinforced through the 19 November 1979 resolution – and as a vehicle for collective expression of the will of the international community, continues to be a very important factor in the effort for the solution of the problem. As a forum for public airing of the issues involved and through its resolutions adopted unanimously or by overwhelming majorities, it provides the principles and the framework within which the problem can be properly solved. It serves the very important purpose of making the governments of the world aware of the continued existence and the international character of the problem, being in its essence a problem of aggression and foreign intervention and not merely an intercommunal dispute as Turkey falsely tries to portray it. The United Nations also highlights the international personality of the Republic of Cyprus and reflects the recognition and support the government of Cyprus enjoys internationally. It is thus common ground that the Cyprus problem is a United Nations problem and its solution can and should be pursued and achieved within the framework of the United Nations. Even Turkey, which understandably is unwilling to accept any third party involvement, has reluctantly agreed to this.

This being the situation as far as the United Nations is concerned, I would now like to examine the role of the United States with regard to the Cyprus problem in its present dimensions. I have already alluded to the salutary effect of the Johnson letter of 1964 and to the constructive and effective efforts of Cyrus Vance in 1967. On both of these occasions, a threatened Turkish invasion of Cyprus, which carried with it a serious risk of a war between two NATO allies, Greece and Turkey, was narrowly averted.

This was not to be the case in the summer of 1974. Despite the efforts of Joseph Sisco, the Turkish army invaded Cyprus, whereupon the American special envoy concentrated his efforts on averting the involvement of Greece which would have brought about a Greek-Turkish war. In this he succeeded and, in the process, the dictatorship fell, and democracy was reestablished in Greece. But it was too late for Cyprus to be saved.

It is not for the present to trace in any detail the United States role in the unfolding of events in the fateful months of July and August 1974. Much has been said and written (e.g., by the late Laurence Stern and by former Ambassador Henry Tasca*) as to successive "tilts" at various turning points

* Laurence Stern, *The Wrong Horse* (New York: Times Books, 1977); and Henry J. Tasca in Martin F. Herz, ed., *Contacts With the Opposition: A Symposium* (Washington, D.C.: Institute for the Study of Diplomacy, Georgetown University, n.d. 1979).

by the United States' top policy makers of the time as the crisis developed. Had the decisions taken then been different, the tragedy from which Cyprus suffers today might have been prevented. There followed the imposition of the embargo by Congress in 1974; its partial lifting in 1975; the election of President Jimmy Carter after his pledge to pursue a solution based on the United Nations resolutions; the Clark Clifford mission early in 1977; the lifting of the embargo (subject to conditions) in the summer of 1978; and, the U.S.-British-Canadian set of suggestions for settlement in November 1978.

More recently, in July this year, President Carter in accepting my credentials stated that he shares our commitment to a united Cyprus. He said, and I quote him:

> Our commitments to Cyprus are the same. We want to see the nation united and human rights honored. Our nation is standing by to help.

On the same occasion, I had stated our conviction:

> ...that Cypriots of Greek and Turkish origin alike can live, work, and prosper together as they have for generations once the foreign interference and troops are moved...We appreciate the fact that the United States has voted for the basic United Nations resolutions (Nos. 3212 and 365) as well as your Government's efforts and we gratefully acknowledge the generous economic assistance provided for the displaced persons. We very much hope and trust that your Government, in accordance with the ideals of the American people and your inspired devotion to the universal respect for human rights, will be able, through its considerable and unique position in world affairs, to play constructively an effective role towards the appropriate direction for the finding of such a just and peaceful solution.

In our considered view, the United States, as a global power and the leader of the western world, has the capability and influence to significantly affect the processes; of reason and justice with regard to achieving a just and lasting solution to the Cyprus problem. In doing so, the United States would not only be acting for reason of moral and legal principles but also for its self-interest.

Allow me, if you will, to elaborate on this point. The United States policy with regard to Cyprus is faced by a three-fold challenge: moral, legal, and geopolitical. Let us first consider the nature of the moral issue.

The United States is today the world's oldest continuous democracy. It is a democracy based essentially on the concept of justice – the pragmatic foundations of which are the Constitution, the Bill of Rights, and the great body of law created by the courts of the land. James Madison, one of the founders of this great democracy wrote in the *Federalist Papers* that "Justice is the end of Government. It is the end of civil society." Let me, then, pose the logical question: Is not a nation founded on and dedicated to the concept of justice morally obligated-especially since it has assumed the burden of world leadership-to foster justice elsewhere? Is not America, which justifiably takes pride in being known as the leader of the "free world," required by its own ideals to help smaller nations, dedicated by free choice to the same ideals? Ought not, to put it bluntly, the United States practice abroad what it preaches at home?

Cyprus, a democratic country founded as a unitary Republic, is today torn apart by an arbitrary line imposed on it illegally by force of arms and by a military occupation which threatens both its present freedom and its future viability. The nations of the world – speaking through the United Nations and elsewhere – have overwhelmingly urged the reunification of Cyprus, the withdrawal of the foreign occupying forces, and the restoration of the basic human rights of the refugees. U.S. policy is committed, in the words of its President, to bring about a united Cyprus where human rights would be honored. The U.S. voted for the basic U.N. resolutions calling for the application of the above principles. The U.S. Administration, in the 1978 Report of the President to Congress, pledged to give increased weight in its national policy to U.N. resolutions adopted by overwhelming majority. Should the U.S. not keep this pledge in the case of Cyprus? Can it be validly argued that the U.S. is under no moral obligation to do so?

If the moral grounds for pressing forward effectively with the quest for a just Cyprus solution are clear-cut, the same can certainly be said for the legal ones. While it is true that no enforcement measures have been taken by the Security Council against Turkey (because of reasons of political expediency which are common in similar cases of non-compliance), nevertheless, under Article 25 of the Charter "the members of the United Nations agree to accept and carry out the decisions of the Security Council in accordance with the present Charter." In the case of Cyprus, the landmark General Assembly resolution 3212, which was unanimously adopted with the positive vote of the U.S., was also unanimously endorsed by the Security Council in its resolution 365, with the U.S. voting in favor. If any doubt existed as to the applicability of Article 25 of the U.N. Charter to such a situation, this was removed by an advisory opinion of the International Court of Justice in the Namibia case. At a time when virtually all nations in the world – and certainly Cyprus – support the applicability of the rules of international law to such glaringly illegal behavior as the taking of diplomatic hostages in Iran, ought not international law be applied equally to all other situations? And, of course, in the case of the Turkish invasion of Cyprus, the violations of the rules of international law by Turkey extend much beyond the violation of the U.N. Charter to the 1949 Geneva Conventions and to virtually all humanitarian law principles and rules.

As one of the great American jurists, former Supreme Court Justice William Douglas, wrote in a 1961 paper: "The United Nations is today the expression of world opinion that the cult of the regime of force must be replaced by a measure of world law." The United States, as a founding member of the United Nations and a permanent member of the Security Council, is legally bound by the Charter and mandatory resolutions such as Security Council resolution 365 (1974) to take appropriate steps for the implementation of such resolutions.

But the legal aspect is not exhausted by the responsibilities undertaken through U.N. membership and the legal validity of the U.N. resolutions. It is also relevant in terms of the violation by Turkey of U.S. legislation and bilateral U.S.-Turkish agreements through the illegal use, in its invasion of Cyprus, of American arms supplied for an expressly different purpose. If I may quote from the testimony of Cyrus Vance and George Ball, testifying in their individual capacity on 10 July 1975 before the Foreign Relations Committee of the House of Representatives:

> That Turkey used the arms we provided in violation of the relevant American laws and of the express language of the bilateral agreement that governed their transfer is not in dispute. That issue has been settled by an opinion of the Comptroller General in unequivocal language.

It was also stated in the same testimony:

> ...that Turkey must make some major concessions in order to create the conditions for long-term stability in Cyprus seems evident.

As we all know, in September 1978 Congress was persuaded by the Administration to lift the embargo against Turkey. This was done by extremely narrow margin in the House of Representatives. The view prevailed that among other reasons, the lifting of the embargo would have resulted in willingness on the part of Turkey to negotiate in good faith towards a just Cyprus settlement. This expectation has not materialized so far, and the conditions laid down by Congress in lifting the embargo, for all practical purposes, remain unfulfilled.

I have elaborated on the moral and legal grounds upon which the United States would reasonably be expected to condition its attitude towards Turkey. In addition, I believe a strong case can be made that a just and viable settlement of the Cyprus problem would also serve the political and strategic interests of the United States without thereby jeopardizing its relations with Turkey.

I am, of course, fully aware of the considerations which are uppermost in the minds of certain "geopolitically minded" policy-makers in the U.S. and other Western countries in determining their policy towards Turkey. We recognize that defense and foreign policy considerations affect each other in the formulation of U.S. policy on any given problem, and that strategic factors have in the past been given much weight in relations with Turkey. Turkey is, of course, a large country and a NATO member. It has an army of some 500,000 men; it borders on the Soviet Union and controls the Dardanelles; and it is in a key position in relation to the Middle East (and hence important with regard to Israel and Middle East oil). Especially in view of the recent developments in Afghanistan and Iran, Turkey's value, in the estimation of these U.S. officials, is further enhanced, taking also into account the existence in Turkey of bases and listening posts for SALT II verification purposes.

I do not intend to deny that Turkey is important to the West, although, at closer examination, the real value of several of these factors may be open to question. But let us remember some facts. Turkey was on the enemy side in the first World War and neutral in the second; the *Minsk* and the *Kiev* were baptized as "cruisers" so as to pass through the Dardanelles despite the Montreux Convention; permission was granted to Soviet planes to use Turkey's airspace in the 1973 Middle East War; and there has been consistent reluctance to allow the use of Turkish airspace for SALT II verification unless the Soviet Union concurs. Let us also remember Turkey's attitude towards Greece's reintegration into NATO; the degree of combat readiness of Turkish armed forces; Turkey's opportunistic flirtation with the Soviet Union and Islamic countries; and its enormous economic, social, and ethnic problems. Among other things, these realities render Turkey's carefully and expensively cultivated image of a "reliable, loyal, and long-time ally" less than certain.

The fact is that, despite the very substantial economic aid Turkey receives from the Soviet Union and certain Islamic countries, the military makes the big decisions in Turkey, and the military will not allow Turkey to leave NATO – now or in the foreseeable future – because it is from NATO and the West that Turkey obtains its sorely needed and massive military and economic aid which it can procure nowhere else. Also, we must not forget that the Turks traditionally fear and distrust the Russians. Indeed, it can be stated with conviction that Turkey needs the United States much more than the United States needs Turkey.

Another important factor, relevant in this connection, is that it is in the interest of the United States that Greece be fully reintegrated into and remain within NATO. Democratic Greece, of course, fully supports Cyprus in its effort to terminate the Turkish occupation and reach a just solution, and the people of Greece are very sensitive to any U.S. action which, positively or negatively, affects the situation in Cyprus. Moreover, it is relevant to remember that, without Greece as the essential geographical link between the Western European NATO countries and Turkey, Turkey's usefulness to NATO and its own defense position would be severely compromised.

Similarly, though Cyprus is a small country and together with the large majority of the Third World countries subscribes to the non-aligned movement, it has always been western in its outlook, its political and social system, and its attitude towards the United States. One could cite many instances where small Cyprus, even from within the non-aligned movement, has taken constructively positions helpful to the West whenever it could do so with a clear conscience. It would be in the interest of the U.S. to ensure, through playing an effective role for the just solution of the Cyprus problem, that Cyprus continues in this course. Conversely, a perpetuation of the Cyprus deadlock, with the frustration mounting and the Turkish occupation continuing under the apathetic eye of the West, might conceivably result in alienation of the people of Cyprus and, worse, a conflagration with unforeseeable consequences for peace not only on the island, but also in the region.

An agreed and just Cyprus solution, brought about with active U.S. assistance within the U.N. framework, would enhance the pro-Western feeling on the island itself. It would also mark a major success for the United States and its administration at a time when the Camp David agreement in its broader aspect is not making any noticeable progress; it would pay handsome dividends in terms of U.S.-Cypriot and, no doubt, U.S.-Greek relations; and it would improve markedly the climate between Greece and Turkey with potentially beneficial results in solving their bilateral problems and ensuring Greece's military reintegration into NATO, thus solidifying the south-east wing of the alliance which for years has remained in disarray.

The main point I would like to make in this connection, however, is this: The United States does not have to *choose* between Turkey and Cyprus (or even between Turkey on the one hand and Cyprus and Greece on the other) in order to play such a role. In my opinion, it is possible for the U.S. to ensure, through effective diplomacy (and we have seen such an example in the November/December 1967 crisis), a just solution to the Cyprus problem without alienating any of the three countries concerned. In fact, the U.S. can earn the gratitude and support of all three. The leverage exists, and the question is whether and to what extent it will be used. This is indeed a case of "where there is the will, there is the way."

It is my view that the finding of such a just and lasting solution, in addition to being in the interest of the United States, would: 1) be in the long-term interest of Turkey itself; 2) benefit NATO and the West as a whole; 3) be conducive to peace in the Eastern Mediterranean region and thus prove beneficial to all the neighboring countries in that strategic and volatile area; and 4) be fair for the wronged and suffering people of Cyprus.

On the basis of a logical analysis, such a solution is not beyond reach. The main elements for such a solution are spelled out in the ten-point agreement of 19 May 1979, reached under the auspices of the Secretary-General of the United Nations, which was accepted by all concerned and expressly supported by the General Assembly resolution of last week. In its broader aspects, this agreement provides, apart from the specific issue of the resettlement of Varosha which is a matter of priority, that the basis for the talks will be the Makarios-Denktash guidelines and the U.N. resolutions; the respect of the human rights of all citizens of the Republic and the demilitarization of Cyprus; adequate guarantees of the independence, sovereignty, territorial integrity and non-alignment of Cyprus, precluding union in whole or in part with any other country and any form of partition or secession; and treatment of all territorial and constitutional aspects through sustained and result-oriented negotiations. No doubt, these points are vaguely worded, and the substantive gap between the two positions is very wide. But with the necessary degree of good will and mutual understanding, a sense of chastisement from the painful experiences of the past, and the provision of some technical and possibly economic assistance by outside interested parties, it will be possible to bridge the gap and reach a solution within the U.N. framework. (It is relevant to remember that so far the concessions have been made by only one of the two sides.)

The main obstacle currently preventing meaningful movement towards a solution is the lack of political will on the part of the Turkish side. Serious difficulties exist also as a result of the perennially unstable political situation in Ankara and the mentality of chauvinism which prevails among certain Turkish and Turkish Cypriot political leaders. The creation of a politically strong government in Turkey would, at this point, seem to be predicated upon early elections which (if present trends continue) would be likely to give Suleyman Demirel absolute majority, thus removing a pretext for Turkish inactivity on Cyprus. Yet, given that Cyprus is classified in Turkey as "a national question," it is the military, acting through the Turkish National Security Council, that, in the final analysis, will have the last word and the decisive voice. The absence of a politically strong government in Turkey is not, therefore, an insuperable obstacle to a solution – even though it might again provide an excuse for inactivity, as happened in 1977 with the Clifford mission. It is well to remember that the modernization of the Turkish army (which is one of the primary objectives of the top military leaders as well as of the new Demirel government) can only be achieved through massive western aid. The situation now calls for a combination of firmness and persuasiveness.

This is where the U.S. can, and if it so chooses may, play an effective role. Seneca, the Roman philosopher, wrote that: "He who has great power should use it lightly." In my opinion, even through such "light use" of U.S. persuasive power and leverage as support of the efforts of the U.N. Secretary-General (who has no real leverage), the desirable fair and mutually agreeable result could come about. If Turkish declarations are taken at face value, a solution as outlined in the ten-point agreement would secure for Turkey most of its professed objectives in Cyprus, as authoritatively stated most recently in the General Assembly last week. A fair and just solution would save Turkey from the considerable expense of maintaining its army of occupation in Cyprus and of subsidizing the Turkish Cypriot budget; it would facilitate the flow into Turkey of sorely needed foreign aid, now impeded because of the repercussions of its actions in Cyprus;* it would substantially improve the atmosphere and prospects for the solution of the bilateral Greek-Turkish problems and could open the way for tourist and other profitable forms of cooperation between the two; it would enhance Turkey's stature in the world by removing the odium of being placed in the dock, year after year, at the U.N. and other international conferences and being condemned by overwhelming negative votes (the one last week was 101 to 4).

I am, of course, in no position to offer advice to the Turkish decision makers. But I believe that, by any reasonable and objective standard, this is a list of substantial incentives. Whether these incentives are sufficient to make the difference will, of course, depend on how effectively the matter is presented and on the degree of reasonableness which Ankara is in a position to display under present conditions (taking also into account the theory that precisely because of Turkey's present ills, the Cyprus problem is being used in Turkey as a rallying point to distract attention from the real internal problems facing it). Judging by the experience of the past, this would not be an easy undertaking. But the alternative of continued deadlock and human suffering on Cyprus, with all the unpredictable consequences which it entails, is by itself a sufficient reason for trying.

For our part, the Cyprus government has every reason to want a fair and just solution which could put an end to the present unacceptable *status quo* and the grave threat of the solidification of the present division. We remain committed to meaningful negotiations for a solution on the basis of the U.N. resolutions and the 19 May 1979 Agreement. At the same time, we have made it equally clear that we shall not accept the legalization of the *faits accomplis* brought about by the illegal invasion or the partition of the island in any form. Our dispute is not primarily with the Turkish Cypriots since the constitutional issues can be worked out within the framework of the

* Demirel, the newly appointed Prime Minister of Turkey, is reported by Reuters to have stated at his press conference on 3 November 1979 that "Cyprus is the focal point of Turkey's difficulties in foreign payments."

elements of the 19 May Agreement. While the Cyprus problem in its essence is one of outside invasion and occupation, and therefore the proper interlocutors should be the government of Turkey and the government of Cyprus, in the practical sense the procedure of the intercommunal talks under the auspices of the Secretary-General of the U.N. is the one which is generally acceptable.

"Politics," it has been said, "is the art of the possible." The attitude at present exhibited by the other side does not leave much room for optimism. However, if a just and fair solution to the problem of Cyprus is not possible today, there is ample scope for carefully conducted, imaginative, principled, and effective diplomacy to make it possible tomorrow. If this can be achieved it would be – let me repeat – in the interest of Turkey; in the interest and in accordance with the moral and legal principles of the United Nations, the United States, and the West; beneficial to peace in the region; and, last but not least, in the interest of the long-suffering people of Cyprus whose plea for justice will have been heeded.

If a just solution is reached, every effort will be made to erase the memories of the recent past. Cyprus will maintain friendly relations and cooperate with all countries in the region, including, of course, Greece and Turkey, on the basis of the principles of sovereign equality and good neighborliness. Cyprus has the economic and human potential as well as the geographical position to become a bridge of peace and understanding in the Eastern Mediterranean region, as Switzerland and Austria are in Central Europe. It is very much our hope that this can become a reality for the benefit of all of the people of Cyprus and for peace and stability in the region.

Cyprus: The International Law Dimension*

From its inception as an independent state in 1960, Cyprus has always endeavored to abide by the rules of international law, to participate constructively in major United Nations Conferences, and to make its contribution internationally in such areas as developing compulsory third party dispute settlement procedures and the adoption of progressive notions of international law such as *jus cogens* (peremptory norms from which no derogation can be allowed by agreement or otherwise).

The all-embracing concern for the people of Cyprus over the past several decades has been what is generally known as the Cyprus problem. Several phases span the years, from the pre-independence anti-colonial struggle in the 1950s, to the present grave dimensions of foreign invasion, continuing occupation, attempted secession, and massive human rights violations. The year 1994 marked the twentieth anniversary of the brutal invasion and occupation of a large part of Cyprus by the Turkish armed forces, with its disastrous consequences in terms of human suffering and its implications for international legal order and for peace in this volatile region. It is the nature and extent of these consequences, together with the wider issues of principle involved, that render the Cyprus problem one of international concern which needs to be urgently addressed and solved. Its continuation is a tragic anachronism in today's world and, even though it may have faded from the daily headlines and more topical international situations have superseded it, the issues of principle involved are as valid today as they were twenty years ago.

The Cyprus problem in its basic dimensions is simple and should be of universal concern. Although it has its constitutional and other aspects, the Cyprus problem in its essence is an international problem of aggression, invasion, occupation, and of massive violation of human rights. It involves the illegal invasion and occupation of a small country by a far larger and militarily much stronger neighbor, bent on imposing by force its arbitrary prescription of a partitionist political solution; it involves attempted secession in violation of international treaties; it involves the systematic destruction of

* Previously published in *American University Journal of International Law and Policy*, Volume 10, Number 4, Summer 1995.

the cultural heritage of an ancient land with thousands of years of history and civilization; it involves "ethnic cleansing" on a massive scale with the forced displacement of practically all of the Greek Cypriot inhabitants of the area under Turkish occupation (constituting eighty percent of the inhabitants of that area and more than a third of Cyprus' total population) and the importation of a large number of colonists aimed at altering the historic demographic composition of the island; and it involves the tragedy of missing persons that raises humanitarian issues of major significance.

Consequently, the Cyprus question is a test-case of the effectiveness of the United Nations and of the universal applicability of many of the most basic rules of international law. There is a solid basis for the proposition that if the international community had taken effective steps in 1974 not to allow the victimization of Cyprus through its forcible division and deliberate massive "ethnic cleansing," similar deplorable actions in the former Yugoslavia and elsewhere would not have taken place. Bad precedents, when tolerated and condoned, tend to be repeated.

Turkey's illegal actions in Cyprus have received universal disapproval from the United Nations and from virtually all other international forums. Turkey's invasion of Cyprus, which was carried out through the use of American-supplied arms in violation of American law and bilateral United States-Turkish agreements, raised the "rule of law" issue and resulted in the arms embargo against Turkey by decision of the United States Congress.

On numerous occasions, the United Nations Security Council called for the withdrawal of all foreign troops from Cyprus, the voluntary return of refugees to their homes, the cessation of all interference in the internal affairs of Cyprus, and respect for its sovereignty, independence, territorial integrity and unity. Turkey chose to ignore the decisions of the international community and did so with impunity. This is a very sad commentary on the state of international legal order.

Despite the international remonstration, the Cyprus Government showed its goodwill, sense of pragmatism, and genuine wish for a peaceful solution by entering into negotiations in the conviction that there is much more that unites all Cypriots than the differences that presently divide us. The Cyprus Government and the Greek Cypriot side made a number of painful concessions in the hope that the Turkish side would respond with reasonable proposals and thus reach a solution. Basically, we asked for the establishment of a viable and genuine federation based on democratic principles, as in the case of all other federal states, and with special provisions to meet the particular circumstances of Cyprus. The demand from the Turkish side called for the establishment of, in effect, two separate states with separate armies, separate treaty-making capacity, and separate economies. In short, while paying lip service to a federal system, the Turkish objective remains a partitionist solution through the legitimization of the internationally condemned invasion.

The Turkish objective is evidenced in the recent position of the Turkish Cypriot leadership as reflected in the resolution adopted in August 1994 by the so-called "Turkish Cypriot Assembly," with the full support of Ankara, to abandon federation as the only solution to the Cyprus problem. This proposition is in direct defiance of United Nations resolutions, including the most recent Security Council Resolution on Cyprus[1] which, in operative paragraph 2, defines very clearly the basis of a solution of the Cyprus problem. It reaffirms:

> the position that a Cyprus settlement must be based on a State of Cyprus with a single sovereignty and international personality and a single citizenship, with its independence and territorial integrity safeguarded, and comprising two politically equal communities as described in the relevant Security Council resolutions, in a bi-communal and bizonal federation, and that such a settlement must exclude union in whole or in part with any other country or any form of partition or secession.[2]

This recent manifestation of Turkish intransigence in flagrant disregard of the international community's position forces current United Nations efforts to an impasse, with ominous implications for the prospects of a negotiated settlement. As the Cyprus Government made clear, there really is no prospect for negotiated progress unless the Turkish Cypriot leadership unequivocally accepts Resolution 939, including paragraph 2.

The position of the Turkish side can be viewed as a continuation of the Turkish intransigence displayed earlier in the year in response to the United Nations' efforts to reach an agreement on a package of confidence-building measures. The Secretary-General concluded in his report to the Security Council that: "[t]he Security Council finds itself faced with an already familiar scenario: the absence of agreement due essentially to a lack of political will on the Turkish Cypriot side."[3] The implications of this conclusion should be clear. Alternative means to implement in practice the many United Nations resolutions on Cyprus and to tackle the overall Cyprus problem, particularly its more substantive aspects, in an effective and result-oriented manner, should now be considered as a matter of utmost importance.

Progress towards a negotiated settlement cannot be expected unless the Turkish side musters up the necessary political will. The necessary political resolve will not be found unless the factors that sustain Turkish intransigence are removed. The primary factor is the overwhelming presence of occupying Turkish troops. The proposal of President Clerides for the demilitarization of the Republic of Cyprus represents a viable resolution to this problem. It is a significant and constructive proposal with far-reaching implications in terms

---

1 Res. 939, U.N. SCOR, 3412th mtg. at 1–2, U.N. Doc. S/Res 939 (1994).

2 *Id.*

3 *Report of the Secretary-General on His Mission of Good Offices in Cyprus*, U.N. Doc. S/1994/629 (1994).

of meeting the perceived Turkish security concerns, and the much more real security concerns of the Republic of Cyprus, and its acceptance would substantially enhance the prospects for a peaceful resolution of the situation.

If Turkey respected the relevant principles and rules of international law, the Cyprus problem, in its basic dimensions of aggression and invasion, continuing occupation, massive violation of human rights, and attempted secession, would not have arisen. By applying international principles and rules, this situation could be resolved in a manner that is fair to all Cypriots and consistent with the legitimate interests of the States involved. The international legal option is particularly relevant in light of the impasse to which the Turkish intransigence has led the negotiating process. Third party determination of the legal issues involved in the Cyprus situation, preferably by the main judicial organ of the United Nations, the International Court of Justice in the Hague, would go a long way towards promoting a just solution. Cyprus would have an iron-clad case before the International Court of Justice. Under the present stalemated situation, recourse to such an international forum offers significant possibilities and could be brought about in the absence of Turkey's consent to adjudication through a request by the Security Council or by the General Assembly of the United Nations for an advisory opinion on the issue by the International Court of Justice.

As early as 1963, the Cyprus Government turned to the United Nations Security Council seeking protection against outside threats and acts of aggression. The present situation in Cyprus – traceable from the July – August 1974 Turkish invasion and continuing occupation, forcible expulsion of one third of the Greek Cypriot population, massive violation of human rights, attempts to alter the demographic composition of the island through the introduction of colonists from Turkey, the tragic issue of missing persons, and the illegal attempt at secession of the occupied area in November 1983 – has global implications going far beyond the narrow geographic confines of Cyprus. This unremedied state of affairs, involving a gross violation of many of the most basic norms of international law, including peremptory norms of *jus cogens*, ought to be of grave concern to all who believe in the universal protection of human rights and the application of democratic principles and the rule of law. The issues involved pose a challenge to the international legal order, to the United Nations, and to the United States as a global power and the leader of the Western alliance.

The criminal coup d'état of July 15, 1974 inspired by the junta then ruling Greece, against the legitimate and democratically elected President of Cyprus, gave Turkey the long-sought opportunity to invade Cyprus in order to impose its will by force of arms which it seized. In July and August 1974, the Turkish army, using 45,000 men and hundreds of jet airplanes, tanks, heavy artillery and napalm bombs, completed, and in fact exceeded, its stated objective and established the notorious Attila Line across Cyprus. The blatant act of aggression, unprecedented in the United Nations era, and paralleled only by Saddam Hussein's invasion of Kuwait in 1990, brought nearly forty percent of the territory of the Republic under Turkish military occupation, including seventy percent of its economic resources. The invasion forcibly uprooted some 200,000 Greek Cypriots from their ancestral homes, rendering many Cypriots destitute refugees. It left several thousand dead and missing. It wreaked havoc with the economy of Cyprus, which had been prospering until then, and entailed massive violations of human rights by the Turkish army.

The Turkish invasion marked the first time since the end of World War II that a member of the Council of Europe and a signatory of the Helsinki Final Act,[4] through the use of armed force, penetrated the borders of another European state, a member of the Council of Europe, an associate member of the European Community and a cosignatory to the Helsinki Final Act. Turkey's attempt to alter systematically the demographic character of the occupied part of the island by importing an alien population from Turkey, expelling the remaining Greek Cypriots from the occupied area, and destroying the cultural and religious heritage of the area under occupation tragically resulted in human suffering, vast material destruction and gross violations of international and humanitarian law.

The current phase, from July 1974 to date, renders Cyprus a test-case of unremedied aggression, continuing occupation, and a massive violation of human rights. Fundamental rules of international law, both customary and conventional, continue to be flouted with impunity, and the United Nations resolutions continue to be ignored by the occupying power.

The government of Cyprus has relied heavily upon international law to pursue its cause of justice. Cyprus presented its position, couched in terms of applicable rules of international law, in all available forums. The United Nations General Assembly, in a landmark resolution, laid down the framework and principles for a just and lasting solution to the Cyprus problem, consistent with applicable rules of international law.[5] The Resolution demanded the withdrawal of the foreign troops, the return of the refugees, respect for the sovereignty, independence, and territorial integrity of the Republic of Cyprus, and called for an end to all intervention and interference in its affairs. Although this unanimously adopted Resolution, endorsed

---

[4] Evgeny Chossudovsky, UNITAR Research Report No. 24, The Helsinki Final Act Viewed in the United Nations Perspective, Towards Strengthening the Continuity and Coherence on Security and Cooperation in Europe, U.N. Sales No. E.80XV.RR/24 (1980).

[5] In its landmark Resolution 3212 of 1974 as well as in many other resolutions and decisions.

by the Security Council in its Resolution 365 (1974) has binding legal force under article 25 of the Charter, it remains unimplemented.

The key issue is whether the Turkish military invasion of July – August 1974 was justified legally under Article 4 of the 1960 Treaty of Guarantee. Article 4 provides in pertinent part:

> [i]n the event of a breach of the provisions of the present Treaty, Greece, Turkey and the United Kingdom undertake to consult together with respect to the representations or measures necessary to ensure observance of those provisions. In so far as common or concerted action may not prove possible, each of the three guaranteeing Powers reserves the right to take action with the sole aim of reestablishing the state of affairs created by the present Treaty.

The clear answer is that this invasion, from which many other illegal consequences flowed, was not justified legally, either in terms of Article 4 or in terms of the peremptory norm in Article 2(4) of the Charter. First, the requirement of consultations under Article 4 was not met. Second, the term "action" could not be interpreted as meaning the use of "armed force." Under the principle of construction *ut res magis valeat quam pereat*, "action" should be interpreted as meaning peaceful action. Third, the Turkish military action, despite some faint lip service at the time, was not taken "with the sole aim of reestablishing the state of affairs created by the present Treaty" but to impose by force Turkey's prescription of a political solution inconsistent with the 1960 Treaty. Even though the removal of the coupist regime and the assumption of power by the constitutional acting President as early as July 23, 1974, reestablished the constitutional order, the Turkish occupying forces remain in Cyprus more than twenty years later.

Under Article 2 (4) of the Charter, the prohibition against the threat or use of force is absolute, and the two exceptions should be interpreted narrowly. Professor Waldock cogently summarizes that:

> The final result is that Article 2(4) prohibits entirely any threat or use of force between independent states except in individual or collective self-defence under Article 51 or in execution of collective measures under the Charter for maintaining or restoring peace. Armed reprisals to obtain satisfaction for an injury or armed intervention as an instrument of national policy otherwise than for self-defence is illegal under the Charter.[6]

Hence, Article 4 of the Treaty of Guarantee did not and could not authorize use of armed force by Turkey against Cyprus. Under the opposite interpretation, Article 4 would conflict with Article 2 (4) under Article 103 of the Charter and would be null and void under *jus cogens*, as defined by the 1969

---

[6] Humphrey Waldock, The Regulation of the Use of Force by Individual States in International Law, in Hague Academy of International Law, 11 Recoueil des Cours 493 (1952).

Vienna Convention. Despite the foregoing, Turkey did not act in accordance with its own interpretation of Article 4, which clearly states that the sole aim of the action is for reestablishing the state of affairs created by the Treaty of Guarantee.

Particular attention should be paid to the findings of the European Commission of Human Rights which, after a quasi-judicial inquiry, found Turkey, as the occupying power, responsible for the infractions in the area of Cyprus under its occupation and found the Turkish army guilty of serious violations of the Rome Convention.

The "declaration of independence" by the Turkish Cypriot leadership and attempted secession of the part of Cyprus occupied by the Turkish armed forces on November 15, 1983, drew immediate condemnation throughout the world. This action, which could not have taken place without Ankara's prior knowledge and approval – indeed Turkey is the only country in the world to have recognized it as an "independent state" – is in flagrant violation of the United Nations resolutions, international law, and more specifically the 1960 Nicosia Treaties, to which Turkey is a signatory, which guarantee that the territory of Cyprus remain "one and indivisible," exclude "separatist independence," and prohibit "any activity aimed at promoting, directly or indirectly… partition of the Island."[7] By promptly recognizing the secessionist entity, Turkey violated its treaty obligations and confirmed its longstanding partitionist designs for Cyprus.

The attempted secession yielded widespread international condemnation. The United Nations, the Council of Europe, the European Community, the Commonwealth Conference, the United States, most other states, and Greece and Britain, cosignatories of the 1960 Treaties, demanded reversal of this situation. Turkey is the only state to recognize the secessionist entity. If any other state legally recognized the secessionist entity, this would raise legal issues against any state that purported to do so under the well established rules of international law on the recognition of states and, in particular, the duty not to recognize situations brought about through the illegal use of force.

The United Nations Code of Crimes against the Peace and Security of Mankind is of particular relevance to the Cyprus situation.[8] In addition to aggression and other crimes listed and defined under this Code, aspects of two other crimes were introduced at the insistence of Cyprus. The first, under Article 21 of the Code, entitled "[s]ystematic or mass violations of human

---

[7] Nicosia Treaties, Resolution 1514 (XV), Dec. 14, 1960.

[8] Comments and Observations of Governments on the Draft Code of the Crimes Against Peace and Security of Mankind Adopted on First Reading by the International Law Commission at its 43d Session, U.N. GAOR, Int'I L. Comm'n, 45th Sess., U.N. Doc. No. A/CN.41448/ Add.l (1993).

rights," is the "deportation or forcible transfer of population." The second, under Article 22 of the Code, entitled "[e]xceptionally serious war crimes," is "the establishment of settlers in an occupied territory and changes to the demographic composition of an occupied territory." As the commentaries to these provisions make clear, these are exceptionally serious crimes and individuals who commit or order the commission of such violations are subject to prosecution and conviction and the state itself may be responsible under the rules of international law.

With regard to prospects for a solution to the Cyprus problem and despite the existing deadlock, there exists both a framework for a solution and a procedure for pursuing efforts to this end.[9] The framework is provided for in the United Nations Resolutions. As for the procedure, the good offices of the Secretary-General and his personal involvement provides a potentially helpful element. The Secretary-General's efforts, in turn, enjoy the support of most states, including the United States and the other permanent members of the Security Council. The political will for a just and lasting compromise solution, as demonstrated in deeds over the years, undoubtedly exists on the part of the Cyprus Government and the Greek Cypriots. The basic difference is that, while the Cyprus Government and the Greek Cypriots aim at reunification of the country within a fair, reasonable and workable federal system, the Turkish side is systematically aiming at consolidation and legitimization of the existing division. The Turkish objective must be overcome and Ankara must be persuaded that it is to its long term benefit to temper its intransigence. If this can be achieved, a just and lasting solution is not beyond reach, for there is much more that unites all Cypriots than the differences that at present divide us. If this does not happen, regrettably, the prospects ahead are for continued confrontation, increasing tension, crisis, and even conflagration which may well spread beyond Cyprus.

Cyprus attaches great importance to the active support of the United States in the efforts to reach a just and viable solution to the Cyprus problem. The United States as a superpower and leader of the West, and as a country with vital interests and influence in the region, is in a unique position to assist. The United States Congress expressed its interest and support in a variety of ways and President Clinton has publicly declared his interest "to work for an end to the tragic conflict in Cyprus, which is dividing too many people in too many ways."

Indeed, some of the many weighted statements offered in the aftermath of Iraq's invasion of Kuwait aptly apply to the Cyprus situation.

---

[9] Notably Resolution 3212 endorsed by the Security Council in its Resolution 365 and reaffirmed by all subsequent resolutions including Resolution 939 of 29 July 1994.

Following his warning to friend and foe alike that the acquisition of territory by force is unacceptable and that aggression will not stand, President Bush stated in his address to Congress in January 1991, that:

> We have before us the opportunity to forge for ourselves and for future generations a new world order, a world where the rule of law, not the law of the jungle, governs the conduct of nations. When we are successful, and we will be, we have a real chance at this new order, an order in which a credible United Nations can use its peacekeeping role to fulfill the promise and vision of the United Nations' founders.[10]

Distinct from the moral and geopolitical reasons for the United States to exercise its influence toward implementation of the United Nations resolutions on Cyprus, a legal case can also effectively be made. As a founding member of the United Nations and a permanent member of the Security Council, the United States is bound under Article 25 of the Charter "to accept and carry out the decisions of the Security Council in accordance with the present Charter."[11]

Moreover, the legal aspect is also relevant to the United States in terms of United States legislation, notably Section 620C of the Foreign Assistance Act of 1961, and bilateral United States-Turkish agreements, because of Turkey's illegal use of American arms supplied for an expressly different purpose in its invasion and continuing occupation of a large part of Cyprus. This rule of law issue resulted in a congressionally mandated arms embargo against Turkey in 1975. Cypriots welcome and appreciate the Administration's repeatedly expressed support for the Secretary-General's efforts regarding a Cyprus settlement, as well as the strengthening of the team dealing with the Cyprus problem through the appointment of a Presidential Envoy.

The situation in Cyprus can be resolved permanently through the application of international rules and principles. It is frustrating that seemingly much more intractable problems such as that of the division of Germany, apartheid in South Africa, and the conflict in the Middle East, are resolved or on their way to a solution, while the situation in Cyprus remains unresolved. It is consoling, however, that only a few years ago no one could have guessed that Germany would be reunified or that apartheid would be peacefully dismantled or that significant progress would occur in the Middle East. Indeed who would have guessed, a few short years ago, that the Soviet Union would no longer exist and that democracy would be the norm in Eastern Europe?

---

10 President Bush Answers American People: We Will Not Fail, Wash. Post, Jan. 17, 1991, at A29.

11 U.N. Charter art. 25.

In October 1990, I was fortunate enough to be present at the historic ceremony in Berlin to mark German reunification. In September of 1993, I was on the White House South Lawn for the signing of the Israeli-Palestinian joint declaration of principles and, in July 1994, I was present at the Joint Session of Congress when King Hussein and Prime Minister Rabin declared that the state of war no longer existed between Jordan and Israel, which led to the conclusion of a Peace Treaty between them. I like to believe that one day in the not too distant future a similarly auspicious event will take place marking the just solution to the Cyprus problem. So, frustrating though it may be, we must persevere, stay the course, redouble our efforts in the conviction that our cause is right and continue to believe that justice and the rule of law will ultimately prevail.

The Cyprus Problem: The International Dimension*

I want to offer a somewhat different, more comprehensive perspective of the Cyprus problem, as seen from Cyprus itself. Representing Cyprus abroad, one learns that the problems of Cyprus may not rank among the major global issues in many minds, nor command the media attention accorded to other regional issues. Yet it nonetheless remains a test case of the effectiveness of the United Nations, and of the application of the basic rules of international law. It is also a tragic anachronism, as has been pointed out, in today's post-Cold War world. It continues to affect adversely the security situation of the whole area, and hence must be addressed as part of the larger effort to build new peace and security structures in the eastern Mediterranean.

It is now nearly twenty-two years since the invasion and occupation of a large part of Cyprus by the Turkish armed forces in 1974, with all its disastrous consequences of human suffering and its deplorable implications for the international legal order of, and peace in, a volatile and strategically significant region. It is neither necessary nor possible here to review in detail the history of the problem. I will simply assert that, in its basic dimensions, the issue of Cyprus presents questions that are straightforward, simple, and properly of universal concern.

Although it has its constitutional, internal, and inter-communal aspects, the Cyprus problem in its essence is an international problem of invasion, occupation, and systematic violations of human rights. Turkey's illegal actions in Cyprus have received universal condemnation, from the United Nations and virtually all other international fora. On numerous occasions, the United Nations Security Council has called for the withdrawal of all foreign troops from Cyprus, the voluntary return of refugees to their homes, the cessation of all interference in the internal affairs of Cyprus, and respect for its sovereignty, independence, territorial integrity, and unity. Turkey has chosen to ignore the decisions of the international community with impunity.

* Previously published in SECURITY IN SOUTHEASTERN EUROPE AND THE U.S.-GREEK RELATIONSHIP, eds. R. Pfaltzgraff and D. Keridis, Brassey's (1997).

Now, over two decades later, the situation on the ground is no different. In fact, it has deteriorated through the massive infusion of Anatolian settlers, the systematic destruction of the cultural heritage of Cyprus, and the attempted secession of the occupied part of the island – while nearly 40,000 heavily armed Turkish troops continue to occupy 37 percent of the territory of the Republic of Cyprus, posing a serious threat to the security and well-being of all Cypriots and to peace and stability in the region.

Despite Turkey's failure to comply with UN resolutions, the Cyprus government showed its good will, its sense of pragmatism, and a genuine wish for a peaceful solution by entering into negotiations with the Turkish-Cypriot side, acting from the conviction that there is much more uniting all Cypriots than dividing us. The Cyprus government and the Greek-Cypriot side made a number of significant concessions, including the acceptance in 1977 of a biregional, bizonal solution (for which no geographical basis had existed prior to 1974), in the hope that the Turkish side would respond with reasonable proposals and thus reach a solution.

What we have sought is the establishment of a viable and genuine federation based on democratic principles, as can be found in other federal systems such as the United States, with special provisions to meet the particular circumstances of Cyprus. We continue to maintain this position. The demand from the other side has been all along the establishment of, in effect, two separate states with separate sovereignties, separate armies, separate treaty-making capacities, and separate economies. In short, while paying lip service to the idea of a federal system, the Turkish objective has always been a partitionist solution through the legitimization of an internationally condemned invasion.

This Turkish intransigence has consistently frustrated all efforts to reach a negotiated settlement in Cyprus. In his May, 1994 report to the Security Council, the UN Secretary-General reached conclusions that accord with what we and many observers have been saying for years: "The Security Council finds itself faced with an already familiar scenario; the absence of agreement due essentially to a lack of political will on the Turkish-Cypriot side."

No progress towards a negotiated settlement can be expected unless the Turkish side finds the necessary political will to engage constructively. The necessary political resolve will not be found unless the factors that sustain Turkish intransigence are removed. Primary among these is the continuing presence and overwhelming military strength of Turkey's occupation force on the island – which prompted the Secretary-General to describe the occupied area of Cyprus as "one of the most highly militarized areas in the world."

The answer to the entire question of security lies in the proposal of the president of Cyprus, Glavkos Clerides, for the demilitarization of the Republic of Cyprus. This proposal was formally submitted to the UN in December of

1993; it has subsequently evolved to cover other aspects of security, including guarantees, and has been reaffirmed on several occasions in a variety of fora. It is a bold, imaginative, significant, and constructive proposal with far-reaching implications for meeting the perceived security concerns of Turkey, and the much more real security concerns of the Republic of Cyprus. It is also in keeping with the spirit of our time, offering the hope of cashing in a peace dividend for constructive development use, the economic benefits of which would redound primarily to the Turkish Cypriots.

The key to the solution of the Cyprus problem, including the acceptance of this crucial proposal, lies in Ankara. Unless Turkish intransigence is moderated no progress can be expected, and the stalemate, with all its risks, is likely to continue. All those who have a role to play – primarily the United States but also the European Union and the UN Security Council – must concentrate their efforts on this objective.

Having said all this, what are the prospects for Cyprus? At the risk of oversimplifying, let me summarize some main points. First, the Cyprus problem is essentially an international problem that needs to be attended to on its own merits, and is a potential threat to peace in the region. But it is a solvable problem, that can and must be solved. The parameters for its solution are provided in the relevant UN resolutions and high-level agreements. The UN Secretary-General's good offices offer a mutually acceptable procedure. Yet the primary reason for the continuance of the problem has been Turkish intransigence and lack of political will, sustained by overwhelming military force. Ankara needs to be persuaded that a compromise solution is ultimately best for its own long-term interests. The demilitarization proposal still on the table provides the answer to the security concerns of all parties involved, and merits general support. Its acceptance will substantially enhance prospects for a peaceful resolution of the problem, and form the cornerstone upon which to build such a solution.

The accession of the Republic of Cyprus to the European Union, a significant prospect, would ensure political and economic benefits for all Cypriots, and further enhance their security. It could also be a catalyst for progress in the talks for a solution to the problem, particularly in solving human rights issues in accordance with European norms and values.

The recent Security Council Resolution 939, stressing the elements of single sovereignty, international personality, and citizenship, reaffirms the proper common basis for a solution; the Turkish side should be pressed by the Council to accept it. The United States can play a major role in the search for a solution within the UN framework and is in a unique position to persuade Turkey to moderate its intransigence.

A just, viable compromise solution would be to the benefit of all parties directly concerned, including Turkey, as well as in the interest of the United States, which shares our concern for peace and stability in the region.

In summary, a united and peaceful Cyprus, free of foreign troops, can be a bridge of peace, instead of a bone of contention, in the region, playing in the eastern Mediterranean the role Switzerland and Austria have played in Central Europe.

Cyprus indeed holds great potential, which could be fully realized with a just and viable solution. Its past and present performance demonstrates that there is room for much pride and satisfaction in what this young and small state, despite all its setbacks, has managed to achieve. Since gaining independence in 1960, the economy of Cyprus has been transformed from that of a colonial backwater with low per capita income and high emigration to a bustling, vibrant, free-market economy with results for everyone to see.

In fact, Cyprus is one of the very few countries in Europe, inside or outside the European Union, that can meet the Maastricht criteria. We have a flourishing cultural life, and are of course intensely proud of our long history, culture, and tradition. We enjoy a democratic system of government, a free enterprise economic system, and an outstanding record in the observance of international standards of human rights. We have a sound civil service, independent judiciary, and full freedom of speech and of the press.

So perhaps there is a silver lining in the heavy clouds above us. It is sometimes frustrating to see such dramatic progress in what had seemed far more intractable problems, such as the division of Germany, apartheid in South Africa, or the conflict in the Middle East; recently, Northern Ireland and even Bosnia have taken considerable steps toward resolution. We rejoice for these accomplishments, of course; but our own difficulties seem nowhere near a solution. It is a consoling thought that a just few years ago hardly anyone could foresee that Germany would have been reunified by agreement, or that apartheid would have been peacefully dismantled. Indeed, who would have guessed, a few short years ago, that today the Soviet Union would no longer exist and that democracy would be the norm in Eastern Europe?

Frustrating though it may be, then, we must persevere, redoubling our efforts in the conviction that justice will in the end prevail. Politics, it has been said, is the art of the possible. If what is possible today is not acceptable, we have no option but to continue to strive in order to make possible tomorrow what is not possible today.

It is perhaps best to conclude by reiterating our own hopes for the future of Cyprus, which have been captured in a recent speech of Richard Boucher, the ambassador of the United States to Cyprus. "We all have an interest in a federal, demilitarized, and European Cyprus. That must be our common goal," wrote the ambassador. Indeed, this encapsulates our own position, objective, and aspiration. If achieved, the future of Cyprus can be bright for all its people and for peace in a volatile region.

The Cyprus Problem*

I am pleased and honored to participate in this important conference and, on behalf of the Government and people of Cyprus, I would like to extend warm congratulations to the American Hellenic Institute and to all the organizers and participants for this timely and significant initiative.

As we are all painfully aware and the title of this conference makes plain, this month marks the twentieth anniversary of the brutal invasion and occupation of a large part of Cyprus by the Turkish armed forces, with all its disastrous consequences in terms of human suffering and its implications for international legal order and for peace in our volatile region.

It is the nature and extent of these consequences, together with the wider issues of principle involved, that render the Cyprus problem one of international concern which needs to be urgently addressed, regardless of how many years have elapsed.

The Cyprus problem in its basic dimensions is simple and should be of universal concern. Although it has its internal, constitutional, and intercommunal aspects, the Cyprus problem in its essence is an international problem of aggression, invasion, occupation and massive violation of human rights. It involves the illegal invasion and occupation of a small country by a far larger and militarily much stronger neighbor, bent on imposing by force its arbitrary prescription of a partitionist political solution; it involves attempted secession in violation of international treaties; it involves the systematic destruction of the cultural heritage of an ancient land with thousands of years of history and civilization; it involves "ethnic cleansing" on a massive scale with the forced displacement of more than a third of Cyprus' population and the importation of a large number of colonists aimed at altering the age-long demographic composition of the island; and the tragedy of the missing persons raises a humanitarian issue of major significance.

---

* Previously published in The United States & Cyprus, Double Standards and the Rule of Law, eds. E. Rossides and V. Coufoudakis, American Hellenic Institute Foundation (2002).

As such, the Cyprus question is a test case of the effectiveness of the United Nations and of the universal applicability of the basic rules of international law.

If in 1974 the international community had taken effective steps not to allow the victimization of Cyprus through its forcible division and the deliberate massive "ethnic cleansing," there is good reason to think that we would not be witnessing today similar deplorable actions in former Yugoslavia and elsewhere. Bad precedents, when tolerated and condoned, tend to be repeated. The disastrous consequences and human suffering caused by the Turkish invasion of 1974 have been and no doubt will be discussed by others during this conference. Suffice it for me to add that, twenty years later, the situation on the ground is no different; in fact it deteriorated through the massive infusion of the Anatolian settlers and the systematic destruction of the cultural heritage of Cyprus.

Turkey's illegal actions and atrocities in Cyprus have received universal disapproval from the United Nations and by virtually all other international forums.

The fact that Turkey's invasion was carried out through the use of American-supplied arms, in violation of American laws and bilateral U.S.-Turkish agreements, raised the "rule of law" issue and resulted in the arms embargo against Turkey by decision of the Congress.

The UN Security Council has repeatedly called for the withdrawal of all foreign troops from Cyprus, the voluntary return of the refugees to their homes, the cessation of all interference in the internal affairs of Cyprus and respect for its sovereignty, independence, territorial integrity and unity. Turkey has chosen to ignore the decisions of the international community and has done so with impunity. This is a very sad commentary on the state of international legal order.

Despite all this, the Cyprus Government showed its goodwill, sense of pragmatism and genuine wish for a peaceful solution by entering into negotiations in the conviction that there is much more that unites all Cypriots than the differences that at present divide us.

The Cyprus Government and the Greek Cypriot side made a number of painful concessions in the hope that the Turkish side would respond with reasonable proposals and thus reach a solution. Basically, what we have asked for is the establishment of a viable and genuine federation based on democratic principles, as in the case of all other federal states and with special provisions to meet the particular circumstances of Cyprus.

The demand from the other side has been all along the establishment of, in effect, two separate states with separate armies, separate treaty-making capacity, separate economies. In short, while paying lip service to a federal system, the Turkish objective has always been a partitionist solution through the legitimization of the results of the internationally condemned invasion.

The Turkish intransigence was again manifest more recently in response to the UN efforts to reach agreement on a package of confidence-building measures. In his report to the Security Council of 30 May 1994, the Secretary-General concluded what many observers have been saying for a long time, that is, and I quote: "The Security Council finds itself faced with an already familiar scenario: the absence of agreement due essentially to a lack of political will on the Turkish Cypriot side."

The implications of this conclusion should be clear. Alternative ways to tackle the Cyprus problem, particularly its more substantive aspects, in an effective and result-oriented manner, should now be considered as a matter of utmost importance. Obviously no progress toward a negotiated settlement can be expected unless the Turkish side finds the necessary political will. And the necessary political will will not be found unless the factors that sustain Turkish intransigence are removed. This is primarily the overwhelming presence of the Turkish troops of occupation and the answer to this is the proposal of President Cierides for the demilitarization of the Republic of Cyprus. It is a significant and constructive proposal with far-reaching implications in terms of meeting the perceived Turkish security concerns, as indeed the much more real security concerns of the Republic of Cyprus, and its acceptance would substantially enhance prospects for a peaceful resolution of the situation.

While we count on the support of all fair-minded people and of all Governments which value international legal order in our efforts to resolve the Cyprus problem, we have looked particularly for support from the United Sates as a superpower – indeed the only superpower now – as the leader of the West and as the country which is in a unique position to assist.

The United States, as the leading member of NATO, has a particular reason to see the rift between two members – Turkey and Greece – healed so as to enhance the solidarity of the NATO Alliance in that turbulent region. The United States is a major source of foreign military and economic aid to Turkey and therefore is in a position of carrying much weight with the recipient of such aid. The United States has declared its dedication to the application of human rights and of the principles of international law in all parts of the world. Therefore, while not oblivious of the importance attached by U.S. policy makers to the bilateral U.S.-Turkish relationship, we feel that the role of the United States can be considerable in bringing the weight of its diplomacy to bear toward a just and lasting solution of the Cyprus problem.

The United States voted in favor of the key UN resolutions for Cyprus and the Administration has followed with close interest the efforts of the Secretary-General and supported them in their various stages. In Congress, there exists much sympathy and support for our position and this has been manifested in a variety of ways. Only last week the House Foreign Affairs Committee passed a significant bill on the issue of the Missing Persons in

Cyprus, while another bill was introduced in the Senate prohibiting all aid to Turkey until Turkey complies with certain conditions relating to its occupation of Cyprus.

These are positive steps in so far as they go. But we strongly feel that more can and should be done in persuading Turkey, and if persuasion does not prove sufficient, to pressure Turkey to comply with the dictates of the international community, withdraw its troops and moderate its position in the right direction. It is frustrating and disappointing to see decisive formulas, such as "by all means necessary," employed in other situations – most recently Haiti – by the Security Council to implement its decisions while on Cyprus there is marked reluctance to do the same.

Through principled, enlightened and effective diplomacy, the United States can undo some of the damage caused in 1974 and help to reach a workable honorable compromise and secure the friendship and appreciation of all the countries involved.

We sincerely appreciate President Clinton's manifestation, both in public and in private, of his personal interest and support for progress on the Cyprus problem. So far it has been primarily concentrated on promoting the acceptance by the Turkish side of the confidence-building measures. We would certainly welcome additional manifestations of this interest and support, not only by the White House but also by the State Department and the Pentagon, through more active U.S. engagement at an appropriately high political level, support by the United States in the UN Security Council for effective measures to implement its own resolutions and support for the significant and far-reaching proposal of President Clerides for the demilitarization of Cyprus. American support for the early admission of Cyprus to the European Union is also very important and we actively seek it.

It has long been my conviction that, if the rules of international law had been applied, the Cyprus problem would not have arisen. And if these rules are applied today, the problem can be solved in a fair and just way for all parties concerned, quickly and permanently. Evidently, other factors also apply – political, economic, psychological factors play their role. But I am fairly confident that the international legal factor is a strong one and that Cyprus would have an ironclad case before the International Court of Justice.

As an elected member of the UN International Law Commission, as well as a delegate to the General Assembly's Legal Committee, I have been actively engaged in the drafting of the statute of the International Criminal Court – which was also proposed by President Clerides at last October's Commonwealth Heads of Government Conference. This important project was completed by the Commission only last week in Geneva and, once finally approved through a treaty, would serve as an important instrument of punishment and deterrence for present and future aggressors, as Turkey is through its actions in Cyprus.

It would also interest you to know that, again with our active participation, the International Law Commission adopted in 1991 on first reading, a "Code of Crimes against the Peace and Security of Mankind" as one of the basic instruments for the jurisdiction of this International Criminal Court. Besides aggression and other crimes listed and defined under this Code, aspects of two other crimes are of particular relevance to the Cyprus situation and were introduced at our insistence. One, under Article 21, of the Code, entitled "Systematic or mass violations of human rights" is the "deportation or forcible transfer of population." The other, under Article 22 of the Code, entitled "Exceptionally serious war crimes," is "the establishment of settlers in an occupied territory and changes to the demographic composition of an occupied territory." This will be taken up by the International Law Commission on second (and final) reading in its session next year.

Cyprus is a party to the Optional Protocol accepting the jurisdiction of the International Court of Justice and has repeatedly challenged Turkey, a non-party to the Optional Protocol, to test this key issue of the legality of Turkey's invasion and continuing occupation and indeed the many other issues of international law raised by the invasion and occupation of Cyprus and the U.D.I. declaration of 1983, so far to no avail. There can be no doubt that the third party determination of the legal issues involved in the Cyprus situation, preferably by the main judicial organ of the United Nations, the International Court of Justice in the Hague, would go a long way toward promoting a just solution. It is my strongly held personal view that this, under the present stalemated situation, offers significant possibilities and one way it could be brought about, in the absence of Turkey's consent to adjudication, is through a request by the Security Council or by the General Assembly of the United Nations for an advisory opinion on the issue by the International Court of Justice.

Here allow me to recall, with tongue in cheek, something I heard from Justice Sandra O'Connor: "If you are strong on the law you argue the law; if you are strong on the facts you argue the facts; and if you are not strong on either the law or the facts, then you cry a lot"! It is good to bear this in mind since in our case we are strong on the law and facts.

The forthcoming Security Council Resolution, in addition to hopefully reaffirming key elements such as the position that the Republic of Cyprus must have a single sovereignty and international personality and a single citizenship with its independence and territorial integrity safeguarded, is expected to open the door for a new process of in-depth reappraisal of the present Cyprus situation and refocusing on ways to tackle more effectively the key elements of the withdrawal of the Turkish troops and settlers, and the other substantive aspects of the problem. The emphasis clearly should be in the acceptance of the demilitarization proposal which has been described by several key Senators and Congressmen including Chairman Pell, Senator Dole, Chairman Hamilton, Congressman Gilman and many others, as positive, constructive, far-reaching, imaginative, and courageous, addressing the basic issue of security for all concerned and promoting the prospects for a peaceful resolution of the overall Cyprus problem.

Utilization of the international legal option offers another promising possibility. The decision of the American Court in the Kanakaria mosaics case in 1989 and the very recent decision of the European Court of Justice on agricultural exports from the occupied part of Cyprus to the European Union are two excellent illustrations of the potential of this option.

But, when all is said and done, the stark reality remains that Turkish military preponderance and lack of political will is likely to prevent any early breakthrough and, realistically, it is not to be expected that sufficient pressure will be applied on Turkey from outside to drastically change this attitude in the foreseeable future. Given this situation, our options are clear: prevent backsliding (such as would occur with "TRNC's" recognition), maintain our economic strength, reinforce our defensive capacity while at the same time pressing for demilitarization, pursue the course of early entry into the European Union and continue the struggle nationally and internationally by all available peaceful means, having faith in the justice of our cause and in the wisdom of our leadership.

This may not be a very rosy picture but it is certainly not hopeless: twenty years after the invasion and eleven years after the UDI, we still maintain international recognition and enjoy international support. Our cause is just, our economy is healthy, international law is on our side and our leadership is responsible and time-tested. It may be frustrating to see what seemed to be much more intractable problems such as that of the division of Germany, apartheid in South Africa and the conflict in the Middle East to have been solved or to be on their way to a solution, while ours is nowhere near to a solution. But it is a consoling thought that a few years ago no one could have guessed that Germany would have been reunified by agreement or that apartheid would have been peacefully dismantled or that significant progress would have been made in solving the problems of the Middle East. Indeed who would have guessed, a few short years ago, that the Soviet Union would no longer exist and that democracy would be the norm in Eastern Europe? So, frustrating though it may be, we must persevere, stay the course and redouble our efforts in the conviction that our cause is right and that justice will at the end prevail. Politics is the art of the possible. If what is possible today is not acceptable, we have no option but to continue to strive in order to make possible tomorrow what is not possible today.

Let me conclude on a personal note: in October 1990 I was fortunate enough to be present at the historic ceremony in Berlin to mark German reunification. Last September I was on the White House South Lawn for the signing of the Israeli-Palestinian joint declaration of principles, and only yesterday, I was present at the Joint Session of Congress when King Hussein and Prime Minister Rabin declared that the state of war no longer existed between Jordan and Israel. I like to believe that one day in the not too distant future a similarly auspicious event will take place marking the just solution to the Cyprus problem.

Cyprus: Prospects for a Solution

Introductory Statement at the Western Policy Center Conference, Washington, D.C., 26 February 2004

I am very pleased to be here at this very timely Conference and to share some views, as a private individual, on the prospects of a solution to the Cyprus problem.

Until two weeks ago it looked as if the Republic of Cyprus was safely headed to full membership of the European Union by 1 May 2004, with the Cyprus problem unresolved and the acquis communautaire not applicable to the Turkish-occupied part of the island (or to the Sovereign British Bases). Its situation would be parallel, though not identical, to that of West and East Germany prior to the 1990 reunification, with some resultant problems, none of them unmanageable, but with strengthened bargaining position vis-à-vis Turkey and its pending application for EU membership. In any case Cyprus, as well as Greece, made it clear that they would not veto Turkey's obtaining a date for commencement of accession negotiations, indeed they would welcome it if the applicable criteria were met.

With the "Friday the 13th" of February agreement (more accurately, the acceptance by the two sides of the UN's communiqué of that day) the situation was – potentially – radically transformed. With the negotiations (in two phases, 19 Feb.–21 March and 22–29 March) and the filling of any remaining gaps by the UN Secretary-General, the "Annan Plan" (with input by many, in the UN Secretariat and outside, extending over many years) will be put to separate referenda on or about 21 April 2004 with a view to the "United Republic of Cyprus" joining the European Union on May 1st, together with the other nine new Members with the problem solved. If either of the two sides (Greek or Turkish Cypriot) votes "no" the situation proceeds as earlier indicated without the UN Plan.

The assumption of many at the United Nations and elsewhere is that, with the combined persuasion/pressure of all actors outside Cyprus (the EU, the US, the UN and probably Greece and Turkey), enough people on each side will vote "yes".

This is the assumption but not a certainty. Much will depend on the final outcome of the negotiations (though, realistically, not very much is expected to change from the present text) and on how public opinion and the attitude of the political parties will evolve between now and then.

Will Mr. Denktash, having earlier declared the plan "dead and buried" but having accepted the UN communiqué of Friday, 13th, continue in his attitude under the control of Ankara and will Ankara's position continue to be steady notwithstanding the earlier attitudes of the Generals, the President, the Opposition and the Foreign Office bureaucracy who, to varying degrees, had manifested different views? Will the Greek Cypriots and Athens (depending also on the outcome of the 7 March 2004 election in Greece) continue their compliance even if their declared aim to "improve" the UN Plan are not satisfied and indeed if there is a "deterioration" towards satisfying the Turkish demands for "improvement"? And how much of a public debate will there be in Cyprus and in Greece once the full implications (political, economic, legal, etc.) of the Plan are further studied, debated and evaluated? We should not forget that the Plan is a very long and complicated document which, in the circumstances of its submission (Nov. 2002), revision (Dec. 2002) and third revision (26 Feb. 2003), was never really studied intensively and in depth, considering the Cyprus Presidential election (28 Feb. 2003) and the Hague collapse (10 March 2003), which seemed to put it on ice as of then.

Undoubtedly Cyprus, as our politicians have been proclaiming for the past several decades, is "going through one of the most critical periods of its long history" – except that at this time it is for real!

It is of course not possible in a 15 minute introductory statement to do justice to the many and difficult issues involved in the Annan Plan.

Soon after it was originally submitted in November 2002, I was asked by Professor Ruth Wedgewood of SAIS to give a briefing to a group of SAIS graduate students who were visiting the UN Headquarters.

I started by saying that any person of good will, especially one who over the years has been associated with the United Nations and conflict resolution (Professor Roger Fisher of the Harvard Law School and the International Peace Academy's Vienna and Helsinki seminars and simulation exercises readily come to mind), who has always stood for rapprochement and good relations within Cyprus between the two (and indeed all) communities and with many Turkish Cypriot friends, would be strongly inclined to be in favour of a peaceful solution of a long-standing international problem, particularly so as a Cypriot diplomat and an international lawyer who throughout his diplomatic career (and even before as a graduate student of international law at Cambridge – February 1959) had formulated and expressed strong views as to what would be a just and lasting solution, in accordance with the UN Charter and Resolutions on Cyprus, the acquis communautaire, public international law and international humanitarian law. I also recalled my own modest role at different junctures – 1963–4, drafting the letter raising the question to the Security Council (S/5488) and articulating on the illegality of the use of force under Art. IV of the Treaty of Guarantee of 1960; in 1974–5 on the key GA Resolution 3212 endorsed by the Security Council in S.C. 365 (1974) and reaffirming the existence of and support for the Cyprus Government in the Security Council and NAM after the disastrous Geneva Declaration of July 30, 1974; in November 1983 in rallying support in Washington in Congress and the Administration against UDI which resulted in the non-recognition and disapproval of the "TRNC", which still holds; from 1990 onwards in promoting Cyprus' course towards the EU; in 1995 in securing support in the United States Congress (and in Canada) for the genuine demilitarization of Cyprus; in 1998 in incorporating in the Statute of the International Criminal Court the provision declaring as an international crime "the establishment of settlers in occupied territory" (co-sponsored by Switzerland, Egypt and Greece), to mention some key developments in a 44 year career, on behalf of the Republic of Cyprus.

Of course, I quite understand – and said so to the SAIS students and now to you – that an agreed solution requires compromise and taking into account other points of view. I do not forget Abba Eban's famous saying that "the Palestinians never lost the chance to miss an opportunity" and that "lawyers and missionaries do not make good diplomats" by insisting on the letter of the law and missing the wider political picture and the need to accommodate the requirements of others if conflict resolution is to succeed.

Over the years, I have stood for compromise and conciliation but within certain parameters so that the result, if not fair, would not be grossly unfair, and if not fully functional would not be evidently dysfunctional. For instance, I was privately in favour of the US-UK-Canadian plan of 1978 (even though the then Cypriot Government rejected it) and in favour of the Perez de Guellar 1984–5 Plan. I had more difficulty with, through no fundamental objection to, the 1992 Boutros Ghali Plan, especially since it genuinely allowed room for improvements through negotiations.

As for the Annan Plan in the form it was presented in November 2002 (it has since been altered in several respects in the 26 February 2003 version, primarily I understand so to secure the support of the Generals in Ankara – and of course the jury is still out on the final outcome of the current version), I observed in my SAIS briefing that I saw flaws and problems in at least three areas:

Firstly: The question of whether, with its complicated provisions of separate majorities and vetoes at the executive and legislative levels, it would be functional, pointing out the lesson of the Zurich-London arrangements which resulted in deadlock and a breakdown of the system. When this occurred, back in 1963/early 1964 (and again in 1974 after the Turkish invasion) the internationally recognized Cyprus Government was able, with international support, to survive and prevail. In this case, by contrast, should the system break down (after all we are Greek and Turkish Cypriots, with a history of strife and mutual suspicions which cannot be completely and immediately obliterated, who are not angels or Swiss or even Belgians!), there is nothing to fall back on since the Republic of Cyprus, as we know it and as is internationally recognized, will have disappeared as of 22 April 2004, with no return. The proposed remedy through the Supreme Court (with its foreign judges, at the level of ICJ judges' salaries I might add at the expense of the Cypriot tax payer) is far from satisfactory. An even more serious situation would develop if, during the long transitional period, Turkey, for whatever reason (including its not being granted by the EU its date in December), declined to proceed with troop withdrawal and/or return of the territory agreed upon. In the absence of such a Government, what recourse would be available and by whom?

Secondly: The financial and economic provisions of the Plan, impose an excessive, unfair and unbearable burden on the public sector and essentially on the Greek Cypriot taxpayer, and this can hardly be offset by any expected increase of economic activity in the private sector.

One of the outrageously inequitable provisions of the Plan is that it imposes, in effect, on the Greek Cypriot taxpayers the enormous cost of compensating the Greek Cypriots who will not be getting back their property in the Turkish Cypriot constituent state and for being deprived of the use of their property for the past 30 years. Turkey (unlike the applicable international law rule on state responsibility under the *Chorzow Factory* (Germany v. Poland, PCIJ, 1928) ruling, as applied most recently by the UN Compensation Commission in the case of Iraq) is obligated to pay nothing, even though the Greek Cypriots affected were deprived of such properties and their use as a result of Turkey's illegal invasion. How such a glaringly unjust and unfair proposal could have been made and, it seems, accepted by our negotiating team, is beyond my comprehension.

The economic cost of the Annan Plan (payment of compensation to property owners, fully funding the cost of the UN Force to be increased to 5,000 troops and 500 policemen, enormously increased bureaucracy, convergence of the Turkish Cypriot with Greek Cypriot per capita income etc. etc.) has been estimated by Government sources at 16.5 billion Cyprus pounds or some 36 billion U.S. dollars, at the current rate of exchange of 2.20. Even if one disputes this figure, a very recent estimate of the Economist Intelligence Unit on the cost of the Annan Plan foresees an increase of 10 billion pounds of the public debt of Cyprus, increase in inflation, reduction of the value of the Cyprus pound and removes into the distant future the prospect of Cyprus joining the European Monetary system which, as things stand now, would happen in 2007. The Central Bank would be subdivided into three and, in the event of a collapse of the system, its foreign exchange reserves, currently estimated 1.3 billion Cyprus pounds (2.8 billion dollars) would presumably be open to division by the two "constituent states" (as with former Yugoslavia, the Czech Republic/Slovakia and other recent such examples). There is much more to be said on this score and there exist serious doubts if the much vaunted "foreign assistance" will amount to more than 500 million dollars (between the EU's 206 million Euros, already allocated to the Turkish Cypriot housing and whether the US, which has currently a lot of economic burdens to bear and a 500 billion deficit, could realistically devote more than at most a few hundred million to Cyprus, given the demands in Iraq, Afghanistan, Liberia, etc.) and the "donor fatigue" which is evident worldwide. However, on the positive side, there would be the savings from the abolition of the military expenditures of National Guard.

Thirdly: In the international legal field – and this is an area I think I can say I know something about – there are at least three points in which the Plan, as it stands, is flawed:

(a) The question of forcible intervention under Art. IV of the Treaty of Guarantee by the Guarantor Powers (which under the Plan would have substantial forces, 6000 each or more as opposed to 950 and 650 respectively under the 1960 Treaty regime, with more extensive rights of intervention than in 1960). Over the years in the Security Council (1964 on), the Law of Treaties Conference (1968–9), the UN Legal Committee, the UN International Law Commission, Cypriot representatives documented the case that under Art. 2 (4) and Art. 103 of the UN Charter and the peremptory norms doctrine of international law (Art. 53 of the 1969 Vienna Convention), Art. IV of the Treaty of Guarantee can only give a right of intervention by peaceful means and have challenged Turkey to test this and other aspects of applicable international law before the International Court of Justice. Apparently, the point was not even raised in the pre-November 2002 negotiations for fear – as I was told – that "it might be interpreted against us"!

(b) The question of the illegality of the presence of the Turkish mainland settlers, as provided in general terms in the 1949 Geneva Convention and in more specific terms (where I might be allowed to say I played a modest role) in the International Law Commission's work on the Code of Crimes against the Peace and Security of Mankind, 1991 and even more explicitly in the 1998 Rome Statute of the International Criminal Court Art. (8 (b) (viii)). This is a question of basic principle, not of numbers, as is now being argued (and is subject only to very strictly circumscribed exceptions for humanitarian reasons).

(c) The question of inalienability of private property. This basic human right, reaffirmed in the *Loizidou v. Turkey case (1996)* by the European Court of Human Rights, was articulated upon by a distinguished group of eminent international lawyers in Geneva in June 1999 – where I was present – and makes clear and even if Governments agree to deprive the owners of their rights, these rights can validly be asserted before the Strasbourg Court under the European Human Rights Convention.

The above are some of the points which constitute flaws that the Annan Plan, most probably introduced by the drafters under the pressure of the need to accommodate conflicting claims and perhaps because our negotiating team did not raise them or did not press them to the extent that they would prevail. Although I was a member of the Greek Cypriot negotiating team at the beginning (December 1999 during the time the Helsinki decision was taken on our EU application) when there was only a meaningless dialogue of the deaf, I was not in the subsequent and decisive phases and so I do not exactly know what transpired. I say this not by way of criticism but so as to avoid letting these flaws, to the extent possible, remain unremedied.

Having said this, I repeat what I said earlier namely that the outcome, is by no means assured.

On the Turkish Cypriot side, there can be no doubt that EU membership with all the benefits that it entails and the prospect of increased prosperity through economic convergence (at present the per capital T/C income is less than one third of that of the Greek Cypriots) will be major factors. The real difficulties, however, of the timely harmonization of the economy in the Turkish occupied part of the island with the EU acquis cannot be underestimated.

On the Greek Cypriot side there are two schools of thought:

There are those who, while not fully satisfied with the Annan Plan, have reasons to feel (some influenced also by considerations of the return of their properties or payment of compensation which under the *status quo* they would not receive) that this is perhaps the last chance to avoid partition and to get a solution, even one which leaves much to the desired. They are content to support the Plan hoping, though not really expecting, for improvements during the current negotiations. Some of them are also influenced by the prospect that with EU membership many of the decisions will be taken not in Cyprus, but in Brussels and some hope that foreign aid will pour in and make things much more easy to apply. Some may even be influenced by such factors as the abolition of military service in the National Guard.

On the other hand, there are those who consider the Annan Plan unfair, undemocratic, inconsistent with the acquis communautaire, human rights, and international law; a moribund monstrosity, prepared by foreigners in pursuit of their own interests and in order to facilitate Turkey's EU aspiration, aimed not at a proper solution but at the dissolution of the Republic of Cyprus. They do not understand why, on the very eve of the Republic's accession to the EU and under asphyxiating time limits, they should consent to its disappearance as a legal entity and its substitution by a scheme which is unfair to them and probably not viable, with no army of its own when there are mainland Greek and Turkish troops, a type of Bosnia-Herzegovina or Kosovo condominium with a disproportionate role played by highly paid UN bureaucrats and with the Greek Cypriot taxpayers subsidizing them and the Turkish Cypriot constituent state – a very peculiar EU member, at best.

For the time being, it appears that the former view is espoused by the majority of the people, as expressed by the leaders of the major political parties, but there have also been polls to the contrary. Whether this will apply after the talks are completed and the final product emerges remains to be seen, although the outside pressures (UN, EU, US), combined with the persuasive influence of Greece and Turkey, may be too much to defy. Yet, it may still prove that "the devil is in the details" and of "people's power" manifesting itself.

Allow me to conclude by quoting from a speech I gave as the then Ambassador of Cyprus to the United States, at the AHI Conference in 1994 on the 20th anniversary of the invasion (The United States and Cyprus, 2002 pp. 226–272):

> In October 1990 I was fortunate enough to be present at the historic ceremony in Berlin to mark German reunification. Last September [1993] I was at the White House South lawn for the signing of the Israel-Palestinian joint declaration of principles and, only yesterday [1994], I was present at a joint session of Congress when King Hussein and Prime Minister Rubin declared that the State of war no longer existed between Jordan and Israel. I like to believe that one day in the not too distant future a similarly auspicious event will take place marking the just solution to the Cyprus problem.

Whether this will be the 1st of May 2004 or some other day remains to be seen.

To my mind it is essential that a solution be functional and that the economic provisions impose the burden where it belongs (Turkey or perhaps any foreign "donors" who are so willing). There should be full demilitarization, no foreign troops, no right of forcible intervention and no settlers (other than those under international humanitarian law). Such a plan would indeed be a proper basis for an agreed, lasting and fair solution. Under these circumstances, everyone should be in favor of reunification and an agreed solution – and I certainly would be.

European Union Expansion: The Old and the New

Introductory Remarks before the San Antonio World Affairs Council, San Antonio, Texas, 24 March 2004

Some years ago – quite a few years ago! – I had the pleasure and the honor to address the San Antonio World Affairs Council as the then Ambassador of the Republic of Cyprus to the United States on the long-standing political problem of Cyprus, an issue involving many political, legal and economic factors and which is still pending despite many efforts for its solution. Should any of you be interested to hear more on its present delicate phase, I would be glad to respond during the "question and answer" period.

What I intend to do today, in response to your kind invitation, is to share this platform with my good friend, Ambassador Jean de Ruyt, the Permanent Representative of Belgium to the United Nations and to address you on a broader topic which has been receiving a good deal of attention worldwide and especially in Europe, namely, the major expansion of the European Union from 15 to 25 Members, due to take place on the 1st of May this year. Ambassador de Ruyt has spoken from the point of view of Belgium, one of the original six members of the European Union (at that time known as the European Economic Community). The ten new members include the key central and east European countries of Poland, Hungary, the Czech Republic, Slovenia and Slovakia; the three Baltic States of Estonia, Latvia and Lithuania; and the two Mediterranean island states of Malta and, my own country, Cyprus.

Before I go any further, I should make it clear that I speak here as a private individual and also that I have no expertise on the particular circumstances of the other nine countries which form part of the present wave of expansion other than in general terms. So I think it would be best that I speak to you about the course taken by Cyprus towards full membership of the European Union in May this year, following the submission of its application in July 1990.

At this stage, perhaps a minor diversion will be in order: The Greek word for Europe is Ευρώπη. According to legend, Ευρώπη/Europa/Europe was a beautiful Phoenician princess (the etymology of her name is "wide-eyed").

Zeus (or Jupiter), the father of the Olympian Gods, who was known for his marital infidelities (a dirty old man you might say, in modern parlance) disguised himself as a bull, lured the innocent girl to ride on his back and abducted her to Greece by way of Cyprus – hence the name of the continent where Greece is located as "Europe". The abduction of Europa by Zeus, was pictured on an ancient coin from Paphos, a city on the west coast of Cyprus, which happens to be my home town, at the period of King Nicocles, 4th Century B.C., and is now reproduced on one of the sides of the 50-cent modem Cyprus coin (worth about one U.S. dollar). I shall be very pleased to present you with one on this occasion as a reminder of the fact that Cyprus, an island located in the eastern Mediterranean at the cross roads of three continents (Europe, Asia and Africa), has a very ancient claim to be associated with Europe dating to the prehistoric period.

Allow me also to mention, on a personal note my own modest involvement in the course of Cyprus' accession to the EU. July 3, 1990, when the then (and now) Foreign Minister of Cyprus, George Iacovou, signed on behalf of the Republic of Cyprus the application to membership, I was the Permanent Secretary (head of the Foreign Service) of the Ministry of Foreign Affairs and naturally played a small role in the taking of this momentous step. Soon thereafter, in early September 1990, I found myself as the Ambassador of Cyprus to the just reunited Germany. Coming from forcibly divided Cyprus, it was a special experience for me to be in the first batch of foreign Ambassadors to present credentials to the Federal President of Germany soon after the reunification ceremony (I recall that some years earlier, in a conversation with my predecessor, President von Weizaecker had remarked that Cyprus was much more likely to be reunited before Germany was – in fact it was the opposite and that was primarily because of Gorbachev and the fundamental changes that occurred in the former Soviet Union, but this is another story!). An important part of my duties in Germany, the largest member of the EEC, and one of its founding members, and indeed in Denmark to which I was also accredited (a member of the EEC since 1973) and to Austria (in the process of accession which occurred in 1995), was to cultivate and promote support for the admission of Cyprus, not an easy task under the then existing circumstances. I recall attending Europe Day events in the historic Aachen Cathedral and, more substantively, the adoption of the momentous 1991 Maastricht Treaty, during my tenure, with its far reaching steps towards Common Foreign and Security policy and the settling of the still applicable criteria leading to the Economic and Monetary Union (EMU) and the European Monetary System. While still on a personal note, I recall being a member of the Greek Cypriot negotiating team for the Cyprus Talks at the United Nations in New York in December 1999, while significant decisions on the fate of the Cyprus application and Turkey's application for membership were being taken in Helsinki by the European Council delinking admission from a solution, which had a direct effect on the New York process and vice versa. I also recall Richard Holbrooke's idea in 1995 of a linkage between the Cyprus admission to the EU, Turkey's admission and a Cyprus problem solution – a parallel as he saw it in Ireland's and the United Kingdom's EU membership and the solution to the Northern Ireland problem.

I will not bore you with the various stages in successive EU meetings having a bearing on the Cyprus 1990 application for membership. Suffice it to say that, in June 1993, the European Commission issued its "Opinion on the Application of the Republic of Cyprus for Membership", confirming the island's European character and vocation and concluding that it was eligible to be part of the Community. In the same Opinion the Commission underscored that the Government of the Republic of Cyprus was "recognized by the European Community as the only legitimate government representing the Cypriot people".

Following substantive discussions, through many working groups and subgroups, covering a broad range of issues, with the participation of public servants and the private sector and extending over a period of several years, the accession negotiations were successfully concluded in October 2002 and it was confirmed by the European Council that Cyprus fulfilled the Copenhagen political and economic criteria.

These criteria (defined by the European Council at its meeting in Copenhagen in December 1993), the Copenhagen criteria, are worth quoting because they are significant as to what the European Union expects from new members:

> Membership requires that the candidate country has achieved stability of institutions guaranteeing democracy, the rule of law, human rights and respect for the protection of minorities, the existence of a functioning market economy as well as the capacity to cope with competitive pressure and market forces within the Union. Membership presupposes the candidate's ability to take on the obligations of membership including adherence to the terms of the political, economic and monetary union.

These requirements set high standards but it is essential that all candidate countries meet them. The 10 countries to join on May 1 have met them. Other candidates (including Romania, Bulgaria and Turkey) need to meet them as a prior condition to membership.

In the particular case of Cyprus, the European Council in December 2002 in Copenhagen reconfirmed its strong preference for the accession of a united Cyprus (i.e. solution of the Cyprus problem in line with the EU principles). This definitely also is the strong preference of the Cyprus government.

At the same time it was decided that, in the absence of a settlement, the Republic of Cyprus would nonetheless become a member of the European

Union, but the application of the acquis communautaire in the northern part of the island would be temporarily suspended. This was done through a Protocol No. 10, attached to the Accession Treaty signed by Cyprus, – and indeed by the other 9 candidates – on 16 April 2003. Similarly the British Bases on the island are exempted from the Accession Treaty's provisions and are specially regulated by another Protocol, No. 3.

The signing of the Accession Treaty (subsequently ratified unanimously by the Cyprus Parliament on 14 July 2003) is a conclusive, collective, political and legal confirmation that Cyprus is part of the European family of nations. All aspects of life on the island – political, economic, social, and cultural – are based on and reflect its European heritage, values and orientation.[1]

Cyprus, with its relatively high per capita income, stable and high economic growth, low unemployment, and low inflation has an open and efficient economic system. With the harmonization process complete – or nearly complete – it is in a position to meet the highest challenge it has been presented since independence in 1960. It is at the same time recognized that EU membership entails both privileges and burdens which can, hopefully, be met successfully for political as well as economic reasons.

Accession to the European Union is a two way relationship. Cyprus has a lot to gain (security, a sense of belonging to a broader unit, high standards in human rights and environment protection etc.) but also to contribute to a united Europe in terms of prosperity and security. Shipping is one area in which Cyprus, with the sixth largest ship registry in the world, can enhance the EU total. Being geographically Europe's last out post in the Eastern Mediterranean Cyprus can make a contribution in the creation of a European security system in the region, because of its location and its traditional good relations with the peoples of the region, including Israel and the Arab countries, in the region and beyond (in addition to its active participation in the Commonwealth). Cyprus can become an economic, political and cultural link and serve as a two way bridge in the region (Europe, the Mediterranean and the Middle East).

Already, many European and multinational firms have chosen Cyprus as a location of their regional headquarters because of its location, the availability of highly educated managerial and technical staff, the excellent transportation and telecommunications system and other infrastructure, including an

[1] [Footnote – Para 44 of the 1993 Opinion is worth quoting:
Cyprus's geographical position, the deep-lying bonds which, for two thousand years, have located the island at the very fount of the European culture and civilization, the intensity of the European influence apparent in the values shared by the people of Cyprus and in the conduct of the cultural, political, economic and social life of its citizens, the wealth of its contacts of every kind with the Community, all these confer on Cyprus, beyond all doubt, its European identity and character and confirm its vocation to belong to the Community].

efficient banking and legal system based on internationally valid principles. The Cyprus pound, now worth about 2.12 U.S. dollars, is tied to the Euro at the same rate as with the ECU (European Currency Unit) since 1992 and it is hoped that it will be part of the EU monetary system in the next 3–4 years. The Cyprus pound is supported by healthy for our size foreign exchange reserves (some 1.3 billion pounds – 2.8 billion U.S. Dollars).

In a united Europe, Cyprus under the Treaty of Nice and subsequent arrangements, would be represented in European organs through its own Commissioner on the European Commission (already selected, Mr. Markos Kyprianou, the Finance Minister), six Members of the European Parliament (elections due on 13 June 2004), a Judge on the European Community's Court, and on the European Central Bank, Civil Service etc. in proportion relating to its population.

In recent years and certainly since the signature of the Accession Treaty in 2003, there has been increasing participation by the Candidate Countries in EU Summits and Ambassadors' meetings in capitals (including Washington) and, almost routinely, Candidate Countries have been associated with the EU positions at the United Nations.

Allow me now to make some brief concluding remarks:

Cyprus's accession to the European Union, as indeed the accession of the other nine countries in the present wave, provides a historic choice and presents major challenges and opportunities. I very much hope – indeed I am convinced – that this major experiment will prove to be a success and it will provide a win-win situation both for the present members and for the new ones, indeed for the world as whole, during these trying times of globalization and the war on terrorism.

It goes without saying that, should there be a solution of the Cyprus Problem on the basis of the UN Plan currently being negotiated, there will be a number of corresponding changes that will need to be taken into account. Belgium might provide some instructive precedents in this respect but – and I stress this – changes must be within the parameters of the acquis communautaire and of international law. Any derogations must be minor and temporary if EU membership will be meaningful for Cyprus and if the EU is to be consistent with its own standards.

Certainly, the entire population will be better off if the island ceases to be a place of arms and of confrontation and the present status quo is replaced by a functional and balanced political order that will allow all Cypriots to live together in peace under conditions of stability and security within the framework of the European Union.

Thank you, for your attention.

Book Review (Excerpt) of *An International Relations Debacle: The UN Secretary-General's Mission of Good Offices in Cyprus 1999–2004* by Claire Palley, Hart Publishing, 2005*

This is not the first time that the American Society of International Law and this Journal have come across the international law issues involved in the Cyprus question.[1] Cyprus is an island of some 3,600 square miles in a strategic location at the crossroads of three continents in the eastern Mediterranean. Its history dates back to 6000 BC, with many foreign occupations, which have left traces of their presence but have not altered Cyprus's unity and ethnological character. Cyprus's native Greek population, whose ancestors came to the island before the Trojan War and who constitute about 80 percent of the island's current population of approximately one million, has retained intact its language, religion, and cultural traditions. The majority population has coexisted with minority communities, the largest of which (18 percent of the population) is that of the Turkish Cypriots, most of whose ancestors arrived on the island after the Ottomans conquered Venetian-controlled Cyprus in 1571.

[...]

Overall, *An International Relations Debacle* is a significant contribution to the understanding of the Cyprus problem in terms of both international politics and international law. It is essential reading for all who have studied or lived through this complicated, but solvable, problem. And for those who would invoke the UN machinery in resolving their conflicts, the book provides lessons concerning what to pursue and also what to avoid in the process of doing so.

* Previously published in *American Journal of International Law*, January 2006, Volume 100, Number 1.

[1] *See, e.g.* 77 ASIL PROC. 99–105 (1983); 78 *id.* 107–32 (1984); M.-Christiane Bourloyannis & Virginia Morris, Case Report: Autocephalous Greek Orthodox Church of Cyprus v. Goldberg & Feldman Arts, Inc., 86 AJIL 128 (1992).

To this reviewer – a former diplomat who was representing the Cypriot government over the course of different phases of the problem's evolution, from 1960 to 1997 – the most salient feature emerging from this account of a truly international debacle is that, through a combination of circumstances (and not only through the ill-advised activities of some in the UN Secretariat) a significant opportunity to reach a fair and agreed settlement of this long-standing international dispute was lost. The Cyprus situation is not, as this reviewer sees it, an "unending problem," and in this respect he differs from Richard Haass, another distinguished author, currently the president of the Council of Foreign Relations, and one of the State Department's special coordinators on Cyprus in the 1980s.[26] In fact, in October 1984, President Reagan's letter to then President Evren did produce some positive movement in the intercommunal negotiations,[37] but not enough to lead to a breakthrough. In fairness, other distinguished personalities who, over the years, dealt with different phases of the problem (George Ball, Dean Acheson, Brian Urquhart, Kurt Waldheim, Xavier Perez de Cuellar, Boutros Boutros-Ghali) have in various ways expressed their frustration with their inability to reach a solution. "Anyone who thinks he understands the situation in Cyprus is misinformed" was the epigrammatic way the matter was put by a former British colonial governor of Cyprus. Anyone who carefully reads Palley's book would not be misinformed.

This reviewer, on the basis of long experience, is of the conviction that, given a minimum of political goodwill, the problem is capable of a compromise solution, provided that such a solution is functional and not incompatible with the applicable rules of international law; there is much more that unites all Cypriots than the differences that at present divide them. Genuine demilitarization, as endorsed by the U.S. House of Representatives in 1995, would be a key ingredient of such a solution. For many years, and in the absence of a practical possibility for resorting to contentious proceedings before the International Court of Justice (ICJ), this reviewer advocated resort to the Court, through a decision of the General Assembly or of the Security Council, for an advisory opinion-one that would clarify the applicable rules of international law on several key aspects of the Cyprus situation. In the view of this writer, such an advisory opinion might address issues concerning unilateral intervention under Article IV of the 1960 Treaty of Guarantee; the 1983 Unilateral Declaration of Independence of the "Turkish Republic

[2] *See* Richard Haass, Conflicts Unending: The United States and Regional Disputes (1990).

[3] For example, the Turkish Cypriot-controlled unit would be reduced to "29 percent plus" of the territory of the federation, and the presidency would have not have to rotate between the communities.

of Northern Cyprus"; "ethnic cleansing" and the establishment of settlers in occupied territory; the applicable rules of state responsibility as they have been applied, for instance, under Security Council Resolution 687 of 1991 (regarding Iraq's invasion of Kuwait); and basic human rights violations. The ICJ's authoritative clarification of the legal aspects of pending political disputes would go a long way toward resolving these disputes in a way consistent with the applicable principles and rules of international law-as recently highlighted by ICJ President Shi in his November 2004 address to the Sixth Committee of the UN General Assembly.

If the ICJ had so acted with regard to Cyprus, if the "fundamental principles" of the EU acquis communautaire had been applied, and if the key relevant resolutions of the Security Council (especially nos. 186 (1964), 365 (1974), 541 (1983), 550 (1984), and 789 (1992) and of the General Assembly (no. 3212 (XXIX) (1974)) had been duly taken into account, the contents of the recent UN plan (Annan V) would have been drastically different. Quite possibly, it would not have been overwhelmingly rejected, thereby becoming defunct by its own terms and ultimately undercutting the process of finding a lasting compromise solution.

It has been argued that politics is the art of the possible and that the Annan Plan in its final form had to incorporate or accede to virtually all the demands ("red lines") put forward by Turkey (concerning, for example, the presence of Turkish troops, right of forcible intervention, stay of Turkish settlers, retention of the Karpas Peninsula), failing which there would have been no agreement. A negotiated solution, no doubt, requires compromises, and involves give and take. But as the tenth anniversary of the Dayton Accords recently served to remind, such a compromise must be functional and be perceived as just. Unlike the circumstances of Bosnia-Herzegovina in 1995, the overriding goal was not "To End a War" (to use the apt title of the 1998 book of Richard Holbrooke, the architect of the Dayton Accords), but to persuade the majority of Cypriots that they should consent to dissolving the Republic of Cyprus on the very eve of its hard-won entry into the EU; but that particular time was one of peace and prosperity, even if of regularized anomaly, in contrast to the economic and political uncertainties associated with the proposed, new "United Republic of Cyprus" (which it could be argued with only a minimum of flippancy was neither united nor a republic). One also needs to include in this mix several elements of the Cyprus situation that arguably violated international law (upon which successive Cypriot governments consistently and strenuously relied and which they invoked since the earliest stages of independence in 1960, in the Security Council in 1964, in the General Assembly in 1965 and in 1974–1983, in the Sixth Committee for decades, and in the Law of Treaties Conference of 1968–1969), as well as the Annan Plan's proposed derogations from the EU *acquis communautaire*.

Taking all of the above into account, is it at all surprising that 76 percent of Greek Cypriot voters rejected the UN plan in the April 2004 referendum? What is essential to realize is that this vote was not, as is sometimes argued, a vote against the unification of Cyprus or even against a bizonal, bicommunal federation. Instead, the vote was a resounding rejection of the particular plan in the terms proposed by the United Nations.

As the impasse on Cyprus continues, Turkey's accession course toward EU membership remains a major factor in the calculations of all concerned. Richard Holbrooke's strategic vision, as early as 1995, was for the Cyprus problem to be solved within the EU. Greece was already a member; Cyprus was likely to become a member; and Turkey itself might eventually become a member. Thus the Cyprus question could be tackled in much the same way as Northern Ireland – by the United Kingdom and the Republic of Ireland as EU members. And, indeed, the situation in Cyprus, especially the Greek Cypriots' rejection of the UN plan in April 2004 and the Republic of Cyprus's accession to full EU membership in May 2004, is currently having a major bearing on Turkey's accession course. Should the outcome such course be Turkey's compliance with European norms of behavior and the "Copenhagen Criteria," it is possible that the UN plan, even if defunct in its own terms, could provide a point of reference and some common ground for fruitful negotiations in the future.

An aspect of Palley's book that deserves particular attention is the acceptance in New York, in February 2004, of the shift from good offices, as properly understood and until then applied, to what was, in effect, arbitration by the UN secretary-general. To some – both at the time and certainly in retrospect – this final leap away from good offices was a major misstep. Palley makes a valiant effort to explain that it was intended to be less far-reaching than it proved to be (and in fairness, the converging political pressures, from many directions were difficult to resist). There can be little doubt, however, that to accept arbitration by the United Nations and, indirectly, by those who influenced UN officials – with their mixed motivations that included their own political objectives as much or more than a fair and workable settlement for the benefit of Cyprus as a whole – was fraught with risk, at least from the point of view of achieving a fair, stable, long-term settlement.

There is one crucial aspect of the Cyprus negotiations that remains opaque in Palley's book: despite the availability of learned opinions by outstanding international lawyers (developed in special sessions held in Geneva in June 1999 and The Hague in December 2000) on the key issues of international law involved, it appears that these formidable weapons in the Greek Cypriot arsenal were not actively used during the 1999–2004 negotiations – except in the very final phase at Bürgenstock, where they were effectively ignored by the UN negotiators as having been put forward too late. The only apparent explanation for this self-inflicted act of omission is that, at the relevant times, the Greek Cypriots' top negotiators decided not to insist on these legal points lest the prospects of a political settlement and EU entry be jeopardized – an attitude that this reviewer finds difficult to accept since it is unlikely that a lasting settlement could be achieved outside the parameters of basic norms of international law.

Palley has written *An International Relations Debacle* in fine style, but it is not light reading, with its massive and detailed footnotes (nonetheless valuable in providing a wealth of information, sometimes anecdotal), many photographs with captions that illustrate the text and several useful annexes. One may or may not share some of the author's evaluations of personalities, but cannot deny the accuracy of her recitation of events, which she lived through closely and intensely. By her own admission, at times she is an advocate and sometimes a passionate one, of points of view that she helped formulate and present during the long periods of the negotiations, but in the considered opinion of this reviewer, she is fair and accurate in presenting views that she sincerely believes in. These views need to be presented to a wider public, especially in order to balance other publications such as David Hannay's *Cyprus: The Search for a Solution* (2005) and the arguably self-serving UN reports on the same facts (particularly UN Doc. S/2004/1437 of May 2004). Palley's excellent book enables the reader to form an objective view of the issues involved in the current Cyprus situation and, yes, to understand it without being misinformed.

Letter to the Editor of the New York Times*

Your editorial "A Clear Assault on the Press" (13 Sept. 2009) is a timely reminder that Turkey has considerable distance to cover prior to meeting the criteria qualifying it for membership of the European Union.

Timely because currently there has been a concerted effort, including by the venerable Mr. M. Ahtisaari ("Cold on Turkey" NYT.com 11 Sept. 2009), the Financial Times ("Engaging Turkey", "Advice for the EU if Cyprus Talks Fail" 9 and 10 Sept, 2009 respectively) to promote Turkey's EU accession course. It is of course up to the EU's 27 members to decide if and when Turkey meets the Copenhagen and other criteria for full membership and it is well known that some member states, including France, Germany and Austria would opt for a "privileged partnership", short of full membership and this for a variety of reasons. December 2009 marks the time when some key decisions will have to be made.

As Mr. Ahtisaari correctly notes, it was in Helsinki in December 1999 that the EU leaders declared Turkey to be a candidate state "on the basis of the same criteria as applied to the other candidate states", coupled with the undertaking to admit the Republic of Cyprus whether its political problem, following the 1974 Turkish invasion and occupation of part of the island, was solved or not (delinking admission from solution).

Strategic thinkers like Richard Holbrooke, as Assistant Secretary of State for Europe at the State Department in the mid-nineties, envisaged a Cyprus solution by analogy to that of Northern Ireland, taking into account that Greece was member of the EU, Cyprus was on its way to doing the same (having applied in 1990 and having satisfied the criteria for membership by 1993) and Turkey would eventually become member if it satisfied these "same criteria as applied to the other candidate states". If I may say, I can speak with some authority on this matter as I was in 1990 the Permanent Secretary of the Cyprus Ministry of Foreign Affairs when the application was submitted, Ambassador of Cyprus in Washington in the mid nineties when the US position as above was formulated and a member of the Cyprus

* Previously published (in edited form) in the New York Times on 24 September 2009.

negotiating team in New York when the Helsinki decision was reached. Cyprus became a full EU member in May 2004.

It is true that in April 2004, the overwhelming majority of the Greek Cypriots (76%) rejected in a democratic vote the Annan Plan for a Cyprus solution thereby rendering it null and void by its own terms, while the Turkish Cypriots (by a smaller margin) accepted it. This is often cited by those supporting Turkey's accession as demonstrating Turkey's good faith in supporting a Cyprus solution. What is not said, however, is that all of Turkey's key conditions (or "red lines") were accepted in toto by Mr. Alvaro de Soto of the UN and incorporated into the Annan Plan. It is easy to support a plan on your own terms, as Turkey did in 2004. It also explains why the overwhelming majority of the Greek Cypriots rejected it and not because they did not want a solution.

An honorable workable compromise, compatible with the applicable rules of international law (Art. 2 (4) of the UN Charter, state responsibility, settlers in occupied territory, human rights), UN resolutions and the acquis communautaire would have been accepted in 2004 and will be accepted by the Greek Cypriots now if such a plan emerges out of the current talks.

The key difficulty now, as it was then, is that Turkey has not moved an inch from its key conditions (Turkey's guarantees including military intervention, legitimization of settlers etc.) as this has been repeatedly stated, including most recently by its Foreign Minister Mr. Ahmed Davutoglu. It was hoped that in light of Turkey's EU accession objectives (subject to a veto by an existing EU member) Turkey would have moderated these anachronistic positions, originally formulated by the all powerful Turkish military, taking also into account that (as Mr. Ahtisaari observes) "the Turkish armed forces have stepped further back from the dominant role they had played in the country's political life since the time of the founding father, Mustafa Kemal Ataturk". Mr. Davutoglu has demonstrated great acumen and remarkable results in his diplomacy (Turkey's election to the UN Security Council, participation in the Dialogue of Civilizations, mediating in the Middle East and the Caucasus, opening to Armenians and the Kurds, concluding key energy agreements with the west and Russia, membership of the G20). One could reasonably ask why it is that only on Cyprus the Turkish position remains inflexible and anachronistic. Indeed Greece as well as Cyprus might ask some such questions on Turkey's actions in the Aegean and the Cyprus Exclusive Economic Zone and yet, both Greece and Cyprus are on record as supporting Turkey's EU accession, in the terms defined in the Helsinki Decision.

Another legitimate question to the EU member states is why do they not react unambiguously to Turkey's refusal to meet its treaty obligations, to the EU as well as to the Republic of Cyprus, under the Ankara Protocol of 2005 (recognizing the Republic of Cyprus, opening its ports, airports and airspace to Cypriot-registered vessels and airplanes). If Turkey's excuse is that it would do so only upon a Cyprus solution, the answer is that a Cyprus solution will be achieved only if Turkey moderates its position on the lines indicated above, thus making it possible for the Greek Cypriots to accept a workable compromise, compatible with international law and the acquis communautaire.

Mr. Ahtisaari and his Independent Committee would be performing a better service to Turkey, as well as to the EU and the international community to which he has offered so much during his distinguished career, if he were to advise Turkey to behave like a European state thereby facilitating its successful accession to the European Union – on Cyprus as well as on the other admission criteria. If this happened, there can be no doubt that the Greek Cypriots would be ready and anxious to respond positively and thus there would be a win-win situation for all concerned.

In October 1990, I had the privilege of being present at the ceremony in Berlin marking German reunification. In September 2003, I was also fortunate to be at the White House lawn in Washington for the historic meeting of Prime Minister Rabin and Chairman Arafat. I would hope and expect that some time in the not too distant future a similarly auspicious event will occur marking the reunification of Cyprus. But for this to happen it will take Turkey to moderate its attitude. If it further delays it will be the fault not of the Republic of Cyprus, but of Turkey. The moment should not be squandered.

Turkish Flexibility Would Solve Cyprus*

Letter to the Editor of the Wall Street Journal

Hugh Pope ("Time Runs Out For Cypriot Solution," op-ed, Oct. 20) makes some valid points. He accepts as anomalous the paradox of Turkey being elected and serving as a nonpermanent member of the United Nations Security Council, while for 35 years denying the Council's calls for Turkey to withdraw troops from Cyprus. All this, while Turkey seeks EU membership, which requires the approval of all EU nations, Cyprus included. He is also right in urging Turkey to live up to its reputation as a peacemaker.

But while it is true that in 2004 the overwhelming majority (76%) of Greek Cypriots voted against the Annan Plan for a Cyprus solution, this was done not because they did not want a solution but because all of Turkey's key conditions were incorporated into the plan. An honorable, workable compromise would have been accepted in 2004 and would be accepted now, if such a plan emerges out of the current talks.

The difficulty now, as then, is that Turkey has not moved one inch from its key conditions, which include a Turkish right to unilateral military intervention, and the legitimization of the mainland settlers. It is true that the Cyprus issue is the main obstacle to Turkish accession to the EU. One could reasonably ask why it is that only with regard to Cyprus does Turkey's position remain inflexible and anachronistic. A moderation of this position sufficient to fit into a solution on the lines indicated above would, I am convinced, result in a win-win situation: The long-sought Cypriot reunification, and bringing Turkey closer to the EU.

As Mr. Pope observes, the alternative could be hostile partition – and this would be in no one's interest.

* Previously published in the Wall Street Journal on 27 October 2009.

Fifty Year Anniversary of the Republic of Cyprus (1960–2010)

Keynote Speech at the American Hellenic Institute Foundation (AHIF) Conference, Washington, D.C., 4 October 2010

I am honoured and delighted to have this opportunity to address such a distinguished audience, including so many friends and colleagues. Tribute is due to the American Hellenic Institute Foundation for organizing this great conference to mark the half century anniversary of the Republic of Cyprus, and to the Greek American community for all you have done for the cause of Cyprus over the years.

In the circumstances prevailing in August 1960, many had misgivings about the future of the new Republic and doubted whether its creation was a cause for celebration.[1] In light of the eventful and turbulent experiences of the past 50 years, it can be stated with conviction that statehood and independence, even subject to the limitations imposed by the Zurich-London Agreements, have been an asset to be treasured and defended against the constant attempts to diminish and destroy it.[2]

In the summer of 1960 I returned to Cyprus, having completed my studies in Law and Public International Law. At the suggestion of Glafcos Clerides, I was appointed by Archbishop Markarios to be a member of the first delegation of Cyprus to the United Nations[3] and was present at the admission of Cyprus to the Organization on 20 September 1960. During the bulk of these 50 years, I had the privilege to represent the Republic of Cyprus in key positions at such bilateral posts as the United States and Germany and

---

[1] Let me remind you that the actual date of independence was 16 August 1960 – it was later that the official National Day was moved to 1 October.

[2] Some may recall the admission in 2006 of "mea culpa" by a former President of Cyprus who, in London in February 1959, was one of the few advisers of Archbishop Makarios to have voted against it.

[3] I was then assigned Cyprus diplomatic passport number 3!

at multilateral positions such as the United Nations and many international conferences.[4]

This, of course, is neither the place nor the time for a personal memoir but perhaps it might be in order to invoke some memories at key turning points to illustrate the contribution of this small newly independent Republic to international political and legal developments, drawing from my personal experience.

But before getting into this, I think it would be appropriate – particularly speaking to an American audience but also objectively – to briefly touch on Cypriot-US relations and the US role in Cyprus developments. There is a tendency among some in Cyprus to, generally and uncritically, take a negative view of the United States. No doubt, there have been many issues on which such criticism is well-founded. The George Ball and Dean Acheson activities in 1964 and certainly Henry Kissinger's policies and "tiltings" in 1974 are such examples and of course Turkey, over the years, has been considered by US policymakers a major factor weighing heavily in their decisions. But it is often overlooked that there is also another side.

Back in 1962, President Kennedy invited President Makarios on a State Visit to Washington with full honours attaching to such visit. It was then that the Archbishop asked me to draft his proposed major speech in Congress. When I, a green 25 year old junior diplomat, appeared overwhelmed by the magnitude of the task, he calmly reassured me: "Just put yourself in my position and write it as if you were Archbishop and President!"[5] There followed several other visits by successive Cypriot Presidents to the White House since then, the last one being that of President Clerides in 1996.

In July 1964, it was President Lyndon Johnson's letter to Premier Inonu that was instrumental in averting the then threatened Turkish invasion.

In 1967, it was Cyrus Vance's dexterous diplomacy that defused the crisis over the Kophinou incident, and averted another threat of an invasion.[6]

In 1972, the US averted an impending coup by the Greek Junta against Archbishop Makarios through the timely action of Ambassador David Popper

[4] I had the extraordinary luck to have served under 5 Cypriot Presidents (Makarios, Kyprianou, Vasiliou, Clerides and, briefly, Papadopoulos) and to have experienced 5 US Presidents (Kennedy, Carter, Reagan, Bush 41 and Clinton) and 6 UN Secretary-Generals (Hammarskjöld, U Thant, Waldheim, Perez de Cuellar, Boutros-Ghali and Kofi Annan).

[5] I drafted many of President Makarios' speeches over the years at the United Nations, at several Commonwealth Conferences, at the Non-Aligned Summit in Colombo, and during his 1966 visits to Latin American states. I also drafted many of the speeches of Presidents Kyprianou and Clerides.

[6] Makarios in New York in 1974 after the coup is supposed to have said to Vance – only half in jest – "If only I had consented in 1967 to the dissolution of the National Guard, we might not have had the coup and the invasion!"

(this, of course, did not happen in 1974 despite the timely warnings of the Cyprus desk officer Thomas Boyatt).

In 1978, the US-British-Canadian Plan could have been, in my view – then and in retrospect – a sound opportunity for progress towards a solution and certainly would have secured the return of Famagusta even if no solution was achieved.[7]

In November 1983, the Unilateral Declaration of Independence (UDI) of the so-called "TRNC" was strongly condemned both by Congress in a joint resolution and by the Administration (including support for SC Res. 541 at the UN and a specially arranged visit by President Kyprianou to the White House to meet President Reagan) and the US was instrumental in averting recognition of this "legally invalid" entity by Islamic countries such as Bangladesh[8] and still does.

In late October 1984, a letter by President Reagan to President Evren, elicited Turkey's acceptance of "29+" on the territorial aspect and the non-insistence on rotating presidency – not enough for a breakthrough in the then ongoing Kyprianou-Denktash talks, but significant concessions nevertheless, as seen in perspective.

In 1995, Richard Holbrooke, as Assistant Secretary of State for Europe, was instrumental in securing the support of the US for the accession course of the Republic of Cyprus to the European Union, a strategic move towards the solution of the Cyprus problem through Greece, Cyprus, and Turkey being (or becoming) EU members, on the parallel of the Northern Ireland situation.

I will not even attempt to relate the numerous ways in which Congress, both the Senate and the House, supported the just cause of Cyprus, other than to mention the congressionally imposed arms embargo on Turkey in 1975 on the "rule of law" issue;[9] the financial aid to Cyprus over the years, being tripled every year by Congress over the Administration's request, which went a long way towards alleviating the suffering caused by the invasion; major initiatives, such as the Pressler-Biden Amendment in 1984 in the wake of the illegal UDI; and the overwhelming support in Congress for the significant resolution in 1995 endorsing the Clerides initiative on the demilitarization of Cyprus.[10]

[7] In fact, Mathew Nimetz's plan.

[8] Whose Ambassador in Washington called me to say that its earlier declared recognition was a private initiative of the then Foreign Minister.

[9] For which many here, John Brademas, Paul Sarbanes, Eugene Rossides, among others, deserve too much credit.

[10] In the Senate it passed unanimously in the Senate Foreign Relations Committee due primarily to the persuasive powers of Senator Olympia Snowe towards Chairman Jesse Helms.

Evidently, in an after dinner speech, it is neither possible nor desirable to make a scholarly presentation (some of you may recall the variation of the Androcles and the lion story: "After dinner, there will be speeches", Androcles is supposed to have whispered to the lion's ear – and the lion didn't eat him!). But I feel that it is both appropriate and fair, at an introspective event such as this to look back and acknowledge that Cyprus owes much to the United States. Indeed, the United States also owes much to Cyprus, for instance, for its helpful role on Lebanon, both in 1983 in the wake of the Marine barracks bombing and, more recently, in 2006 with the US citizens' evacuation, its cooperation in fighting terrorism and drug trafficking and in other substantial ways such as providing FBIS facilities (Foreign Broadcast Information Service).[11]

Preserving the independence of Cyprus and defending the legitimacy of its government has not been easy. Much is owed to the United Nations for the stand it took when repeatedly Turkey and the Turkish-Cypriot leadership challenged it.

The first time this happened was in December 1963, in the wake of the intercommunal fighting, when Turkish jets flew menacingly over Nicosia on Christmas day and Turkish naval vessels moved threateningly close to the northern coast of Cyprus. The Cyprus delegation to the UN asked for an emergency meeting of the Security Council[12] asking for protection against these threats of force. Ambassador Rossides's credentials were challenged by the then T/C Vice-President F. Kutchuk, who invoked his right of veto under the Cyprus Constitution against the recourse. The Security Council brushed aside this objection and accepted the credentials of the Permanent Representative of Cyprus acting on behalf of President Makarios. Thus, a significant precedent was created which has been followed ever since.

During the subsequent full consideration of the Cyprus recourse by the Security Council, in February and March 1964, Cyprus was represented by its delegation headed by Foreign Minister Spyros Kyprianou. In the resulting significant Security Council resolution 186 (1964), the Cyprus government was fully recognized and referred to as any other government of a UN member state, fully empowered to give is consent to the establishment and operation of the UN Force in Cyprus and the appointment of a U.N. Mediator.

Another key stage was reached after the 1974 invasion. In the Geneva declaration of 30 July 1974, at Turkey's insistence, there was no reference to the "Government of Cyprus" but only to the "two communities". Not even in the landmark GA Res. 3212 was there an explicit such reference, even though it

[11] Aptly summarized in the recent publication in major American newspapers.

[12] I remember drafting on Christmas day what became SC document S/5488 – Ambassador Rossides was in Washington at the time.

contained many other strong provisions. The term "Government of Cyprus" reappeared in the December 1974 renewal of UNFICYP at the insistence of the Permanent Representative of Cyprus.[13] The 6 monthly SC Resolution renewing UNFICYP's operation has since then, as always since 1964, included without any disputation except by Turkey, the term "Government of Cyprus" – including most recently last June (SC Res. 1930) when Turkey voted 14 to 1 against the resolution it would otherwise support, because of the reference to "Government of Cyprus".

I related all this in order to underline that our statehood and governmental status are valuable assets which we should preserve at all cost, unless and until there is an agreed solution on the basis of the evolution of the Republic of Cyprus to the United Republic of Cyprus.

In the diplomatic field, the Republic of Cyprus has had a proud record of achievements, despite its small population and resources.

At the United Nations, especially during the period 1960–1963 when it started with a clean slate unencumbered by a problem of its own, Cyprus was a factor to be reckoned with in UN affairs. During this formative period, Cyprus made the United Nations and the principles of its Charter central to its foreign policy. Its views, as a small, non-aligned, developing, newly independent state having just emerged from colonial rule after a liberation struggle, under the towering figure of Archbishop Makarios, were carefully listened to and given considerable weight. Through active participation before UN organs, Cyprus played a role considerably exceeding that which would be expected from a state of its size. Whatever the issue, whether disarmament, decolonization, and also international law – to which I shall return – but also specific issues such as Algeria, Korea, Palestine, South Tyrol, Cuba, the Cyprus delegation was consulted, its assistance was sought and its positions listened to and given considerable weight. In the UN, where each state has one vote in the General Assembly, the Cyprus delegation under its articulate and energetic Ambassador Rossides played an active role. The credit it built through such activities proved to be valuable when, from the end of 1963 onwards, it laboured under a major problem of its own – and in a sense, Cyprus became a ward of the United Nations. Through such landmark Security Council resolutions as 186,541, 789, 1521 among many others, and major General Assembly resolutions (such as 2077, 3212, 37/253), the United Nations backed and reinforced our position internationally. It took a firm stand by calling for the withdrawal of all foreign troops of occupation; for the voluntary return of the refugees to their homes in safety; for the

[13] Who rejected a mere reference to the "Republic of Cyprus" since, he said, he tried to telephone the Republic to get instructions but could not do so, he could only reach the "Government of Cyprus"!

preservation of the demographic composition of Cyprus, for the respect for its sovereignty, independence and territorial integrity; excluded any form of partition or secession; declared the "TRNC" legally invalid and called on all states not to recognize it.[14]

Strong endorsements of these positions were also obtained in successive Commonwealth Heads of Government Meetings[15] and Non-Aligned Summits[16] and other international fora.

All of these provisions, skillfully obtained with much effort, dedication and a sense of mission, should be remembered and highlighted as these, together with the issue of proper guarantee if any is needed, are the bulwark of our diplomacy. In more recent years, the focus has been on the internal issues (constitution, territory, property, economy), which are of course also important and relevant. But, in my view, it is essential in a future settlement to preserve the hard fought positions indicated above, which were achieved through the United Nations.

Another major achievement was marked in 2004 through the accession of the Republic of Cyprus to the European Union, in a process which started in July 1990[17] with the submission of its application of membership. It gradually gathered support, with intensive diplomatic work in European capitals as well as in the United States, resulting – also with the active engagement of Greece – in the 1999 Helsinki decision, prior to full membership in 2004.

Looking back in retrospect, one may be permitted some degree of satisfaction by how much was achieved in the international field against so many odds by this small and embattled state.

But, for the sake of objectivity, it also has to be acknowledged that in recent years and currently, matters in the diplomatic field are less positive. At the United Nations, Turkey succeeded two years ago to get elected as a nonpermanent member of the Security Council by a record 151 (out of 192) votes, without Cyprus lifting a finger to avert it by reminding the electors that dozens of Security Council resolutions on Cyprus have been contemptuously ignored by Turkey with impunity. Our silence has also been deafening in the General Assembly on the annual adoption of the Law of the Sea Resolution, where Turkey is the only state to vote against it every year. At

---

[14] It also established the UN Force in Cyprus, UNFICYP, to help maintain the peace, always with the consent with the Government of Cyprus, as it is still doing. And, through the Plaza Report in 1965, it provided the outline for a proper solution of the overall problem which regrettably was not acted upon.

[15] Starting from that in Jamaica in 1975.

[16] Especially in Colombo, Sri Lanka in 1976.

[17] When I served as Permanent Secretary of the Ministry of Foreign Affairs in Nicosia, I was also a member of the Cyprus negotiating team in 1999 in New York, during the Helsinki Decision.

the European Union the threat of the so called "direct trade" is looming in the European Parliament.[18] Our position in the European Commission and Council has been significantly eroded.[19] In the European Court of Human Rights, the great successes we had through, for instance, the *Loizidou v. Turkey* case (1996) have been recently weakened by the *Demopoulos* and other cases (2010). The picture is not all bleak in the legal field as we can also point to the recent *Orams* case in the British Courts, the not so recent *Kanakaria Mosaics* case before the federal Court of Indianapolis and the reassuring paragraphs 81 and 114 of the recent *Kosovo* Advisory Opinion of the International Court of Justice.

But recent developments in the Islamic Conference and with the active policies of Turkey towards the Arab world and the Balkans and its declared policy of "zero problems" towards its neighbours, Turkey's membership of the G20 etc, the bitter truth that this is no time for complacency. If the current inter-communal talks produce no results – the prospects at present are far from bright – the Republic of Cyprus at 50 will be faced with new challenges and dangers. I can only express the fervent hope that its diplomacy will be up to the task.[20]

If time allowed, much could be said about the successes of the Cyprus economy over the past half century and of its achievements in the cultural and several other areas. Alas, it does not. I trust that the success of the current excellent Smithsonian exhibition will mark a major contribution in our cultural diplomacy – the kind which, on a much smaller scale, we attempted through our presentation of the Cypriot Amphora to the Eisenhower Theater of the Kennedy Center (a fine instance of bipartisanship, I might add!) and the major success of the return of the Kanakaria Mosaics to Cyprus, through the proper use of the American justice system.

But, I trust that you will allow me to take a few minutes on Cyprus's contribution to public international law. It so happens that, in addition to being a diplomat for the bulk of the past 50 years, I have also been and still am an international lawyer for an even longer period. I recall participating in a seminar at Cambridge University in early 1959 and outlining to the participants[21] the legal aspects of the just concluded Zurich-London

[18] And more worrisome, is that it appears that our responsible officials were not even aware of it until 3 months after it arose.

[19] Partly, it seems, because of positions we take on such issues as Gholan Heights, Abkhazia-Ossetia and Kosovo, valid though they may be, but not shared by the majority of the EU member states and this influences negatively their attitude on our own issue.

[20] German reunification was made possible by the statesmanship of M. Gorbachev and also W. Brandt and H. Kohl. No such prospect is in sight in our situation as far as Turkey is concerned.

[21] Including the future president of the ICJ Rosalyn Higgins.

Agreements (February 1959) pointing out, already then, that if Article 4 of the draft Treaty of Guarantee purported to give the three Guarantor Powers a unilateral right of forcible military intervention this would be contrary to Article 2 (4) of the UN Charter. An attempt to amend this wording during the preparatory stage was not accepted and our position on these lines was articulated before the Security Council in February 1964 and has been a mainstay of our position ever since. At our insistence, it was articulated at the 6th (Legal) Committee of the UN and the Vienna Conference on the Law of Treaties (1968–1969) which adopted the notion of *jus cogens* (peremptory norms intemationallaw) from which no deviation is permitted by treaty. It was also considered by the American Society of International Law in 1984[22] but, regrettably, it was never referred to the ICJ for an Advisory Opinion (as suggested by U Thant already back in 1964 and as I repeatedly urged) and therefore was not authoritatively interpreted and still remains an issue in the current stage of the Cyprus negotiations.[23] If it had been referred to the ICJ, I am convinced that it would have been decided in favour of Cyprus, as indeed the issue of legality of the UDI, as recently authoritatively commented upon by the Court in its Kosovo Advisory Opinion (22 July 2010), clearly distinguishing (in its paras 81 and 114) the case of Kosovo's independence declaration from that of the "TRNC"[24] and affirming the territorial integrity of the Republic of Cyprus.

Another major area of the contribution of Cyprus to international law is in the Law of the Sea. Through its active participation in the UN Law of the Sea Conference (1973–1982), Cyprus played a key role in the formulation and adoption of such issues as the full entitlement of islands to the zones of maritime jurisdiction (Art. 121), enclosed and semi-enclosed seas (Art. 122–123), the median line of delimitation of zones of maritime jurisdiction especially of territorial waters and the exclusive economic zone, all of which are of major importance in safeguarding the interests of Cyprus (and indeed of Greece, as acknowledged at the time). In view of the current situation in our EEZ, what would be more sensible than to declare our willingness to resort to third party settlement (ICJ, ITLOS, or arbitration) even if Turkey was unwilling to do so?[25]

---

[22] Mr. Nimetz was one of the panelists and Marcos Kyprianou, a student at the time, was one of the attendees.

[23] The 2000 Hague Opinion by distinguished international lawyers completely endorses our position.

[24] Citing the 1960 Treaties and the relevant SC Resolutions 541 and 1251, explicitly rejecting "any form of partition or secession" – in addition to SC Res 774, 789 and others.

[25] My statement at ERPIC of 23 June 2009 "Current trends in the Law of the Sea and their relevance to Cyprus".

Moreover, in the area of state responsibility (as in the Iraq case paying billions of dollars to Kuwait for its illegal aggression as compensation) and international criminal jurisdiction (resulting in the establishment in 1998 of the International Criminal Court), in declaring that the establishment of settlers in occupied territory is a war crime, as well defining aggression, Cyprus and its representatives have left their mark in the formulation of the relevant rules of international law.[26] If these rules had been given due weight by the framers of the Annan Plan, the result could have been different – although, of course, these were not the only weaknesses of that Plan. These rules have to be included in any future settlement if it is to be viable.

In concluding, may I leave you with two messages: The one is that the Republic of Cyprus at 50, despite its ups and downs during its turbulent existence, has much to be proud of. The other is that, unless and until there is a proper resolution of the presently outstanding issues which will enable the people of Cyprus – all of the people of Cyprus – to live in peace and prosperity, we must do our utmost to defend and preserve what was achieved in the past fifty years.

[26] Let me also cite the fact that successive Permanent Representatives of Cyprus have served as Chairmen of the Host Country Relations Committee at the UN; two were elected as members of the UN International Law Commission; and Cyprus was an active contributor from its inception to the Programme of Assistance for the teaching and promotion of international law and the rule of law worldwide.

Turkey Needs to Be Sincere on Cyprus*

Letter to the Editor of the Financial Times

David Hannay (Letters, November 19) makes a valid point in stressing that Turkey's accession to the European Union is – potentially – in the interest of Cyprus. Cyprus as well as Greece supports such accession. But, in urging "all parties" to inject some "new thinking" into the UN-sponsored negotiations, he ignores the fact that while substantial concessions have been made by the Greek-Cypriot side (including, most recently, accepting a rotating presidency and 50,000 settlers), not an inch has been given by the other side (in effect, Turkey).

If Turkey negotiates in good faith within the agreed framework, complies with its legal obligations to Cyprus and the EU under the 2005 Ankara protocol and stops interfering forcibly in the Cyprus exclusive economic zone, the road would be opened wide to further progress in Turkey's accession and to a viable Cyprus compromise solution.

* Previously published in the Financial Times on 24 November 2010.

Letter to the Editor of Foreign Affairs*

Mr. Hugh Pope of the International Crisis Group makes several interesting observations under the intriguing heading "Pax Ottomana?" (November/December 2010 issue). However, the article also calls for some comments and corrections.

I had occasion, in a lecture back in 1991 at Humboldt University in Berlin as Ambassador to just-reunited Germany, to observe that what the world needs in the era of the United Nations is a peace based on the UN Charter (a "Pax Unitarum Nationum"), in preference to "Pax Romana" of the distant past or to "Pax Britannica" of the more recent past or "Pax Americana" as some had been proposing. Considering that, as Mr. Pope observes, Turkey succeeded in being elected to a rotating seat of the UN Security Council 2009–10 (and in fact President Gul chaired last September a Summit level debate on the Council's "effective role in maintaining international peace and security") it might be assumed that Turkey's policies would be guided by the UN Charter principles. How this can be reconciled with its continued occupation by more than 40,000 troops of a large part of the territory of a UN (and, since 2004, EU) member state, despite numerous Security Council Resolutions, since the July 1974 invasion, calling for their immediate withdrawal and for respecting the territorial integrity of the Republic of Cyprus, is something that your readers may wish to think about.

Mr. Pope writes that "in 2003 the [AKP] party reversed traditional Turkish policy by agreeing to endorse the UN plan to reunify" Cyprus. What he does not say, however, is that the plan in its latest version (Annan V), incorporated in toto Ankara's demands. It is easy to endorse a plan made in your own terms. Whether it was politically and economically viable or compatible with basic norms of international law is another matter. In any case, the result of the April 24 2004 referendum rendered the Annan plan null and void.

Mr. Pope makes an unfounded assertion in stating that "since joining the EU in 2004, Cyprus has pulled all available levers to block Turkey's own accession to the Union." This is simply not so. If it were so, Turkey would

* Previously published (in edited form) in Foreign Affairs May/June 2011.

not in 2005 have been endorsed by the European Council as a candidate for membership since such a decision required unanimity and Cyprus could have exercised its veto. There followed the Ankara protocol of 2005 and the indisputable fact is that Turkey does not comply with its legal obligations to Cyprus and to the EU under its terms, in addition to forcibly interfering with Cyprus' rights in its exclusive economic zone of maritime jurisdiction under the 1982 Law of the Sea Convention.

Many of us welcomed Mr. Davutoglu's declared goal of the "settlement of disputes" that "directly or indirectly" concern Turkey and the "zero problem" policy towards Turkey's neighbors (see e.g. my letter to the New York Times dated 15 September 2009 and to the Wall Street Journal dated 20 October 2009). Yet, other than paying lip service to supporting the process of the UN sponsored intercommunal talks on Cyprus, Turkey (which, as everyone knows, calls the tune for the Turkish Cypriots, whether Mr. Talat or Mr. Eroglu) has on substance not conceded an inch so as to meaningfully contribute towards a solution within the agreed framework. If it does, even at this late stage (the UN Secretary-General's report of 24 November 2010 gives a clear signal that a crucial stage has been reached which requires decisive steps forward) and a solution is reached, Turkey will find the way wide open to its European accession as far as Cyprus (and Greece) is concerned. Of course (as the perceptive 14 – page Special Report on Turkey, The Economist, October 23, 2010 indicate), other considerations also have bearing on Turkey's prospects of EU membership.

Mr. Pope says, correctly, that "the AKP's zero-problem policy has been largely beneficial and has gone a long way towards defining a new national role for Turkey" and toward "win-win outcomes." If the Cyprus problem is solved through a viable compromise settlement with Turkey's constructive contribution, Turkey will gain more than removing a major obstacle to its EU accession course. A reunited and peaceful Cyprus, free of foreign troops, will be transformed into a bridge of peace instead of a bone of contention and will cooperate with Turkey as well as with Greece (within the EU or otherwise) through trade, tourism, finance and, quite possibly, through mutually beneficial water and energy projects. This can be achieved through good neighborly relations on the basis of the UN Charter principles and the acquis communautaire, not through occupation, domination and Pax Ottomana.

(23 November 2010)

Part C

Related Topics

Remarks at the 75th Anniversary Commonwealth Day Celebration of the British Officers' Club of Haverford

Pennsylvania, 15 April 1994

Thank you for inviting me to address this distinguished gathering on this very special occasion. I am honoured to do so as the Ambassador of my country, Cyprus, which had the privilege of hosting the most recent Commonwealth Heads of Government Conference (CHOGM, for short). And, I was delighted to accept since I was fortunate enough to have participated in six previous CHOGMs, represented Cyprus in several capitals of Commonwealth countries and most recently served as a member of the Appraisal Group, a think tank on the future of the Commonwealth.

The most recent CHOGM was held in Limassol, Cyprus, during 21–25 October and the retreat was in the beautiful and historic resort area of Paphos – if I may be permitted the commercial interruption, as they say on television, since I am from Paphos! Her Majesty the Queen was, as customary, present. It was a successful Conference which resulted in the adoption of a far ranging Final Communiqué summarizing the commonly held views of the Commonwealth leaders on the major political and economic issues of the world today. It included a strong paragraph expressing the collective position of all the participating Heads of Government on the situation in Cyprus following the 1974 Turkish invasion and the visiting dignitaries had the occasion of being reminded of and seeing for themselves some of the disastrous consequences of this internationally condemned invasion.

Since, very fortunately, what had been in past such Conferences the major issue, viz apartheid in South Africa was no longer an issue – indeed South Africa is expected to rejoin soon the ranks of the Commonwealth under a democratic system –, the emphasis for practical action was on international economics and particularly the GATT Agreement. It is hoped that the conclusion reached by the Heads of Commonwealth after due deliberation, on all issues, political and economic as well as legal, will be pursued by each of the participating Governments with consistency and tenacity in all other forums where they are raised and not be allowed to be in abeyance until the next Conference.

I presume that speaking to you on the merits of the Commonwealth is like trying to convert the Pope to Catholicism! I take it for granted that we all share support and commitment to this unique and remarkable concept of an extended family of nations.

Indeed, there are many similarities between the Commonwealth structure and that of families. Some members of the family are strong and flourishing; others are barely surviving and poor; some are psychologically and physically healthy; others suffer from a variety of diseases; some are secure; others are threatened and abused by outsiders and, just like so many other families, there may be the occasional black sheep!

In the case of the Commonwealth family we all share a common heritage, having been at some stage, whether by choice or otherwise, a part of the British Empire which stretched over the globe and over which, it was said, "the sun never sets".

We share a common language and a healthy respect for, among other things, the rule of law, for democratic institutions, for freedom of the press, for an independent civil service. We also share an undefinable and vague, yet unmistakable, bond of common attitudes and sense of values so that we can feel at home with each other, speak to and understand each other with much more ease than with other groups of countries and with individuals of different cultures.

For example in my travels from Nairobi to New Delhi, to Colombo, to Georgetown, to Nicosia, I could see the same type of familiar district commissioner's office, the same type of court-house, the same type of police station and other government buildings. We have the same basic legal system – indeed we constitute a principal legal system in the world – and the same civil service terminology and grades, not to mention driving on the left! Even in terms of diplomatic nomenclature, we apply our own rules. As you know, members of the Commonwealth do not exchange "Ambassadors". We share "High Commissioners". Currently, for instance, in addition to being Ambassador to the United States, I am non-resident High Commissioner to Canada, Jamaica and the Bahamas and my Letters of Credence were addressed to the same Sovereign, Her Majesty Queen Elizabeth II, but in each case respectively as Queen of Canada, Jamaica and the Bahamas.

While still on the subject of nomenclature, strictly speaking Foreign Ministries of Commonwealth countries should be, and in some cases are, termed Ministries of *External* Affairs since they deal not only with *foreign* countries but also with Commonwealth countries and the latter are "external" but not "foreign".

Which reminds me of the story of the elderly English gentleman who did not travel abroad much and upon arriving at Stockholm's airport was confronted by two signs marked, respectively "Swedish citizens" and "Foreigners". He looked puzzled, he paused and then he approached the nearest airport official and said, "excuse me, Inspector, but I'm afraid I do not understand these signs. There seems to be nowhere for me to go. I am not a Swedish citizen and I am certainly not a foreigner".

In a more serious vein, let me briefly deal with these questions: What is the Commonwealth? How did it originate? What purpose does it serve? How does it function? And, what does it mean particularly to you here and to us in Cyprus?

In the declaration of Commonwealth principles, adopted in 1971, the Commonwealth of Nations is defined as "A voluntary association of independent sovereign states, each responsible for its own policies, consulting and cooperating in the common interests of their peoples and in the promotion of international understanding and world peace".

As early as the imperial conference of 1926, which preceded the enactment of the statute of Westminster, its members were stated to be "equal in status, in no way subordinated to one another in any aspect of their domestic or external affairs, though united by common allegiance to the Crown and freely associated as members of the British Commonwealth of Nations".

As with so many institutions, it has evolved pragmatically and, through a historic process of several phases, it was transformed from the British Empire to the present voluntary association of independent states, no longer bound by allegiance to the Crown but merely recognizing the Queen as the Head of the Commonwealth.

As an institution, the Commonwealth has marched with the times, both structurally and qualitatively, and in the process it has shown an adaptability and dynamism which has enabled it to survive situations which could have brought about its demise.

Wisdom and statesmanship have played an important role in ensuring this process of adjustment. Today, the Commonwealth has grown in numbers and importance. It consists of 50 members and is still growing. It encompasses a diversity of peoples of many races, spread allover the globe, rich and poor, strong and weak.

In terms of population, the Commonwealth nations range from minute to the second most populous country in the world; and in terms of area from mere specks in the sea to an island continent. Combined we represent one quarter of the entire world population.

We share memories of a common rule. Some of these memories are pleasant, others are less so – indeed, some of the leaders of our nations shared the common experience of having served in a colonial jail.

Even though the colours of our skin differ as do our religions, mores and the languages we speak when we are not using English, we have, as I said before, a common heritage and can understand each other through sharing this common heritage and certain fundamental values. It is in this context that it has been aptly said that "the Commonwealth cannot negotiate for the world: but it can help the world negotiate".

Today, the symbolic task of linking us together is performed by the Queen as the Head of the Commonwealth and, on the more practical level, through the activities of the Commonwealth Secretariat – currently headed by a distinguished Nigerian diplomat, chief Emeka Anyaokou – with its competent staff, drawn on an equitable basis, from all member countries.

The periodic Heads of Government meetings, usually held every two years in rotation in different member countries, provide the main occasion to exchange views at the highest level on the political and economic problems of the world, renew personal friendships and chart the way for future cooperation.

Having myself had the privilege of participating in six such conferences, I can say with conviction that their value is inestimable. In addition, many other conferences, meetings and seminars, in particular fields such as law, economics, arts and health are being periodically held in different Commonwealth capitals, and these provide more opportunities for constructive cooperation in these specialized fields. Cyprus, in fact, had the privilege of hosting several such meetings last year, besides the Heads of Government conference.

This brings me closer to home and to the relationship of Cyprus with the Commonwealth. Cyprus is strongly committed to the values and ideals of the Commonwealth and, because of its particular situation and background, deeply appreciates the significance of it as an Institution and a multi-national forum for cooperation and solidarity. Ours has not been a typical case of evolution of self-government leading to independence within the Commonwealth, as has been the general rule in most other cases.

The explanation lies in history – and we in Cyprus are proud of our history which goes back to six thousand years B.C. – and to the circumstances under which Cyprus came under British administration in 1878 and subsequently achieved its independence in 1960.

Yet, the fact of having cultural and ethnic ties which pointed to different directions and the bitterness of the anti-colonial struggle of the 1950's was no obstacle to our joining the Commonwealth by our own free choice in 1961, soon after our independence.

This has been a decision we have not regretted. We are proud to be a member of the Commonwealth, to share in its traditions and to contribute as best as we can to its deliberations and decisions. And, in an hour of need, we sought and received support from our fellow Commonwealth countries.

Let me conclude on a personal note: as one who has studied law in one of the ancient institutions of higher learning in England, as a member of the foreign service of my country for more than three decades, and who has participated in several of the Commonwealth's activities and represented my country to six Commonwealth capitals, I have found time and again the Commonwealth factor to have been invaluable in many small and large ways.

The indefinable bonds, which are based on common language and a shared sense of values, make contact easier and understanding and willingness to help more forthcoming.

This is particularly useful in multilateral diplomacy, at the united Nations and at major conferences such as that of the Law of Treaties and the Law of the Sea, but can also be extremely helpful in bilateral contacts.

For smaller countries in particular, it gives a sense of belonging which is much more valuable than simply membership of a club.

I would certainly not suggest that Commonwealth membership is a panacea. Admittedly, there are no easy solutions to the complex problems which face Commonwealth nations, as indeed the rest of the world. But even in some of these – Rhodesia, now Zimbabwe, being a case in point – just solutions can be found through collective wisdom and statesmanship.

Unity and a sound sense of values within the Commonwealth gives us all, large and small countries, strength and confidence and enhances our ability to cope with difficult situations. And so, on this occasion of Commonwealth Day, we can all join in celebrating an Institution which we can all share and cherish.

Remarks at the Kennedy Center on the Occasion of the Presentation of an Ancient Amphora by the Cyprus Government

Washington, D.C., 14 May 1981

It gives me great pleasure to present, on behalf of the Government and people of Cyprus, this ancient amphora from our small island, to share space in this modern edifice of your great country.

It is a token from the people of Cyprus to the people of America, expressing friendship and a sincere wish to enlarge and strengthen the ties between them – hence the welcome presence here of several members of the newly formed "American Friends of Cyprus" association.

It is right and fitting that this concrete reminder of these feelings should be exhibited at this unique center of culture which bears the name of the late President Kennedy. I recall with emotion the memory in 1962 when, as a junior official, I participated in Washington in the ceremony in which President Kennedy received with great honours our late President and founder of the Republic of Cyprus, Archbishop Makarios.

This amphora, recently uncovered in the island, dates back to the eighth century B.C., and is of the Cypro-Geometric Period. Amphoras of this type were extensively used in the ancient world of the Eastern Mediterranean. This was a time of prosperity and, I may even say, of glory for Cyprus, which was described as "Mistress of the Seas" during that period! Our teeming forests provided ample timber for the construction of sailing ships and our abundant mines furnished the copper by which weapons and other implements were made. In those ancient times, the Cyprus city states were famous and prospered through shipping and commerce.

Cypriot men sailed and oared their ships to every port of the known world. Amphoras, such as the one you see, were used to transport everything imaginable that could be contained in them -olive oil, wine, grain, fruits and even coins: They were the forerunners of the container transports used by today's shipping men.

The word "ancient" is, of course, a relative term. In this great new land of America, where the landing of Christopher Columbus and the arrival of the "Mayflower" are some of the outer landmarks, twenty eight centuries seems like a very long time ago. In the world of the Mediterranean – and I do not mean to be complacent or patronizing –, with traceable signs of civilization going back to 6000 years B.C., it seems much more recent.

Throughout these eight thousand years, many civilizations and cultures have had their influence on Cyprus. And today, antiquities and ancient artifacts are ubiquitous. A plow turning up a furrow, not uncommonly, discloses some concrete remembrance from our long and eventful past; and many a diver or swimmer in the blue Mediterranean waters, which surround the island, has turned up ancient treasures – some of you may have seen the film "The Kyrenia Shipwreck".

During these centuries, conquerors came and went leaving behind some monuments and traces of their passing but never transforming the basic ethnological and cultural character of the island. The strategic location of Cyprus and its beauty and prosperity left it exposed to settlers and invaders from the three continents at the crossroads of which it lies – Europe, Asia, and Africa. But Cyprus, having become part of the Greek world of antiquity through emigration by the Mycenaeans in the 14th Century B.C., to be followed by new waves of colonizers from Greece after the Trojan War, retained its basic character, language and traditions ever since. As it appears in the Iliad, Kinyras, the King of Paphos, was invited by Agamemnon to participate in the expedition against Troy. Following the Trojan War, Agapenor, King of Arcadia, founded Nea Paphos and Teucer, brother of the legendary Ajax and son of the King of Salamis in Greece, founded the great city state of Salamis in Cyprus (the present-day Famagusta).

At the risk of being accused as a name-dropper, let me drop a few more names which, over the centuries, have been associated with Cyprus and its history so that you might see our island in its broader perspective.

As most of you of course know, according to legend, the Greek Goddess of Love and Beauty, Aphrodite (or Venus, to use also her Latin name) emerged from the foam of the beautiful sea near Paphos – and, because of this the ancient poets referred to her as "ΚΥΠΡΙΣ"[1] and "ΠΑΦΙΑ".[2] From throughout the eastern Mediterranean, the faithful came to pay homage to her in the place of her birth.

What is less well known is that Zeno, the founder of the Stoic School of Philosophy, was a Cypriot from Kitium (today's Larnaca); that the Cypriot

[1] Of Cyprus.
[2] Of Paphos.

kings, having been freed from Persian domination by Alexander the Great, were instrumental in his taking the fortified City of Tyre by contributing 120 ships as well as the Admirals who led his fleet in his campaign all the way to the Punjab in India and helped his army cross the great rivers along his way; that Cleopatra, herself a descendant of Ptolemy, one of Alexander's generals, was offered Cyprus as a gift of love successively by both Julius Caesar and Mark Anthony; that Cicero served as a benign Roman Pro-Consul; that St. Paul, accompanied by the Cypriot-born St. Barnabas, visited the Island and converted to Christianity not only many Cypriots but also the then Roman Pro-Consul Sergius Paulus; that St. Helena, mother of Constantine the Great, stopped in Cyprus on her way back from the Holy Land and founded the Monastery of Stavrouvouni – which still exists – and endowed it with a piece of the Holy Cross (hence the name of the monastery); that Umm-Haram, a close relative of Prophet Mohammed, died while visiting the Island in the seventh century and a holy place was established in her memory near Larnaca, the Umm-Haram Tekke, which also still exists as a Moslem holy shrine; that Richard the Lionheart, on his way to the Crusades, stopped in Cyprus, defeated the local ruler Isaakios Komnenos (whom he put in silver chains, having promised as a condition of his surrender not to put him "in irons") and proceeded to marry Berengaria of Navarre in a romantic setting near Limassol; that Guy de Lusignan, having been dispossessed as King of Jerusalem by Saladin, became King of Cyprus and established a model feudal kingdom which lasted for more than three centuries, the last ruler of this dynasty being Caterina Cornaro, famous patroness of the arts who was declared "Daughter of Venice" and ceded her crown to the Venetian Republic; that Othello, the Venetian Governor of Cyprus according to Shakespeare did what he should not have done to Desdemona at Othello's Tower, near today's Famagusta.

This of course is not a historical account. For this, anyone interested can consult such authoritative works as the four-volume "History of Cyprus" by Sir George Hill. But I think I have dropped enough names – some of you may think too many – in these random vignettes to give you an idea of the rich and varied background of the Island. Of more recent vintage are names such as Lawrence Durrell, who made Cyprus widely known through his "Bitter Lemons", and Lord Caradon who, as Sir Hugh Foot, was the last British Governor of the Island – and thus a successor of both Cicero and Othello!

Today, Cyprus is where the ancient mingles with the modern against a beautiful background of blue sea, green mountains and fertile valleys and plains. Ancient Greek temples and agoras, Roman period villas and mosaics, Byzantine churches and monasteries, Crusaders, castles and abbeys, Gothic churches and Ottoman minarets, Venetian fortifications, modern hotels, excellent beaches and new buildings all blend together to make it a most remarkable Island.

Cyprus has had a rich past and now faces a difficult present. But, with the proper spirit on the basis of the lessons learned from the past and the efforts of all those – within and outside the Island – who are concerned for a brighter tomorrow for all its people, it can look to a better future.

Let this small present, which I am privileged to unveil today, serve as a token of our appreciation for the understanding and help we received from the people of this great country; as a symbol of our friendship; and as a reminder that we share so many values and ideals.

The United Nations Programme of Assistance in the Training, Study, Dissemination, and Wider Appreciation of International Law*

Statement to the Sixth (Legal) Committee at the 58th Session of the UN General Assembly on agenda item 149: "United Nations Programme of Assistance in the Training, Study, Dissemination and Wider Appreciation of International Law" on the United Nations Programme of Assistance in the Training, Study, Dissemination and Wider Appreciation of International Law, New York, 4 November 2003

The purpose of my brief statement is to place on record our recognition of the value of the United Nations Programme of Assistance in the Teaching, Study, Dissemination and Wider Appreciation of International Law; to express our deep appreciation for the efforts of the UN Secretariat (and in particular Mr. George Korontzis), of UNITAR and UNESCO; and to reaffirm our support for the Programme.

Allow me, Mr. Chairman, to recall that we have been among those who, recognizing the desirability and need for such a Programme, together with such legal luminaries and then members of the International Law Commission Codjo Dadzie and Abdul Tabibi took the initiative more than three and a half decades ago to establish it through General Assembly resolution 2099 (XX) in 1965. Cyprus has served on the Advisory Committee for the bulk of this period and we have endeavoured, in our very modest way, to contribute to its successful conduct financially and through its inclusion under the UN Decade of International Law (1990–1999), of which it formed an important part.

Having myself had first hand knowledge of how some parts of the Programme function, including lecturing twice at the Geneva International Law Seminar as a member of the International Law Commission[1] and the Hague

---

* Previously published in the records of the General Assembly, United Nations, 4 November 2003.

1 "Three Aspects of the Law of the Sea – Islands, Delimitation and Dispute Settlement", 1982 and "The Role of Diplomacy in International Law", 1991.

International Law Fellowship Programme[2] conducted by UNITAR, among other such activities, I am convinced of its great value for advanced students, law professors and government officials, primarily from developing countries, in updating and deepening their knowledge of developments in international law, in exchanging and sharing information and in familiarizing themselves with the legal work of the United Nations and its associated bodies. Of particular interest are also the Programme's activities concerning the Law of the Sea and Ocean Affairs, notably the Amerasinghe Memorial Fellowships on the Law of the Sea and those concerning Trade Law and the valuable work of UNCITRAL.

Indeed, all the activities of the Programme, as summarized in the Secretary-General's Report (A/58/446), deserve the support of Member States. We endorse the recommendations regarding the continuation of the Programme in the biennium 2004–2005 and we urge its full financial backing, both through the UN regular budget and through voluntary contributions by States.

Additionally, in our view, the possibility should be seriously considered, explored and promoted of obtaining voluntary contributions from foundations, institutions and individuals who can be convinced of the utility and importance of the Programme, under the appropriate modalities. Much is contributed yearly, especially by foundations, for other worthy purposes. Why not also towards the teaching, study, dissemination and wider appreciation of international law, thereby contributing towards international legal order and the rule of law among nations? Should these efforts prove fruitful, we would envisage a substantial expansion of the Programme's activities in the years ahead.

Finally, we shall be pleased to support the draft resolution just proposed by the Chairman of the Advisory Committee.

---

[2] Special Seminar on "Alternative Means of Dispute Settlement: The United Nations Compensation Commission and the Claims Resolution Tribunal for Dormant Swiss Accounts" 2000.

Index

AAA (American Arbitration Association), 128, 265
AALCC (Asian-African Legal Consultative Committee), 238, 246
Accession Treaty (EU), 338, 339
Acheson, Dean, 354
Acquis communautaire, 343
"Agenda for Peace" (Boutros-Ghali), 196
Agreement on the Delimitation of the Exclusive Economic Zone (Cyprus-Egypt), 77–78, 109–110
AHIF (American Hellenic Institute Foundation), 353
Ahtisaari, M., 347, 349
Aiken, F., 167
Akashi, Yasushi, 195
Albright, Madeleine, 195
Alford, Roger, 211, 213
Amerasinghe Memorial Scholarship, 84, 235, 244, 380
American Arbitration Association (AAA), 265
American Friends of Cyprus association, 375
American Hellenic Institute Foundation (AHIF), 353
"American Interests and UN Reform" (U.S. Congress), 142
American Journal of International Law, Kanakaria Mosaics in, 236
American Society of International Law (ASIL)
  Annual Meeting of, 113, 133, 232–233
  Cyprus problem and, 341
  international law and diplomacy and, 256
  jus cogens and, 360
  outreach program of, 138
  UN anniversary and, 142
Amphora, ancient, 375–378
Annan, Kofi
  on ICJ, 145
  international law, role of, 125, 131, 252
  on rule of law, 85
  terrorism and, 211, 213, 257
  on UN reform, 142
Annan Plan
  acquis communautaire and, 344
  Cyprus problem, solution for, 329–333
  international law rules and, 361
  rejection of, 327–328, 344, 348, 351
  state responsibility and, 145
  Turkey's interests in, 110–111, 365
Anyaokou, Emeka, 126, 246, 372
Anzilotti, Dionisio, 20
Arab Commission of International Law, 238
Arafat, Yasser, 349
Arctic, global warming and, 117–118
Arctic Climate Impact Assessment, 79
Articles on Responsibility of States for Internationally Wrongful Acts. *See* Draft Articles on Responsibility of States for Internationally Wrongful Acts
ASA (Swiss Arbitration Association), 129, 265
Asian-African Legal Consultative Committee (AALCC), 238, 246
ASIL. *See* American Society of International Law
Assistance Fund for the Fish Stocks Agreement, 79
Ataturk, Mustafa Kemal, 348
Attila Line, 186, 279, 292, 309
Austro-German Customs Union (1931), 20

Ball, George, 299, 354
Baltic Marine Environment Protection Commission, 82
Barbados/Trinidad and Tobago (2006), 268
Baxter, Richard, 11
Bekker, Pieter, 211
Bin Laden, Osama, 140
Biodiversity, 81–82
"Bitter Lemons" (Durrell), 377
Blum, Yehuda, 146
Bolton, John, 195
Bottom-trawling fishing practices, 80, 81–82, 83
Boucher, Richard, 318
Boutros-Ghali, Boutros, 145, 196, 197, 200
Boutros Ghali Plan (1992), 329

British Officers' Club, 369
The Brown Journal of World Affairs on UN peacekeeping, 195, 197
Buergenthal, T., 69, 92
Bush, George H.W., 313

C.V. Starr Lecture, 255, 256
Cameroon v. Nigeria (2002), 92, 105–106, 113, 268
Caminos, Hugo, 107
Canadian Armed Forces, 205–207
Caradon, Lord (Hugh Foot), 184, 377
Careers in diplomacy and international law, 1–6
Caribbean Community (CARICOM), 76, 77
The Caroline doctrine, 262
Carter, Jimmy, 297
Center for International Law (New York Law School), 255
Central Treaty Organization (CENTO), 285
Certain Expenses of the United Nations (1962), 167
"Challenges for the Present and Solutions for the Future" discussion, 106
Charter of Paris (1990), 239
Charter of the United Nations. *See* United Nations Charter
CHOGM (Commonwealth Heads of Government Conference), 258, 369–370
Chorzow Factory (1928), 259
Churchill, Winston, 142–143
Claims Resolution Tribunal for Dormant Accounts, 265–266
Clark, Joe, 207
"A Clear Assault on the Press" (editorial), 347
Clerides, Glafcos
  demilitarization proposal of, 201, 206, 307, 316, 321, 322, 356
  Makarios and, 353
  at Security Council, 161
  U.S. visit of, 354
Climate change, 79, 117–118
Clinton, Bill, 312, 322
Code of Crimes against the Peace and Security of Mankind (ILC)
  international criminal court and, 61, 323
  international law and, 62, 237, 248, 331
  state responsibility and, 11, 236
Collective security, 152–153, 177
Commission on Security and Cooperation in Europe, 239
Commission on the Limits of the Continental Shelf, 78, 81
Committee on the Elimination of Racial Discrimination, 279
Commonwealth Day Celebration, 369–373
Commonwealth Heads of Government Conference (CHOGM), 258, 369–370
Commonwealth of Nations, 371–373
Conference of Maritime Delimitation in the Caribbean, 80
Congress on Public International Law, 245
Contiguous zone, 99, 103
Continental shelf, 78, 81, 99–101, 103
Continental Shelf Commission, 78, 81
Convention and Management of Highly Migratory Fishstocks, 81
Convention on Offences and Certain Other Acts Committed on Board Aircraft, 214
Convention on the Elimination of All Forms of Racial Discrimination. UN, 294
Convention on the Means of Prohibiting and Preventing the Illicit Import, Export and Transfer of Ownership of Cultural Property (UNESCO Convention for the Protection of Cultural Property), 138
Convention on the Recognition and Enforcement of Foreign Arbitral Awards (New York Convention), 136–137
Convention on the Settlement of Investment Disputes Between States and Nationals of Other States (ICSID Convention), 136–137, 212, 264–265
"Copenhagen Criteria," 344
Corell, Hans, 211, 234–235, 245
Corfu Channel (1949), 35
Corporate governance, 266–267
Countermeasures, state responsibility and, 12
Counter Terrorism Committee, 214
Crawford, James, 12, 260
Crimes against humanity, 259
Cuellar, Perez de, 182
Customs Union Agreement (Cyprus – European Community), 191
Cyprus: The Search for a Solution (Hannay), 345
Cyprus and Cyprus problem, 273–366. *See also* United Nations Force in Cyprus
  amphora, presentation of ancient, 375–378
  anniversary of republic of, 353–361
  book review on, 341–345
  EEZ and, 77–78, 109–110, 118–122
  EU accession and, 317, 322, 327, 332–333, 335–339, 348, 358
  General Assembly, UN, 52–54, 278, 282, 291, 302, 309
  international law and, 234–236, 243–244, 305–318
  international legal order and, 227–228, 229

law of the sea and, 87–88, 89, 92, 108–111, 115–122, 267–268, 360–361
Non-Aligned Movement and, 187, 188, 281, 301, 329
peacekeeping and, 179–193
Security Council, UN, 50–52, 276–278, 280–281, 283, 290, 306–310, 316–317, 320–321
as small state, 129–130, 149–178
solution, prospects for, 289–304, 316–318, 327–333, 351
Turkey, EU accession of, 363
United Nations and, 273–287, 291, 293–294, 296, 356–357
Zurich-London 'Agreements' and, 39–55, 290

Dadzie, Codjo, 379
Davutoglu, Ahmed, 348, 366
Decade of International Law, United Nations, 243–249
international law and, 57, 231, 238, 242
jus cogens rules and, 64
Non-Aligned Movement and, 238
permanent international court and, 63
state responsibility and, 11
Declaration of Intent and Memorandum of the Cyprus Government (UN General Assembly), 278
Declaration on Friendly Relations and Cooperation in Accordance with the Charter of the United Nations, 253
Declaration on the Conduct of Parties in the South China Sea, 81
Declaration on the Inadmissibility of Intervention in the Domestic Affairs of States and the Protection of Their Independence and Sovereignty, 35
de Gaulle, Charles, 138
Delimitation (law of the sea), 93–94, 97–101, 103–106, 267
Demirel, Suleyman, 302
Denktash, Rauf, 182, 184, 191, 295, 328, 355
de Ruyt, Jean, 335
de Soto, Alvaro, 348
Diplomacy
careers in, 1–6
international law and, 58–59, 231–242, 255–269
Diplomatic Corps (Washington DC), 217–223
Dirksen, Everett, 264
Dispute settlement
international dispute resolution tribunals, 133–140
law of the sea and, 93–94, 102–103, 106–108
peaceful settlement of international disputes, principle of, 30, 32–34, 49–54
state responsibility and, 12–13
UNCLOS III and, 69–73
Dobrynin, Anatoliy, 217
Douglas, William, 299
Draft Articles on Responsibility of States for Internationally Wrongful Acts (ILC), 11–14, 21–23, 25, 26–27, 54
Draft Code of Crimes against the Peace and Security of Mankind. *See* Code of Crimes against the Peace and Security of Mankind
Durrell, Lawrence, 377

Eban, Abba, 329
ECHR (European Court of Human Rights), 137, 266
Economic and Monetary Union (EMU), 336
EEZ. *See* Exclusive Economic Zone
Egypt, Arab Republic of, delimitation issues and, 92, 109–110, 118, 268
Eisenhower Theater, 359
El Erian, A., 23
Eliasson, Jan, 142, 146
EMU (Economic and Monetary Union), 336
EOKA B extremists, 291
Erga omnes obligations, 61–62, 236, 260, 261
Ethnic cleansing, 306, 319–320, 343
European Commission of Human Rights, 311
European Committee on Legal Cooperation, 238, 246
European Convention on Human Rights, 294, 332
European Council, 337
European Court of Human Rights (ECHR), 137, 266
European Monetary System, 336
European Rim Policy and Investment Council, 115
European Union (EU), 335–339
agricultural exports to, 324
Cyprus, accession of, 317, 322, 327, 332–333, 335–339, 348, 358
direct trade and, 359
expansion of, 335, 337
law of the sea debate and, 76
Turkey, accession of, 347, 348–349, 351, 365–366
Evren, Kenan, 183, 342, 355
Ex aequo et bono, 33, 108, 264
Exclusive Economic Zone (EEZ)
continental shelf and, 99–101, 103

Cyprus agreement on, 77–78, 109–110, 118–122
evolution of, 80
median line and, 92

Factory at Chorzow (1928), 259
Federalist Papers (Madison), 297
Fife, Rolf Einar, 106
Financial Times, letter to editor of, 363
Fish Stocks Agreement (1995), 79, 81, 83
Foreign Affairs, letter to editor of, 365
Foreign Aid Bill (U.S.), 184
Foreign Assistance Act of 1961 (U.S.), 313
Framework Convention for the Protection of National Minorities, 138
A Future for Small States: Overcoming Vulnerability (Commonwealth Secretariat), 126

General Assembly, United Nations
Cyprus problem and, 52–54, 278, 282, 291, 302, 309
law of the sea discussions in, 75–85
peaceful settlement of disputes and, 33
state sovereignty and, 35
Geneva Convention on the Continental Shelf (1958), 96, 102
Geneva Convention on the Territorial Sea and Contiguous Zone (1958), 96, 97, 98, 99, 100
Geneva Conventions on the Law of the Sea (1958), 93, 94
Geneva International Law Seminar, 379–380
Genscher, Hans-Dietrich, 237, 239–240
Glaberson, William, 139–140
"Global Humanitarian Emergencies 1996" (U.S. Government), 196
Globalization, 125–126, 133–134
Global Marine Assessment mechanism, 79
Global warming. *See* Climate change
Gorbachev, Mikhail, 192, 336
Goulding, Marrack, 198
Governance of High Seas Fisheries conference (2005), 78
Greenstock, Jeremy, 136
Gromyko, Andrei, 152
Group of Eight Major Industrialized Countries (G-8), 214
Guellar, Perez de, 329
Guggenheim, Paul, 19
Guillaume, Gilbert, 92, 104–106, 107, 127, 137
Gyani, Prem Singh, 164, 276

Haass, Richard, 342
Hague Conventions on the Pacific Settlement of International Disputes, 249
Hague International Law Fellowship Programme, 380
Hamilton Shirley Amerasinghe Memorial Fellowship. *See* Amerasinghe Memorial Scholarship
Hammarskjöld, Dag, 150, 162–163, 164
Hannay, David, 345, 363
Heffter, A.W., 18
Helsinki Decision, 348, 358
Helsinki Final Act, 309
Higgins, Rosalyn, 266, 359
Hill, George, 377
History of Cyprus (Hill), 377
Holbrooke, Richard, 337, 343, 344, 347, 355
Holtzmann, Howard, 139
Human rights, 240, 253, 278, 292–293, 308–309, 323
Human Rights Commission, UN, 278, 279, 282
Hussein, Abdullah II bin al-, 314, 325, 333
Hussein, Saddam, 309

Iacovou, George, 336
ICC. *See* International Chamber of Commerce; International Criminal Court
ICJ. *See* International Court of Justice
ICSID (International Centre for Settlement of Investment Disputes), 264–265
ICSID Convention. *See* Convention on the Settlement of Investment Disputes Between States and Nationals of Other States
ILC. *See* International Law Commission
IMO (International Maritime Organization), 77, 118
Individuals, international criminal liability of, 259
INF Agreement (Intermediate-Range Nuclear Forces Treaty), 192
Injurious Consequences Arising Out of Acts Not Prohibited by International Law, 11–12
"In Larger Freedom" (Annan), 142, 143–144, 213, 257
Inonu, Ismet, 354
Institute for the Study of Diplomacy (ISD), 142, 251
Inter-American Juridical Committee, 238, 246
Intermediate-Range Nuclear Forces Treaty (INF Agreement), 192
International Centre for Settlement of Investment Disputes (ICSID), 264–265
International Chamber of Commerce (ICC), 265
International Convention for the Suppression of Acts of Nuclear Terrorism, 257–258

International Convention for the Suppression of the Financing of Terrorism, 214
International Court of Justice (ICJ), 141–146
advisory function of, 122, 254, 263
compulsory jurisdiction of, 228, 235, 243
international law, role of, 60
law of the sea disputes in, 71, 85, 94, 102, 106, 113–114, 122
Optional Protocol of, 323
peaceful settlement of disputes by, 33
Statute of, 101
use of force and, 262
International Criminal Court (ICC), 135, 247–248, 258–259, 322–323
International Crisis Group, 365
International dispute resolution tribunals, 133–140
"International Law: 100 Ways it Shapes Our Lives" (ASIL), 256
International law, careers in, 1–6
International law, role of, 57–65, 231–242
International Law Commission (ILC). *See also* Code of Crimes against the Peace and Security of Mankind; Draft Articles on Responsibility of States for Internationally Wrongful Acts
Decade of International Law and, 248–249
"Fragmentation of International Law" agenda, 261
international criminal jurisdiction and, 258
international law, role of, 58, 61–64, 241–242
international legal order and, 227
jus cogens and, 17, 21–25, 27
relations with other organizations, 238
state responsibility and, 236
"International Law on the Eve of the Twenty-First Century" (ILC), 248
International legal order, 225–230
International Maritime Organization (IMO), 77, 118
International Plan of Action for the Conservation and Management of Sharks, 76
An International Relations Debacle: The UN Secretary General's Mission of Good Offices in Cyprus 1999-2004 (Palley), 341–345
International Seabed Authority, 76, 79, 83, 87–89
International Tribunal for the Law of the Sea (ITLOS)
dispute settlement in, 102
establishment of, 88, 247
expansion of, 146
international law, contributions to, 113–114
Sea-Bed Disputes Chamber, 71
UN General Assembly law of the sea debate and, 76, 83
Yankov on, 108
International tribunals and small states, 125–131. *See also specific tribunals*
International Union for the Conservation of Nature (IUCN), 76, 83
Iraq, UN Compensation Commission and, 13–14
ISD (Institute for the Study of Diplomacy), 142, 251
Islamic Conference, 359
Islands, regime of, 92, 93–97, 103, 104, 116–117, 267
Israel, withdrawal of forces of, 283
ITLOS. *See* International Tribunal for the Law of the Sea
IUCN (International Union for the Conservation of Nature), 76, 83

Jan Mayen (1993), 105, 268
Jennings, Robert, 245, 263
Johnson, Lyndon, 354
Jus cogens
defining of, 63–64, 238
international law rules under, 27–38, 248–249
state responsibility and, 13
treaties conflicting with, 17–55, 310–311
Vienna Convention on the Law of the Treaties and, 13, 61, 63–64, 236, 248, 260–261, 311, 360
Zurich-London 'Agreements' and, 27–54

Kanakaria Mosaics, recovery of, 130, 138, 236, 244, 324, 359
Karamanlis, Konstantinos, 40
Kellogg-Briand Pact, 19, 20, 30
Kelsen, Hans, 20
Kennedy, John F., 274, 354, 375
Kennedy Center, 359, 375
Khrushchev, Nikita, 274
Kiev (cruiser), 300
Kissinger, Henry, 195, 196–197, 354
Koh, T., 101
Korontzis, George, 379
Kosovo Advisory Opinion (2010), 359, 360
Kutchuk, F., 40–41, 42, 49–50, 356
Kyprianou, Spyros, 294, 295, 355, 356

Lauterpacht, Eli, 113
Lauterpacht, Hersch, 19, 20, 23, 37
Law of the sea, 91–111. *See also* International Tribunal for the Law of the Sea; Third United Nations Law of the Sea

Conference; United Nations Convention on the Law of the Sea
overview, 91–94
contiguous zone and, 99, 103
continental shelf, 99–101, 103
Cyprus problem and, 87–88, 89, 92, 108–111, 115–122, 267–268, 360–361
delimitation and, 93–94, 97–101, 103–106
developments subsequent to 1982, 104–108
dispute settlement and, 93–94, 102–103, 106–108
EEZ and, 92, 99–101, 103, 109–110
international law and diplomacy and, 267–268
islands, regime of, 92, 93–97, 103, 104
territorial sea and, 97–99
UNCLOS, rules of, 94–104
UN General Assembly debate (2004) on, 75–85
Law of the Sea Convention. *See* United Nations Convention on the Law of the Sea
Law of the Sea Tribunal. *See* International Tribunal for the Law of the Sea
League of Arab States, 35
League of Nations, 19, 20, 30
Legal Adviser of the State Department, U.S., 139, 233, 246
Legal and Scientific Aspects of Continental Shelf Limits Conference (2003), 84
Legal Committee, UN. *See* Sixth (Legal) Committee
Legal Consequences of the Construction of a Wall in the Occupied Palestinian Territory (2004), 145
Legal order, international, 225–230
Leigh, Michael, 122
Leigh, Monroe, 135
Lex specialis, 137, 138, 266
Libya v. Malta (1985), 105, 268
Lima Declaration (1975), 281
Li Peng, 139
Loizidou v. Turkey (1998), 130, 137, 266, 332, 359
London Court of International Arbitration (LCIA), 265
Lugar, Dick, 201

Maastricht criteria, 318
Maastricht Treaty, 336
MacDonald, Ronald, 214
Madison, James, 297
Makarios III
Clerides and, 353
coup d'état against, 291–292, 355
Kennedy and, 354, 375
Kutchuk and, 40–41, 42, 49
leadership of, 357
Rossides and, 356
13-point proposals of, 290
Treaty of Alliance and, 48
at UN, 274, 281, 286
Makarios-Denktash guidelines, 302
Malone, David, 214
Manner, E., 101
Marschik, Axel, 214
Martin, Paul, 205
Martola, A.E., 164
Mauritius International Meeting, 80
Mayer, Howard, 263
Maynes, Bill, 195
McHenry, Don, 198
McMahon, John, 149
McNair, A., 19–20
Median line principle, 98, 101, 103, 116–117, 268
Menderes, Adnan, 40
Military forces for peacekeeping, 157–159
Milosevic, Slobodan, 140
Minsk (cruiser), 300
Missing Persons in Cyprus bill (U.S.), 321–322
Montreux Convention, 300
Moore, John Norton, 113
Morelli, Gaetano, 19
Mugabe, Robert, 140

NAM. *See* Non-Aligned Movement
Nandan, Satya N., 83, 113
NATO. *See* North Atlantic Treaty Organization
Natural gas resources, 119–120
Nelson, L. Dolliver M., 83
New York Convention (Convention on the Recognition and Enforcement of Foreign Arbitral Awards), 136–137
Nicaragua v. Honduras (2007), 113–114
Nicosia Treaties, 51–52, 160, 180, 182, 311
Nobel Peace Prize, 188, 190, 196, 229
Non-Aligned Movement (NAM)
Belgrade Conference of 1961 and, 274
Coordinating Committee of, 280
Cyprus problem and, 187, 188, 281, 301, 329
Decade of International Law and, 246
international law and, 58, 238–239
Meeting on Peace and International Law (1989), 244
Non-intervention in internal state affairs, principle of, 30, 34–35, 43–46, 54
Nordquist, Myron, 113
North Atlantic Treaty Organization (NATO), 160–161, 183, 207, 285, 300–301, 321

North Sea Continental Shelf (1969), 96, 105
Nuclear weapons, 77

Observer forces, 156–157
Oceans and the Law of the Sea, Omnibus Draft Resolution on, 76, 84
"Oceans and the Law of the Sea" debate (2004), 75–85
O'Connor, Sandra, 262, 323
Oil resources, 119–120
ONUC, United Operation in the Congo (ONUC). *See* United Nations Operation in the Congo
"Opinion on the Application of the Republic of Cyprus for Membership" (European Commission), 337
Oppenheim, L., 37
Organisation of African Unity, 35
Organisation of American States, 35
Organization for Security and Cooperation in Europe, 64
Oscar Chinn Case (1934), 20
Overfishing problems, 76, 83–84
Ozal, Turgut, 191

Pacific Islands Forum, 76
Pacta sunt servanda rule, 49
Palley, Claire, 341, 342, 344–345
Pallieri, Balladore, 20
Parry, Clive, 231
"Pax Ottomana?" (Pope), 365, 366
Pax Romana, 239, 263, 365
"*Pax Unitarum Nationum*", 239, 263
Peaceful settlement of international disputes, principle of, 30, 32–34, 49–54
Peacekeeping and peacekeeping operations, 151, 154–178, 179–193, 195–203, 228–229. *See also specific operations*
Pell, Claiboene, 324
Pepin, Jean-Luc, 207
Pepperdine University, 211
Peremptory norms of international law. *See Jus cogens*
Permanent Court of Arbitration, 129, 265
Pickering, Tom, 251
Piracy, 77, 78, 118
Plaza, Galo
  report of, 52, 206, 277, 291
  as UN mediator, 180, 189, 201–202
Pope, Hugh, 351, 365, 366
Popper, David, 355
Pressler-Biden Amendment (U.S.), 355
Project of State Responsibility for Injury to Aliens (Harvard Law School), 11
Project on International Courts and Tribunals, 129

Qatar v. Bahrain (2001), 92, 104–105, 106, 113, 268

Rabin, Yitzhak, 314, 325, 333, 349
Ranjeva, Raymond, 106, 107
Reagan, Ronald, 183, 187, 342, 355
Reagan-Gorbachev Summit, 192
Rebus sic stantibus doctrine, 49
Reed, Lucy, 133, 134, 136, 137–139, 140
Regional Cooperation Agreement on Combating Piracy and Armed Robbery, 79
Report of the UN Secretary-General's High Level Panel (HLP) on Threats, Challenges and Changes, 212, 251–252, 257
Reservations to the Genocide Convention (1951), 20–21
Responsibility to protect, 253
Rhodes Academy for Maritime Law and Policy, 117
Rio Group, 76
Robinson, A.N.R., 237
Rolandis, Nicos, 119
Rolz-Bennett, José, 157
Rome Statute of the International Criminal Court, 258–259, 331
Rosenne, Shabtai, 29–30, 106, 107
Rossides, Zenon, 356, 357
Rousseau, Charles, 19
Rule of law, 58–59, 355

S. S. Wimbledon (1923), 36
SALT II, 300
San Antonio World Affairs Council, 335
Sarbanes- Oxley Act (U.S.), 267
Schucking, Walther, 20
Schwarzenberger, G., 19, 20, 36
Schwebel, Stephen, 263
Secretary-General, United Nations, 34
Security Council, United Nations
  collective security and, 153
  Cyprus problem and, 50–52, 276–278, 280–281, 283, 290, 306–310, 316–317, 320–321
  expansion of, 145–146
  international law, role of, 60
  nuclear weapons and, 77
  peaceful settlement of disputes and, 33
  peacekeeping and, 198–200, 205
  terrorism and, 211, 213–214, 258
  UN Compensation Commission and, 13–14
  UN reform and, 142
Self-determination, right of, 36
Seneca, 302–303
Sharks, conservation of, 76

Shi Jiuyong, 144, 145, 254, 263, 343
Shultz, George, 187
Sixth (Legal) Committee (UN General Assembly)
  international criminal jurisdiction and, 258
  international law, role of, 60, 63
  jus cogens and, 17, 29
  state responsibility and, 11
  terrorism and, 211–212, 252, 257
Small states, role of, 149–178
  collective security and, 152–153
  general conclusions on, 172–178
  international tribunals and, 125–131
  military forces and, 157–159
  observer forces and, 156–157
  peacekeeping operations, ad hoc, 156–159
  UNFICYP and, 159–172
  UN peace force, proposals for permanent, 154–155
Sohn, Louis B., 11, 69–71, 249
Sovereign equality of all states, principle of, 30, 36–38, 43–46, 54
Starr Lecture, 255, 256
State responsibility, 11–14, 61–62, 236, 248, 259–260. *See also* Draft Articles on Responsibility of States for Internationally Wrongful Acts
State sovereignty, 30, 36–38, 43–46, 54
Stern, Lawrence, 184
Stewart, Potter, 212
'Suggested Measures to Facilitate the Smooth Functioning of the State and to Remove Certain Causes of Intercommunal Friction' (Cyprus), 49–50
Sustainable Fisheries, Draft Resolution on, 76, 79, 84
Swiss Arbitration Association (ASA), 129, 265

Tabibi, Abdul, 379
Teaching, Study, Dissemination and Wider Appreciation of International Law, UN Advisory Committee on the, 244
Territorial seas, 97–99, 267
Terrorism, 135–136, 140, 211–214, 252–253, 257–259
Thatcher, Margaret, 140, 264
Thimayya, Kodendera Subayya, 164
Third United Nations Law of the Sea Conference (UNCLOS III), 69–73, 94–96, 98, 102
To End a War (Holbrooke), 343
"Towards a More Effective U.N.: Prospects for Peace-keeping" (Jacovides), 188
Training, Study, Dissemination and Wider Appreciation of International Law, UN Programme of Assistance in the, 5, 379–380
Treaties. *See also specific treaties*
  jus cogens, conflicting with, 17–55
  unequal, 42–43
Treaty of Alliance (Cyprus-Greece-Turkey), 45, 48–49, 50
Treaty of Guarantee (Cyprus-Greece-U.K.-Turkey)
  conflict over, 50
  constitutional force of, 45, 49
  unilateral intervention under, 342, 360
  use of force and, 46–47, 235, 310–311, 331
  validity of, 254, 276
  violation of, 48
Treaty of Lausanne, 39
Treaty of Nice, 339
TRNC. *See* Unilateral Declaration of Independence
Trudeau, P., 167
Truman, Harry, 253
Trust Fund to Assist States in the Settlement of Disputes through the International Court of Justice, 144, 235, 244
Tuerk, Helmut, 113, 114
Tunkin, G. I., 20
Tuomioja, Sakari, 201, 277
Turkey. *See also* Cyprus and Cyprus problem; United Nations Force in Cyprus
  Annan Plan and, 110–111, 365
  EU accession and, 347, 348–349, 351, 363, 365–366
  flexibility of, 351
  on Security Council, 365
  UNCLOS and, 120–121
  UNFICYP and, 159–160, 170
  Zurich-London 'Agreements' and, 39–45, 47–53
"Turkish Cypriot Assembly," 307
Turkish National Security Council, 302

UDI. *See* Unilateral Declaration of Independence
UNCC. *See* United Nations Compensation Commission
UNCLOS. *See* United Nations Convention on the Law of the Sea
UNCLOS III. *See* Third United Nations Law of the Sea Conference
UNEF. *See* United Nations Emergency Force
UNESCO Convention for the Protection of Cultural Property (Convention on the

Means of Prohibiting and Preventing the Illicit Import, Export and Transfer of Ownership of Cultural Property), 138
UNFICYP. *See* United Nations Force in Cyprus
Unilateral Declaration of Independence (UDI), 254, 329, 355, 358, 360
United Kingdom
UNFICYP and, 170
Zurich-London 'Agreements' and, 41, 43, 45
United Nations. *See also* General Assembly, United Nations; Security Council, United Nations
Cyprus problem and, 273–287, 291, 293–294, 296, 356–357
international law, role of, 60–61
international legal order and, 226–227
Islamic Group of, 212
peacekeeping, 151, 154–178, 179–193, 195–203
reform of, 141–146, 251–254
small states and, 149–151
United Nations Charter
Article 2(1), 36
Article 2(4), 12, 13, 30–32, 161, 169, 198, 226, 235–236, 261–262, 310
Article 3, 26–27
Article 14, 24
Article 25, 298, 313
Article 33, 33, 38, 50
Article 40, 168–169
Article 51, 30–31, 253, 261–262, 310
Article 103, 26–27, 32, 37, 53
collective security under, 152–153
jus cogens and, 19
UN reform and, 141
United Nations Code of Crimes against the Peace and Security of Mankind, 311–312
United Nations Commission for Indonesia, 157
United Nations Committee on the Peaceful Uses of the Seabed and the Ocean Floor Beyond the Limits of National Jurisdiction (Seabed Committee), 94, 96, 98
United Nations Compensation Commission (UNCC), 13–14, 265
United Nations Convention on the Law of the Sea (UNCLOS)
Annex VII arbitral tribunals, 108
Annex VIII special arbitral tribunals, 108
coming into force of, 247
contiguous zone and, 99, 103
continental shelf, 99–101, 103
delimitation and, 93–94, 97–101, 103–106
dispute settlement and, 93–94, 102–103, 106–108
EEZ and, 92, 99–101, 103, 109–110
Implementation Agreement of, 82, 88
International Seabed Authority and, 87–89
islands, regime of, 92, 93–97, 103, 104
rules of, 94–104
territorial sea and, 97–99
third-party dispute settlement and, 62, 72
UN General Assembly debate on, 75, 78–79, 81–82, 84
UNCLOS III and, 69–73
United Nations Emergency Force (UNEF), 157–158, 164, 167, 169
United Nations Force in Cyprus (UNFICYP)
assessment of, 172, 199–200
Canadian Armed Forces and, 205–207
complexity of, 158–159
composition, direction, and control of, 162–164, 206
creation of, 159–162, 188, 276–277, 291
Cyprus problem and, 188–190, 197–200
duration and financing of, 166–168, 190, 199–200, 201, 206
East European Secretariat participation in, 175
legal framework for, 168–169
mandate of, 164–166, 190, 199, 278, 281, 357
operation of, 170–172
political basis for, 169–170
"United Nations Global Counterterrorism Strategy" (UN General Assembly), 258
United Nations India-Pakistan Observation Mission, 157
United Nations Military Observer Group in India and Pakistan, 157
United Nations Observation Group in Lebanon, 157
United Nations Operation in the Congo (ONUC), 158, 167, 169
United Nations Special Committee on the Balkans, 156–157
United Nations Temporary Executive Authority, 156–157
United Nations Truce Supervision Organization, 157
United Nations Yemen Observation Mission, 157
United States
Cyprus problem and, 183–184, 187, 296–304, 312–313, 321–322, 356
Diplomatic Corps, 217–223
peacekeeping and, 197
UN reform and, 251–254
United States Association for the United Nations, 142

Uniting for Peace resolution, 173
Universal Declaration of Human Rights, 277
Universal suffrage, principle of, 44
University of Cambridge, 231
University of Indianapolis, 225
Urquhart, Brian, 195
Use of force, prohibition of
 international law and, 252–253, 264
 jus cogens and, 4–5, 261–262
 Zurich-London 'Agreements' and, 30–32, 46–47, 54
U Thant
 ICJ Advisory Opinion and, 122
 on peacekeeping, 155, 156, 172
 on Third World, 150
 UNFICYP and, 163, 170, 205
Ut res magis valeat quam pereat principle, 310

Vance, Cyrus, 195, 299, 354
Vassiliou, George, 184, 187, 191, 192
Vattel, Emeric, 18
Verdross, A., 20, 24, 25
Vienna Convention on the Law of the Treaties (1969)
 jus cogens and, 13, 61, 63–64, 236, 248, 260–261, 311, 360
 third-party dispute settlement and, 62
Vienna Convention on the Law of Treaties between States and International Organizations (1986), 64, 248

Waldock, Humphrey, 21, 27, 262, 310
Washington Convention. *See* Convention on the Settlement of Investment Disputes Between States and Nationals of Other States
Washington Diplomatic Corps, 217–223
Washington Times on peacekeeping costs, 200
Webster, Daniel, 289
Wedgwood, Ruth, 134, 328
Weizaecker, Richard von, 336
Western and Central Pacific Tuna Commission, 80
Western Policy Center Conference (2004), 327
Weston, Tom, 251
Wolfensohn, James, 125, 133
Wolff, Christian, 18
World Bank, 185, 186, 264–265
World Summit Outcome (2005), 143–144, 146
World Trade Center attacks, 140. *See also* Terrorism
The Wrong Horse (Stern), 184
Wulfrum, Rudiger, 114

Xydis, Stephen, 273

Yankov, Alexander, 107, 108, 114
Yemen/Eritrea (1999), 104, 106, 268

Zurich-London 'Agreements,' 17–55
 Cyprus, independence of, 290
 historical background and recent developments, 18–21
 International Law Commission and, 21–25
 lesson of, 329
 limitations of, 353
 non-intervention in internal state affairs, principle of, 30, 34–35, 43–46, 54
 peaceful settlement of international disputes, principle of, 30, 32–34, 49–54
 peremptory norms and, 21–54
 sovereign equality of all states, principle of, 30, 36–38, 43–46, 54
 termination and change of circumstances of, 47–49
 treaties, unequal, 42–43
 treaty provisions, conflict of, 38–39
 UN Charter Article 103 and ILC Article 37, 26–27
 use of force norms and, 30–32, 46–47, 54